AF560012

PROBLEMS OF TRIBAL GIRL STUDENTS

PROBLEMS OF TRIBAL GIRL STUDENTS

By

Dr. V. Durga Prasad

M.A., M.Sc., M.A., IRPM, M.Ed., Ph.D.

Principal

Bhakt English Medium School

Kakrolia - 389 390, Panchamahal District

Gujarat (India)

&

Prof. Digumarti Bhaskara Rao

M.Sc., M.A. M.A., M.Ed., Ph.D.

Dean, Faculty of Education

Member, Academic Senate

Ex-Chairman, Board of Studies in Education

Member, Research Advisory Committee

Acharya Nagarjuna University

D-13, S.V.N. Colony

Guntur - 522 006 (India)

DISCOVERY PUBLISHING HOUSE PVT. LTD.

NEW DELHI-110 002

Published by:

Tilak Wasan

DISCOVERY PUBLISHING HOUSE PVT. LTD.

4383/4B, Ansari Road, Darya Ganj
New Delhi-110 002 (India)
Phone : +91-11-23279245, 43596064-65
Fax : +91-11-23253475
E-mail : discoverypublishinghouse@gmail.com
sales@discoverypublishinggroup.com
web : www.discoverypublishinggroup.com

***First Edition:* 2016**

ISBN: 978-93-5056-399-1

Problems of Tribal Girl Students

© Digumarti Bhaskara Rao
V. Durga Prasad

All rights reserved. No part of this publication should be reproduced, stored in a retrieval system, or transmitted in any form or by any means: electronic, mechanical, photocopying, recording or otherwise, without the prior written permission of the author and the publisher.

This book has been published in good faith that the material provided by authors is original. Every effort is made to ensure accuracy of material, but the publisher and printer will not be held responsible for any inadvertent error(s). In case of any dispute, all legal matters are to be settled under Delhi jurisdiction only.

Printed at:
Infinity Imaging Systems
Delhi

Dedicated

To

My Revered Mother

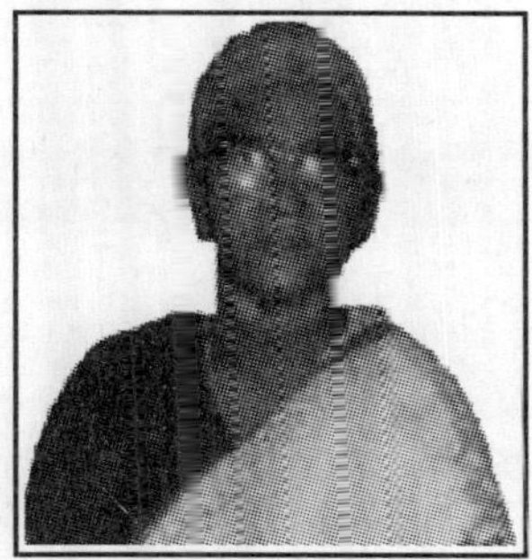

(Late) Mrs. V. Lakshmi

&

To

My Affectionate Wife

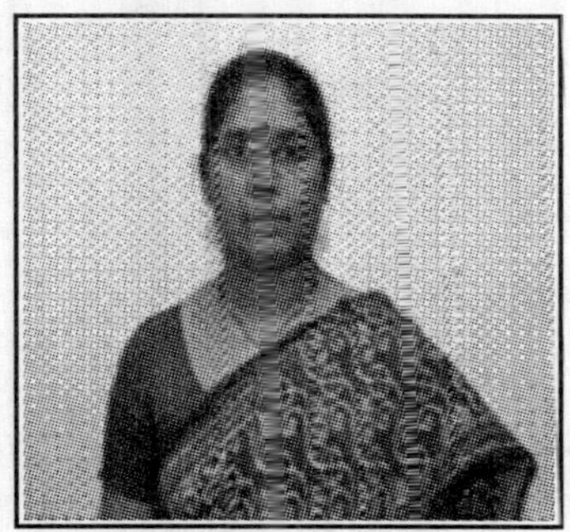

Mrs. V.V.V. Lakshmi

(The Fountain of Inspiration

Foreword

Tribals constitute a substantial portion of India's population. In many respects, they lag behind their non-tribal counterparts. To ameliorate their condition, much attention has been given to their education. The Government of India and constituent state governments have launched a good number of schemes to promote education among the tribal children, especially the girls. In addition, separate schools have been established under ITDA (Integrated Tribal Development Agency projects, in order to promote literacy among tribals. Inspite of several efforts, the growth of education in terms of tribal girls' participation and rate of literacy among them were found to be low.

According to a study, tribal women, who do not want to send their daughters to the school, said it is because of household work, labour, cattle grazing and distance of the school. Half of the tribal women feel that their habitations have no school. Those who have the school have their own reasons for liking and disliking for girls' education. Lack of adequate facilities, lack of good teaching, irregular attendance of teachers, etc., are some of the reasons for disliking the school. More than half of them knew about the teachers and only two thirds of the teachers were found to be regular to the school. More than half of them like to have a non-tribal teacher as these teachers do well in schools as teachers. The tribal women want their daughters to have formal education along with some vocational components. Half of the tribal women like the environment of the residential schools though they are located quite away from their residential places.

Under these circumstances, the present study was aimed at identifying the problems of tribal girl students of secondary schools. All the tribal girl students are having several problems with regard to their education. The tribal girl students of urban areas, uneducated father and mother, aided schools and Gujarati medium of instruction are facing more problems than their counter parts. The economic status of the family, religion, class studying and day or residential system have no effect on the problems of tribal girl students though they have many problems.

Efforts are being put-forth by the Government of India along with State Governments to establish schools for the tribals and educate them on par with other citizens of the nation. In spite of the plans and programmes envisaged, this has not been carried out to the extent possible to facilitate education to tribal girl students. Hence, the central and the state governments should start as many schools as required to tribal girl students on war-footing in order to support the education of tribal girl students.

Dr. Digumarti Bhaskara Rao
digumartibhaskararao@rediffmail.com
Tele-Mobile: +91 949 3333 555

Contents

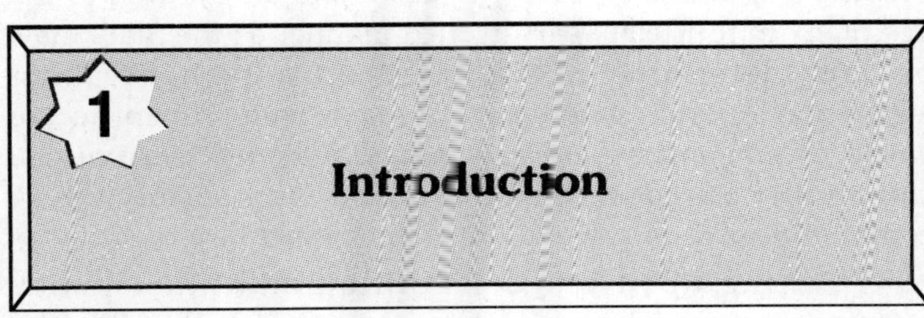

1 Introduction

EDUCATION IS A MODERN WORD which is derived from the Latin word 'educare', means to nourish, to cause to grow. Education also prevails in illiterate societies, where it is imparted orally and by mass behaviour. A member of primitive society learns to earn his livelihood, to do good works, to obey spiritual beings and also superstitions, etc., from the elders of the society and bind by its laws and regulations. These are the education for them. We, the modern people, do mean "education as reading and writing". This is also true. By modern education, a person can able to increase his knowledge and expand his vision and avail the fruits of development. Hence, modern education can play the role of catalyst in bringing changes in the spheres of social, political, and economic fields. One of the important reasons for failure of developmental activities in the society by various developmental agendas is the prevalence of acute illiteracy and ignorance, combined with superstitions among the rural masses. Hence, to ward off economic backwardness, social deprivation spreading of education is regarded as one of the most effective and forward-looking instruments. Another reason for failure of education is superstition among the tribal. Superstitions like "reading would make their eyes drop out of their sockets", etc., is also responsible for not spreading of education, so no remarkable progress could be achieved within next 10 years..

The 86th Constitutional Amendment Act, 2002 has made elementary education, a Fundamental Right for children in the age group of 6-14 years by providing that "the State shall provide free and compulsory education to all children of the age of six to fourteen years in such manner as the State may, by law, determine". This has been a path breaking legislation in India, where such a major commitment to the cause of elementary education has bound governments, community based organizations and civil society into a common resolve to achieve universal elementary education.

Drawing upon the Constitution and other policy statements articulated in the years that followed, the Government of India in partnership with State Governments has designed different strategies, interventions, schemes and programmes with specific objectives that impinge on girls' education.

Constitutional and Policy Framework

The Constitution of India in Article 15(1) on right to equality provides the basic policy framework that enshrines the vision of girls' education and the spirit, in which their education is to be provided. Until 1976, education was a State subject. Since its transfer to the Concurrent List by the 42nd Constitutional Amendment in 1976, the Central Government has played a more proactive role in the sector through several centrally sponsored schemes that had a distinct bearing on promoting education for girls.

A new thrust was provided to girls' education in the National Policy on Education 1986, (as modified in 1992), which provided a holistic vision for the education of women and girls and recognized the cross cutting issues that inhibited the realization of this goal. It aims at using Education as an agent of basic change in the status of women in society. Education of girls, especially those belonging to the scheduled castes and scheduled tribes, is the primary focus in Sarva Shiksha Abhiyan. Efforts will be made to mainstream gender concerns in all the activities under the Sarva Shiksha Abhiyan programme. Mobilization at the habitation/village/urban slum level, recruitment of teachers, upgradation of primary into upper primary schools, incentives like mid-day meal, uniforms, scholarships, educational provision like text books and stationary, will all take into account the gender focus. Every activity under the programme will be judged in terms of its gender component. Besides mainstreaming, special efforts like the Mahila Samakhya type of mobilization and organization, back-to school camps for adolescent girls, large-scale process based constitution of Mahila Samoohs, will also be attempted. The selection criteria take into account the low female literacy among the scheduled caste and scheduled tribe women.

The Sarva Shiksha Abhiyan recognizes the need for special efforts to bring the out-of-school girls, especially from disadvantaged sections, to school. This would require a proper identification of girls, who are out of school in the course of micro planning. It also calls for involving women through participatory processes in the effective management of schools. Experiences across the states under Mahila Samakhya and under the District Primary Education Programme have suggested the need for a clear perspective on women's issues. The provision for girls' education would have to be situated in the local contexts and interventions designed to suit the specific community needs in this regard. Special interventions need to be designed to address learning needs of girls and relating education to their life. The Sarva Shiksha Abhiyan is committed to make these interventions possible.

Educational Provisions for Tribal Children in India

Free and compulsory education to all children upto the age of fourteen years is the constitutional commitment in India. At the time of adoption of the Constitution in 1950, the aim was to achieve the goal of Universalisation of Elementary Education (UEE) within the next ten years *i.e.,* by 1960. Keeping in view the educational facilities available in the country at that time, the goal was far too ambitious to be achieved within a short span of ten years. Hence, the target date was changed a number of times. Till 1960, all efforts were progressed on provision of schooling facilities. It was only after the near realization of the goal of access that other components of UEE, such as universal enrolment and retention, started receiving attention of planners and policy-makers. It is the quality of education, which is focused on all programmes relating to elementary education in general and primary education in particular.

Education of Tribal Children

In traditional tribal societies, there was no formal system of education. The knowledge cultivated upto that generation was to be handed over to the upcoming next generation. The necessity of transfer of knowledge has led them to invest some novel methods of education. For acquiring technical knowledge the youngsters had to do the same work under supervision of an elder or elders through participation. The art of ploughing, weaving, making of tools and weapons, works of art, house building, cooking etc., have been categorized. Human feelings and literary knowledge is more of a subtle nature. The feelings need a smoother medium for expression. The songs may be the songs of planting, harvesting, childbirth, love and marriage, which are examples of this generation. To catch the young minds and to train them for a better understanding of surrounding environment, art and other essential riddles were a modest method of education.

Educationally, the tribal population is at different levels of development but overall the formal education has made very little impact on tribal groups. Earlier Government had no direct programme for their education. But in the subsequent years the reservation policy has made some changes. There are many reasons for low level of education among the tribal people. Formal education is not considered necessary to discharge their social obligations. Superstitions and myths play an important role in rejecting education. Most tribes live in abject poverty. It is not easy for them to send their children to schools, as they are considered extra helping hands. The formal schools do not hold any special interest for the children. Most of the tribes are located in interior and remote areas where teachers would not like to go from outside.

Many tribal schools are plagued by high dropout rates. Children attend for the first three to four years of primary school and gain a smattering of knowledge, only to lapse into illiteracy later. Few who enter continue up to the tenth grade; of those who do, few manage to finish high school. Therefore, very few are eligible to attend institutions of higher education, where the high rate of attrition continues. Members of agrarian tribes like the Gonds often are reluctant to send their children to school, needing them, they say, to work in the fields. On the other hand, in those parts of the northeast where tribes have generally been spared the wholesale onslaught of outsiders, schooling has helped tribal people to secure political and economic benefits. The education system there has provided corps of highly trained tribal members in the professions and high-ranking administrative posts. An academy for teaching and preserving Adivasi languages and culture was established in 1999 by the Bhasha Research and Publication Centre. The Adivasi Academy is located at Tejgadh in Gujarat.

Extending the system of primary education into tribal areas and reserving places for tribal children in middle and high schools and higher education institutions are central government policy, but efforts to improve a tribe's educational status have had mixed. Recruitment of qualified teachers and determination of the appropriate language of instruction also remain troublesome. Commission after commission on the "language question" has called for instruction, at least at the primary level, in the students' native tongue. In some regions, tribal children entering school must begin by learning the official regional language often one completely unrelated to their tribal tongue. The experiences of the Gonds of Andhra Pradesh provide an example. Primary schooling began there in the 1940s and 1950s. The government selected a group of Gonds who had managed to become semiliterate in Telugu and taught them the basics of written script. These individuals became teachers who taught in Gondi, and their efforts enjoyed a measure of success until the 1970s, when state policy demanded instruction in Telugu. The switch in the language of instruction both made the Gond teachers superfluous because they could not teach in Telugu and also presented the government with the problem of finding reasonably qualified teachers willing to teach in outlying tribal schools.

The commitment of tribes to acquiring a formal education for their children varies considerably. Tribes differ in the extent to which they view education positively. Gonds and Pardhans, two groups in the central hill region, are a case in point. The Gonds are cultivators and they frequently are reluctant to send their children to school, needing them, they say, to work in the fields. The Pardhans were traditionally bards and ritual specialists, and they have taken to education with enthusiasm. The effectiveness of educational policy likewise varies by region. In those parts of the northeast where tribes have generally been spared the wholesale onslaught of outsiders, schooling has helped tribal people to secure political and economic benefits. The education system has provided corps of highly trained tribal members in the professions and high-ranking administrative posts.

Composition and Location of Tribal Population in India

There is a substantial list of Scheduled Tribes in India recognized as tribal under the Constitution of India. Tribal people constitute roughly 8 per cent of the nation's total population, nearly 68 million people according to the 1991 census. 8.2 per cent over 84.2 million people according to the 2001 census. One concentration lives in a belt along the Himalayas stretching through Jammu and Kashmir, Himachal Pradesh, and Uttarakhand in the west, Assam, Meghalaya, Tripura, Arunachal Pradesh, Mizoram, Manipur and Nagaland in the northeast. In the northeastern states of Arunachal Pradesh, Meghalaya, Mizoram, and Nagaland, more than 90 per cent of the population is tribal. However, in the remaining northeast states of Assam, Manipur, Sikkim and Tripura tribal people range from 20 per cent to 30 per cent of the population.

Another concentration lives in the hilly areas of Central India (Chhattisgarh, Madhya Pradesh, Orissa and to a lesser extent in Andhra Pradesh); in this belt, which is bounded by the Narmada River to the north and the Godavari river to the southeast tribal people occupy the slopes of the region's mountains. Other tribals, including the Santals, live in Jharkhand, Bihar and West Bengal. Central Indian states have the country's largest tribes and taken as a whole roughly 75 per cent of the total tribal population live there, although the tribal population there accounts for only around 10 per cent of the region's total population.

There are smaller number of tribal people in Karnataka, Tamil Nadu and Kerala in south India; in western India in Gujarat and Rajasthan and in the union territories of Lakshadweep and the Andaman Islands and Nicobar Islands. About one per cent of the population of Kerala and Tamil Nadu are tribal whereas about six per cent in Andhra Pradesh and Karnataka are members of tribes.

The extent to which a state's population is tribal varies considerably. In the northeastern states of Arunachal Pradesh, Meghalaya, Mizoram and Nagaland, upward of 90 per cent of the population are tribal. However, in the remaining northeast states of Assam, Manipur, Sikkim and Tripura, tribal peoples range from 20 to 30 per cent of the population. The largest tribes are found in central India, although the tribal population there accounts for only around 10 per cent of the region's total population. Major concentrations of tribal people live in Maharashtra, Orissa and West Bengal. In the south, about 1 per cent of the populations of Kerala and Tamil Nadu are tribal, whereas about 6 per cent in Andhra Pradesh and Karnataka are members of tribes.

There are some 573 communities recognized by the government as Scheduled Tribes and therefore eligible to receive special benefits and to compete for reserved seats in legislatures and schools. They range in size from the Gonds (roughly 7.4 million) and the Santals (approximately 4.2 million) to only eighteen Chaimals in the Andaman Islands. Central Indian states have the country's largest tribes and taken as a whole, roughly 75 per cent of the total tribal population live in their own places.

The 1991 Census figures reveal that 42.02 per cent of the Scheduled Tribes population was main workers of whom 54.50 per cent were cultivators and 32.69 per cent agricultural labours. Thus, about 87 per cent of the main workers from these communities were engaged in primary sector activities. The literacy rate of Scheduled Tribes is around 29.60 per cent, as against the national average of 52 per cent.

More than three-quarters of Scheduled Tribe women are illiterate. These disparities are compounded by higher dropout rates in formal education resulting in disproportionately low representation in higher education. Not surprisingly, the cumulative effect has been that the proportion of Scheduled Tribes below the poverty line is substantially higher than the national average. The estimate of poverty made by Planning Commission for the year 1993-94 shows that 51.92 per cent rural and 41.4 per cent urban Scheduled Tribes are still living below the poverty line.

The Constitution of India incorporates several special provisions for the promotion of educational and economic interest of Scheduled Tribes and their protection from social injustice and all forms of exploitation. These objectives are sought to be achieved through a strategy known as the Tribal Sub-Plan strategy, which was adopted at the beginning of the Fifth Five-year Plan. The strategy seeks to ensure adequate flow of funds for tribal development from the State Plan allocations, schemes/programmes of Central Ministries/ Departments, financial and Developmental Institutions.

The cornerstone of this strategy has been to ensure earmarking of funds for TSP by States/UTs in proportion to the ST population in those State/UTs. Besides the efforts of the States/UTs and the Central Ministries/Departments to formulate and implement Tribal Sub-Plan for achieving socio-economic development of STs, the Ministry of Tribal Affairs is implementing several schemes and programmes for the benefits of STs.

Table 1.1: ST population in different States/UTs as per census 2011

Sl. No.	State	Percentage
1.	Madhya Pradesh	14.51
2.	Maharashtra	10.17
3.	Orissa	9.66
4.	Gujarat	8.87
5.	Rajasthan	8.42
6.	Jharkhand	8.40
7.	Chhattisgarh	7.85
8.	Andhra Pradesh	5.96
9.	West Bengal	5.23
10.	Karnataka	4.11
11.	Assam	3.92
12.	Meghalaya	2.36
13.	Nagaland	2.10
14.	Jammu and Kashmir	1.31
15.	Tripura	1.18
16.	Mizoram	1.00
17.	Bihar	0.90
18.	Manipur	0.88
19.	Arunachal Pradesh	0.84
20.	Tamil Nadu	0.77
21.	Kerala	0.43
22.	Uttarakhand	0.30
23.	Himachal Pradesh	0.29
24.	Dadra and Nagar Haveli	0.16
25.	Sikkim	0.13

Tribes (STs)

Traditionally referred as Adivasis, vanbasis, tribes, or tribals, STs constitute about 8 per cent of the Indian Population. According to the Indian Education Report 2002, there are 573 Scheduled Tribes living in different parts of the country, having their own languages different from the ones mostly spoken in the state where they live. There are more than 270 such languages in India.

Realizing that Scheduled Tribes are one of the most deprived and marginalized groups with regard to education, a host of programmes and measures were initiated ever since the Independence. Elementary education is a priority area in the tribal sub-plans from the 5th Five-year Plan. Education of ST children is considered important, not only due to the constitutional obligation but also as a crucial input for total development of tribal communities.

Another important development in the policy towards education of tribal population is the National Policy on Education (NPE), 1996. For the improvement in the education among the tribal people, the NPE specified the following:

1. Priority will be according to opening of primary schools in tribal areas.
2. There is need to develop curricula and devise instructional material in tribal languages at the initial stages with arrangements for switchover to regional languages.
3. ST youth will be encouraged to take up teaching in tribal areas.
4. Ashram schools/residential schools will be established on a large scale in tribal areas.
5. Incentive schemes will be formulated for the STs, keeping in view their special needs and lifestyle.
6. Since wastage is maximum in the lower classes, the curriculum should be slightly changed instead of elementary science and social studies, if they are taught about the tribal life and culture with an emphasis the history and achievements of the tribal people of the area

where the school is located, the tribal children will be more inclined towards their studies.

7. Wastage is a phenomenon in, which the number of students suddenly drops in higher classes. It is natural that in tribal areas, not all students proceed to the higher classes and that they become a drop out before reaching a particular stage in their educational career.

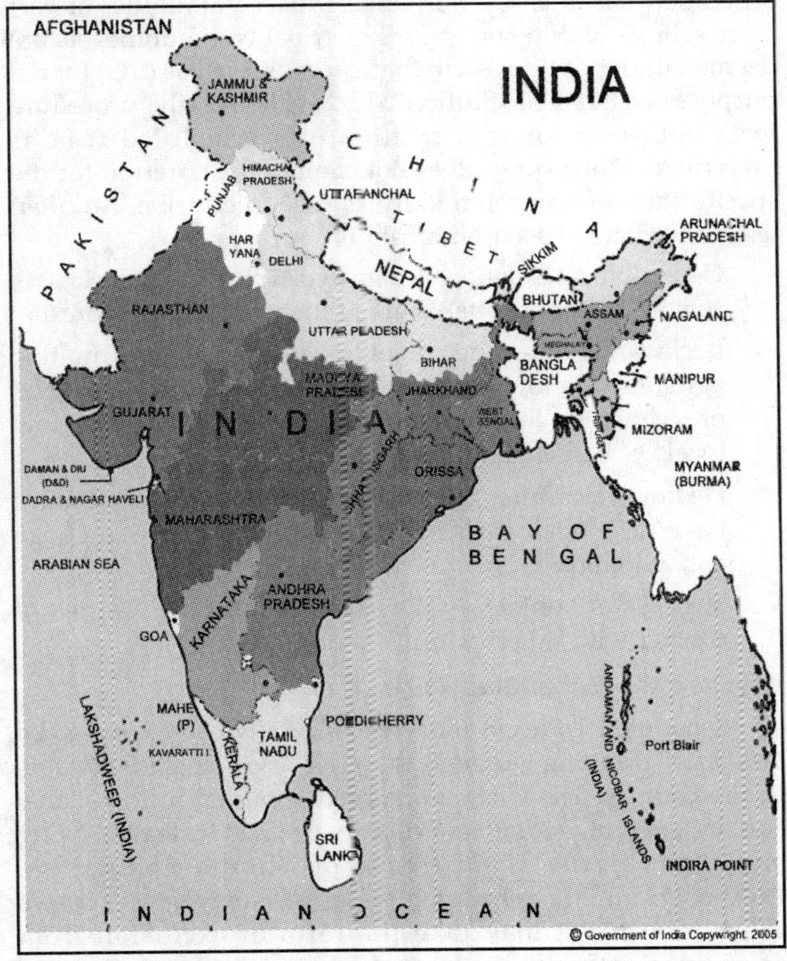

Map No. 1: Map Indicating Tribal Areas in India

Scheduled Tribes

A tribe is a group comprising families, alone, or generation having its own customs, occupying a specific geographic territory and being independence of or having little contact with the dominant national society of the country in which they live with their environment.

The Constitution of India, Article 366 (25) defines Scheduled Tribes as "such tribes or tribal communities or part of or groups within such tribes or tribal communities as are deemed under Article 342 to the Scheduled Tribes (STs) for the purposes of this Constitution". In Article 342, the procedure to be followed for specification of a scheduled tribe is prescribed. However, it does not contain the criterion for the specification of any community as scheduled tribe. An often used criterion is based on attributes such as:

- Geographical isolation — they live in cloistered, exclusive, remote and inhospitable areas such as hills and forests.
- Backwardness — their livelihood is based on primitive agriculture, a low-value closed economy with a low level of technology that leads to their poverty. They have low levels of literacy and health.
- Distinctive culture, language and religion — communities have developed their own distinctive culture, language and religion.
- Shyness of contact — they have a marginal degree of contact with other cultures and people.

Who are the Scheduled Tribes?

Scheduled Tribes in India are generally considered to be 'Adivasis,' meaning indigenous people or original inhabitants of the country. The tribes have been confined to low status and are often physically and socially isolated instead of being absorbed in the mainstream of Hindu population. Psychologically, the Scheduled Tribes often experience passive indifference that may take the form of exclusion from educational opportunities, social participation and access to their own land. All tribal communities are not alike. They are products of different historical and social conditions. They belong to different racial stocks and religious backgrounds and speak different dialects. As a result of being distanced by the Hindu population, many tribes have retained their social, religious, and cultural practices as well as their distinctive languages. Discrimination against women, occupational differentiation, and emphasis on status and hierarchical social ordering that characterize the predominant Hindu culture is generally not present among the tribal groups. Though there was trade between the Adivasis and the mainstream society, any form of social intercourse between the two groups was discouraged by the Hindus. Adivasis are not as a general rule regarded as unclean or polluted in the same way as the Scheduled Caste population is perceived by the mainstream Hindus. However, the mainstream Hindu population considers the general tribal population as primitive, technologically backward and illiterate. Since the 16th century, the tribes have been perceived as sub-humans who live under primitive conditions (Xaxa, 2005). They have often been portrayed as 'daityas,' 'rakshasas' (demons), and 'vanaras' (monkeys) in Indian epics. The tribal population constitutes a majority in the northeastern states of Mizoram (94.5%), Meghalaya (85.9%), and Nagaland (89.1%). Tribal men and women in Mizoram, Meghalaya and Nagaland are isolated from the mainstream Hindu population, their cultures and practices. Although tribes comprise a large proportion of the total population in the northeastern states, they account for a small (12%) per cent of the tribal population in India. Numerically, the tribal population is very high in the central state of Madhya Pradesh and the western states of Gujarat, Rajasthan, and Maharashtra. Together the four states account for about 50 per cent of the total tribal population in India. However, in these states tribes constitute a small per cent of the total Hindu population (Census of India, 2001).

Due to the lack of exposure to the mainstream Hindu population, the tribes in northeastern India have not been influenced or pressurized to adopt Hindu social and cultural practices and have maintained their heritage and social practices. On the other hand, many tribes in central and western India who are in close proximity to the mainstream population have adopted many Hindu practices in order to be accepted by the higher caste population. Differences in tribal religions also affect their educational attainment and attitudes towards female literacy. The vast majority of the tribal population in Mizoram, Meghalaya, and Nagaland are Christians. Christian missionaries.

Encouraged the tribal population in these states to pursue education and emphasized the importance of becoming literate. On the other hand, the literacy rates among the Hindu and Muslim population in India are relatively lower. The vast majority of the tribes in central and western India are Hindus.

Primitive Tribes

The Scheduled Tribe groups, who were identified as more backward communities among the tribal population groups have been categorized as 'Primitive Tribal Groups' (PTGs) by the Government at the Centre in 1975. So far seventy-five tribal communities have been identified as 'primitive tribal groups' in different States of India. These hunting, food-gathering and some agricultural communities, who have been identified as more backward communities among the tribal population groups need special programmes for their sustainable development. The primitive tribes are awakening and demanding their rights for special reservation quota for them.

Tribes and their Literacy

The literacy rate for scheduled Tribes has gone up from 8.5 per cent (male – 13.8%, female – 3.2%) in 1961 to 29.6 per cent (male – 40.6%, female – 18.2%) in 1991 and to 40 per cent (male – 59%, female – 37%) in 1999-2000 as per the 55th Round of National Sample Survey (NSS). According to Indian Education Report 2002, states with large proportion of STs like Mizoram, Nagaland and Meghalaya have high literacy rate while states with large number of tribal people like Madhya Pradesh, Orissa, Rajasthan and Andhra Pradesh have low tribal literacy rate. For instance, tribal literacy in Madhya

Pradesh was 7.6 per cent in 1971, 10.7 per cent in 1981, 21.5 per cent in 1991 and 36 per cent in 1999-2000 (NSS 55th Round) – all below the national average for tribal literacy rate is high ranging from 82 per cent in Mizoram to 17 per cent in Andhra Pradesh.

Table 1.2: Literacy rate in india: census 2011 (general population)

State/UT Code	India/State/UT	Literate Persons (%)	Males (%)	Females (%)
1.	Jammu and Kashmir	68.74	78.26	58.01
2.	Himachal Pradesh	83.78	90.83	76.60
3.	Punjab	76.68	81.48	71.34
4.	Chandigarh	86.43	90.54	81.38
5.	Uttarakhand	79.63	88.33	70.70
6.	Haryana	76.64	85.38	66.77
7.	NCT of Delhi	86.34	91.03	80.93
8.	Rajasthan	67.06	80.51	52.66
9.	Uttar Pradesh	69.72	79.24	59.26
10.	Bihar	63.82	73.39	53.33
11.	Sikkim	82.20	87.29	76.43
12.	Arunachal Pradesh	66.95	73.69	59.57
13.	Nagaland	80.11	83.29	76.69
14.	Manipur	79.85	86.49	73.17
15.	Mizoram	91.58	93.72	89.40
16.	Tripura	87.75	92.18	83.15
17.	Meghalaya	75.48	77.17	73.78
18.	Assam	73.18	78.81	67.27
19.	West Bengal	77.08	82.67	71.16
20.	Jharkhand	67.63	78.45	56.21
21.	Orissa	73.45	82.40	64.36

Contd..

State/UT Code	India/State/UT	Literate Persons (%)	Males (%)	Females (%)
22.	Chattisgarh	71.04	81.45	60.59
23.	Madhya Pradesh	70.63	80.53	60.02
24.	Gujarat	79.31	87.23	70.73
25.	Daman and Diu	87.07	91.48	79.59
26.	Dadra and Nagar Haveli	77.65	86.46	65.93
27.	Maharashtra	82.91	89.82	75.48
28.	Andhra Pradesh	67.66	75.56	59.74
29.	Karnataka	75.60	82.85	68.13
30.	Goa	87.40	92.81	81.84
31.	Lakshadweep	92.28	96.11	88.25
32.	Kerala	93.91	96.02	91.98
33.	Tamil Nadu	80.33	86.81	73.86
34.	Pondicherry	86.55	92.12	81.22
35.	Andaman and Nicobar Islands	86.27	90.11	81.84
	India	**74.04**	**82.14**	**65.46**

Table 1.2: Shows the literacy rates of males and females for selected states in India as per 2011 Census

The literacy rate among tribal women in urban areas in Mizoram is the highest in the country and even surpasses the literacy rate of tribal urban women in Kerala, which is considered to be a model state in literacy rates of women in the country. Some contend that since the northeastern states are isolated and not exposed to the social and cultural norms of the Hindu population, the former do not follow the common trend of downplaying the importance of literacy attainment among girls. Thus the "convergence effect" of following the mainstream norm of encouraging gender inequality in education is absent among the tribal women in some of the northeastern states of India. The influence of Christianity in the northeastern states also played a significant role in encouraging high literacy rate among tribal women. Conversely, in the central state of Madhya Pradesh and the western states of Gujarat and Rajasthan, as well as the eastern states of Bihar, Orissa, and West Bengal, female literacy rate is significantly lower than the northeastern states. Unlike the northeastern states, the tribal population in the central, eastern, and western states constitutes a minority as a percentage of the total Hindu population. In these states, tribal groups are regularly exposed to the social and cultural practices of the mainstream Hindus and their discriminatory practices against women.

Many scheduled tribes imitate the practices and traditions of Hindus in order to gain acceptance in larger society. Next to the northeastern states, the state of Kerala shows relatively high literacy rate among tribal women in urban areas. Kerala ranks the highest in the country in terms of women literacy rate and gender development index. Although the tribal population is very small in Kerala, their exposure to the general trend of high female literacy rate in the state and the high status of women in Kerala may have partially contributed to the high literacy rate among tribal women.

Gross Enrollment Ratio and Drop-out Rates for Scheduled Tribes in India Gross Enrollment Ratio (GER) is the number of students enrolled in different levels of education (whether or not they belong to the relevant age group for that level), as a percentage of the population in the relevant age group for that level.. In general, we find that as the level of education increases, the GER decreases for both boys and girls. This clearly demonstrates that poverty is a significant deterrent to enrollment as both boys and girls are needed in household and family work, and families cannot afford to send their children to schools because these families do not have the economic resources. It is also interesting to note that the GER of boys and girls are comparable in classes I-IV but the gender gap increases significantly with higher levels of education. This may be indicative of the conservative social fabric of the

Hindu society, where girls are expected to get married early and boys are given preference over girls in a family's decision to allocate resources for their children's education. We find that the northeastern states show a different trend in GER of girls and boys than some of the other states in India. In the northeastern state of Meghalaya, the GER of girls is higher than boys in both levels of schooling. In Mizoram, the GER of girls is higher than boys in classes I-V and comparable in grades VI-VIII. In Nagaland, more girls than boys are enrolled in classes VI-VIII. The GER for tribal girls in Mizoram in both classes I-V and VI-VIII far surpasses the GER for girls in the general population in both categories.

In contrast to the northeastern states, the eastern state of Bihar shows a dismal picture. Here, the enrollment ratio for girls in higher levels of education is only 8.53 per cent for the tribal population and 18.77 per cent for the general population. Orissa and West Bengal also show a low GER for girls in classes VI-VIII among tribal women. The state of Kerala in South India shows a very high GER for girls in higher classes both among tribal women and the general population. Kerala is an outlier in India in terms of its literacy and educational attainment of women and clearly this has a spillover effect among other groups of population. In general, there are vast differences in the enrollment patterns of tribal women across the different states in India. Some of the differences can be attributed to poverty and lack of resources among various tribal groups; however other factors such as the social and cultural fabric of the society and the status of women among various tribal groups also account for the differentials in the enrollment patterns of women in some states.

There are now 194 Integrated Tribal Development Projects (ITDPs) in the country, where the ST population is more than 50 per cent of the total population of the blocks or groups of block. During the Sixth Plan, pockets outside ITDP areas, having a total population of 10,000 with at least 5,000 scheduled tribes were covered under the Tribal Sub-Plan under Modified Area Development Approach (MADA). So far 252 MADA pockets have been identified in the country. In addition, 79 cluster with a total population of 5,000 of which 50 per cent Scheduled Tribes have been identified.

In order to give more focused attention to the development of Scheduled Tribes, a separate Ministry, known as the Ministry of Tribal Affairs was constituted in October 1999. The new Ministry carved out of the Ministry of Social Justice and Empowerment, is the nodal Ministry for overall policy, planning and coordination of programmes and schemes for the development of Scheduled Tribes.

The mandate of the Ministry includes social security and social insurance with respect to the Scheduled Tribes, tribal welfare planning, project formulation research and training, promotion and development of voluntary efforts on tribal welfare and certain matters relating to administration of the Scheduled Areas. Each Central Ministry/Department will be the nodal Ministry of Department concerning its sector. Ministry of Tribal Affairs supports and supplements the efforts of State Governments/UT Administrations and the various Central Ministries/Departments for the holistic development of these communities.

Tribal Literacy Rate

Delivering inaugural address at the International Seminar on "Adivasi/ST Communities in India: Development and Change" organized by the Institute for Human Development, Indian Vice President, Mr. M. Hamid Ansari said that the literacy rate of the Schedule Tribes (STs) at 47.1 in the 2001 Census is far below the national literacy rate of 64.84. Tribal children suffer from high drop out rates and low female literacy. They also have high infant mortality rates and malnutrition as compared to other population groups. "If there is any group of Indian people that has been shabbily treated is the 'Adivasis' (tribals). They have been disgracefully treated, neglected for the last 6,000 years," Ansari said. "The reality is unpalatable and the data speaks for itself. Compared to other sections of our society, the tribal population has the lowest Human Development Index. The literacy rate of the STs at 47.1 in the

2001 Census is far below the national literacy rate of 64.84. Tribal children suffer from high drop out rates and low female literacy. They suffer from geographical and social exclusion, high poverty rates and lack of access to appropriate administrative and judicial mechanisms. Low level of infrastructural endowments and growing gap in infrastructure creation in tribal areas, as compared to the rest of India, has further diminished prospects for progress.

The Vice-President opined that the Forest Rights Act of 2006 represents an important step in attempting to reverse the marginalization of our tribal people. It gives legislative teeth to the Constitutional provisions for protection and development of Scheduled Tribes, provides them a level playing field and casts tribal rights in a new matrix based on community control and customary access. It acknowledges the immense hardship caused to the Scheduled Tribes due to insecurity of tenurial and access rights and forced relocation due to State development interventions.

Over 80 per cent of the Scheduled Tribes population works in the primary sector, with 45 per cent of them being cultivators and 37 per cent being agricultural labourers and thus represents the most important source of livelihood, emotional attachment and social stability in tribal communities. It is critical for cultivation, horticulture, forestry and animal husbandry. The Draft National Tribal Policy testifies to it and notes that "alienation of tribal land is the single most important cause of pauperization of tribals, rendering their vulnerable economic situation more precarious."

Quick implementation of the provisions of this Act by various State Governments would go a long way in realizing the vision of our Founding Fathers and ensuring that economic development and social progress is inclusive.

Literacy Trends among Tribal Women

Literacy is an important indicator of development among tribal groups. Among women in general, high literacy rates lead to lower infant mortality rates, reduce the number of pregnancies and enhance the status of women both in domestic life and society. Additionally, the mother's literacy status and educational attainment have significantly positive effects on the child's human capital attainment (Sengupta and Guha, 2002; Colclough, 1982). During the Post-Independence period, the Indian government implemented legislation and allocated funds to facilitate access to enrollment in primary education (grades I-V) in India. As a result, both literacy rates and gross enrollment ratios of boys and girls across the general population have increased substantially during the past 50 years. The tribal population, in general, lags behind the Hindus and the Scheduled Caste population both in literacy and educational attainment. This discrepancy in human capital attainment between the mainstream population and the tribes is particularly marked among tribal women. However, the literacy rates for scheduled tribes in India have also improved substantially from 1961 (8.54%) to 1991 (29.60%) for both males (13.83% to 40.65%) and females (3.16% to 18.19%).

Factors Contributing to the Low Literacy Rates among Tribal Women in India

Socio-economic factors contribute significantly to disparities in literacy and educational attainment among women in rural and urban areas. The Scheduled Caste and Scheduled Tribe population have been discriminated against and confined to the lowest rungs of social and economic hierarchies. As Dreze pointed out, "educational disparities, which contribute a great deal to the persistence of massive inequalities in Indian society, also largely derive from more fundamental inequalities such as those of class, caste and gender." High poverty rates and dependence on agriculture call for increasing rates of child labor force participation among many of the tribes in India. The tribal dropout rate is extremely high relative to the mainstream population. Children often enroll in primary education and then drop out of school in order to help the family. This applies more to females than males both among the mainstream Hindu population and the tribal groups because girls are expected to help out with domestic chores more than boys at a very early age. Traditionally, the Hindu society has demonstrated its preference for sons and has treated boys and girls differently based on social and cultural norms. Parents often allocate their scarce resources towards the schooling of their sons. For the poorer sections of the population, it is worthwhile investing in the son's education, as that would generate income for the family in the future. Daughters are expected to get married early, and parents have to save money for dowry payments. Further, parents do not want to invest in their daughters' schooling because the latter have limited labour market opportunities and earning potential. For the poorer sections of the Indian community, education for girls is often considered to be consumption good rather than an investment good. This perception is partly justified in light of the poor labour market prospects for women in many states and especially in rural areas. This leads to a significant gender gap in investment in education in India although recent trends show that wealthy and educated families in urban areas are allocating resources equally between their sons and daughters.

The tribal society in general is characterized by lack of discrimination against women and tribal women participate in all spheres of economic and social lives. This is particularly true among the matrilineal tribal groups in the northeastern states of Mizoram, Nagaland, and Meghalaya. Unlike Hindus, most tribal societies value girls, as shown by the high female sex ratio (females per 1000 males) among the vast majority of tribes in India (Census of India, 2001). The negative relationship between poverty and literacy attainment can often be overcome if women are considered to be an important part of society and if the social and cultural norms are in favor of women's human capital attainment. Some unique obstacles faced by tribal women in addition to the high poverty rates are insufficient numbers of schools in many tribal areas, lack of resources in tribal schools, significant language barriers in schools where the teachers are not fluent in tribal languages (Srivastava, 1997), and the problems in social adjustment faced by many tribal boys and girls who are often discriminated against by upper-caste children.

Status of Tribal Women in India

Decisive elements giving these societies are stability and cohesiveness. Emphasis on gender, a relational concept provides opportunities for looking at full range of social and cultural institutions, which reproduce gender hierarchies and gender-based inequalities. The cultural interpretation of gender is central to the identity and status of women that entails web of Relationships. The conceptual framework to analyse women's status comprise the seven roles women play in life and work - parental, conjugal, domestic, kin, occupational, community and as an individual. In order tc appraise the social status of women in these diverse ecological areas, the findings have been divided in to subsequent categories:

(a) a girl/daughter/a unmarried woman;

(b) a married woman;

(c) a widow;

(d) divorcee; and

(e) a barren woman.

Apart from the social status, women role in the social sphere; her political domain; religious sphere; economic activities; and decision-making.

What is considered as a special joyful moment in any traditional Hindu family in the country? Well, the birth of a son! But this is not the case in the tribals in India, as girls and boys are both considered equal. In most of the so-called 'modern' Indian families, women are susceptible to undergo an abortion as soon as they come to know that the foetus is that of a girl child. Women undergo number of pregnancies just because they want a boy and not a female child. Well, modern women should and must learn something from the tribal society regarding this. A tribal woman declares her pregnancy with pride and does not welcome her husband till she is willing to conceive again. Delivery is without the assistance of a midwife and mother herself cuts the umbilical chord. The mother nurses the baby with her milk, carries it everywhere in a piece of old cloth hanging from her shoulder. She puts her child to sleep in a bamboo cradle. Older sisters attend to their younger siblings.

Girls' and Women's Education

World Education has a long history of successfully working with local partners to design, execute, manage and evaluate participatory, community-based initiatives to advance the conditions of girls and women. World Education's programmes help girls enrollment and stay in schools and help women gain access to or create new educational, financial, and social resources in their communities. World Education programmes help girls and women improve their own lives, the lives of their families and the conditions in their communities. For parents, and especially mothers — this means creating conditions that ensure their daughters have equal access to basic education, are able to make informed decisions about their futures, and are able to protect themselves from trafficking, sexual exploitation, HIV and AIDS.

By improving educational opportunities for girls and women, World Education helps women to develop skills that allow them to make decisions and influence community change in key areas. In turn, these programmes have a positive impact on some of the most profound issues of our time: population growth, HIV and AIDS, peace and security, and the widening gap between the rich and poor.

Drop-out Rates among Scheduled Tribe Girls

The dropout rates for the tribal population for 2002-03 indicates rates for both boys and girls increase sharply as their educational level increases. Among the general population, the drop out rate in classes I-V during 2002-03 was 35.85 per cent among boys, while it was 33.72 per cent among girls. Among all tribal groups, the dropout rate in classes I-V was 41.13 per cent among boys and 41.91 per cent among girls. At lower levels of education when the children are relatively young, there is no significant gender discrepancy in the dropout rates among all groups. However, as the level of education increases, the gender gap becomes much more pronounced among the tribal groups. The dropout rate among tribal boys in classes 1-VIII is 66.86 per cent while it is 71.17 per cent among girls. The dropout rate among boys in the general population is 50.82 per cent, while it is 52.10 per cent among girls.

The high costs of providing education and the need for children to work contribute to the high dropout rates in higher levels of education. This is particularly true for girls as poor families with limited resources would invest money in their son's education rather than in their daughter's education for reasons discussed earlier. While education at the lower level is free, there are other costs, including books and learning materials, which impose a significant financial burden on low-income tribal families (Ramachandran 2003). Thus, the supply of human capital is constrained by poverty, lack of resources, shortage of schools, inadequate infrastructure, and low emphasis on education, especially in rural areas. The demand side of the labour market also has a feedback effect on the investment decisions of tribal groups in education. The vast majority of Scheduled Tribes rely on agriculture and forestry for their livelihood and a few are employed in skilled jobs. Table 1.3 demonstrates a great deal of variation in the tribal dropout rates in the different states in India. The gender discrepancy in the dropout rate is relatively lower in the northeastern states of Mizoram, Nagaland, and Meghalaya. The dropout rate among tribal girls in classes I-VIII is the lowest in the states of Himachal Pradesh and Uttar Pradesh in northern India, followed by Kerala in south India and Nagaland in northeastern India. Interestingly enough, the dropout rates among tribal girls in the above states are far below the national average among the general population in this category (53.45%).

Table 1.3: Dropout rates in classes I-V, I-VIII and I-X std students year 2009-10

Sl. No.	State/UTs	Classes I - V	Classes I- VIII	Classes I- X
		Girls	Girls	Girls
1.	Andhra Pradesh	39.64	69.36	78.07
2.	Arunachal Pradesh	38.14	48.09	65.21
3.	Assam	31.41	67.43	79.53
4.	Bihar	15.64	56.95	98.12
5.	Chhattisgarh	39.53	52.93	—
6.	Goa	87.1	—	—
7.	Gujarat	50.89	58.25	74.92
8.	Haryana	—	—	—
9.	Himachal Pradesh	3.77	16.31	9.95
10.	J and K	31.88	67.64	72.40
11.	Jharkhand	36.24	77.77	—
12.	Karnataka	22.54	31.37	50.73
13.	Kerala	12.33	4.76	15.01
14.	Madhya Pradesh	17.76	43.38	85.04
15.	Maharashtra	23.07	51.83	74.23
16.	Manipur	60.43	80.13	72.55
17.	Meghalaya	48.18	7.91	76.29
18.	Mizoram	47.84	54.03	61.14
19.	Nagaland	39.01	31.64	66.09
20.	Odisha	32.04	74.91	85.13
21.	Punjab	—	—	—
22.	Rajasthan	52.61	64.92	79.43
23.	Sikkim	12.07	-7.15	65.50
24.	Tamil Nadu	1.85	51.32	-2.34
25.	Tripura	38.14	62.61	74.39

Contd...

Sl. No.	State/UTs	Classes I - V	Classes I- VIII	Classes I- X
		Girls	Girls	Girls
26.	Uttar Pradesh	214.59	47.33	67.61
27.	Uttara Khand	19.31	33.90	—
28.	West Bangal	39.76	67.37	82.65
29.	A and N Islands	8.79	11.98	36.40
30.	Chandigarh	—	—	—
31.	D and N Haveli	23.56	61.06	72.32
32.	Daman and Diu	7.65	28.44	53.11
33.	Delhi	18.35	47.16	6.48
34.	Lakshadweep	9.24	5.55	18.30
35.	Puducherry	—	—	—
	India	**33.72**	**60.64**	**75.85**

Upswing in Girls' Enrollment

Growth in access to schooling has been matched by a steady increase in enrollment with the most dramatic upswing since 1990 in girls participation levels. From 13.8 million boys and 5.4 million girls enrolled at the primary level in 1950-51, the number rose to 69.7 million boys and 61.1 million girls in 2004-05. At the upper primary level, the enrolment increased from 2.6 million boys and 0.5 million girls to 28.5 million boys and 22.7 million girls.

The proportion of girls in the total enrollment has also been growing. Girls' enrolment at the primary stage increased from 28.1 per cent in 1950-51 to 46.7 per cent in 2004-05. At the upper primary stage, girls' enrollment rose from 16.1 per cent in 1950-51 to 44.4 per cent in 2004-05. The overall improvement in girls' enrollment with respect to total population of girls clearly shows that there is a near universal enrollment at primary level. The gap and challenge exists now at upper primary stage, but there too the gap is narrowing steadily.

Enrollment of Scheduled Caste and Scheduled Tribe girls poses a greater challenge to India's education administrators. Survey data, however, revealed that the participation of these disadvantaged girls in basic education, has grown steadily over the years. G.E.R. for SC girls at primary level have climbed up from 64.8 per cent in 1986-87 to 106.6 per cent in 2004-05 and at upper primary stage, from as low as 26.6 per cent in 1986-87 to 61.5 per cent in 2004-05. In the case of ST girls, the Gross Enrollment Ratio (GER) at primary level have gone up from 68 per cent in 1986-87 to 115.5 per cent by 2004-05 and from 21.9 per cent in 1986-87 to 59.5 per cent in 2004-05 for upper primary level.

The overall gender gap in enrollment at the primary stage has dropped to 4.6 percentage points and that at the upper primary level has reduced to 8.0 percentage points in 2005. There are only 48 districts out of a total of 600 districts in India, with a gender gap above 10 percentage points at the primary stage. Focused attention is being targeted to these districts by education policy planners, in order to address the barriers in specific terms.

Declining Drop-Out Rates and Out-of-School Girls

Providing access and enrolment to schooling facilities are only a part of the story. Our aim is also to help the students to continue their studies. Although the phenomenon of drop outs continue to be a serious problem in India's education scenario, the drop out rates in elementary education have been on the decline, more sharply so for girls. Girls drop out rate in 2004-05 was lower than for boys, at primary level *i.e.,* 25.42 per cent compared to 31.81 per cent for boys. Since 2000, girls drop out rates have fallen by 16.5 per cent points in just four years, compared to a reduction of only 4.1 per cent points over the entire last decade (1990-2000).

With respect to the situation inside the school it is found that the repetition rates have been fast declining for girls. Two clear messages that underlie this trend are: one that girls who enter the school system do not leave easily and two, school efficiency is gradually improving with girls completing the elementary cycle of education in lesser time.

The number of out of school children has also been declining rapidly, from 32 million in 2001-02 to 7.5 million in 2006-07. Of the total age cohort of girls in the 6-14 years age group, 3.9 per cent are reportedly out of school. In the 6-11 years age group, out of school girls are 3.34 per cent and in the 11-14 years age group they are 5.3 per cent. The inclusion of these 'hard to reach' and older girls, who have remained excluded from the education net is being addressed through context specific strategies and interventions presently.

More Girls Move to Upper Primary Classes

The trends in transition rates from Primary to Upper Primary are also positive. The transition rate has improved from 71.98 in 2003 to 80.64 in 2005. The gains in the transition rates of girls (8.6 percentage points) have been higher than that of boys (7.65 percentage points). This has led to sharper decline in the gender gap in transition rates from 4.03 percentage points to 3.02 percentage points.

In the case of SC girls, the transition rate has increased from 80 per cent in 2004-05 to 83 per cent in 2005-06 leaving a gender gap of 3 percentage points. The picture is comparable in the case of ST girls for whom the transition rate has increased from 85 per cent in 2004-05 to 88 per cent in 2005-06 leaving a gender gap of 2 percentage points.

Problems of Tribal Education in India

1. Location of Schools - Rural and Urban

Rural habitations and access to secondary level schooling facilities is one of the important problems. Secondary level schools in rural areas having *kutcha* buildings are facing many problems, especially during rainy seasons. Non-availability of drinking water facility is also hampering the interest of the students in Secondary schools. There is an acute shortage and non availability of Toilet (Urinal and Lavatory) facilities in secondary schools in rural areas is also an important problem. The girls are very much deprived of the basic amenities in most of the schools in tribal areas. Many of the schools situated in tribal rural areas do not have *Pacca* buildings and the students are compelled to adjust with Kutcha buildings which are lagging with basic requirements. Though the urban schools are equipped well than their counter parts in several infrastructural and instructional aspects. Schools located at interior villages have severe disadvantages because of lack of proper communication facilities. The students belonging to this area are less exposed to the outside world and also the level of awareness and assimilation of new ideas through formal education is apparently low compared to the students, who are at schools situated at the road side.

The girls are very much deprived of the basic amenities as most of the schools in tribal areas are not equipped with Urinal and toilets.

2. *Economically Backward Families*

In most of the tribal families income is one of the important factors which construed to be a deciding feature for their girl child to be educated. Tribal girl has become a home maker to look after the siblings, apart from assisting her parents in working environment also like daily labour in construction works, agricultural labour, etc., in many of the families. Hence, the parents do not want to loose her participation in home survival.

3. *Teacher Related Problems*

The relationship between teachers, schools and the villagers is quite thin. In tribal villages, villagers have virtually no relationship with the teacher. Teachers do not get any accommodation facility in the village, which makes them irregular, ultimately hampers to normal routine of a school. Further, the apathetic attitude of the villagers and their simplicity provide ample scope to the teachers to act according to their wish and will.

The appointment of untrained teachers in tribal areas diminishes the values of education.

Lack of special incentives for the teachers in tribal areas serve as a demotivating factor for the teachers and degrades their efficiency.

Teachers have a pre-conception that tribal children are average students; so they don't take special care in promoting tribal education. The pre-conceived notions of the teachers that the urban children cannot grasp anything beyond nature. The non-tribal teachers adopt an attitude of indifference of tribal languages, traditions, cultural and life style. They fail to perceive human values ingrained in these folk culture .When they try to impart an education, which neglects these human values and culture, they fail to make it interesting for the tribal children.

The ideas of non-tribal teachers about tribal environment and culture are narrow and hallow. For this, they fail to cite examples from the surrounding and make the concepts complicated for the tribal students. The inbuilt creativity of tribal children remains unknown to the teachers.

Teachers face wide gulf between the language used in the books and the native uses while teaching the tribal students. They simply opine that the content of the text books is beyond the comprehension of the students so teaching becomes futile.

Children's engagement in household works, agricultural coupled with parent's indifference towards their children's studies, deprives the teachers to render their services in the class room. No efforts are made on the part of the higher authorities and the tribal masses to curb the frequent and recurrent inspection mechanism, no doubt aggravates the situation.

Many of the schools situated in tribal areas do not have adequate number of teachers. Even in some schools, there are untrained teachers. Most of the teachers working in secondary schools in tribal region do not reside in the same village. Hence they have a little association with the students and their parents. Interaction between teacher and tribal students is very much minimal. Non-tribal teachers show negative attitude towards tribal learners. Non-tribal teachers are unable to mingle with the tribal students due to their cultural and ethnic difference. Inadequate number of female teachers at secondary schools is also a problem for tribal girl students.

The girl students prefer female teachers. The tribal girl students feel that non-tribal teachers show discriminatory attitude towards tribal students.

4. Teaching Learning

The languages used in the books are beyond the understanding of the tribal children. Sometimes the local teachers also get confused by the bookish language and do not try to communicate in the tribal languages. As a result, teaching seems to be artificial for the tribal children. The contents of the primary school books are fewer practices oriented and are more factual and abstract. Teaching at primary schools ignores the local nature, culture and environment. There is dearth of study materials and kits in the class rooms.

The kits that are provided to the schools under the Operation Black Board Scheme are not properly utilised by the teachers. Books are not supplied to the schools at the session beginning by the Tribal Welfare Department. This irregularity found in the supply of books creates problems both for the teachers and students. Further, stipends are not being given in due time.

5. Parents

An educated parent seem to influence their children to be well educated and prefer white collar occupations like teaching and medicine; those more committed to educate their children have wards, who find enough time to study outside school hours and are less likely to discontinue their school studies for immediate employment. The effect of parental education on the middle class aspirations and academic habits of their children is evident. On the issue of parental attitude towards education and educating the child, it is observed that the tribal parents are not in a serious mood about the education of their children. They do not like that their educated children should leave their family in search of jobs and leave agriculture as their profession. The educational background of the parents is one of the key factors in determining the development of education of tribal children. Hence, the parents need to be encouraged to get education through non-formal means. They will in turn automatically encourage the education of their children.

6. *Social Aspects*

The enrollment of girls has been a low compared to boys. The tribal communities are not showing interest to educate their girl children due to some traditional inhibitions. Parents have a great appreciation about the attitude of educated youth. In contrary to this, they have a fear that they may not be able to find an educated groom for their girl child, if she is educated. It is due to that the educated tribal youth have come to a stage to prescribe some yardsticks for the selection of their life partner. For the tribal girl, 'husband' needs to have education, employment and free from all sorts of vices.

7. *Peer Group*

Tribal girls students studying in urban schools feels that they are ill-treated/defamed by their co-students of other communities due to their social strata, appearance etc., tribal girl students are inferior to their poor communication skills and low social status.

8. *Learning Experiences*

Educational infrastructure at schools such as teachings aids, laboratories and libraries are either inadequate or not present in some schools. Text books are based on urban middle class, non-tribal culture. Text books, which are prescribed, are not catering to the needs of tribal culture, tradition. The tribal schools are not having curriculum based on their local culture, tradition. Hence, the tribal girl students are unable to show interest in pursuing secondary education. Due to routine curriculum, which is being neglected, is not giving scope for the tribal girls to peruse the secondary education. No learning experiences are provided in tribal mother tongue. This can be treated as a bottleneck in the spread of tribal girl education. Many tribal girls are not appreciating the learning experiences and not willing to sit among four walls of a class room due to the tribal concept of pleasure.

9. *Physical Aspects*

Many of the tribal girl students expressed that the teaching on health and hygienic habits has to become a part of curricula in the schools.

Suggestions for Solving Educational Problems

Though the Government has done much to solve the educational problems of the tribal students, still it should take the following steps for ameliorating the problems that are remained;

1. At least in pre-primary and primary schools, the teachers should be preferably of the same tribe and locality in which the school is located, so that they may have a sense of self-involvement in the betterment of the school and in teaching the students, whom they know from their very birth. The teacher's responsibility does not cease after the enrollment drive at the beginning of the school session. It should be made duty of the teachers to visit the homes of children and to find out the reasons for their absence. Such frequent visits of the teachers will bring them nearer to the parents as well as the students. There should be some kind of reward and punishment to the teachers. If a bulk of students become a drop-out, there should be curtailment in the salary of teachers and on the contrary, if at a school the percentage of drop outs and stagnation is very much less, the teachers as well as the students should be given incentives in the shape of extra-allowance to the teachers and prizes to students.
2. In tribal areas having difficult terrain, there should be primary school in each and every village, so that the children may not have to cover long distance every day for going to the school.
3. Holidays and vacations should be allowed during all local festivals and during sowing and harvesting seasons. Instead of giving holidays on every Sunday, it should be given on weekly market days. The weekly holidays would therefore vary from school to school.
4. At least in the lower primary stage, the tribal children should be taught through the medium of their own tribal language. This is possible only when the teacher himself knows both the languages, the tribe as well as official regional language. After a year or two of schooling at

the primary stage, the regional and other languages should be introduced gradually.

5. Modern educational theory does not hold yearly examination in the primary stage necessary for promotion. The entire three years period should be regarded as unit and the progress made by the students should be finally tested at the end of this period. In between, there should be simple tests, which would help the teachers asses the caliber of each student as well as the progress made by him. Thus, the problem of stagnation in the primary stage would disappear. At the end of the primary stage, only such students as can bear the burden of higher education should be promoted." (Sachchidanada; 1967:211).
6. Since wastage is maximum in the lower classes, the curriculum should be slightly changed. Instead of elementary science and social studies, if they are taught about the tribal life and culture with an emphasis the history and achievements of the tribal people of the areas, where the school is located, the tribal children will be more inclined towards their studies.
7. Wastage is a phenomenon in which the number of students suddenly drops in higher classes. It is natural that in tribal areas, not all students proceed to the higher classes and that they drop out before reaching a particular stage in their educational career. Some of them give up study as it does not interest them; others leave it because of poverty. The extent of wastage can be reduced by providing adequate hostel accommodation, larger number of stipends, book grants, mid-day-meals and the provision of other educational facilities. We have also to remove the fear in the minds of parents that if they give higher education to the children, the latter would be lost to home and in that case they would not like to stay in their father's occupation but would prefer to look for petty jobs in the town. Many children are not allowed to pursue higher studies for this reason." (Sachchidananda; 1967:211).

8. The general complaint of the tribal students and their guardians is that the disbursement of scholarship is not regular in schools and colleges. Due to administrative and procedural delay, the scholarships are paid after five-six months or even more. Because of these delays either the tribal students or guardians are compelled to borrow money at heavy rate of interest. In many cases it so happens that after the student gets a consolidated amount as scholarship for several months, they have to pay-back the loans with huge interest and are left with little money for their study. They get their scholarship at a time when their needs have been satisfied or they have left their studies in despair. Therefore, it is suggested that payment of scholarship should be released on time and the Head Masters, Principals and all other heads of educational institutions should ensure to grant scholarships from the very month the student joins their institution and for this purpose, necessary fund should be placed at their disposal well in advance of the academic year. This should be done on the basis of previous years grant with a margin of increase. Scholarship may be paid to every student along with the salaries of teachers, so that every student gets the scholarship in the beginning of the month. Secondary, considering the price-rise; the amount of scholarship granted to the tribal student is very low. Scholarships should be increased to cover all necessary expenses while the student is studying at school and college and not merely a part of expenses because most of the tribal students have not any private resource to cover the huge cost incurred in education.
9. As the tribes are inhibiting in the small, scattered habitations, deep in the forest, the Government has to start more number of schools in these habitations and also establish Ashram schools and tribal welfare residential schools for further studies.
10. It is true that the majority of the tribals are illiterate, ignorant, living in deep forest without any communication with the general population. In order to, improve

these people, schools are to be established in the tribal hamlets and for those, who have reached the maturity and certain level of education, Residential schools for tribal girls are to be established.

11. In order to attract and to retain the tribal children in the residential schools, the Government has to create and establish tribal educational complexes and provide homely atmosphere with local teachers, even summating the tribal languages to be used at the initial stages. In order to find out the physical facilities made available for the comfortable stay of the girls, living accommodation, number of bathrooms and other facilities are to be made available for study and quality of the food to be served and to maintain cleanliness etc.

12. In some of the Hostels, the living accommodation available for the girls is ranged from two rooms to fifteen rooms for the students ranging from 52 to more than 300. This clearly shows that the extent of accommodation available for the girls is very low and they were made to adjust and share in a less place.

The number of bathrooms available in the hostel is also ranged from two to ten. This clearly shows that each bathroom has to be used by not less than 20 pupils. And this creates a lot of problems in terms of time and health. The class room accommodation, living place, bath rooms and toilets available for the girls reveals the putative situation of managing the schools. This type of environment clearly develops a negative attitude among the children and it may lead to the withdrawal of the children from the schools. To curb the above problems the Government has to chalk out plan and programme in Five-year Plan to allocate more funds to establish Hostels exclusively for the tribal girls students.

13. In most of the residential schools for girls, there are problems of toilet blocks, study rooms and recreation facilities, which will inspire them to stay and study. Hence, the Government attention is required in this direction to improve the educational environment in the schools so as to retain the tribal girls who are different from non-

tribal girls. Once, these girls drop out from such an environment, it is difficult to bring them back. Hence, suitable measures to improve the situation are called for.

14. Free supply of text books will also create an interest among the girl students to continue their studies, despite the fact that they are unable to purchase the books.
15. Teaching aids are required to make the learning easy. They not only help the teacher in his communication in teaching but also help the students in grasping the subject taught clearly. Hence, efforts may be made to make use of the teaching aids by all the teachers in all the subjects.
16. Most of the tribal girls are unable to understand the lessons which are in other than their language and also in difficult level. In the context, grouping the students as below average and above average and provide remedial coaching would be more worthwhile for below average students.
17. In addition to the regular teaching in the class room, assigning home work to the students is normal in any school. In the case of residential schools there is a provision for tutor directed learning to stabilize what they have already learned. Cross checking the home work and counseling on the mistakes they committed will also improve their standards.
18. In order to understand the desire of the tribal girls in pursuing their future education, interest to be generated among them by providing basic amenities in the school environment.
19. It is generally assumed that majority of the tribal parents may not be willing to send their children particularly the girls away from their house by foregoing some assisting hands to a newer environment. The parents of the tribal girls should be educated through various programmes with respect to future job aspiration of tribal children.
20. In a rationalistic and culture valued country like us, the parents desire to have male children than the girl is more. The parents also treat their children based on sex the

male children are treated superior than girls which is also reflected in the day to day treatment. This point need to be taken care of by the government seriously and implement certain motivational schemes like fixed deposit scheme for the single girl child, scholarships schemes for the higher studies etc.

Tribes of Gujarat

Tribes of Gujarat are primarily resided in the rugged regions of Aravallis, Vindhya, Satpura and Sahiyadri ranges. There are several tribal groups in Gujarat.

Tribes of Gujarat have an interesting history. The Ramayana and the Mahabharata make several references to the hill tribes. The reference to the Bhil hunter mistakenly slaying Lord Krishna at Prabhas Patan shows that the tribe had freedom in this region. In the character of Shabri, Valmiki's Ramayana portrays the simple and hospitable nature of the Bhil women.

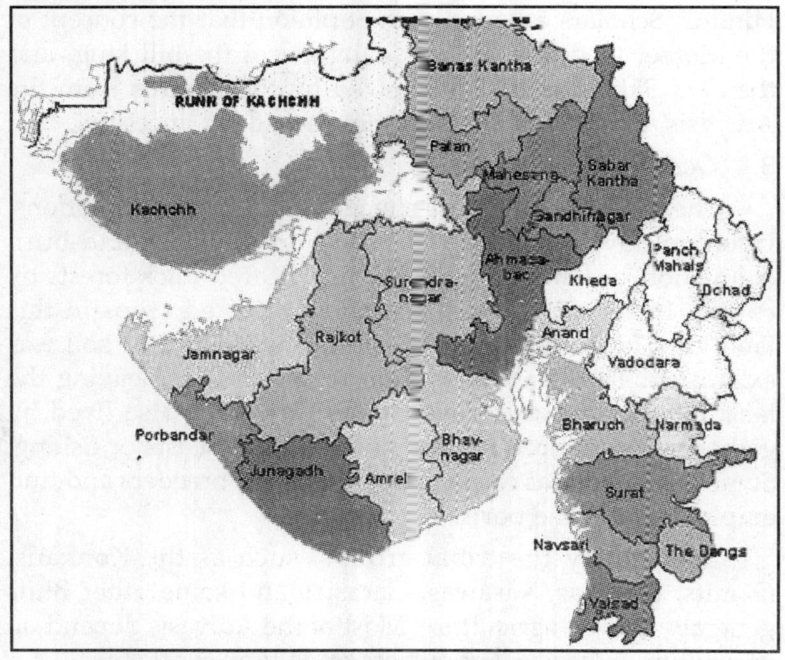

Map No. 2 Map Indicating Tribal Area in Gujarat

1. *Demographics*

There are over 5 million Adivasis or tribal communities in Gujarat. Tribes with Bhil features account for more than 50 per cent of the Gujarat's Adivasi population. Most of the Adivasi sects claim descent from clans, such as, the Rathod, Solanki, Chauhan, Parmar and Makwana. The colourful ghagra, the jhulki, the sallo and the jewellery worn by the Bhil Garasia women reveal Rajput influence as well.

2. *Culture*

The tribal people of Gujarat are religious and are animistic in religion. They worship animals, such as the tiger, crocodile and snake as Gods and also worship some plant Gods and a hill God (Thumbi Dev). They also have many Gods in common with the Hindus such as Chamunda, Kalika, Amba, *Lord Hanuman* and *Krishna*. Their greatest festival is *Holi*.

It is said that festivals such as *Diwali*, originally belonged to these aborigines, were in due course of time adopted by the Hindus. Scholars are also of the opinion that the concept of the Mother Goddess, *Parvati* (daughter of the hill king) and the *Lord Shiva* has been borrowed by the Hindus from the Adivasis. The tribals also worship their dead ancestors.

3. *Occupation*

The tribes of Gujarat are engaged in different occupations. In olden days the Bhils depended on the slash-and-burn cultivation system under which they cleared thick forests by cutting trees or burning them and cultivated crops in this land for a few years until the natural fertility of the soil was exhausted. They then moved on to new forests, leaving the land fallow for it to recover its fertility. They also lived by gathering forest produce and hunting wild beasts or fishing. Some tribes work as casual labourers, cattle breeders and find employment in the ports.

Even today the tribal groups, such as the Konkans, Gamits, Dhodias, Vasawas, Garasias and some other Bhils generally live on agriculture. Most of the Adivasis depend on agriculture either as landowners or as farm workers.

4. *Tribal Life*

Early man in Gujarat probably roamed about at will along the river valleys with the advent of Aryan tribes with their superior striking power. The tribes that we find today have probably descended from them.

The important tribes present today are Bhil, Charan, Dhanka, Dhodia, Dubla, Bharwad, Gamti, Kali, Kolcha, Parashi, Rabari, Siddi, Vasava, Vagari and Wari, etc.

The Dangs district is a short drive from Bulsar as well as Surat. The Dangs is forest area where the Adivasi tribal community lives. Waghai to Saputara, a distance of thirty two miles, the river Ambica playing hide and seek alongside, one become aware of awesome bounty of nature everywhere.

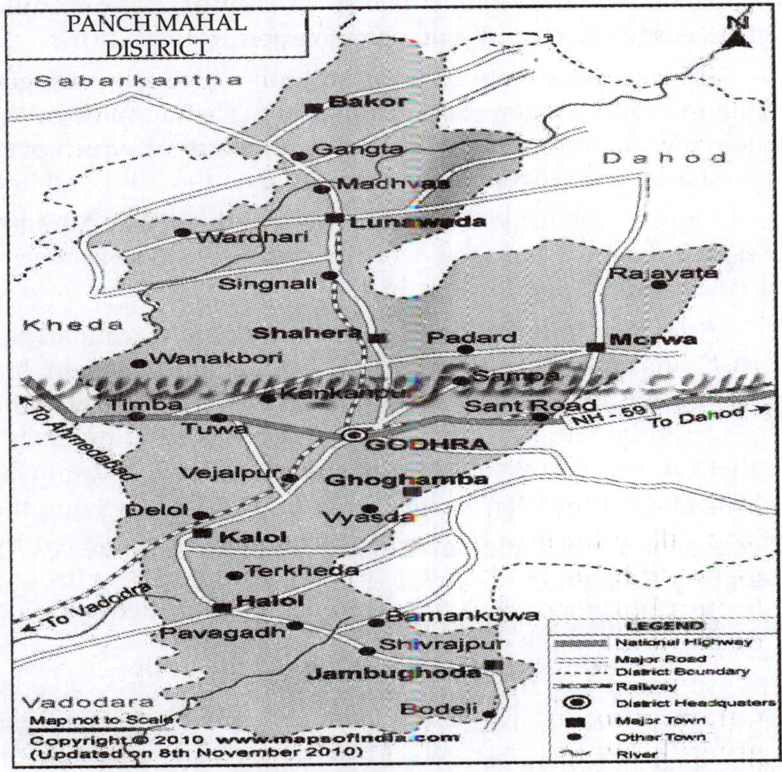

Map No. 3: Map Indicating Tribal Area in Panch Mahal

The tribals in their response to their surroundings have evolved a pattern of relationship with their environment and of the utilisation of natural resources, getting a bare survival. As food quest takes most of tribal time for survival, his entire social life revolves round it.

Tribal art is not aesthetic but mainly utilitarian, apart from satisfying a deep-rooted want, art has helped to integrate the people and enrich their life. The artistic activities are mainly plastic and graphic art, Music and dance and Oral literature.

Perhaps the oldest form of art in which primitive man first expressed himself is dramatic art. Occasion like marriages and festival like Holi provide them opportunities or the development and expression of dramatic talent among tribal people of Gujarat. During Holi festival, their dramatic groups visit nearby towns and give performance.

Dancing as a form of art is still alive in Gujarat tribal. Both men and women dress aesthetically. They have devised their own native musical instruments, some of which are marked by their inventive and originality.

During Holi festival Dongi tribal have their "The Annual Festival of Fance" and song, which is known as 'Dang Darbar', is celebrated during Holi festival.

Adornment of the body is very popular in which the artistic impulse of the tribal people has found expression. In work of clay, wood and stone important aspect of their artistic talent can be felt. The cult objects in clay and the funerary pillars in stone are examples of their artistic impulse and expression of their way of life.

Programme and Policy of Gujarat State for Effective Primary Education

1. *Girl Child Education in Gujarat*

Primary education is the backbone of the comprehensive development of a country. What do we mean by primary education? 'Stage between pre-primary and secondary education is known as primary education. It is thus called because, for majority of the people, it is of prime importance and the basic requirement of education'. As it is in 1882, the Hunter commission suggested primary education into the concept of people's education. Realizing the worth of primary education, the Indian constitution has made primary education compulsory and free for the age group between 6 to 14, by article 45. When Indian constitution was adopted in 1950, it was resolved that by 1960 the goal of primary education to all children between 6-14 years must be achieved. But till date it has never happened. UNESCO had noted, 'The percentage of the Indian population who are literate has gradually increased from 27.8 per cent in 1961 to 54.3 per cent in 1996, but a large part of the Indian population is still illiterate. According to UNESCO figures for 1995, the number of illiterates stood at 265 million, corresponding to 48 per cent of the adult (age 15 and older) population'. The ultimate goal of primary education shall be called achieved when all eligible and able children between 6 to 14 years not only get enrolled to class 1st but they essentially complete class 7th without dropping on in middle of the education.

Primary education is made compulsory and free for children. These children are segregated in the different groups to achieve success such as: urban and rural, backward area, tribal area further grouped into boys and girls. The enrollment of students in tribal area was only 12.4 per cent in 1961 in the state of Gujarat. In India, in 1965-66, the literacy ratio between boys and girls was 90 per cent and 47.6 per cent respectively. The literacy ratio between urban and rural area was 80.06 and 59.21 in 2001 in India. According to official statistics collected from census and national sample surveys, the literacy rate among scheduled castes and tribes are significantly lower than for the rest population – 37 per cent for scheduled castes and 30 per cent for scheduled tribes. Enrollment figures for primary education are also lower for these groups than for the rest of the population. There has been a caste gap of 10-20 per cent and a tribe gap of 15-20 per cent. This depicts that even after 58 years of independence we have not gained success in the field of primary Education. However, each State Government can turn the picture into bright colours. Gujarat government has understood it well in time in last 8 years and has under taken various glorious steps to see Primary Education dream of success in own state. To take measures to check the rate of drop outs and to increase enrollment Gujarat Government has involved a number of professionals, social workers, educationalist, sociologist and expert, and has come out with a number of schemes which helped in resulting into encouraging results.

2. School Entrance Celebration Programme

To encourage 100 per cent enrollment of an eligible child to the school this unique scheme has been introduced. The school staff goes house to house and felicitate child with kumkum and sweet. The child is brought to the school in decorated camel or bullock cart, tractor or other vehicle. There after the child enters the school. The whole atmosphere becomes a celebration.

In many countries, school enrollment is a monotonous or perhaps a dull process. But in Niloshi village of Gujarat it was quite the opposite. To the sound of traditional music and drumming, about 30 children, all under 6 years, were registered as first-graders and received their textbooks. Navsu Bhoya, mother of five-year-old Manisha, said: 'without the 'Shala Pravesh Utsav' [enrollment drive], I would not have known that it was time for Manisha to join school. I always thought she was too small and could wait for a couple more years", say the website of UNICEF.

3. Girl's Education – Rath Yatra

Gujarat state holds 15th place in the country for literacy rate, and 21st place for female literacy in 2001. Hence the state Government has introduced girl's education, 'Rath Yatra' with an intention of putting the state amongst the first few in the literacy rate and to improve the female literacy rate in villages having less than 35 per cent female literacy rate to achieve 100 per cent enrollment of girls in std. 1st. The main aim of Girl's Rath Yatra is that, all children eligible for enrolment, especially girls, where enrolled in Primary schools, and those children who had left the schools those re-enrolled.

This scheme concentrated in 2002 at the places, which had less than 20 per cent female literacy rate, and in 2005 less than 35 per cent female literacy rate. This celebration of Rath Yatra goes on three days to bring awareness in parents and girl students. With a view to render social service in active manner to the Girls' Education and School Entrance Celebration, Chief Minister and other ministers, District collectors, District Development Officers, I.A.S., I.P.S. officers, officers of Secretariat, officers of the Education Department and other departments moved from one village to another. Local MP and MLA and also various officers of taluka and district level, joined Girls' Education Rath Yatra programme and had sincerely contributed to the efforts of the state government to raise the female literacy level to the highest point.

Government Initiation Towards Girl Child Education

The Gujarat State Government has seen primary education as a grass-root sector and initiated mass movements. The Government's efforts have succeeded in increasing school enrollments and bringing down school drop-out ratio, the two major concerns in primary education. Educating the Girl Child: 'Kanya Kelavani' Attention and priority given by Narendra Modi to education as compared to any other past Chief Minister of the state is noteworthy. His realization that no amount of economic, industrial or commercial resurgence can be sustained on a long-term basis without the foundation of proper academic and professional education has made him re-work the whole system of education in Gujarat state. Successive annual campaigns for enrollment of all children in schools, with a special focus on enrollment of the girl child have brought lakhs of children back to school, which otherwise would have been left out. The concern of the CM for education of the girl child is reflected in the fact that he has specially created a fund called 'Kanya Kelavani Nidhi'. Now it is a well-known fact that all the gifts received by Narendra Modi are auctioned and the funds are credited to the government treasury for the cause of girl child education. Within a span of 41 years, his 13 predecessors had deposited a meager amount of Rs. 4.55 lacs, whereas the present Chief Minister has raised.

In fact, the CM has set-up a separate fund for it and raised Rs. 44 crores himself through auction of gifts. Thus, he has set a unique trend of adding to the state exchequer. Kanya Kelavani Nidhi has been created with a long-term goal that no girl child in Gujarat remains illiterate and the efforts have started yielding results. In 2006-07, the dropout rate of the girl child had dwindled to 3.68 per cent from 20.81 per cent in 2000-01 (Std. 1 to 5) and to 11.64 per cent from as high as 36.30 per cent (Std. 1 to 7). The current year has seen the drop-out ratio fall even further to an all-time low of 2 per cent. The focus now is to bridge this 2 per cent gap during 9th Kanya Kelavani Rath Yatra: truly, a mass movement The dwindling drop-out rates are equally supported by new enrollments through Kanya Kelavani Rath Yatra (girl child enrolment drive), a unique initiative in Gujarat. Since 2003, every year in the month of June, the Chief Minister along with his team travels to remote villages to encourage parents to enroll their children in schools. It is a three day long statewide drive covering all the villages and the urban areas in the scorching summer heat. An atmosphere of festivity and celebration is created. Young children now wait with keen interest to get in themselves enrolled into schools. Chief Minister Narendra Modi himself led Team Gujarat this year, to cover select 32,772 primary schools in all the 18,000 villages, 151 municipalities and eight municipal corporations during the 9th Kanya Kelavni Yatra (Girls' Education) and Shala Praveshotsav Abhiyan (School Enrollment Movement). They were held in two phases from June 16 to 18 in rural areas and from June 23 to 24, 2011 in urban areas.

The Team Gujarat includes the entire Council of Ministers and all Secretaries, besides other officers and people's representatives. The Gujarat Team was divided into small groups of five, as each group fanned out to the entire state, visiting five schools daily during the six-day movement. These efforts of the team are geared towards pushing up people's participation in making primary education quality and result oriented. The twin movements which entered the seventh year have already started paying dividends in the form of higher enrollment, greater spread of education among girl child and qualitative improvement. As per the comparative figures of Census 2001 and 2011 reports, Gujarat state has showed more than 13 per cent increase in Female literacy in the last decade, one of the highest among Indian states, and decreased school drop-out ratio by 29.77 per cent. Mr. Narendra Modi believes that the most heartening aspect of the twin movements is the people's all round support, down to the village level, replacing the complacency with awareness and positive action.

Yet another initiative is the Vidyalaxmi Yojana, introduced in the villages where female literacy rate is lower than 35 per cent and in urban areas for girls belonging to BPL families. This innovative scheme provides with Rs. 1,000 bond to every girl child who enrolls in the first grade in villages with a low female literacy rate. The girl child gets the money once she completes class VII, with interest accrued on Rs 1,000 for seven years. Rs. 11 crores has been disbursed through this scheme that has attracted countrywide attention. A Vidyalaxmi bond of Rs. 1000/- is given to girl students who take admission to the 1st Std. and 8th Std. The girl receives the amount of the bond along with interest on completion of Std. 7th and 10th respectively.

This ensures higher retention rate. Families having only daughters will receive Rs. 1,000 as incentive if their girls are enrolled to school. The school which has 100 per cent registration of girls and zero dropout rates receives an award of Rs. 25,000. Teachers of such schools also receive appreciation certificates. Other initiative in Primary Education 'Gunotsav' was carried out to upraise the quality of all 33,376 schools of the State in 2009. Results of Gunotsav-2009 were assessed by UNESCO and recognized gradation method adopted by Education Department as unique and innovative. The Gujarat state government has initiated a pilot project to ensure full enrolment of all eligible students and to reduce dropout rate in primary schools. The pilot project covers 680 primary schools, 70 Cluster Resource Centres (CRCs) and 4 Block Resources Centres (BRCs) in Narmada district, one of the most backward districts of Gujarat having predominant tribal population and low literacy. It will cover around 2,508 teachers and 76,000 students. Addition of nutrients in the mid-day-meals and regular health checkup of students has had their pleasant fallouts too, through qualitative improvement in the education and health of children. All the above initiatives taken by the Gujarat government should herald a new path towards higher Human Development in the state.

The population of Gujarat is about 5 Crore and 6 Lakhs and out of it 14.76 per cent people belong to the Scheduled Tribes. Most of them are either farmers or engaged as farm labourers, and they find it difficult to run their families throughout the year. This is also because whatever land they have, that is also rocky, sloppy, eroded, forested and moreover less productive. Most of the farmers possess less than 5 acres of land per head. The landless Adivasis' condition is more pitiable and problematic apart from the problems of small farmers who have land. In some villages such people don't get daily wages work in their own villages and neighborhood. In order to earn livelihood and to run their families, most of the Adivasis migrate to distant places which are non-Adivasi. They also migrate to different parts of the state in search of work for the reasons like less amount of agricultural land, low-productivity of soil, inadequate and uncertain rainfalls, and distribution of land among their heirs. They find whatever odd jobs they get to the places they migrate to. These include, labour work on farms, work in factories, construction of buildings and roads, in tobacco fields and in small industries. They also carry their wives and children along with them. Sometime natural factors also create hardships for them. In such a time, due to their poverty or financial crisis, the Adivasis migrate to nearby urban centers to get employment.

Problems and Challenges of Migratory Adivasi Women

As mentioned earlier, the Adivasis migrate along with their children and wives. Their children have to leave studies from their present schools in between which results into continuous absenteeism or in irregularity.

Despite the education being a man's fundamental right, the Adivasi girls are not able to get admission and if they get it, they leave their studies in between. The system of male domination influences the society of the Adivasis. They are not interested to educate their daughters much. They allow their daughters to attend the schools available in their villages but they don't show any mental preparations when they have to send them to some other place.

In the Adivasi community the girls are engaged in domestic chores when they attain the age of 10 to 12 years, mainly to look after their siblings to fetch water, to cook food or to buy things from the market. Moreover, they are not able to get more education since the Adivasi areas lack in the educational environment. Therefore, their education at development doesn't take place.

The Factors that Hinder Education of the Migratory Adivasi Females

1. Due to their migration, parents do not realize the importance of the girls as they expect them to do house hold works and to look after their young ones. Being illiterate they overlook it and don't show their readiness to educate their girls.
2. The low-level of education makes them more stagnant as the girls are asked to look after their young ones and to accompany their parents to work at the age of getting education or going to school.
3. Lack of special education training for the migratory Adivasi female workers.
4. Their problems of socialization and education to their children and mainly for the girls' care.
5. To reside in a new or unknown place of migration becomes a serious problem for the women. They have to run from pillar to post with their bags and baggage.
6. The Adivasi families find themselves in wretched condition despite their efforts to find place to live in.

7. To reach the economic responsibilities, females accept migratory occupations.
8. The young women are abused or sexually harassed of their migrated places and women having small children don't get work easily.
9. The migrating females have to play double role apart from their traditional and socially accepted roles. It includes.
   (i) to assist males apart from their domestic chores;
   (ii) to earn livelihood along with males; and
   (iii) to earn wages by doing other works traditionally.

In the above works, the occupations workload increases add to their family life and they find it difficult to satisfy both the roles.

10. Such women can't keep in touch with their family members or relatives as they are not able to spare time which often results into broken relationships.
11. They don't get proper wages as per their work and they are exploited financially.
12. Moreover, there arises the shortage of basic amenities and compulsion increases their whole life is adversely affected by their migration. Their girls (daughters) are also not able to complete or continue their studies because of the same problem of migration. It comes in the way of their educational progress.

Suggestions for Educational Upliftment of the Migratory Females

1. The proportion of migration in Adivasi tribes is more so, for such migrating labourers provision of housing, education and health should be made available.
2. For their educational upliftment local environment and materialistic facilities should also be made available.
3. Due to this problem the education of children is badly affected and often admissions are withdrawn from their schools. Child labour is a big problem in Gujarat and

mainly among the Adivasi children such children can't study so, each and every school is provided with boarding facilities, which would rely the migrating Adivasis to keep their children there to get education.

4. Child-Care Centers, Aganwadis, Balwadis, etc., help such children to keep in touch with education, so that, they do not remain illiterate. They should be provided with 'Bridge – Cards' in case of their migration to some other place to get admission in any nearby school.
5. The migratory Adivasis should be allowed to get admission in government run primary schools or Balwadis and should be provided the certificate when they leave for their own native place.
6. Special programmes to be held to enhance the skills of the Adivasi females. They should be informed about the different government schemes meant for their upliftment. Proper guidance and encouragement should be given for the educational development of their children.
7. Human Resource Development Ministry should start the optional arrangement of Kasturba Gandhi Balika Vidyalaya so there; they can continue their studies by getting admission in between the academic year.
8. To teach reading and writing to the migratory females, the arrangement 'Bal Sakhi' should be made to take care of their children and to create simple education facility for them.
9. According to Mahila Samakhya 2004-05, programmes regarding initial schooling, hygiene, nutritious diet etc., should be organized. The children below 5 years should be taken care by the Bal Sakhis.
10. Employers should be compelled to satisfy the basic needs of the migratory labourers.
11. According to the Factory Act. 1948, - the provision for a crèche should be made if more than 30/40 females are working.

12. Along with education such women should be trained in tailoring, patch work, embroidery, toy-making and other forms of vocational fields.

The government has launched many schemes for the upliftment of women. If they are made fully benefited by such schemes, then their economic and education status can be improved further. If they are guided properly to develop their lives then many of their problems can be solved.

1. The gap between literacy rate of general population and STs has increased from 20 per cent in 1981 to 23 per cent in 1991. The position is still worse in case of ST females, which is only 18.19 per cent as against 39.23 per cent for non-STs.
2. At Secondary education, the drop out has been increased from 9 per cent to 11 per cent for Scheduled Tribes. Female drop out rate is still a higher and alarming picture.
3. At Higher Education level, the participation of ST girls amounts to less than 3.9 per cent as against an average of more than 8 per cent.
4. The enrollment ratio of SC girls in Secondary Schools have continued to show a progressive trend, whereas it is quite opposite in the case of ST girls.
5. The other prevailing factor is that at Primary level, ST girls show a better progress than SC girls, 43 per cent over 29.7 per cent, it is reversed in Secondary level.
6. In Gujarat, tribal population comprises 7.5 million people accounting for about 15 per cent of the State's population. The developmental indicators of tribal talukas in economy and education of Dahod and Vadodara districts of Gujarat are the lowest among others.

Women were expected to earn, perform domestic chores and to bring up their family members. The basis of the division of labour was thought to be their sex, relationship and authority.

Education is an important avenue for upgrading the economic and social conditions of the Scheduled Tribe women. This study will helping identifying the root causes for the problems girl students studying in the secondary schools of Gujarat.

STATEMENT OF THE PROBLEM

A Study of Problems of Tribal Girl Students of Secondary Schools.

NEED FOR THE STUDY

The women have been given an important place in tribal communities. In the different areas of social life the attitude of females, their duties are related to their position in the society. All the ancient societies have high respect for woman. It is far from the truth. Both the genders are given equal rights in the tribal communities residing in India.

In education among different tribes is a very critical question in huge Nation like India. Spread of education is an urgent need for the overall development and economic prosperity of our country. The educational problems among the ancient tribes should not be limited for them to mere knowledge of reading and writing but they should be given equal opportunities.

No organized efforts were taken to provide education to the Adivasis before the independence, several efforts were made by the Christian Missionaries and some individuals to some extent. Religion was at the focal point in the spread of education among the tribals by the Christian missionaries. In those days, revered Thakkar Bapa showed a strong determination in this regard and established a residential school (Ashram Shala) to provide basic education to the Scheduled Castes and Scheduled Tribes.

The Adivasis were injustice or ignored before independence and they were exploited economically. No body raised their voice against it. Mahatma Gandhiji awakened the latent feelings, aspirations by drawing attention towards, the 'Harijans', Adivasis and discriminated tribal races. He made an appeal to fight against this injustice and gifted our nation with the constructive programme. He made successful efforts and laid strong foundation of education by establishing the Kochrab Ashram, Harijan Ashram and the same in Wardha.

The Adivasis are very backward socially, economically and educationally compared to other communities. And for this, the educational backwardness is responsible to a great extent. Therefore, education has been given more importance in the Indian Constitution to bring social and economic change. It has been emphasized in the Article – 45 of the Directive Principles and in the Articles — 29, 30, 45 and 46 to provide free education to each child up to the age of 14 years.

Though the primary education has been made compulsory by the constitution, despite of the provision of special facilities, many Adivasi males and females are yet to see any school.

Education is a very import aspect of human development. An individual intellect, logic and creativity can be developed through education only. Education helps in bringing awareness to develop society. According to the declaration of the Human Rights, every one has the right to get education.

About 70 per cent of the Indian populations live in villages only. In many rural areas, the Adivasis live in backwardness it is due to their ignorance and illiteracy. The benefits of urban areas of educational development achieved after the independence have not been received by the Adivasis, while in rural areas they are still caught in bondages due to ignorance and their faith in superstitions social traditions, customs, rituals which have hindered their education at development beyond the expectation. There exists a great inequality of education between Adivasi males and females.

Table 1.4 as mentioned above show that the percentage of education among the females compared to that of the males. There is a difference between the percentage of literacy rate of males and females. The number of schools or educational institutions in Adivasi areas was quite low in 1961. Afterwards, there has been improvement in the literacy rate due to gradual increase in the number of educational institutions. The improvement in their literacy rate is visible due to implementation of educational programmes and other welfare schemes to boost the overall development of the Adivasis as their prime objective of education and economic factors are directly related to each other Therefore, the Adivasis, show very cold attitude to educate their girls (daughters). Unfortunately, more than 50 per cent of the Adivasi females are illiterate in Gujarat.

Table 1.4 : The details about the educational development of adivasi - females

Year	Literacy Rate in Gujarat			Literacy Rate and The Adivasis		
	Males	Females	Total	Males	Females	Total
1961	41.13	19.10	30.45	19.06	4.03	11.69
1971	46.11	24.75	35.79	28.83	6.15	14.12
1981	54.44	32.30	4.70	30.41	11.64	21.14
1991	60.99	40.62	5115	39.37	19.65	29.67
2001	88.03	79.02	85.03	59.18	36.02	47.74
2011	87.23	70.73	79.31	*Not yet finalized*		

The women have been given an important place in tribal communities. All the ancient societies have high respect for women. Both the genders are given equal rights in the tribal communities residing in India.

SCOPE OF THE STUDY

The present study intends to find out the level of the problems of tribal girl students, studying in secondary schools only. The researcher has taken into consideration the variables such as locality of the school, management of the school, exclusive or co- of the tribal girls, economic status of the family, education of the parents, school-leaving class and non-school-leaving classes. The study is confined to the state of Gujarat, India.

OBJECTIVES OF THE STUDY

The following are the objectives of the present study.

1. To find out the level of the problems of tribal girl students of secondary schools.
2. To find out the difference in the problems of tribal girl students of rural and urban secondary schools.
3. To find out the difference in the problems of tribal girl students of economically forward and economically backward families.
4. To find out the difference in the problems of tribal girl students of educated and uneducated mother.
5. To find out the difference in the problems of tribal girl students of educated and uneducated father
6. To find out the difference in the problems of tribal girl students of educated and uneducated parents
7. To find out the difference in the problems of tribal girl students of aided and unaided secondary schools.
8. To find out the difference in the problems of tribal girl students of Hindu religion and Christian religion.
9. To find out the difference in the problems of tribal girl students of Gujarati medium and English medium secondary schools.
10. To find out the difference in the problems of tribal girl students of school-leaving class and non- school-leaving classes of secondary schools.
11. To find out the difference in the problems of tribal girl students of day and residential secondary schools.

EDUCATIONAL IMPLICATIONS

Education is the most important means by which individuals and society can improve personal endowments, build capacity levels, overcome barriers, and expand opportunities for a sustained improvement in their well-being.

In the context of tribal education, finding a balance between preserving tribal cultural identity and mainstreaming for economic prosperity means building education programmes that ensure a tribal child's success in mainstream schools. Recognizing that the education system is currently designed for the dominant group, there is a need to invest in creating support mechanisms that supplement the integration of tribal children into the formal education system.

In the present study, after completion of a systematic survey, the researcher will find the information related to the problems of tribal girl students studying in secondary schools. These findings will help the policy makers, administrators, teachers and families in helping the tribal girl students do their best in their academic endeavours.

2

Review of Related Literature

THE ACCUMULATION of scientific knowledge is a slow and gradual process in which an investigator depends on the work of the past and this serves as a starting point for future research. The more the links that can be established between a given study and other studies or a body of theory, the greater the contribution (Karma, 1987).

By reviewing the related literature, the researcher can avoid unfruitful and useless problem areas. The researcher can select those areas in which positive findings are very likely to result and his endeavours are likely to add to the knowledge in a meaningful way. Through the review of related literature, the researcher can avoid unintentional duplication of well established facts. It is of no use to replicate a study when the stability and validity of its results have been clearly established.

The review of related literature gives the researcher an understanding of the research methodology, which refers to the way the study is to be conducted. It helps the researcher to know about the tools and instruments, which proved to be useful and promising in the previous studies. It also provides an insight into the statistical methods through which the validity of the results is to be established.

Good, Barr and Scates (1941) analyzed the purpose of the review of related literature as given herewith: to show whether the available evidence material solves the problem adequately without further investigation; to provide ideas, theories, explanations or hypotheses valuable in formulating the present study; to suggest the research methods concerned to the problems; to locate comparative data useful in the interpretation of the results; and to contribute to the general scholarship of the investigator. It helps the research worker to find out what is already known, what others have attempted to find out, what methods of attack have been promising or disappointing and what problems remain to be solved. It furnishes him with indispensable suggestions about comparative data, good procedures, likely methods and tried techniques. It makes him alert to research possibilities that have been over looked and research approaches that have proved to be sterile, and it prevents pointless repetition of research.

The review of related literature provides a comprehensive understanding about what has already been known about a topic. It forms the basis for subscribing rationale for having chosen the problem for the study. Review of related literature allows the researcher to acquaint himself with the current knowledge in the field or area in which he is going to conduct his research. It enables the researcher to define the limits of his study. It also helps the researcher to delimit and define his problem. The knowledge of the related literature brings the researcher up-to-date on the work, which others have done and thus state the objectives clearly and concisely.

As such, there is a vast but incoherent and unsynthesized literature, containing stereotyped views about the state of affairs pertaining to the social, economic and cultural worlds of tribals. The attitudes, views, perspectives or the way they looked at life in general, say modern or contemporary life of non-tribes, need to be studied. Most of the researchers, right from independence till recently, did not go beyond taking up peripheral issues of life. In fact, they lacked depth, but trucking only the surface. All of them can be tracked together for their maypole approach to the problems of modernization, progress and industrialization in relation to education.

This demands close and deeper attention to the problems of the tribes. Hence, the necessity of a fresh approach and a brocade framework for studies. The present work attempts precisely to do this. A new perspective, more rational and pragmatic, has been opened up. In the related research studies, tribal problems were categorized and studied in relation to different aspects in the contest of their problems concerned to tribal education, particularly that associate with the problems of tribal girls' education.

Problems of Tribals

Dutt (1977) studied the problems like population pressure, occupational structure, solid cultural contexts, etc., which are to be tackled in order to raise the economic standard of tribal population.

Shah, V.P. and Patel, T. (1977) studied about the secondary education of Scheduled Tribes in Gujarat and made a remark that encouraging inbuilt and self-learning would be effective.

Shyamlal (1987) found that tribal children experienced considerable problems in their studies. Analyzing the nature of educational hardship of Scheduled Tribes, he reported that a major proportion of students felt problems in learning English (67.30%) and Mathematics (29.4%). Thirty eight per cent of students blamed the teachers for their low quality teaching.

Mahendra Kumar Mishra (1996) in his study on 'Strategies of Tribal Education for Intervention (District Primary Education Programme)' envisaged improvement of tribal education and girls' education in backward regions of India to reduce social disparities.

Lalan P. Gupta (2004) proposed that a dual programme will have to be undertaken for promoting education of tribal communities; one is a long term programme of conventional education and the other is short term programme to meet urgent and specific needs of their areas.

Nayar (1975) confirmed that the number of repeaters in the class increased with the increase in the level of the class. Similarly, it has been reported that drop-out rate among STs was higher at primary level. It decreased with increase in the class of study.

Social Change in Tribals

Shah (1967) concluded that the growth of education was slow in tribals due to poor socio-economic and cultural environment of their life, but not much in their cultural and social values.

Patrick and Patrick (1968) opined that consequent to modern change in Indian society, especially since Independence, tribes appear to be in transition and were increasingly adopting the legitimate means of achieving goals and seeking more identity with the large society.

R. K. Gulati (1970) described social change occurs due to education among the Bhils of West Khandesh district.

Cyril S. Belshaw (1970) studied through comparative methods of several kinds of economies from primitive to modern, similarities and dissimilarities and concluded that all social relations involve exchange transactions in tribal communities.

S. M. Dubey (1972), V. Rama Rao (1988), Satyanarayanan Murthy and Vijaya Laxmi Kumari (1974), Martin Oraon (1959), and Mutatkar (1973) considered education as an important variable for social change in any community, including tribal populations.

B. D. Sharma (1974-75) noticed that tribal areas stand at a much lower level in terms of literacy and enrolment of school-going children compared to other areas.

Mishra (1974-75) explained that the question of formal education has not been touched in tribal communities, which is certainly an important requisite in the process of planned growth of any community.

Harman (1975) observed tremendous change in the Naga way of life, and informed that many earlier salient features of Naga life have been disappeared. A new standard of living has been adopted by the Nagas, which is at times not in tune with their own traditional ways.

Kumar (1975) discussed the status of women in tribal society and found very low literacy rate due to various social taboos and scarcity of educational facilities nearby.

K. L. Kothari (1978) studied the social change in tribals and observed that the tribals lived happily in isolation with their own mythology,

Bhandari (1978) showed the position of the Indian tribal societies vis-à-vis the peasantry.

K. S. Nair and others (1979) noticed that the inter-tribal differences in educational achievement were directly related to their socio-economic levels and to the size of the family.

Sibir R. Das (1979) stated that the tribals were more concerned about their food rather than attendance in the educational institutions.

Mittal (1979) explained that the tribals have strong faith in their own traditional methods, and the Santhals have neither use nor respect for modern medicines.

Roy Choudhary (1978) presented an account of the life style of the tribals of Bihar in all aspects including their food habits, clothing, marriage, customs, family life and the economic and social activities. According to him, Christian Missionaries have been largely responsible for spreading literacy, education and sanitation among the tribes.

Economic Change in Tribals

Das and Banerjee (1962), Vidyarthi (1964), Majumdar (1956), N. Prasad (1961), Sachchidanand (1965), and Martin Oraon (1966) studied the impact of industrialization on the life of tribal communities and noticed its impact on their life and living.

Satyanarayanan Murthy and Vijaya Laxmi Kumari (1974) explained the modern impact on the life Koyas of Andhra Pradesh.

N. N. Vyas (1975) described the fact that the State Governments have initiated action to restore the tribal lands already transferred to non-tribals.

N. N. Vyas (1975) concluded that Kathodis of Rajasthan have different stages of development according to their occupation.

Ratna Bhattacharya (1977) concluded that in order to raise the social status through economic development as well as to adjust themselves for the wave of modernization, appropriate agricultural procedures must be adopted for the better use of land.

Abbasayulu (1978) stated that by the implementation of community development programmes among the Gonds of Adilabad, the Government of Andhra Pradesh had created a situation of exposer of the people to the way of living of non-tribals.

Sachchidanand (1978) explained that the forces of modernisation at work in tribal societies have produced a two-fold trend.

Martin Oraon stated that modern education has eliminated bad social practices and has provided a booster to opt for new occupations by tribals.

B. D. Ray (1979) had completed a research project on the occupational mobility among the Khasis of Shillong and concluded that the occupational opportunity was greatly motivated by the availability of occupational opportunity in urban areas.

Gopal Rao (1979) examined the process of transfer of land from tribals to non-tribals and various factors influencing it and noticed its influence on the life styles of tribals.

Umanand Phuken (1979) discussed the structural changes in tribal society and found the influence of modernity in the structural change of tribal communities.

Purohit (1979) noticed the fact that the criminality of the tribes of Rajasthan tended to undergo a major change in automated and unplanned fashion.

Chanda and Loknath Soni (1982) tried to analyse the impact of development activities and found that a bulk of tribal population as a whole was still living below the subsistence level.

Mishra (1983) dealt with the socio-economic and political aspects of Nishing tribe of Arunchal Pradesh and tried to analyse the economic aspects of social revolution, which has emerged out of new economy-based life of the tribal society and observed that the economic levels helped in the social revolution of tribal societies.

Satyanaryanan (1989), in his study on tribal development, concluded that because of the development programmes, the living condition of tribals has improved, but not to the desired level.

Cultural Change in Tribals

B. H. Mehta (1965) studied the dynamics of Gond society with special reference to its habitat, socio-economic conditions, religion and culture and informed that several of the Gond populations were living in primitive living conditions.

Hari Mohan (1969) had conducted a research on the style of living, the means of subsistence, trade, market and indebtedness, family and kinship, crime and punishment, religion, magic, etc., of Parhariya tribe and noticed that their tribal culture was strongly playing its legitimate role with regard to the above aspects.

Mishra (1972) and G. N. Chaudhari (1997) compared the cultural status on the basis of their customs and way of life and noticed that customs and way of life are interwoven.

J. K. Doshi (1974) described the social structure and cultural change of a Bhil village and concluded that the process of change has accelerated with the improvement in communication channels and State intervention on account of welfare programmes.

Eswara Reddy (1975) used the term "Sanskritization" to study the direction of change in customs, rituals, ideology and way of life and understood that the phenomenon of Sanskritization helped in modifying the above systems of tribal communities.

K. L. Sharma (1975) stated that cultural change is impossible without economic progress in tribal populations.

K. B. Srivastava (1977) attempted to study the origin of the tribals of Chotanagpur, their fusion into the rest of the non-tribal society and their role in the development of Indian culture and by this study it was concluded that these tribals tried to certain extent to mingle with the non-tribal societies.

Vidyarthi (1977) observed that unlike some tribes, which have achieved a high level of socio-cultural integrations, the conditions of others such as the Birhor, Hill Kharia, Korwa and Pahariya tribes were rather disturbing from demographic and economic points of views,

K. S. Singh (1978) described the nature of colonial transformation of tribal society in relation to the political system, social stratification, Sanskritisation, Christianity, economic transformation, agrarian restructuring and tribal movements.

Mahapatra (1979) found an inverse relationship between technology and tribal cultures.

Anita Horsey (1979) focused the impact of modernisation on the socio-cultural life of the Warli tribes, and observed that Warlis were politically backward and were not aware of the meaning of citizenship, rights and duties.

Political Change in Tribals

Roop Singh (1970) found two similar movements, *viz.*, Bhagat and non-Bhagat movements, among the Bhils.

S. P. Sinha (1971) reviewed the election scene in tribal areas and found that the participation in elections was not so encouraging.

Sachchidanand (1972) discussed the pace of change and the role played by leadership in the tribal societies and the resistance encountered from traditional leadership; and observed that the younger generations were coming forward to play leadership roles due to their exposure to modern societies when compared to the older generations.

R. S. Mann examined the relationship between the leadership and political change in tribal Rajashthan and noticed that there was a lower relationship between leadership and political change in tribals.

Ranjit K. Bhandra (1977) analyzed the sociological significance of the revitalization movements among Gonds and found that these movements helped in upgrading their social status.

John Macdongall (1977) attempted to describe the differences in two different types of social movements that occurred among some Adivasi (indigenous) people of Bihar during 1858-95 and noticed that these movements helped them to certain extent in getting their legitimate rights as tribal communities.

S. L. Doshi (1978) believed that political unification need not imply corresponding unification in social and cultural spheres.

Udayon Mishra (1978) examined the historical and sociological basis for the persistent consciousness among the Nagas.

L. M. Prasad (1981) suggested representative bureaucracy to bring about a change in their attitude.

Chandra Mohan Reddy (1981) described the fact that the tribal communities in India have been undergoing a variety of socio-political changes for the last two centuries.

Padam Nabh Gautam (1987) emphasized the role of administration as an instrument for socio-economic development among tribals.

Ajit K. Pandey (1987) concluded that the traditional patrimonialism of the Oraons and their heads has certainly been weakened and gradually has been replaced by modern political machineries.

Renuka Patnaik (1995) in her studies on nomadic tribal movements among the tribals of Mayurbanj district of Orrisa concluded that these movements helped them to settle at a particular place with some social and economic security.

Other Changes in Tribals

Maheswari Prasad (1976) analyzed the factors determining the spatial distribution of tribes of Jharia town in

Chotanagpur district and noticed that means of income was the prime cause for spatial distribution of tribes.

Jaganath Pathy and others (1976) proposed that tribes be studied not as homogenous units, but as a class of societies internally and otherwise.

Krishna Sharma (1978) studied about the fertility and mortality of the tribal community of the Konds of Orissa and reported that both fertility and mortality in them were more.

Michael York (1979) dealt with the organizational aspects of Raj Gonds and made some points specially related to marriage.

Naidu (1979) found that in Banspar block of Keonjhar district, people's response to family planning was neither very impressive nor varied.

Ramesh P. Sinha (1979) proved that tribals were not exposed to mass communication.

W. G. Archer (1984) has presented a report on tribal law and justice.

Suar (1984) informed that the three major factors, viz., education, infrastructure and urbanization, were helpful to a considerable extent in the developmental situation of tribes.

Role of Parents in the Education of Tribals

Srivastava (1981) studied the problems of early schooling of tribal children and the attitude of their parents and found that economic hardships, domestic engagements and superstitions affected the education, particularly, the education of girl children.

Mathur (1994) studied various dimensions of school education of tribals, role of parents, role of Government agencies, social workers and others, and emphasized the need for popularizing the vocational education.

Khan (2008) investigated the parents' attitudes towards their daughters' education in tribal areas of Dera Ghazi Khan district. His findings disclosed the parents' positive perceptions toward their daughters' education. He recommended several empirical steps to overcome the problems including provision of new school locations and ensuring the availability of school buildings, supporting infrastructure and teachers for already functioning schools in the area. Financial aid for poor students was also proposed in the study.

Academic Achievement in Tribal Students

M. R. Pandey (1981), in his study on social aspects of academic achievement and aspirations of scheduled tribe students, concluded that the educational opportunity provided to tribals by the formal educational set up could not be of benefit due to their socio-cultural backwardness, gap between the school environment and family, and low achievement of the tribal students.

T. Singh (1981) concluded that the educated tribes tend to become more pragmatic and composed, and they appeared to be more shrewd, worldly and socially aware. The motivation and the achievement of the tribal students of class IX and X were positively related.

S. C. Prince (1981) found that the family background, cognitive aspects and personality factors influenced the level of aspiration for education of tribal pupils.

Mishra found that the rural disadvantaged children seemed to be better than their urban and tribal counterparts in verbal creativity scores. Educational achievement was significantly related to creative thinking.

S. K. Jasuja (1983) in a study on frustration, level of aspiration and academic achievement in relation to age, education and sex differences among adolescents, conducted that girls achieved higher in the academic field and were less frustrated as compared to boys, and frustration and level of aspiration were positively related.

M. B. Desh Pandey (1984) in an analytical study on cognitive and affective development of tribals and non-tribals of the Chattisgarh region of Madhya Pradesh concluded that the main scores of non-tribal students were significantly higher than those of the tribal students on the entire cognitive test and tribal girls were found more social, stable and emotionally well developed than non-tribal girls. Tribal girls had a more favourable attitude than non-tribal girls towards schooling. Rural tribal boys and girls were emotionally better developed and more social than urban tribal boys and girls. Rural tribal boys and girls had a more favourable attitude than urban tribal boys and girls. Tribal students were more educationally backward than non-tribal students.

S. P. Singh (1986) in a study on Harijan students, their values, problems and level of frustration, found that Harijan students were significantly higher on economic and religious values, and lower on social, political, theoretical, moral and aesthetic values.

R. S. Thakur (1992) studied the scholastic achievement of secondary school tribal pupils in Bihar and concluded that the group performance in all the branches of scholastic achievement did not differ significantly. Physics was found responsible for lowering the standard of scientific achievement. For classes VIII to XI, it was observed that there was stagnation in the most probable performance in the field of language. The level of the most probable performance in social science improved from classes VIII to IX. The group performance of boys was superior to that of girls in all branches. The best group performance of upper middle class was found to be followed by middle class, upper class, lower middle class and lower class. Scholastic achievement and intelligence were significantly associated. The correlation between achievement motivation and science aptitude was significant for boys only.

Manjulatha (1997) has taken up a study to compare the academic achievements of tribal and non-tribal students in Ranchi and found that isolation from home and other social factors as the reasons for poor attendance and drop-outs among tribal and achievement of non-tribal students was high than that of tribal students.

Literacy Rates and Schooling in Tribals

Aparna Mitra and Pooja Singh have studied the trends in literacy rates and schooling among the Scheduled Tribe women in India. High poverty rates pose to be significant obstacles in attaining literacy and education among tribal women in India. However, large differences in literacy rates in various states of India show that social and cultural norms, proximity to the mainstream, Hindu culture, and the role of women were also important determinants in achieving literacy among tribal women.

Naidu and Pradhan (1973) found that the enrolment of tribal girls in Tribal Development Blocks of Andhra Pradesh was miserably low in Government Schools compared to Missionary Schools.

P. K. B. Nayar (1975) worked on the SC and ST girl students of high schools in Kerala and made objective evaluation of the Government Policies, Programmes and Schemes that were concerned to tribal girl education.

Dixit Asha (1975) studied the educational need patterns of adults in urban, rural and tribal communities of Rajasthan and concluded that there are little or no educational opportunities in rural and tribal communities.

Srivastava (1981) studied the problems of early schooling of tribal children and the attitude of their parents and found that economic hardships, domestic engagements and superstitions affected the education of girl children.

Joshi (1984) tried to evaluate the development of education in the tribal areas of Dhule district and noticed inadequate provision of schools, irregular supply of incentives, transfer of teachers, high dropout rate, etc., were the root causes to the slow down of the development of tribal education in the district.

Mathur (1994) studied various dimensions of school education of tribals, role of parents, role of government agencies, social workers and others, and emphasized the need for popularizing the vocational education among tribal populations.

Manjulatha (1997) compared the academic achievements of tribal and non-tribal students in Ranchi and found that the isolation from home and other social factors as the reasons for poor attendance and drop-out.

Formal and Non-formal Education of Tribals

Renuka Ray Committee (1959), Elwin Committee (1960) and Dhebar Commission (1962) suggested that opening of Ashram (residential) schools as an improvement over the existing pattern of education in Scheduled Tribe areas.

Verrier Elwin Committee (1960) stated that a great deal of effort was necessary for starting compulsory education for the tribes.

L. R. N. Srivastava and others (1964) pointed out that the slow progress of education among the tribals in India was due to inadequate provision of schools for these communities.

Sachchidananda (1967), Ambasht (1970) and Das Gupta (1963) pointed out that retardation in education among tribal communities was due to apathy, indifferent attitude and lack of motivation for education, which arise due to two main reasons, viz., firstly, the formal education system is alien and not adjusted to their socio-economic and cultural needs; secondly, the tribals have certain prejudices and cultural suspicions towards sincerity of non-tribals.

A. B. Bose (1970) stated that the states with higher literacy in general population also have higher literacy in tribal population. According to him, there were variations in the literacy levels among different tribes in each region.

G. P. Reddy (1970) found that the causes for wastage in tribal education in Andhra Pradesh were poor economic conditions of the tribals and indifferent attitude of tribal parents towards education

Tribal Cultural Research and Training Institute, Hyderabad (1971) revealed that there were rampant absenteeism, stagnation, and dropout among the Chenchu schools in Andhra Pradesh. These triple evils were largely due to the constraints of poor economic condition, ingrained apathy towards education and lack of proper incentives to Chenchu students to make education attractive.

G. K. Khurana (1978) pointed out that, in spite of all the efforts to reduce the illiteracy among the scheduled tribes, the gap existed because of their poverty and backwardness coupled with ignorance and lack of educational facilities. He argued for the need-based education for adult tribals and alternative education methods for school-age children.

Ratnayya (1978) in his study on structural constraints in tribal education in Andhra Pradesh found that geographical barriers and inadequate number of schools and hostel facilities in tribal areas were largely responsible for the poor progress of education among tribal communities.

M. Rebellow (1978) found that curriculum was the main reason for high drop-out rate in tribal areas at the primary stage and suggested that the curricula should be need-based keeping in view of the local conditions.

K. Sujatha (1980) concluded that household work, agricultural work and lack of interest on the part of Yanadi (tribal) children for education were the main reasons for the poor enrolment in schools.

M. L. Sharma (1980) revealed that in most cases of the drop-outs from primary schools, young women and those from lower socio-economic level including tribes were not provided any education; the adults were attracted only to the programmes concerned with literacy and numeracy.

V. G. Dave (1981) recommended that there should be one supervisor for every tribal education centre and good system of training to the instructors.

S. P. Mullick (1981) reported that the teacher trainees felt that tape-sliced materials were useful for non-formal education meant for tribal communities, and making the lesson interesting and more useful in the large classes.

R. Y. Kumar (1981) studied the cause for non-enrolment, absenteeism and wastage among tribal girls and noticed that the schools were not so effective and the school system did not show any impact on the students and parents.

Dutta (1983) revealed that teaching and learning strategies need to be different for tribals.

Daljit Gupta (1983) found that attendance of children at the non-formal educational centres was found to be satisfactory.

Prabhakar Reddy (1983) studied the non-formal educational needs of the rural community and found that caste was perceived as a main source of social evils, the community felt that education was must for a better livelihood, and the tribals generally opined that they were not properly educated about development programmes that were meant for them and the tribals also felt that they had no access to formal education due to economic reasons.

R. Bhatnagar (1985) revealed that most of the tribal girls preferred to study in the afternoon or evening and wanted practical knowledge about knitting, embroidery, and home science and drawing. Girls wished to have radio, television sets and film shows at the non-formal centres.

N. K. Sivarajan (1985) concluded that most of the respondents were aware of the pitiable social and educational conditions of Harijans and of the attempts made at improving their lot. The studies of Hebsur (1981), Laxminarayana (1983) and Rao (1983) had also established the above fact.

Lakshmaiah and Yadappanaver (1986) observed that the schools, hostels and Ashram schools were neither both properly equipped and maintained nor the available institutions were adequate to meet the requirements.

Lakshmaiah (1987) identified the medium of instruction, lack of sufficient financial support, mis-utilisation of stipend and scholarship, improper implementation of incentives and conflicting relations between the government and its agencies as the problems of tribal schools in Bihar.

P. L. Mahapatra (1987) found that a low payment of monthly remuneration to the Instructors was very discouraging, and location of the centres at a long distance away from their homes was causing disturbance in the working conditions of women Facilitators. The centres have poor physical facilities in terms of building, ventilation furniture, and storage and display of materials.

Shymlal (1987) found that the unfavourable geographical conditions and low socio-economic level of the tribal families acted as the constraints and, as such, there was more educational wastage among those living in the interior tribal areas. The single teacher schools were to be the most important cause for drop-outs in tribal areas.

Joshi (1999) found that majority of the tribes were very backward in their socio-economic and educational conditions and this contributed for low levels of education.

D. Taradutta (2001) revealed that the tribal girl child was viewed as a security and asset to the family, and so, the parents did not allow the girls to study. The parents would like to give their sons better education. If the school language was changed into mother tongue and the syllabus was in tune with tribal culture, stories of tribal heroes who fought for Indian freedom are included or modes such as storytelling, showing video films, etc., are added, it will generate more interest for the pursuit of education among tribal communities.

Medium of Instruction

Nayar (1975) concluded that 80 per cent Scheduled Tribes felt the difficulty in following the class-room lessons in some of the subjects due to medium of instruction.

Mahajan observed that tribal students did not understand English, Mathematics and Science so easily. They, therefore, lag behind.

Basu, Biswas and Aiyappan discussed the importance of mother tongue as the medium of instruction. In their opinion, scientific collection of vocabularies of tribal children should be done and accordingly proper planning of tribal education be made.

Chottopadhyay explained that the problem of instruction, preparation of script in mother tongue, type of school, training of teachers, etc., were the root causes for the problems of tribal education and strongly advocated to have the local tribal language as the medium of instruction.

Sen, Sexena and Srivastava emphasised the need of education for tribal children and suggested that the best medium of educating them would be their own languages.

Tapase stressed that, for the first two standards, the education of tribal children should be imparted in tribal dialects and can be changed thereafter.

Chaliha pointed out that, for tribal pupils, after primary stage, the medium of instruction should be Hindi till textbooks and other literature become available in the tribal language.

Vinoba Gautam (2001), in his study on "Education of tribal children in India and the issue of medium of instruction", explained that most tribal children did not understand the textbooks that were generally in the regional language, and appointment of non-tribal teachers in schools meant for tribal children was another problem as the teachers do not know the language the children speak and children do not understand the language the teacher speaks.

Pamela J. MacKenzie (2009), in a study on "Mother tongue - First Multi-lingual Education among Tribal Communities in India", concluded that the education that was conducted in a language that they do not understand due to unfamiliar cultural context is a wasteful effort and suggested an improved quality of education and meeting the challenges of success and sustainability.

Mahendra Kumar Mishra (2009) noticed that the medium of instruction that was not in their own language prevented access to education.

Tribal Development

Bibhuti Mishra (2004) reported that an implicit stratification system was emerging within the tribal society on the basis of education, income, status and power. With modern education, modern values came into existence and clashed with the age-old traditional values of tribal society and this led to the tribals being antagonistic to modern education.

Jancy Gregory (2007) summarized that the tribal development has been a major challenge for the policy-makers and development planners for its multiple approaches and inherent complexities. Considering the significance of education in any development process, it has also posed a major challenge with regard to the nature and form of education that is most appropriate and befitting to tribal development in a meaningful way.

Dominic M. D'Souza (2007) highlighted the Indian constitutional measures that provided for tribal education and made recommendations for achieving not only equity in learning outcomes but in providing education that is more culturally attuned to the experience and context of tribal peoples in India.

Teachers and Tribal Education

Rath and Mishra (1974) confirmed that majority of Scheduled Tribe students felt themselves that they were neglected by their teachers.

Pratap (1971) observed that most of the Ashram schools were having non-tribal teachers with low educational qualifications. Thus, inadequate number and incompetent teachers in tribal schools were important reasons for slow progress of tribal education.

Desai and Patel (1981) reported that attitude of teachers towards tribal children was not healthy.

Joshi (1981 reported that the heads of the tribal families expressed that teachers did not show favourable attitude towards their children. It was observed that majority of the teachers had no special training for working in backward areas, particularly in tribal areas. As they belonged to upper caste groups, their prejudices towards SC/ST students influenced highly their behaviour with them.

Pathak (1991) found that 55 per cent of the ST students expressed positive attitude, whereas 33.75 per cent of the ST students had negative attitude towards their teachers.

Shah reported that ST students did not feel any problem in adjusting with their teachers. The ST students expressed that they never experienced any partiality by their teachers. In a mixed tribal and non-tribal student class, it was found that about one-third of the questions were posed to tribal students for better understanding of the lesson.

Educational Status of Tribal Families

Srivastava, Dubey, Rath and Mishra found that tribal students usually had poor family educational background.

Joshi (1980) observed that 85 per cent of the fathers (below 45 years of age) and 95 per cent of the mothers from tribal populations had practically no education in schools.

Pathak (1981) found that 42 per cent of tribal parents were educated, but only 9 per cent had education above intermediate (+2) qualification.

Lakshmanna concluded that 28.3 per cent of tribal fathers were high school pass and 14 per cent had received college education.

SCERT reported that, the distribution of parents from tribal families, according to the level of education, was primary 12.3 per cent, middle school 9.8 per cent, high school 7.55 per cent, higher education 2.5 per cent and illiterate about 60 per cent.

Thus, the review of the related research helped in developing a clear insight into the problem and in selecting the present research study to study the problems related to the education of tribal girls.

3 Research Methodology

RESEARCH IS A SYSTEMATIC enquiry seeking facts through objective verifiable methods in order to discover the relationship among them and to deduce from them the broad principles or laws. Therefore, the very success of a research work depends upon collecting the necessary information. Several methods of collecting information are developed to assist the research. Every expert has his own idea in selecting the best method for the collection of information. But, it cannot be uniform to all studies. Selection of the method depends on the type of information to be gathered and the sources of information to be consulted. For the present study, the normative survey method was chosen.

Survey means viewing and interpreting things rigorously and comprehensively. Now-a-days, survey method is a popular way of collecting data and analyzing the results statistically and systematically. This method is suitable to this study as this one is a status study meant for the study of the problems of tribal girl students with regard to their education.

OPERATIONAL DEFINITIONS OF KEY TERMS

The operational definitions of the important key terms used in the present study 'A Study on Problems of Tribal Girl Students of Secondary Schools' are defined here under:

1. *Tribal girl students:* The girls who are obtaining education in secondary schools belonging to tribal community are called tribal girl students.
2. *Rural secondary schools*: The secondary schools located in rural settings are called rural secondary schools.
3. *Urban secondary schools:* The secondary schools located in urban areas are called urban secondary schools.
4. Economically forward families: The families of the tribal students having annual income more than Rs. 30,000 are called economically forward families as per government norms.
5. *Economically backward families:* The families of the tribal students having annual income less than Rs. 30,000 are called economically backward families as per government norms.
6. *Educated parents:* The parents of the tribal girl student who are having some educational background.
7. *Uneducated parents*: The parents of the tribal girl student who are not having any educational background.
8. *Educated father:* The father of the tribal girl student who is having some educational background.
9. *Uneducated father:* The father of the tribal girl student who is not having any educational background.
10. *Educated mother:* The mother of the tribal girl student who is having some educational background.
11. *Uneducated mother:* The mother of the tribal girl student who is not having any educational background.
12. *Educational problems:* Things that become hindrances in obtaining education by the girl students are referred to as educational problems.
13. *Aided private schools:* The schools that are funded by Government and managed by a private Trust or Society are called aided private schools.

14. *Unaided private schools:* The schools that are fully funded and managed by a private Trust or Society are called unaided private schools.
15. *Hindu tribal girl students*: The tribal girl students believing and practicing Hinduism are called Hindu tribal girl students.
16. *Christian tribal girl students*: The tribal girl students believing and practicing Christianity are called Christian tribal girl students.
17. *Gujarati medium of instruction*: The tribal girl students get their education in Gujarati medium.
18. *English medium of instruction*: The tribal girl students get their education in English medium.
19. *School-leaving class tribal girl students*: The tribal girl students studying tenth class are considered as school-leaving students.
20. *Non-school-leaving class tribal girl students*: The tribal girl students studying eighth and ninth classes are considered as non-school-leaving students.
21. *Day-scholar tribal girl students*: The tribal girl students who are studying in day (secondary) schools are referred to as day-scholar students.
22. *Residential tribal girl students:* The tribal girl students who are studying in residential secondary schools are referred to as residential students.

VARIABLES OF THE STUDY

Variables are the conditions or characteristics that the experimenter manipulates, controls or observes. There are mainly three types of variables, namely, independent, dependent and intervening. The independent variables are those variables which do not change on manipulation by the experimenter. The dependent variables are those variables which change on manipulations made by the experimenter. The intervening variables are those variables which are dependent both on dependent and independent variables.

For the present study, the following independent variables were chosen.

1. Locality of the Secondary School

The geographical location affects the girls' education as the economic and social statuses vary form one geographical area to the other and these shall influence the education of the girl students of tribal communities. Urban and rural schools were selected under locality of the school. Urban schools are well equipped in many aspects when compared with rural schools. The facilities like buildings, libraries, laboratories, teaching staff, educational atmosphere, competitive spirit among pupils exposure to workshops etc., are different from one to the other. The work, living and academic atmosphere at home also differ from urban to rural settings. These amenities provided to the tribal girl students may make them to develop better or deprive worstly. So, locality was selected as a variable to compare the problems of tribal girl students of rural and urban secondary schools.

2. Economic Status of the Families of the Tribal Girl Students

Economic status of the families greatly influences the education of the tribal girls. The economically forward families try to send their children to schools and the economically backward families try to involve their children in income-yielding or domestic activities without sending them to schools. So, economic status (economically forward and backward) of the family of the tribal girl students was taken as a variable for comparison.

3. Educational Background of the Parents of the Tribal Girl Students

The educational background of the tribal girl students also influences their education. Most of the educated families try to provide education to their children, but some uneducated families also try to educate their children as they experience the benefit of education and enjoy the fruits of their education. So, education of the parents (both father and mother) was taken as a variable for the present study.

4. Educational Background of the Fathers of the Tribal Girl Students

Education of father of tribal girl students plays an important role in the educational opportunities of the tribal girl students as he understands the problems of his daughters and provides the required opportunities for their education by earning the needed money and extending the needed support in every aspect. Of course, now-a-days, uneducated fathers also encouraging their children to go to schools and colleges as they are suffering a lot due to their illiteracy. Hence, this variable (educated father and uneducated father) was taken as one of the variable to study.

5. Educational Background of the Mothers of the Tribal Girl Students

The role of mother plays a vital role in the education of the girl child and in identifying the problems of tribal girl students of secondary schools as has quoted by many authors that an educated mother can educate the entire family and this is opposite to an uneducated mother. So, the education of the mother (educated mother and uneducated mother) was taken as a variable to study the problems of tribal girl students studying in secondary schools.

6. Aided versus Unaided Secondary Schools

The reputation of unaided private schools is generally considered superior when compared with that of aided private schools. Unaided private school students are exposed to better study atmosphere with the facilities like laboratories, libraries, individual class rooms, teaching aids, language labs, etc., when compared to aided private schools as the former schools get higher fees and the later schools get low fees. The quality of teaching is also supposed to be better in unaided private schools since the standards of teaching and the physical facilities are supposed to be different in private unaided schools. This variable was taken up to study the difference in the problems of tribal girl students studying in aided and unaided private secondary schools since the unaided schools are financially self-sustained, the quality in all respects varies from aided schools to unaided private schools.

7. Religion of the Tribal Girl Students

Religion, as one of the factors that contribute for educational opportunities, will help the children in getting quality education. Both religions have varied aspects that contribute to the education of their followers. In the present study, the students belonging to Hindu religion and Christian religion were taken as sample to compare their problems as the religious beliefs and obligations contribute differently to the education of tribal girl students.

8. Medium of Instruction of Tribal Girl Students

Medium of instruction plays a legitimate role in encouraging the tribal girl students in getting education without any communication barriers as these students understand the subjects without any hurdles and when the instruction is in their well-known language. Hence, medium of instruction (Gujarati medium and English medium) was taken as a variable to see whether it has any role in contribution to the problems of tribal girl students.

9. School Leaving and Non-leaving Class Tribal Girl Students

Tribal girl students studying in school-leaving 10th class and studying in non-school-leaving 8th and 9th class were considered as a variable as these students will have certain educational problems with regard to pass or fail, promotion or retention, age, selection of future courses, etc., after leaving the secondary school, etc.

10. Day and Residential Secondary School Tribal Girl Students

The students who are studying in residential schools are much brighter than the day-school students as the residential school environment is catering to the better study environment. Hence, this variable is considered to find out the difference in the problems of students studying day-scholar and residential secondary schools.

HYPOTHESES OF THE STUDY

The hypothesis is a tentative answer to a question. It is a hunch or an educated guess, to be subjected to the process of verification or confirmation. It is a supposition or provisional guess, which explains the situation under observation.

Hypotheses are suggested problem solutions, which are expressed as generalizations or prepositions. They are the statements consisting of elements expressed in an orderly system of relationships which seek to describe or to explain events that have not yet been confirmed by facts. They may provide the conceptual elements that complete the known data, conceptual relationships that systematize unordered elements or conceptual meanings and interpretations that explain the unknown phenomena. By logically relating the known facts and intelligent guesses to unknown conditions, the hypotheses can extend and enlarge our knowledge.

John W. Best identifies four basic characteristics of a good hypothesis: it should be reasonable, it should be consistent with known facts or theories, it should be stated in such a way that it can be tested and found to be probably true or probably false, and it should be stated in the simplest possible terms.

Hypothesis is the most important step in the research process. The following hypotheses were formulated based on the variables and stated in null hypothesis form. The null hypothesis states that there is no significant difference or relationship between two or more parameters. It concerns to a judgment whether apparent differences or relationships are true or whether they merely result from a sampling error.

For the present study, the following Null hypotheses were put-forth:

1. There are no problems to tribal girl students of secondary schools.
2. There are no problems to tribal girl students of secondary schools at high level.

3. There is no significant difference in the problems of tribal girl students of rural and urban secondary schools.
4. There is no significant difference in the problems of tribal girl students of economically forward and economically backward families.
5. There is no significant difference in the problems of tribal girl students of educated and uneducated father.
6. There is no significant difference in the problems of tribal girl students of educated and uneducated mother.
7. There is no significant difference in the problems of tribal girl students of educated and uneducated parents.
8. There is no significant difference in the problems of tribal girl students of aided and unaided private secondary schools.
9. There is no significant difference in the problems of tribal girl students of Hindu religion and Christian religion.
10. There is no significant difference in the problems of tribal girl students of Gujarati medium and English medium secondary schools.
11. There is no significant difference in the problems of tribal girl students of school-leaving class and non-school-leaving classes of secondary schools.
12. There is no significant difference in the problems of tribal girl students of day-scholar and residential secondary schools.

SAMPLE OF THE STUDY

A population is any group of individuals that has one or more characteristics in common. The population may be all the individuals of a particular type or a more restricted part of that group.

A sample is a small proportion of a population selected for observation and analysis. It is a collection consisting of a part or subset of the objects or individuals of population that is selected for the express purpose of representing the population. By observing the characteristics of the sample, one can make certain inferences about the characteristics of the population from which it is drawn.

After finalizing the variables, consideration was given to whether the entire population is to be made the subject for data collection or a particular group is to be selected as representative of the whole population. The entire population here refers to all the tribal girls studying in secondary schools of Panchmahal district of Gujarat State.

The selection of a group as a representative of the whole population was found to be more convenient and suitable. The technique leads to a considerable saving of time, effort and finance. The number of students selected will be small in order to make a detailed and intensive study. This generally leads to more accurate and reliable results. As this sampling has many advantages, it was selected for the collection of data.

After finalizing the variables of the present study, consideration was given to whether the entire population is to be made the subject for data collection or a particular group is to be selected as representative of the whole population. Here, population refers to all the tribal girl students of the secondary schools located in Panchmahal district of Gujarat. Of the two techniques, the second one, namely, the selection of a group as a representative of the whole population was found to be more convenient and suitable. This technique leads to a considerable saving of time, effort and finance. The number of students selected is small, and so it is possible to make a detailed and intensive study. This generally leads to more accurate and reliable results. As this sampling technique has many advantages, it was selected for the collection of data. Sampling is simply the process of learning about the population on the basis of a sample drawn from it.

In any social research, various methods are utilised for selection and drawing of samples. After a detailed study of all these methods and considering the variables selected for the research work, the stratified sampling method was found to be most suitable.

In the stratified sampling method, the entire population will be divided into smaller homogeneous groups (John W. Best) or strata, and then the sample is selected within each group. Every sampling unit in the population is placed in one of the strata prior to the selection of the sample so that the sum of the strata is identical with the population.

Stratified sampling method has certain merits and advantages as a technique of sampling. Auck of has rightly said that stratified sampling enables the researcher to make a comparison of properties or traits as well as to estimate population characteristics (Kerlinger, 1964)..

In stratified sampling method, the investigator has greater control over the selection of the sample when compared with random sampling. In random sampling. although every group has a chance of being selected and included in the sample, there is every possibility and sometimes it does happen that certain important groups are left unrepresented. But, in stratified sampling method other than stratified sampling method, no important group is likely to be left out.

Stratified sampling method is the ideal one when comparison between different variables has to be made. For example, if comparison has to be made between alcoholic and non-alcoholic students, it would be very difficult to select the required number of units through any other method of sampling. If any other method is used, the problem of bias and prejudice creeps in.

Replacement of units is also possible in the stratified sampling method. Normally, if a particular unit is not accessible for a study, it is difficult to replace it by another but in this method it is possible. Stephen states that stratification automatically brings about a replacement of persons lost to the sample by persons of the same stratum, thus partly correcting the bias that would result if there were no replacement of losses. As the entire population is divided into particular strata, it is easy and convenient to replace an inaccessible one by an accessible one.

In stratified sampling method, much depends on the stratification process. The following precautions were taken while stratifying the population: the variables involved in the study were taken note of, care was taken to see that each stratum in the universe was large enough in size so that selection of items could be done on random basis, the strata formed were definite and clear and each stratum was 'free from the 'influence of others'; and that 'there was no over lapping'. Before actually selecting the sample, certain fundamental principles were considered to make the sample scientific and clear-cut.

Firstly, the 'universe' was clearly defined. In the technical phraseology of research, the whole population out of which the samples are selected is known as the 'universe'. For the present research work, the universe includes all the tribal girls studying in secondary schools of Panchmahal district of Gujarat State The study was limited to a particular geographical area to facilitate appropriate sample selection and to avoid bias and prejudice.

Secondly, decision has to be made about the units of the sample. A unit of sample may be a house, a family, a group of individuals or a single individual. A good unit should possess these characteristics:

1. *Clarity*: The unit should be clearly defined in unambiguous terms. This would make the study easy and efficient. For the present research work, a sampling unit was defined as a tribal girl student studying in any secondary school of Panchmahal district of Gujarat State.
2. *Suitability:* A good unit should be well suited to the problem under study. Since the study is on the problems of tribal girl students of secondary schools of Panchmahal district, the unit selected is well suited to the problem.
3. *Accessibility:* The unit selected should be easily accessible to the researcher. If the units selected are difficult to reach and if the researcher fails to make use of them, the study would be vitiated. The selected sample unit, *i.e.,* tribal

girl student studying in any secondary school of Panchmahal district, is easily accessible since she could be approached in any secondary school.

Thirdly, consideration should be given to the preparation of the source list. This is an important factor that makes representative selection possible. A source list is the list, which contains the names of the units of the universe from which the sample may be selected. It may exist even before the beginning of the project or it may be prepared afresh by the investigator himself. Without a source list, study through a sampling technique is not possible. For the parent research work, a source list consisting of the names of schools in Panchmahal district was used. Care was taken to see that the source list was up-to-date and valid and that there was no repetition of names of the schools. This source list was found to be relevant and suitable because it included secondary schools as the study deals with the tribal girl students of secondary schools.

Besides considering these principles, it is extremely important to think about the size of the sample to be selected. If the sample is either too small or too large, it will make the study difficult and also make the results untenable. An optimum sample in survey is one which fulfils the requirements of effective representativeness, reliability and flexibility. The sample should be small enough to avoid intolerable sampling error. The size of sample for the present research work was decided after considering the following factors.

Since an intensive study was planned, a very large number of samples were not selected. In case of an intensive study, very large numbers of samples are not so useful as they involve huge consumption of resources. A smaller sample is very much convenient. In the present case, it is highly difficult to get large member of sampling units as tribal girl students are limited in number when compared to general category girl students.

The size and selection of the samples will also be influenced by the nature of the universe. If the universe is homogenous, even a small-sized sample may yield dependable and required results. If the universe is heterogeneous, small - sized samples may not be useful. In case of the present study, the heterogeneous universe will be split into smaller homogenous groups and the samples will be selected from these strata. For example, all the tribal girl students will be broadly grouped under urban and rural tribal girl students. Required sample will be selected from each of these two groups.

The investigator needs to determine the number of groups to be formed. In case the number of groups proposed is large, the size of the samples shall have to be large so that every group should be of proper in size and suit to the requirements of the study. In case the number of groups proposed is small, even small-sized samples can fulfill the requirement. In case of the present study, the groups into which the universe was divided are urban and rural tribal girl students, tribal girl students from economically forward and economically backward families, tribal girl students of educated and uneducated father, tribal girl students of educated and uneducated mother, and tribal girl students of aided and unaided private schools, etc. Since the number of groups is moderate, a reasonably large sample was selected from each of these groups.

Practical considerations and accuracy will also play a vital role in determining the size of the sample. Every study is guided by certain practical considerations such as time, resources, accessibility of data, etc. Generally, it is believed that a large-sized sample is more representative and generally produces accurate results. This, of course, depends upon the technique of sampling used. If the technique is scientific, even small-sized sample can produce dependable and accurate results. While selecting the size of the sample for the present study, practical considerations like the availability of resources and time were taken into consideration. Care was taken to make the sample selection technique as scientific as possible.

The size of the sample is also governed by the size of the tools to be used. In case the tools are short and the questions asked pertain to certain limited factors, a large sample can be selected. In case the tools are large and the questions complicated, the sample should be small in size so that, from administrative point of view, the investigator may not be put to unnecessary troubles. In the present study, the tool was quite elaborate and needs care; hence a very large sample was not selected.

The sampling method also determines the size of the sample. When random sampling method is used, the samples have to be large. On the other hand, if samples are selected through stratified sampling method, the reliability can be achieved even with the help of the small-sized samples.

After taking into consideration all these factors, which influence the size of the sample it was decided that an ideal sample would consist of 712 secondary school tribal girl students. This sample is small enough to avoid unnecessary expenditure and large enough to avoid intolerable sampling errors.

After deciding about the sampling method and the size of the sample, the universe selected was divided into urban and rural tribal girl students, tribal girl students from economically forward and backward families, tribal girl students of educated and uneducated father, tribal girl students of educated and uneducated mother, and tribal girl students of aided and unaided private schools, etc.

The following sample division shows the final variable-wise distribution of tribal girl students studying in secondary schools of Panchmahal district Gujarat.

Total secondary school tribal girl students: 712.

(i) Locality of the secondary school: Rural: 481, Urban: 231.

(ii) Grant-in-aid of the secondary school: Aided: 640, Un-aided: 72.

(iii) Medium of instruction: English medium: 176. Gujarati medium: 536.

(iv) Type of the secondary school: Day-scholar: 587, Residential: 125.

(v) Religion of the tribal girl student: Hinduism: 599, Christianity: 113.

(vi) Economic status of the tribal girl student: Economically forward: 67, Economically backward: 645.

(vii) Education of the father of the tribal girl student: Educated: 436, Uneducated: 276.

(viii) Education of the mother of the tribal girl student: Educated: 171, Uneducated: 541.

(ix) Education of the parents (both mother and father) of the tribal girl student: Educated: 170, Uneducated: 542.

(x) Class of the tribal girl student: School-leaving class: 216, Non-school-classes: 496.

TOOL OF THE STUDY

A research tool plays a major role in any worthwhile research as it is the sole factor in determining the sound data and in arriving at perfect conclusions about the problem or study in hand, which, ultimately, helps in providing suitable remedial measures to the problem concerned.

A great variety of research tools has been developed to aid in the acquisition of data. These tools are of many kinds and employ distinctive ways of describing and quantifying data. Each tool is particularly appropriate for certain sources of data, yielding information of the kind and in the form that would be most effectively used, like the tools in the carpenter's chest, each is appropriate in a given situation.

The selection and use of tools can be done in two ways.

The first one is to construct a tool independently by the investigator for his own study. Here, there are many problems in doing so. Preparation and standardization of a perfect tool itself is a major task, and one can easily say that it is a doctoral study itself. On construction of their own tools, Anand and Padma (1987) felt that "A note of caution has to be taken when a researcher develops a tool for his study by merely pooling up some items and does not subject it to the sophisticated techniques of tool construction. The result would be then, obviously, a poor quality research." With this, one can say that preparation and standardization of tools is a major task, and one should take care in aspects like selection of area and sample, pooling up of statements related to the area and sample, consulting the experts, and application of sophisticated statistical techniques.

The second way of selection and use of tools is right selection of tools from already standardized ones available in the field of study. Here also it involves a tedious job in locating the tools and identifying their usefulness to the study on hand. Even then, this technique is very useful when a research work is taken to study in depth and when the research work involves a good number of variables. Some people believe that some of the instruments available do not measure up to their standards. Hence, new ones. In some instances, consideration should be given to the logistics of the situation. Lacking of time and financial resources, many researchers cannot expect to produce a better instrument. In these cases, the most logical procedure that one can follow is to choose the best instrument available for his purpose.

As no ready-made research tools concerned to the problems of girl students of Gujarat were available, the researcher constructed a rating scale by following the appropriate research and standardization procedures, which is explained here under, for identifying the problems of tribal girl students.

Standardization of the Rating Scale: Problems of Secondary School Tribal Girl Students

For the purpose identifying the problems of tribal girl students of secondary schools of Gujarat state, the researcher has developed a rating scale, *viz.*, Problems of Secondary School Tribal Girl Students, by following the necessary tool standardization procedures.

Pre-test and Final-test Forms

In order to achieve the set objectives of the study, the social, economical, educational and physical aspects have been taken into consideration. Various items were included while preparing the statements such occupation, religion, family income, educational status, social status, type and size of family, reasons for not attending the schools, methods of improving the children, attitude of parents towards education, difficulties concerned to school and teachers in study, motivating factors behind the education, etc.

Taking above issues into view, the rating scale with 160 statements has been drawn and sent to eight subject experts of the following universities/institutions to seek their expert opinion on the sustainability regarding validity and reliability of each test item:

1. Faculty of Education and Psychology, M. S. University, Baroda.
2. Department of Education, Sardar Patel University, Vallabh Vidhyanagar, Anand.
3. Department of Education, South Gujarat University, Surat.
4. Department of Education, Navrachana College of Education, Baroda.

The experts have reviewed the draft rating scale on the lines of its relevance, clarity, purpose and language used. Based on the experts' recommendations, the rating scale was again reviewed by the researcher by eliminating certain irrelevant statements as suggested by the experts and then 135 statements were retained in the rating scale.

A Pre-test was conducted on 52 tribal girl students; with varied economic, social and educational backgrounds; studying 8th, 9th and 10th classes in M. B. Vidhyalaya, a secondary school, Kandivav, Gujarat. On receipt of the responses on all the 135 statements, it was opined, by putting each test item to item analysis, that on some statements do not be hold good for the tool and hence, 10 statements have been removed from the rating scale and final rating scale is confined to 125 statements in six areas.

The following are the areas chosen for the study and the test items included in each area of the study.

1. *Economics*

20 statements have been drawn on economic problems of tribal girl students, which have been covered all the financial constraints responsible for study. These have been worked out keeping in view the responses may be useful for the Researcher to give some suggestions for the remedy.

2. *Social Concerning to Education*

20 statements have been drawn on social problems concerning to education of tribal girl students, which includes the tribal social strata leads to education and its hurdles.

3. *Concerning to School Teachers*

20 statements have been drawn on the problems of school teachers, where the tribal girl students are studying in the schools.

4. *Created by Peer Group*

20 statements have been drawn on the problems created by co-students/peer group, which includes the statements related to the attitudes of non-tribals and indicative of social status, dialects, etc.

5. *Text Books and Learning Experiences*

25 statements have been drawn on text books and learning experiences, which are also important factors for the problems of tribal girl students.

6. *Physical Problems*

20 statements have been drawn on physical problems of tribal girl students, which have been covered all the problems related to physical constraints responsible for study. These have been worked out keeping in view the responses may be useful for the Researcher to give some suggestions for the remedy.

Reliability and Validity

After finalizing the final rating scale, the same has been administered on small sample of 100 tribal girl students studying in different schools and calculated for the scale's validity and reliability.

Since reliability is the most essential and significant feature of a test/scale, the Split-Half and Test-Retest reliabilities have been calculated for this scale battery. For calculating the split-half reliability, Guttmann and Spearman Brown's prophecy formula have been used which yielded the coefficient of correlation as +0.852 and +0.911 respectively when this test was administered to a sample of 100 tribal girl students. These reliability coefficients reveal that the present scale is highly reliable. As for the test-retest reliability, the present scale was administered twice to a sample of 100 tribal girl students with a time lapse of two weeks and the co-efficient correlation was found to be +0.895.

With regard to the validity of the scale, only highly discriminating items are included in the rating scale following item analysis (Garrett, 1961). The upper 27 per cent and lower 27 per cent served as criterion groups (Kelly, 1939). The face validity of the measures is very high. The content validity is ensured as the items for which there has been 100 per cent agreement in final rating scale amongst the judges (again refered to the judges who initially rendered their expertise) regarding their relevance to the problems of tribal girl students are included in the rating scale.

Scoring

Each statement is followed by three alternative responses. One score will be given to Agree, two scores to Undecided, and three scores to Disagree. All the statements are given in positive way.

Necessary instructions are given in the rating scale for following the rating scale scrupulously.

Administration of the Tool and Data Collection

The rating scale developed for the study was administered personally on 712 school-going tribal girl students of 8th, 9th and 10th classes studying in 14 secondary schools in 4 talukas (a cluster of villages is nomenclatured as a taluka by the government) of Panchmahal district of Gujarat state, and the sample was asked to respond to the statements. Before giving the tool to the sampling units, the researcher explained the purpose of the present investigation. Directions given on the cover sheet were read out to the sample and specific instructions were given. Then the sample answered the scale comfortably.

4

Analysis of Data

ANALYSIS OF DATA is the most skilled task of all the stages of research. Analysis of data means studying the tabulated material in order to determine inherent facts or meanings. It involves breaking down complex factors into simple ones and putting the parts in new arrangements for the purpose of interpretation.

The first step in the analysis of data is a critical examination of the assembled data in tabular form. Tabulation is a means of recording and classification of data in a compact form in such a way so as to facilitate comparisons. Data is arranged in rows and columns to facilitate mathematical and statistical operations. It is of great help in analysis and interpretation of data. While tabulating the data, the purpose of the study has to be kept in mind.

The method of analysis chosen for a particular study depends upon the nature of objectives formulated, hypotheses to be tested, and usefulness of the study. Statistical methods are the mathematical techniques used to facilitate the interpretation of numerical data secured from groups of individuals or group of observations or a single individual. For the present study entitled "A Study of Problems of Tribal Girl Students of Secondary Schools", several statistical techniques were used to perform the analysis.

After collecting the data from 712 tribal girl students of secondary schools, the analysis was performed keeping in view the objectives formed, hypotheses formulated, type of data collected, type of tool used, etc. To find out the problems faced by each sub-samples as well as the whole sample, the total scores of problems faced by each tribal girl student was taken into consideration.

There are 125 items in the rating scale, *viz*., Problems of Secondary School Tribal Girl Students. The minimum and maximum score one can get for each item was 1 and 3 respectively according to the norms of the scale. Therefore, the highest and the lowest scores of the problems faced by a tribal girl student can be 375 and 125 respectively.

For the purpose of classification of the level of problems of secondary school tribal girl students, the problems were divided into three categories, namely, problems at low level (1-125 scores), problems at average level (126-250 scores), and problems at high level (251-375 scores).

The mean scores were used to identify the level of problems of secondary school tribal girl students and to compare the sub-sample variation. The values of standard deviation were used to measure the spread or dispersion of scores in the distribution (Garret, 1979). The critical ratios were calculated to test the significant difference in the means of the sub-samples of each variable. The null hypotheses formulated for this study were accordingly accepted or rejected.

The chi-square test of independence was applied for comparing the experimentally obtained results with those to be expected theoretically.

Hypothesis 1

There are no problems to tribal girl students of secondary schools.

To test the above hypothesis, the following calculations were made.

Table 4.1: Problems of tribal girl students of secondary schools

Sample	Sample Size	Mean	Standard Deviation
Whole	712	255.12	42.43

As per the values of Table 4.1, the secondary tribal girl students were facing problems at high level. The problems were dispersed widely in secondary school tribal girl students as per the Standard Deviation value cited in the table.

The chi-square test of independence was applied to test the divergence of observed results from those expected on the hypothesis of normal probability of distribution of the problems in the sample.

Table 4.2: Distribution of problems in secondary school tribal girl students

Sample Size	Low	Average	High	Chi-square Value
712	f_o 76 f_e 75.99	424 4222.99	212 212.99	32.32 *

df = 2, *p at 0.05 level 5.99* * *Significant at 0.05 level*

f_o = Frequency of observed or experimentally determined facts.

f_e = Frequency of expected on some hypothesis.

It is clear, from Table 4.2, that the distribution of the problems of tribal girl students in the whole sample was nearly normal.

The hypothesis that "there are no problems to tribal girl students of secondary schools" can be accepted as the secondary school tribal girl students were possessing problems at high level.

Hypothesis 2

There is no significant difference in the problems of tribal girl students of rural and urban secondary schools.

To test the above hypothesis, the following calculations were made.

Table 4.3: Comparison of problems of tribal girl students of rural and urban secondary schools

Variable	Sample Size	Mean	SD Diff	Mean	SED	CR
Rural girls	481	247.94	39.29	21.11	3.49	6.01*
Urban girls	231	269.05	45.53			

df = 2, p at 0.05 level 1.96 — ** Significant at 0.05 level*

As per the values of Table 4.3, the tribal girl students of both rural and urban secondary schools were facing problems with a significant difference. The tribal girl students of urban secondary schools were facing problems at high level and the tribal girl students of rural secondary schools were facing problems at an average level. The problems of tribal girl students were spread widely in both rural and urban secondary schools.

Further, the chi-square test was applied to test the divergence of observed result of the problems of tribal girl students of rural and urban secondary schools from those expected on the hypothesis of normal probability.

Table 4.4: Distribution of problems of tribal girl students of rural and urban secondary schools

Variable	Sample Size		Low	Average	High	Chi-square Value
Rural girls	481	fo	70	290	121	32.31*
		fe	51.34	285.76	143.89	
Urban girls	231	fo	6	133	92	
		fe	24.65	137.23	69.1	

** Significant at 0.05 level*

The chi-square value suggests that there was a significant difference in problems of tribal girl students of rural and urban secondary schools.

The hypothesis that "there is no significant difference in the problems of tribal girl students of rural and urban secondary schools" can be rejected as there was a significant difference in the problems of tribal girl students of urban and rural secondary school.

Hypothesis 3

There is no significant difference in the problems of tribal girl students of economically forward and economically backward families.

To test the above hypothesis, the following calculations were made.

Table 4.5: Comparison of problems of tribal girl students of economically forward and economically backward families

Variable	Sample Size	Mean	SD	Mean Diff	SED	CR
Economically forward families	67	255.49	58.12	0.78	7.28	0.11#
Economically backward families	645	254.71	40.65			

 # Not significant at 0.05 level

As per the values of Table 4.5, the tribal girl students of both economically forward and economically backward families were facing problems at high level without any significant difference. Problems of tribal girl students were spread widely in economically forward and economically backward families.

Further, the chi-square test was applied to test the divergence of observed result of the problems of tribal girl students of economically forward and economically backward families from those expected on the hypothesis of normal probability.

Table 4.6: Distribution of problems of tribal girl students of economically forward and economically backward families

Variable	Sample Size		Low	Average	High	Chi-square Value
Economically forward families	67	fo	12	34	21	4.75#
		fe	7.15	39.8	20.04	
Economically backward families	635	fo	64	389	192	
		fe	67.78	377.25	189.96	

 # Not significant at 0.05 level

The chi-square value reveals that there was no significant difference in problems of tribal girl students of economically forward and economically backward families.

The hypothesis that "there is no significant difference in the problems of tribal girl students of economically forward and economically backward families" can be accepted as there is no significant difference in the problems of both the sub-samples.

Hypothesis 4

There is no significant difference in the problems of tribal girl students of educated and uneducated father.

To test the above hypothesis, the following calculations were made.

Table 4.7: Comparison of problems of tribal girl students of educated and uneducated father

Variable	Sample Size	Mean	SD	Mean Diff	SED	CR
Uneducated father	276	265.21	37.73	17.02	3.10	5.49*
Educated father	436	248.19	44.12			

** Significant at 0.05 level*

As per the values of Table 4.7, the tribal girl students of both educated and uneducated father were facing problems with a significant difference. The tribal girl students of uneducated father were facing problems at high level and the tribal girl students of educated father were facing at an average level. Problems of tribal girl students of both educated and uneducated father were spread widely in the sub-samples.

Further, the chi-square test was performed to test the divergence of observed result of the problems of tribal girl students of educated and uneducated father from those expected on the hypothesis of normal probability.

Table 4.8: Distribution of problems of tribal girl students of educated and uneducated father

Variable	Sample Size		Low	Average	High	Chi-square Value
Uneducated father	276	fo	10	161	105	64.43*
		fe	29.65	163.78	82.57	
Educated father	436	fo	66	262	108	
		fe	46.85	258.72	130.43	

** Significant at 0.05 level*

The chi-square value suggests that there was a significant difference in the problems of tribal girl students of educated and uneducated father.

The hypothesis that "there is no significant difference in the problems of tribal girl students of educated and uneducated father" can be rejected as the tribal girl students of uneducated father are facing more problems than those of educated father.

Hypothesis 5

There is no significant difference in the problems of tribal girl students of educated and uneducated mother.

To test the above hypothesis, the following calculations were made.

Table 4.9: Comparison of problems of tribal girl students of educated and uneducated mother

Variable	Sample Size	Mean	SD	Mean Diff	SED	CR
Uneducated mother	541	257.58	39.45	11.64	3.71	2.9[illegible]*
Educated mother	171	245.94	50.24			

** Significant at 0.05 level*

As per the values of Table 4.9, the tribal girl students of both educated and uneducated mother were facing problems with a significant difference. Tribal girl students of uneducated mother were facing problems at high level and the tribal girl students of educated mother were facing at an average level. Problems of tribal girl students of both educated and uneducated mother were spread widely in the sub-samples.

Further, the chi-square test was performed to test the divergence of observed result of the problems of tribal girl students of educated and uneducated mother from those expected on the hypothesis of normal probability.

Table 4.10: Distribution of problems of tribal girl students of educated and uneducated mother

Variable	Sample Size		Low	Average	High	Chi-square Value
Uneducated mother	541	fo	38	331	171	64.45*
		fe	58.02	320.43	161.54	
Educated mother	171	fo	39	91	42	
		fe	18.48	102.06	51.45	

** Significant at 0.05 level*

The chi-square value suggests that there was a significant difference in the problems of tribal girl students of educated and uneducated mother.

The hypothesis that "there is no significant difference in the problems of tribal girl students of educated and uneducated mother" can be rejected as the tribal girl students of uneducated mother are facing more problems than those of educated mother.

Hypothesis 6

There is no significant difference in the problems of tribal girl students of educated and uneducated parents.

To test the above hypothesis, the following calculations were made.

Table 4.11: Comparison of problems of tribal girl students of educated and uneducated parents

Variable	Sample Size	Mean	SD	Mean Diff	SED	CR
Uneducated parents	542	265.51	37.75	21.34	4.76	4.48*
Educated parents	170	244.17	51.27			

** Significant at 0.05 level*

As per the values of Table 4.11, it is clear that tribal girl students of both educated and uneducated parents were facing problems with a significant difference. The tribal girl students of uneducated parents were facing problems at high level and the tribal girl students of educated parents were facing problems at an average level. Problems of tribal girl students of both educated and uneducated parents were spread widely in the samples.

Further, the chi-square test was applied to test the divergence of observed result of the problems of tribal girl students of educated and uneducated parents from those expected on the hypothesis of normal probability.

Table 4.12: Distribution of problems of tribal girl students of educated and uneducated parents

Variable	Sample Size		Low	Average	High	Chi-square Value
Uneducated parents	542	fo	88	74	96	21.78*
		fe	110.48	65.91	81.61	
Educated parents	170	fo	88	31	34	
		fe	65.52	39.09	48.39	

*Significant at 0.05 level

The chi-square value suggests that there was a significant difference in problems of tribal girl students of educated and uneducated parents.

The hypothesis that "there is no significant difference in the problems of tribal girl students of educated and uneducated parents" can be rejected as the tribal girl students of uneducated parents are facing more problems than those of educated parents.

Hypothesis 7

There is no significant difference in the problems of tribal girl students of aided and unaided secondary schools.

To test the above hypothesis, the following calculations were made.

Table 4.13: Comparison of problems of tribal girl students of aided and unaided secondary schools

Variable	Sample Size	Mean	SD	Mean Diff	SED	CR
Aided private school students	640	257.43	41.69	26.14	5.35	4.88*
Unaided private school students	72	231.29	43.2			

* Significant at 0.05 level

As per the values of Table 4.13, tribal girl students studying in both aided and unaided schools were facing problems with a significant difference. The tribal girl students of aided secondary schools were facing problems at high level and the tribal girl students of unaided secondary schools were facing problems at an average level. Problems of tribal girl students of both aided and unaided secondary schools were spread widely in the sub-samples.

Further, the chi-square test was performed to test the divergence of observed result of the problems of tribal girl students of aided and unaided secondary schools from those expected on the hypothesis of equal probability.

Table 4.14: Distribution of problems of tribal girl students of aided and unaided secondary schools

Variable	Sample Size		Low	Average	High	Chi-square Value
Aided private School students	640	fo	55	380	205	35.13*
		fe	68.31	380.22	191.46	
Unaided private School students	72	fo	21	43	8	
		fe	7.68	42.77	21.54	

** Significant at 0.05 level*

The chi-square value suggests that there was a significant difference in problems of tribal girl students of aided and unaided schools.

The hypothesis that "there is no significant difference in the problems of tribal girl students of aided and unaided secondary schools" can be rejected as the tribal girl students of aided secondary schools are facing more problems than those of unaided secondary schools.

Hypothesis 8

There is no significant difference in problems of tribal girl students of Hindu religion and Christian religion.

To test the above hypothesis, the following calculations were made.

Table 4.15: Comparison of problems of tribal girl students of hindu religion and christian religion

Variable	Sample Size	Mean	SD	Mean Diff	SED	CR
Hindu students	599	254.34	43.75	2.82	3.80	0.7429#
Christian students	113	257.16	35.60			

 # Not significant at 0.05 level

As per the values of Table 4.15, it is clear that, both Hindu and Christian tribal girl students were facing problems at high level without any significant difference. The problems of both Hindu and Christian tribal girl students were spread widely in the sub-samples.

Further, the chi-square test was applied to test the divergence of observed results of problems of tribal girl students of Hindu and Christian religions from those expected on the hypothesis of normal probability.

Table 4.16: Distribution of problems of tribal girl students of hindu religion and christian religion

Variable	Sample Size		Low	Average	High	Chi-square Value
Hindu students	599	fo	72	346	181	8.24*
		fe	63.94	355.87	179.20	
Christian students	113	fo	4	77	32	
		fe	12.06	67.13	9.87	

** Significant at 0.05 level*

The chi-square value suggests that there was a significant difference in the problems of tribal girl students of Hindu and Christian religion with regard to distribution from low level to high level.

Hence the hypothesis that "there is no significant difference in problems of tribal girl students of Hindu and Christian religions" can be accepted as there is no significant difference in the problems of tribal girl students of Hindu religion and Christian religion.

Hypothesis 9

There is no significant difference in the problems of tribal girl students of Gujarati medium and English medium secondary schools.

To test the above hypothesis, the following calculations were made.

Table 4.17: Comparison of problems of tribal girl students of gujarati medium and english medium secondary schools

Variable	Sample Size	Mean	SD	Mean Diff	SED	CR
Gujrati medium	536	265.57	44.16	14.32	3.66	3.91*
English medium	176	251.25	41.44			

** Significant at 0.05 level*

As per the values of Table 4.17, it is clear that tribal girl students of both Gujarati medium and English medium secondary schools were facing problems at high level with a significant difference. Though both were facing problems at high level, the tribal girl students of Gujarati medium were facing more problems than the tribal girl students of English medium. The problems of tribal girl students of both Gujarati medium and English medium were spread widely in the samples.

Further, the chi-square test was applied to test the divergence of observed result of the problems of tribal girl students of Gujarati medium and English medium secondary schools from those of expected on the hypothesis of normal probability.

Table 4.18: Distribution of problems of tribal girl students of gujarati medium and english medium secondary schools

Variable	Sample Size		Low	Average	High	Chi-square Value
Gujrati medium	536	fo	68	324	144	15.36*
		fe	57.21	318.44	160.35	
English medium	176	fo	8	99	69	
		fe	18.79	104.56	52.65	

* *Significant at 0.05 level*

The chi-square value suggests that there was a significant difference in the problems of tribal girl students of Gujarati and English medium secondary schools

The hypothesis that "there is no significant difference in the problems of tribal girl students of Gujarati medium and English medium secondary schools" can be rejected as the tribal girl students of Gujarati medium are facing more problems than those of English medium.

Hypothesis 10

There is no significant difference in the problems of tribal girl students of school-leaving class and non-school-leaving classes of secondary schools.

To test the above hypothesis, the following calculations were made.

Table 4.19: Comparison of problems of tribal girl students studying in the school-leaving class and non-school-leaving classes

Variable	Sample Size	Mean	SD	Mean Diff	SED	CR
Non-school-leaving classes	496	256.11	43.85	4.36	3.32	1.31#
School-leaving class	216	251.75	39.33			

\# *Not significant at 0.05 level*

The values of Table 4.19 reveal that tribal girl students studying in both the school-leaving class and non-school-leaving classes were facing problems at high level without any significant difference. Problems of tribal girl students studying in both school-leaving class and non-school-leaving classes were spread widely in the samples.

Further, the chi-square test was applied to test the divergence of observed results of problems of tribal girl students studying in the school leaving class and non-school-leaving classes from those expected on the hypothesis of normal probability.

Table 4.20: Distribution of problems of tribal girl students studying in school-leaving class and non-school-leaving classes

Variable	Sample Size		Low	Average	High	Chi-square Value
Non-school-leaving classes	496	fo	51	289	156	1.88#
		fe	52.94	294.67	148.38	
School leaving class	216	fo	25	134	57	
		fe	23.06	128.33	64.62	

 # Not significant at 0.05 level

The chi-square value suggests that there was no significant difference in the problems of tribal girl students studying in the school leaving class and non-school-leaving classes with regard to the distribution of problems in the sub-samples.

The hypothesis that "there is no significant difference in problems of tribal girl students of school-leaving class and non-school-leaving classes" can accepted as there is no significant difference in the problems of school-leaving and non-school-laving class students.

Hypothesis 11

There is no significant difference in problems of tribal girl students of day-scholar and residential secondary schools.

To test the above hypothesis, the following calculations were made.

Table 4.21: Comparison of problems of tribal girl students of day-scholar and residential secondary schools

Variable	Sample Size	Mean	SD	Mean Diff	SED	CR
Day students	587	253.69	43.12	6.26	3.96	1.58#
Residential students	125	259.94	39.51			

 # Not significant at 0.05 level

From the values of the Table 4.19, it is clear that tribal girl students of both day and residential secondary schools were facing problems at high level without any significant difference. The problems of tribal girl students were spread widely in the sub-samples.

Further, the chi-square test was applied to test the divergence of observed result of problems of tribal girl students of day and residential schools from those expected on the hypothesis of normal probability.

Table 4.22: Distribution of problems of tribal girl students of day-scholar and residential secondary schools

Variable	Sample Size		Low	Average	High	Chi-square Value
Day students	587	fo	70	345	172	5.55#
		fe	62.22	348.74	175.61	
Residential students	125	fo	6	78	41	
		fe	13.34	74.26	37.39	

 # Not significant at 0.05 level

The chi-square value suggests that there is no significant difference in the problems of tribal girl students of day and residential secondary schools in respect to the distribution in the samples.

The hypothesis that "there is no significant difference in the problems of tribal girl students of day and residential secondary schools" can be accepted as there is no significant difference in the problems of tribal girl students of day and residential secondary schools.

5 Summary, Conclusions and Discussion

EDUCATION is not only a means for betterment of one's position in life but is also indicative of the socio-economic status of an individual, a group or a community. Educational advancement can be taken to be the best indicator of the development of a community. The exact measure of educational development has become a critical question for the analysis of any traditional society. It is perhaps due to the fact that educational development of any society is greatly affected by cultural, social and political forces that operate in the environment. The different subtle overt and covert mechanisms, such as race, sex and socio-economic conditions become powerful determinants of educational attainment.

Education constitutes the most important constituent in the development of any community, particularly in tribal areas where new developmental programmes are being taken up. It is associated with the quality of life, related to production and interlinked with the promotion of social and national integration. Realizing the importance of education for a democratic country, the Constitution of India enshrines certain provisions which promise 'equality of opportunity for education' at all levels and also guarantee the educational advancement of the Scheduled Castes and Scheduled Tribes, because they constitute the core among the weaker sections in the country.

On the basis of a recent estimation, UNICEF claims that secondary education is attained by only 43 per cent of girls of the appropriate age in today's developing world. There are multiple reasons for this. There may be simply no secondary school for girls to attend or the absence of the single sex schools exclusively for girls. Many developing countries and donors have traditionally focused on offering unmoral primary education and neglected to allocate resources to increase the enrolment and attendance especially of girls in secondary education. The parents of girls may conclude that they cannot afford secondary education or may take the traditional view that marriage should be the limit of her ambitions.

Tribals constitute a substantial portion of India's population. In many respects, they lag behind their non-tribal counterparts. To ameliorate their condition, much attention has been given to their education. But, in spite of such several attempts, education has made little progress among tribals.

The independent India has assured equality in all spheres to all groups. Groups like the Tribals and Dalits, who have suffered centuries of discrimination and neglect, have been granted special protection for their educational, economic and social development. Further, the Constitution also accorded provision for positive discrimination by providing reservations in education and employment to satisfy the principle of equity and social justice required for development of these groups. Equality in education implies that communities that have suffered from an iniquitous social structure cannot merely be given equal opportunity in education but requires affirmative action within the institution to remedy past injustice (Nandission, 1996).

The Government of India and respective state Governments have launched a good number of schemes to promote education among the tribal children, especially the girls. In addition, separate schools have been established under ITDA (Integrated Tribal Development Agency) projects, in order to promote literacy among adults. The adult literacy programmes have been organized. Inspite of this kind of several efforts, the growth of education in terms of tribal girls' participation and rate of literacy among the women were found to be low.

The major sources of the income of the family are agricultural products, minor forest produces, labour, and domestic animals. The girls are found to be contributing to the family through all these sources. More domestic and agricultural work was assigned to the girls. The girls are assigned with domestic, agriculture and forest work in order to train them for their future roles.

According to a study, women, who do not want to send their daughters to the school, said it is because of household work, labour, cattle grazing and distance of the school. Half of the women feel that their habitations have no school. Those who have the school have their own reasons for liking and disliking for girls' education. Lack of adequate facilities, lack of good teaching, irregular attendance of teachers, etc., are some of the reasons for disliking the school. More than half of them know about the teachers and only two thirds of the teachers were found to be regular to the school. More than half of them like to have a non-tribal teacher. The women want their daughters to have formal education along with some vocational components. Half of the women like the environment of the residential schools though they are located quite away from their residential places. Given a chance, women would like to continue their education through non-formal means.

The pattern of tribal girl dropouts shows that majority of them have dropped out from the school before the completion of the fifth standard. All the drop-outs are either working in their own houses or as labourers in agriculture.

Indian constitution gives privileged status to the disadvantaged groups, namely, scheduled tribes and scheduled castes due to some historical reasons. The content and orientation of tribal education has to be geared up according to the social conditioning in which the tribals live. One of the foremost condition of the tribals in the country has been their pattern of habitation. They are pre-Drawidian and pre-Aryan groups of people inhabiting this country since the dawn of civilization. They are the original settlers of this country. The Adivasis, as the first settlers of this country, they lived in forests and hills. Because of this, they are also called the hill-dwellers and/or forest-dwellers. The tribal educational situation has, therefore, to be analyzed in terms of the social condition of the people in the past.

Prior to schools and formal systems of education, tribal societies had their own informal system of imparting education to their children. In that system, learning from the habitat, family and kin group was dominant. The main objectives of these traditional tribal institutions have always been to educate or train their children in economic pursuits or make them skilled in traditional occupations followed by specific tribes.

Since many of the tribal communities have only a dialect and not always a written language, most of the training and education were conducted through non-literacy or non-reading methods. The vocation and craft related information regarding designs and techniques, which had to be disseminated orally, was memorized by the trainees or learners. In spite of the disadvantages of not having a written medium, this probably was the only way of continuing with a certain socio-cultural and socio-economic form of education and training in an isolated community.

The traditional institutions of education in tribal communities in the past were of different kind. Learning activities in them generally started from the childhood through the process of enculturation, socialization and assimilation of knowledge and skill from the family, kin and peer group. There existed youth dormitories like the 'Ghotul' of Muria, 'Rangbang' of Bhotia, 'Moruang' of Oraon and 'Dhangarbassa' of Bhuiya. They were the institutions of learning in these societies. These dormitories performed various functions, but their main function was that of teaching and learning. They initiated adolescents of both sexes in their adult roles by providing them opportunities of learning various skills of hunting, fighting, dancing, decoration, etc. However, these institutions gradually disintegrated due to the rapid social changes, which followed industrialization and the resultant changes in the mode of production.

In the early years of independence, there was a deep controversy among social workers in tribal areas about the relative importance of education and economic development. Today, with highly advanced technology and means of transport and communication, it has become difficult for the tribals to remain unaffected by the process of industrialization and modernization. Thus, education is becoming an important condition for obtaining occupational opportunity; such a formal training is of use in tribal traditional occupation as well. It leads vertical mobility in the absence of which, it is horizontal mobility with better know how.

The Education Commission (1964-66) observes in terms of Scheduled Tribes that "In regard to tribal education, provision of facilities at the primary stage should be improved and Ashram schools should be established in distantly populated areas. The medium of instruction for the first two years of the school should be the tribal language and during this period the children should be given oral instruction in the regional language and by the third year the regional language should become the medium of Instruction".

According to the National Policy on Education (1986), the state governments would accord priority in the opening of primary schools in tribal areas including the construction of school buildings. In order to provide identity to the tribal ethnicity, efforts would be made to develop curricular and devise instrumental materials in tribal languages at the initial stages with arrangements for switching over to the regional language. Efforts would also be made to prepare schedule tribe youths to take up teaching jobs in tribal areas. The Policy puts a premium on starting residential schools for tribals including Ashram Schools. Looking to the need structure of the tribals, special efforts would be made to bring them to accept technical, professional and para-professional courses as a new deal for their future.

According to the 4th All India Educational Survey, only 83 per cent of the tribal population was covered by primary schools within the habitats or within 1 km of the habitat. Thus, about 17 per cent of the tribal population depended on elementary schools, which were more than 1 km away from their habitats; out of these 13.96 per cent did not have a school within 1.5 kms and 8.37 per cent did not have a school within 2 kms.

The enrolment in classes I and II was not the real indicator of the achievements on the educational front. What is important is how many children are reaching the middle and secondary school levels and passing out of them. It is argued that in tribal people do not send their children to schools and, hence, there are heavy drop-outs as they do not come out of their domestic and agricultural work. This is not true wholly. It is also due to apathy towards education, lack of interest in education and awareness of the importance of education.

The drop-out rates among the tribal girls were found highest in Rajasthan (94.37%), Tripura (93.44%), Bihar (93.64%) and Madhya Pradesh (92.15%). It is interesting to note that West Bengal has the highest rate of drop-outs amongst tribal girls and boys, *i.e.,* 92.74 per cent and 92.35 respectively. Though, West Bengal is one of the progressive states in India, the drop-out rate among non-tribal students is 52.47 per cent. On the other hand, Maharashtra is also one of the progressive states, but is having the 86.18 per cent drop-out rate among tribal students between I to IXth standard classes.

Like all other sectors of socio-economic life, educationally, the tribal people are at different levels of development; but on the whole, formal education has made very little impact on tribal groups. In the light of the past efforts, it is not shocking because prior to 1950, the Government of India has no direct programme for the education of the tribals. With the adoption of the constitution, the promotion of education of STs has become a special responsibility of the central as well as of the state governments.

The primary concern of the Government was to establish a school in every village. Tribal village had lesser ratio of schools per village. The 'day schools' or 'schools of basic education' established in tribal areas were oriented to basic education,

Under these circumstances, the topic selected for the present investigation was "A Study of Problems of Tribal Girl Students of Secondary Schools". The study was aimed at identifying the problems of tribal girl students of secondary schools.

The present study is planned to proceed with the objectives:

1. To find out the problems of tribal girl students of secondary schools.
2. To find out the problems of tribal girl students of rural and urban secondary schools.
3. To find out the problems of tribal girl students of economically forward and economically backward families.
4. To find out the problems of tribal girl students of educated and uneducated mother.
5. To find out the problems of tribal girl students of educated and uneducated father.
6. To find out the problems of tribal girl students of educated and uneducated parents.
7. To find out the problems of tribal girl students of aided and unaided secondary schools.
8. To find out the problems of tribal girl students of Hindu religion and Christian religion.
9. To find out the problems of tribal girl students of Gujarati medium and English medium secondary schools.

10. To find out the problems of tribal girl students of school-leaving class and non-school-leaving classes of secondary schools.
11. To find out the problems of tribal girl students of day and residential secondary schools.

The variables chosen for the present study are:

1. Locality,
2. Economic status of the family,
3. Educational background of the mother,
4. Educational background of the father,
5. Educational background of both the parents,
6. Grant-in-Aid status of the school,
7. Religion (Hindu or Christian) of the student,
8. Medium of instruction (Gujarati versus English),
9. School-leaving class and non-school-leaving classes,
10. Day and residential secondary schools.

The hypotheses formulated for the investigation are:

1. There are no problems to the tribal girl students of secondary schools.
2. There is no significant difference in the problems of tribal girl students of rural and urban secondary schools.
3. There is no significant difference in the problems of tribal girl students of economically forward and economically backward families.
4. There is no significant difference in the problems of tribal girl students of educated and uneducated father.
5. There is no significant difference in the problems of tribal girl students of educated and uneducated mother.
6. There is no significant difference in the problems of tribal girl students of educated and uneducated parents.
7. There is no significant difference in the problems of tribal girl students of aided and unaided private secondary schools.

8. There is no significant difference in the problems of tribal girl students of Hindu religion and Christian religion.
9. There is no significant difference in the problems of tribal girl students of Gujarati medium and English medium secondary schools.
10. There is no significant difference in the problems of tribal girl students of school-leaving class and non-leaving classes of secondary schools.
11. There is no significant difference in the problems of tribal girl students of day-scholar and residential secondary schools.

The sample of the study selected through stratified random sampling method consists of 712 tribal girl students of 14 schools located in 4 Talukas of Panchmahal district, Gujarat State. The following sample division shows the final variable-wise distribution of tribal girl students studying in secondary schools: Total secondary school tribal girl students: 712; Locality of the secondary school: Rural: 481, Urban: 231; Grant-in-aid of the secondary school: Aided: 640, Un-aided: 72; Medium of instruction: English medium: 176, Gujarati medium: 536; Type of the secondary school: Day-scholar: 587, Residential: 125; Religion of the tribal girl student: Hindu religion: 599, Christian religion: 113; Economic status of the tribal girl student: Economically forward families: 67, Economically backward families: 645; Education of the father of the tribal girl student: Educated father: 436, Uneducated father: 276; Education of the mother of the tribal girl student: Educated mother: 171, Uneducated mother: 541; and Education of the parents (both mother and father) of the tribal girl student: Educated parents: 170, Uneducated parents: 542.

As no ready-made research tools concerned to the problems of girl students of Gujarat were available, the researcher constructed a rating scale, *viz.*, "Problems of Secondary School Tribal Girl Students" by following appropriate research methods and tool standardization procedures.

The collected data was analyzed by employing statistical techniques like Mean, Standard Deviation, Critical Ratio and Chi-square test.

The following are the conclusions drawn from the analysis of data and the conclusions are discussed in the context of tribal education.

CONCLUSIONS AND DISCUSSION

The following conclusions are drawn from the present study on "A Study of Problems of Tribal Girl Students of Secondary Schools". The conclusions are analyzed here under in order to utilise them for exploring the remedies to the problems of tribal girl students.

1. **The secondary school tribal girl students are possessing problems at high level.**

The problems being faced by tribal girl students in secondary schools are heterogeneous in nature as these are due to various constraints like economical, social, physical and psychological aspects and also due to other problems related to teachers, peer group, etc.

Punalekar reported that non-enrolment was highest in Rajasthan villages (47%) compared that in Maharastra (44%) or Gujarat (34%) villages. All the states taken together, more tribal children (56%) than non-tribal children (25%) remained away from the school and school education.

Naidu (1975) confirmed that the number of repeaters in the class increases in the level of class. Similarly, it has been reported that drop-out rate among STs (Scheduled Tribes) was higher at primary level. It decreased with increase in the class of study.

Shyamlal (1987) found that tribal children experienced considerable difficulties in their studies. Pratap and others have reported that the curriculum of Ashram schools, which was specially framed for tribals, was almost similar to that of other primary schools, except for the teaching of craft. Similarly, Solanki observed that the text books did not properly reflect the special needs of tribal children. Singh found that a majority of ST students felt problems in learning of English and Mathematics due to poor handwriting.

Analyzing the nature of educational hardships of Scheduled Tribes, Shyamlal (1987) reported that a major proportion of students felt problems in learning English (67.30%) and Mathematics (29.40%). 38 per cent students blamed the teachers for their low quality teaching.

Regarding adjustment with school and home work, Nayar found that SC (Scheduled Caste) and ST students usually give three or four hours to complete their home work and studies. Rajagopalan's study contradicts this finding. He reported that domestic work seemed to come in their way of education. Most of the students felt difficulties in completing their home work due to lack of guidance/help available from the family.

ST students usually hesitate to go to their teachers for guidance and help. This indicates the problems of adjustment between teachers and ST students. Singh (1987) observed that due to over-crowded classes, teachers failed to pay proper attention to the ST students. Desai and Patel (1981) reported that attitude of teachers towards the tribal children was not healthy. Joshi (1981) reported that the heads of the tribal families expressed that teachers did not show any favorable attitude towards their children. It was observed that majority of teachers had no special training for working in backward areas as they belong to upper caste groups, and their prejudices towards SC/ST students highly influenced their interaction with them. Rath and Misra (1974) also confirmed that majority of ST students felt themselves neglected by their teachers.

Pathak (1991) found that 55 per cent of the ST students expressed positive attitude whereas 33.75 per cent had shown negative attitude towards their teachers. Shah reported that ST students did not feel any problem in adjusting with their teachers. They expressed that they never experienced any partiality by their teachers. In a mixed tribal and non-tribal student class, it was found that about 1/3rd of the questions were asked by the tribal students for better understanding of the lesson.

As regards to the problems of adequacy and suitability of teachers, Bihari found that higher the percentage of single teacher schools, the lower was the percentage of school-going children. The inadequacy, inefficiency and insincerity on the part of the teachers were the main factors responsible for wastage and stagnation.

Pratap and others (1971) observed that most of the Ashram schools were having non-tribal teachers with low educational qualifications. Thus, inadequate number of teachers and incompetent teachers in tribal schools were important reasons for the slow progress of tribal education.

There is a need for specialized teacher education programmers directed towards the preparation of teachers and administrators for working within the tribal system of education. These programmes should be inter-disciplinary, enabling the students to undergo courses in various fields, such as applied anthropology, sociology, psychology, political science, economics, commerce and geography.

Most of the tribal communities tend to migrate from one place to the other, which is a common phenomenon, and this is hampering their educational progress.

Talesara (1989) noticed that the tribal students lag behind considerably as compared to non-tribal students. On the contrary, Desai observed that the number of tribal students is increased at all the levels of education. This is largely due to the educational facilities provided by the government to the tribal students.

Desai and Patel (1984) found that the percentage of drop-out among girls was significantly higher than among boys as the tribal parents are in dire need of assistance in their household or economic activities, and hence withdraw the female children from schools after some education when they feel that the children are suitable for their desired activities.

The subjects like English and Mathematics to be taught in very informal way by using the examples of tribal culture and way of life. The teachers need to acquire a special training in this regard.

The tribal girl students should be treated on par with the non-tribal students by the teachers, as imparting education to the pupils is no way concerned with the discrimination of tribals and non-tribals.

In the text books, that are meant for tribal students, steps have to be taken care of about inclusion of tribal culture, traditions, taboos, customs and history as topics so as to create interest among tribals and make them learn education through their culture.

Suitable and adequate libraries are not available in schools, and even if available, they are non-functional. This leads to the development of poor study habits among the students. The library services should be the focal point of the school and continuous help should be given to the students in the use of library for specific reading purposes.

The vacations and holidays of schools do not fit in with the agricultural pursuits and the social festivals of the tribal communities. So, the holidays should match with their work culture and social activities.

Tribals generally live in small and scattered villages. Tribal students have inadequate space and facilities for study at home. Sachchidananda reported that the cause of low caliber in the SC/ST students was the absence of conducive atmosphere at home. Masavi found that the pattern of tribal residence as a hurdle in tribal education. Shah (1989) observed that like non-ST students, ST students had unanimously admitted that they had adequate space and other facilities in their homes and they did not feel any severe problem in their studies at home due to inadequate space or insufficient facilities.

Regarding the question of distance between home and school as a barrier for schooling, Rathnayya found that due to long distances, tribal parents found it inconvenient to send their children to school. Shah (1989) confirmed that ST students were facing considerable obstacles in their studies due to long distances between home and school. Patel (1984) revealed that a major constraint of the tribals living in small communities is that they do not have a school in their own residence and their children have to walk for far distances to attend the school in a nearby village, and, if the teacher in such a school happens to come from another place, his irregularity in attendance leads inevitably to irregularity and lack of interest among tribal students.

Srivastava found that 97 per cent teachers and 95 per cent tribal parents were of the opinion that the superstitions and rigidity of the community hindered the schooling of the tribal children; the problems of economic hardship of the tribal parents and its adverse effects was supported by 98 per cent teachers and 90 per cent parents; 97 per cent teachers and 96 per cent tribal parents perceived the problems of girls education in the tribal areas; the medium of instruction was not a barrier in the early schooling of the tribal children as it was supported by only 37 per cent teachers and 10 per cent tribal parents; unproductive and traditional type of educational system for the tribal was the cause of the indifferent attitude of the tribal parents towards the education of their children which was supported by 87 per cent teachers and 95 per cent tribal parents; lack of necessary facilities and equipments of teaching was the cause of lack of motivation for education among the tribals.

The Government, central or state, may introduce vocational training programmes in the tribal schools at secondary and higher secondary levels as this might prove to be particularly attractive to the tribal youth, who can enroll themselves to learn some skills, for which they could not afford to pay otherwise. An expanded scheme of scholarship and vocational training programmes for tribal youth would pay a positive role in the development of tribal education. There is a need to develop in the tribal children the requisite skills and attitudes that directly or indirectly affect their academic programmes. The most important academic skills are ability to read and write and communicate, which may suitably develop positive attitude towards education in tribal children. The schemes envisaged for tribal students by the government should be extended impartially.

Education must be accorded the highest priority in coming years in the tribal areas, since the tribal communities must be enabled to satisfactorily negotiate the transitional phase in their social-economic change and take advantage of the new investment under economic programmes. The role of education in pre-development phase of a community has not been properly appreciated so far. Therefore, the prescriptions tend to confirm to the concept development with reference to more advanced rural areas where common man, even though illiterate, has able to acquire considerable information and is long used to the process of change and development.

Das reported that since after being educated in new generations, the tribal parents did not like to tie up with the traditions of their society, and did not like to give their traditional education to their children. Similarly, Shah and Patel observed that tribal parents had indifferent and apathetic attitude towards education and on the other hand, Bhattacharya has pointed out that the tribal guardians were found very eager to send their children to school.

With the above discussion, we can suggest that the administrators, the teachers and parents should find out the reasons for the problems of tribal girl students and should try to solve them with urgency in order to facilitate them in getting quality education without any hurdles in their way.

2. **The urban and rural tribal girl students are facing problems at high level. The tribal girl students of urban secondary schools are facing more problems than the tribal girl students of rural secondary schools with significant difference between them.**

Many of the schools situated in tribal areas do not have adequate number of teachers unlike the urban schools. Even in some tribal schools, there are not-so-much useful for teaching un-trained teachers, who do not know either about teaching learning process or about psychological aspects of the students.

In most of the schools that are situated in urban areas, the students are not homogeneous in nature, in terms of life style, economic status, social and cultural affiliations, educational background of the parents, etc. Hence, several of the tribal students are in isolated state of mind from the majority group. The peculiar problems, which are being faced by the tribal students, are not the problems of the main stream students such as accessibility of the school, low social strata, worrying financial status, unable to mingle with the main stream students, etc.

Mishra found that the rural disadvantaged children seemed to be better than urban and tribal counterparts in verbal creativity scores, and their educational achievement was significantly related to creative thinking.

Though the urban schools are equipped well than their counter parts in several infrastructural and instructional aspects, this study indicates that the problems that are faced by the urban tribal girl students are more than the problems of rural tribal girl students, which is an astonishing one. It is very much required that the schools, wherever they may be situated, should reduce the problems of tribal girl students. The heads and the teachers of these schools should try to reduce the problems of tribal girl students related to school and education.

3. **The tribal girl students of economically forward families and economically backward families are facing problems at high level without any significant difference in their problems.**

Economic status is one of the determining factors in anybody's livelihood. Likewise, financial strata are apparent features in the tribal's day-to-day livelihood, which will play a dominating role in strengthening their educational growth and development. The economic constraints are resisting the tribal girls from participating in various educational activities such as exhibitions, excursions, etc., which are not becoming the sources of motivation of tribal girl students. Some of these constraints may demoralize the girl students to associate with their classmates and develop sociability that helps them in educating themselves with great interest and efficiency.

Tribal girls, like several other girls, usually assist their parents in their day-to-day livelihood, and this one is also a deterrent factor of education for the school-going girls. Due to economic problems, many of the tribal girl students are unable to equip themselves with their required educational needs that enhance their interest towards education.

The older girls of the family stay at home to take care of the younger siblings when mothers are away from houses and stay at work. Tribal girls do attend work in order to help in augmenting the family income. Early marriage is quite common in case of tribal girls. Social customs hinder the mobility of tribal girls after their maturation. Several facilities in the form of school building, hostel, women teachers, etc., are also some of the common problems of tribal girl students in having the required education.

Satyanarayanan (1989) concluded that because of the development programmes, the economic condition of tribals has improved but not to the desired level. Apart from non-tribal exploitation, there is intra-tribal exploitation also. There is a wide gap between the power of the elite and the folks, resulting in quick development of certain tribes and under-development of several tribes.

Bhattacharya (1977) concluded that in order to rise the social status through economic development as well as to adjust themselves to the wave of modernization for the purpose of surviving, the Bhils are trying to give scientific basis to the agricultural procedures for the better use of land.

Shah concluded that like other benefits, education has not been evenly distributed among all social and economic strata of the tribal societies. The middle and rich farmers have taken greater advantage of the educational facilities than the poor cultivators and labourers.

Chandu and Loknath (1982) tried to analyze the impact of development activities and found that bulk of tribal population as a whole is still living below subsistence level. Moreover, they are not in a position to find out an alternative way to come out from their poor socio-economic condition. The developmental and welfare activities of the governments are very slow and unrealistic.

Singh (1981) reported that the majority of tribal students belonged to agricultural class, and their family size varied from 5 to 8 members in large number of cases. Approximately, 30 per cent parents were below the poverty line.

Chitnis mentioned that a higher proportion of ST students came from disadvantaged homes and most of them belonged to rural occupations. On the large, the SC/ST students come from average economic status families and they believed that their status was still lower than that of their classmates belonging to other castes. Sachchidananada (1964) had supported the finding that their status had improved but not to the extent of Hindus.

Parents with higher socio-economic status support children in their schooling and would not want to discontinue their studies for a workforce. However, the students with such parents prefer farming less, read less and are less aware of government concessions given to scheduled tribes in education and employment. The effect of parental socio-economic status then is somewhat ambiguous. They are supportive of their children's education in a general way. The Adivasis will have larger agricultural assets and the non-Adivasis will have business and this is contributing for the education of their children.

Special financial assistance to the meritorious students belonging to ST communities is to be extended. Vocational facilities should be provided like agricultural training, industrial trade, plantation work, sports, craft, tailoring, embroidery, etc., so that the services become actually available to the tribals in the periphery of the growing industrialization and other developing worlds. Education is the only investment, which would enable the concerned tribal communities to take the advantage of new opportunities. Pre-metric and post-metric scholarships and stipends are being disbursed by the government to students belonging to ST communities, but there have been complaints in distribution of so much so that on account of late availability of the installments, some students have been unable to join the institutions, as they have no funds to make advance payments of the initial fees, caution money, hostel fees, etc. Therefore, scholarships and stipends should be disbursed as per the requirement at a required date in order to meet such contingency expenditure.

4. **The tribal girl students are facing problems at high level and there is a significant difference between the problems of tribal girl students of educated father and uneducated father. The tribal girl students of uneducated father are facing more problems than the tribal girl students of educated father.**

The educational background of the father plays a vital role in providing education to their wards. As one of the important factors, the education of the father is affecting the girl's education.

The government schemes, plans and programmes should be chalked out in such a manner that the fathers of the tribal families acquire sufficient knowledge about the ways and means of advantages available for the girl students who get education. Since father being the family head, through Adult Literacy classes and Literacy Awareness programmes, the government and voluntary organizations should come forward and educate the fathers of the tribal girls.

5. **The tribal girl students are facing problems at high level and there is a significant difference in the problems of tribal girl students of educated mother and uneducated mother. The tribal girl students of uneducated mother are facing more problems than the tribal girl students of educated mother.**

As it was quoted by several personalities, if a woman is educated, the entire family is educated. Mother's illiteracy, undoubtedly, brings out a negative impact on girls education. If the uneducated mothers are educated through non-formal means, they will try to provide education to their girl children as they understand the importance of education.

Puberty is one of the important hurdles for the tribal girl education, wherein the mother will resist the girl to attend to the school. Of course, this is quite common in several other communities also. In this connection, women education plays a vital role in promoting the education of girls.

As mothers education plays a prominent role in providing education to their daughters, educating the mothers of tribal girls, initially, need to be taken care of.

6. **The tribal girl students are facing problems at high level and there is a significant difference in the problems of tribal girl students of educated parents and uneducated parents. The tribal girl students of uneducated parents are facing more problems than the tribal girl students of educated parents.**

Srivastava, Dubey and Rath, and Misra found that tribal students usually had poor family educational background. Joshi (1980) observed that 85 per cent of fathers (below 45 years of age) 95 per cent of the mothers of school-going children had practically no education. Pathak (1981) found that 42 per cent parents were educated but only 9 per cent had education above Intermediate level. Similarly, Lakshmanna concluded that 28.3 per cent fathers were high school pass and 14 per cent had received college education. On the contrary, in a study conducted by the SCERT, it was reported that the distribution of parents according to the level of education was primary 12.3 per cent, middle school 9.8 per cent, high school 7.5 per cent, higher education 2.5 per cent and illiterate about 60 per cent.

Several other researchers have pointed out that tribal girls came for education in a very low proportion. On the contrary, some other studies have reported that the rate of enrolment of girls as well as total ST students is increasing satisfactorily.

However, Patel (1985) studies the time series enrolment rates for the period 1964 to 1980 and showed that about 25 per cent to 50 per cent of the tribal girls enrolled in standard-1 dropped out at the very next stage of primary education. Srivastava and Joshi concluded that inadequate schools and poverty in the tribal region, insufficient learning material, language difficulty, inadequate schools, ignorance of parents, child labour and parents compulsion were the causes responsible for the non-enrolment as for dropping out of ST students from the school. A variety of reasons are advanced to explain the drop-out behaviours of ST students. The foremost reason is that the family, kin, clan and village atmosphere is not conducive for a tribal student to continue his education. Economic backwardness is also one of the important reasons of development.

Better educated parents seem to influence their children to read more and prefer white collar occupations like teaching and medicine; those more committed to educating their children have wards who find enough time to study outside school hours and are less likely to discontinue their school studies for immediate employment. The effect of parental education on the middle class aspirations and academic habits of their children is evident.

On the issue of parental attitude towards education and educating the child, it is observed that the tribal parents are not in a serious mood about the education of their children. They do not like that their educated children should leave their family in search of jobs and leave agriculture as their profession.

The educational background of the parents is one of the key factors in determining the development of education of tribal children. Hence, the parents need to be encouraged to get education through non-formal means. They will in turn automatically encourage the education of their children.

7. **The tribal girl students are facing problems at high level and there is a significant difference in the problems of tribal girl students of aided and unaided secondary**

schools. The tribal girl students of aided secondary schools are facing more problems than the tribal girl students of unaided secondary schools.

The aided schools are financially supported by the concerned governments and the un-aided schools are not. As the un-aided schools collect fees as per their wish to meet the every requirement of the school and the student, they provide better facilities than the aided schools, which is not possible in case of aided schools where fees cannot be collected from the students. This may be the reason for having a significant difference in the problems of tribal girl students of aided and un-aided secondary schools.

The secondary schools, irrespective of aided or un-aided, should meet all the requirements of the tribal girl students in order to make them cope up with the non-tribal girl students in every walk of education. As both of them are managed by the private managements, they may raise funds getting from philanthropists and support the girl students.

8. **The tribal girl students are facing problems at high level and there is no significant difference in the problems of tribal girl students of Hindu religion and Christian religion studying in secondary schools.**

Sachchidanand pointed out that due to the efforts of Christian missionaries, education has reached to the interior areas of the country. It not only resulted in increased literacy among lower castes and tribes, but also influenced all aspects of their life.

Lakra has traced the progress of education of the tribes before and after independence. He pointed out that the Christian missionaries did some laudable efforts to spread education among tribes and protected them from the clutches of money lenders. Greater importance was given by them to girls' education.

Rudolf C. Heredia (1992) reported that Christian students are less aware of the educational and employment concessions given to tribals by the government.

The educational authorities and the tribal parents of different religions need to look into the aspects that contribute for the quality and equity of education of tribal girl students and do the needful.

9. The tribal girl students are facing problems at high level and there is a significant difference in the problems of tribal girl students of Gujarati medium and English medium secondary schools. The tribal girl students of English medium secondary schools are facing fewer problems than the tribal girl students of Gujarati medium secondary schools.

The medium of instruction is a significant determinant of education. Basu, Biswas and Aiyappan have discussed the importance of mother tongue as the medium of instruction. In their opinion, scientific collection of vocabularies of tribal children should be done and accordingly proper planning of tribal education is needed. Chattopadhyay has discussed the problem of instruction, preparation of script in mother tongue, type of school, training of teachers, etc., and emphasized that the problems of using tribal/regional language as medium of instruction must be removed.

Nayar (1975) concluded that 80 per cent STs felt difficulty in following the class-room lessons in some of the subjects. Mahajan observed that tribal students do not understand English, Mathematics and Science easily. They, therefore, lag behind.

Sen, Saxena, and Srivastava have emphasized the need of education for tribal children and suggested that the best medium of education for them would be their own language.

Tapase stressed that, for the first two standards, the education of tribal children should be imparted in tribal dialects and can be changed there after.

Chaliha pointed out that, for tribal pupils, after primary stage, the medium of instruction should be Hindi till textbooks and other literature become available in the tribal language.

In brief, it can be said that the research findings support the view that the medium of instruction up to primary level should be in local dialect. But, at later stages, the medium of instruction can be changed over to the regional language.

It is very difficult for the tribal students studying in schools to learn the regional language and understand the lessons, which are taught in the class generally through regional language. The Article 350A of Indian Constitution states that it shall be the endeavor of every state and every local authority within the state to provide adequate facilities for instruction in the mother tongue to children belonging in linguistic minority groups. It may, therefore, be suggested that the Union Ministry of HRD might ask the states to what extent it has been possible for them to provide instruction in the mother tongue to the tribal children, and if, the provision has remained largely inoperative for want of books, teacher, etc., necessary steps need to be initiated.

The concerned authorities should take care of the situation and make arrangements to provide instruction in the medium in which the tribal girl students can understand the subjects well and cope up courageously with other students.

10. **The tribal girl students are facing problems at high level and there is no significant difference in the problems of tribal girl students of school-leaving class and non-school-leaving classes of secondary schools.**

The tribal girl students of school-leaving class and the non-school-leaving classes study tenth class, and eighth and ninth classes respectively. The problems of these classes differ significantly because of students' class, age, physical and psychological maturity, facilities accorded at home and school, attitudes and aptitudes of students, etc. But, the problems of tribal girl students of all these classes are at the same high level without any significant difference, which need the attention of the administrators, teachers and parents to solve them with competency and comfort.

11. **The tribal girl students are facing problems at high level and there is no significant difference in the problems of tribal girl students of day and residential secondary schools.**

The infrastructural and instructional facilities differ significantly in residential and day (non-residential) schools. The residential school students get all the required space for study after their regular instruction in classrooms when compared to the students study at, probably, congested spaces at home. The residential school students study in the morning and evening under the supervision of qualified teachers, which is not possible to the students of the day schools. Even then, the problems of the tribal girl students are high and equal both in the students of residential and day schools.

Efforts are being put-forth by the Government of India along with state governements to establish residential schools for the tribals. In spite of the plans and programmes envisaged, this has not been carried out to the extent possible to facilitate residential secondary schools to the tribal girl students. Hence, the central and the state governments should start residential schools to tribal girl students on war-footing in order to support the deprived tribal girls for quite a long time.

SUGGESTIONS FOR FUTHER RESEARCH

The present study, A Study of the Problems of Tribal Girl Students of Secondary Schools, brings to light a good number of new areas to be studied by future researchers. The areas and variables that are not covered by this study may be put to test to enlighten the other associated factors. So, the researchers may think of the following areas of study in detail.

1. Studies may be taken up to study the impact of psychological factors on the problems of tribal girl students of secondary schools.
2. Studies may be taken up on experimental basis to inculcate, nourish and promote achievement motivation and academic achievement in order to overcome certain

educational problems of tribal girl students of secondary schools.

3. Studies may be taken up to suggest suitable measures to avoid and or nullify the problems of tribal girl students of secondary schools.
4. Studies may be conducted on how to enhance the academic achievement irrespective of the problems of tribal girl students of secondary schools.
5. Studies may be taken up to know the effect of factors like age, stage of education, attitude, adjustment, creativity and other factors on the problems of tribal girl students of secondary schools.
6. Studies may be undertaken to find out the influence of school environment, home environment, teachers and co-students on the problems of tribal girl students of secondary schools.

Bibliography

Adane, Taye (1992), *A Historical Survey of State Education in Eritrea* (Vol. V, No. 1). Africa EMPDA.

Ambashi, N. K. (1971), *A Case Study of Tribal Education*, New Delhi: S. Chand and Co.

Ambashi, N. K. (2001), *Tribal Education: Problems and Issues*, Vol. 10, No. 3. New Delhi: Census of India.

Bapat, V. (1961), Tribal Education — A Problem. *Vanyajati*, IX (1), pp. 37-39.

Baskaran, K. (1991), *Achievement Motivation, Attitude towards Problem-Solving*, New Delhi: NCERT.

Bhagirath, G. S. (1978), *Correlates of Academic Achievement as Perceived by the Teachers and Students of High Schools*. In Buch.

Bhaskar Rao, Digumarti, Editor (1996), *Global Perceptions on Peace Education*, (3 Volumes). New Delhi: Discovery Publishing House.

Bhaskara Rao, Digumarti, C. A. P. Swamy and B. S. V. Dutt (1997), *Self - Evaluation in Student Teaching*, New Delhi: Discovery Publishing House. ISBN 81-7141-374-9.

Bhaskara Rao, Digumarti, Editor (1997), *Success Story of A Primary Education Project*. New Delhi: APH Publishing Corporation.

Bhaskara Rao, Digumarti, Editor (1997), *Education for the 21st Century*, New Delhi: Discovery Publishing House. ISBN 81-7141-389-7.

Bhaskara Rao, Digumarti, Editor (1998), *Community and School Nutrition Education,* New Delhi: Discovery Publishing House.

Bhaskara Rao, Digumarti, Editor (1998), *District Primary Education Programme,* New Delhi: Discovery Publishing House. ISBN 81-7141-396-X.

Bhaskara Rao, Digumarti, Editor (1998), *Teacher Education in India,* New Delhi.

Bhaskara Rao, Digumarti, Editor (2001), *Distance Education in Different Countries,* New Delhi: APH Publishing House.

Bhaskara Rao, Digumarti, Editor 2001), *Decentralised Management of Education,* New Delhi: Discovery Publishing House. ISBN 81-7141-617-9.

Bhaskara Rao, Digumarti, Editor (2001), *World Conference on Science,* New Delhi: Discovery Publishing House. ISBN 81-7141-612-8.

Bhaskara Rao, Digumarti, Editor (2001), *World Conference on Higher Education,* New Delhi: Discovery Publishing House. ISBN 81-7141-610-1.

Bhaskara Rao, Digumarti and Sridhar, D. (2002), *Job Satisfaction of School Teachers,* New Delhi: Discovery Publishing House. ISBN 81-7141-645-4.

Bhaskara Rao, Digumarti, Editor (2003), *Inspiring Experiences in Teacher Education,* New Delhi: Discovery Publishing House. ISBN 81-7141-656-X.

Bhaskara Rao, Digumarti, Editor (2003), *International Studies in Education,* 3 Volumes, New Delhi: Discovery Publishing House.

Bhaskara Rao, Digumarti, Editor (2003), *World Education Forum,* New Delhi: Discovery Publishing House. ISBN 81-7141-639-X.

Bhaskara Rao, Digumarti, Editor (2003), *Education, Employment and Human Resource Development,* New Delhi: Discovery Publishing House. ISBN 81-7141-681-0.

Bhaskara Rao, Digumarti, Editor (2003), *Successful Schooling,* New Delhi: Discovery Publishing House. ISBN 81-7141-677-2.

Bhaskara Rao, Digumarti, Editor (2003), *European Education and Teachers,* New Delhi: Discovery Publishing House. ISBN 81-7141-702-7.

Bhaskara Rao, Digumarti, Editor (2003), *Teachers in Changing World,* New Delhi: Discovery Publishing House. ISBN 81-7141-694-2.

Bhaskara Rao, Digumarti and E. Sreekanth Babu (2004), *Educational Interests of School Students,* New Delhi: Discovery Publishing House. ISBN 81-7141-837-6.

Bhaskara Rao, Digumarti and M, A Fayaz (2004), *Problems of Primary School Drop-outs,* New Delhi: Discovery Publishing House. ISBN 81-7141-834-1.

Bhaskara Rao, Digumarti and S. A. Khader (2004), *Problems of Private School Teachers,* New Delhi: Discovery Publishing House. ISBN 81-7141-838-4.

Bhaskara Rao, Digumarti and S. A. Khader (2004), *School Education in India,* New Delhi: Discovery Publishing House. ISBN 81-7141-849-X.

Bhaskara Rao, Digumarti and SK. Johni Basha (2004), *Teachers' Population Education Awareness,* New Delhi: Discovery Publishing House. ISBN 81-7141-832-5.

Bhaskara Rao, Digumarti and D, Naresh Kumar (2004), *School Teacher Effectiveness,* New Delhi: Discovery Publishing House. ISBN 81-7141-880-5.

Bhaskara Rao, Digumarti, Editor (2004), *General Secondary Education in the 21st Century,* New Delhi: Discovery Publishing House. ISBN 81-7141-885-6.

Bhaskara Rao, Digumarti, Editor (2004), *Reforming Secondary Education,* New Delhi: Discovery Publishing House. ISBN 81-7141-843-0.

Bhaskara Rao, Digumarti, Editor (2004), *Technical and Vocational Education and Training in the 21st Century,* New Delhi: Discovery Publishing House. 81-7141-984-4.

Bhatnagar, R. (1985), *The Expectations of Girls Studying at Non-formal Education Centres*, Jaipur: SIERT.

Bhusari, C. V. (1988), *Intelligence of Scheduled Castes and Scheduled Tribes Students and Its Correlation with Scholastic Achievement in Vidharba*, New Delhi: NCERT.

Bose, A. B. (1970), *Problems of Education*, Ohio: Charles E. Merill Publishing Company and A. Bell and Howell Company.

Brown, F. G. (1970), *Principles of Educational and Psychological Testing*, Illinois: The Dryden Press Inc.

Bruner, J. S. (1962), *Process of Education*, Ohio: Charles E. Merill Publishing Company and A. Bell and Howell Company.

Cronbach, L. J. (1960), *Essentials of Psychological Testing*, New York: Harper and Brothers Publishers.

D. J. (1969), *The Research Process in Education*, New York: Holt, Rinehart and Winston.

Darchin, P. (1989), *A Study of Achievement Science Attitude and Problem Solving Ability Among the Secondary School Students*, New Delhi: NCERT.

Das, Gupta (1964), *Problems of Tribal Education and the Santhals*, New Delhi: Bharatiya Adimjati Sevak Sangh.

Desai, S.D. (1979), *A Study of Class Room Ethos, Pupils Motivation and Academic Achievement*, New Delhi: NCERT.

Devi, U. A. (1990), *Pupil's Academic Achievement in Relation to their Intelligence, Neurotism and Locus of Control*, New Delhi: NCERT.

David, R.G. (2004), *Eritrean Voices: Indigenous Views on the Development of the Curriculum Ten Years after Independence*, International Journal of Education Development, 24, pp. 437-450.

Devy, G. (2008), *The Tribal Situation in Higher Education*, New Delhi: Department of Elementary Education, Government of India.

Dhebar, U. N. (1962), *Report of the Commission for Scheduled Tribes*, Vol. 1, New Delhi: Ministry of Home Affairs, Government of India.

Dreze, J. and Sen, A. (2002), *India: Development and Participation*, New Delhi: Oxford University Press.

Gange, R. M. (1977), *Conditions of Learning*, New York: Rinehart and Winston.

Ghurye, G.S. (1959), *The Scheduled Tribes*, England: Oxford University Press.

Good, C. V. (1973), *Dictionary of Education*, New York: McGraw-Hill Book Company.

Goode, William J. and Paun, K. Hatt (1952), *Methods in Social Research*, Tokyo: Kogakusha Company Ltd.

Gourikutty, A. J. (1992), *A Study of Certain Abilities Correlates of Secondary School Mathematics Achievement Measured using Bloom's Taxonomy*, New Delhi: NCERT.

Government of Eritrea (2003), *Education Sector Improvement Project, Environmental and Social Management Framework*. Eritrea: The Government of Eritrea.

Govinda, R. (2002), *India Education Report: A Profile of Basic Education*, New Delhi: Oxford University Press.

Hambly, W. D. (1960), *Origin of Education Among Primitive Peoples*, New York: The MacMillan Company.

Haq, N. (1988), *A Study of Academic Achievement of the Students of the Higher Secondary Stage in Relation to Achievement Motivation and Socio-economic Status*. New Delhi: NCERT.

Haris, K. (1997), *Education and Knowledge: The Structured Misinterpretation of Reality*, London: Routeldge and Keyan Paul.

Harlen and Wynne (1989), *Recent Developments in Primary and Lower Secondary School Science*, New Delhi: Sterling Publications.

Heda, H.C. (1965), *Tribal Education: Integration Aspect*, Hyderabad: Adimjati Sevak Sangh.

Hurd, Paul Dehart (1969), *New Directions in Teaching Secondary School Science*, Chicago: Rand Mc Nally and Co.

Jha, J. and Jhingaran, D. (2002), *Elementary Education for the Poorest and Other Deprived Groups*, New Delhi: Centre for Policy Research.

Jha, J. and Jhingaran, D. (2002), *Review of Elementary Education for Poorest and Other Disadvantaged Groups: The Real Challenge of Universalisation,* New Delhi: Centre for Policy Research.

Jhingaran, D. (2000), *Janshala — Main Streaming Out of School Children through Bridge Courses,* New Delhi: Monthly News Letter of the joint GOI-UN System Educational Program.

Joshi and Vidyut (1984), *A Century of Tribal Education in Gujarat,* Surat: Centre for Social Studies.

Joshi, R. R. (1983), *An Investigation into the Interest of Higher Secondary School Going Pupils in the Context of Some Psycho-Socio Variables,* New Delhi: NCERT.

Kar, L. N. (1957), Patterns of Tribal Education: A Psychological Approach, *The Journal of University of Gauhati,* 8, pp. 59-72).

Kaul, S. K. (1967), *Existing Facilities, Wastage and Utilization of Financial Assistance in Respect of Tribal Education,* New Delhi: NCERT.

Koppikar, G. K. 1956), *The Education of Adivasis,* New Delhi: Government of India.

Lakra, S. (1976), *Impact of Education on the Tribals of Ranchi. Patna District,* Unpublished Ph.D. Thesis, Education.

Madan, T.N. (1952), *Education of Tribal India,* India: Asia Publishing House.

Maharatna, A. (2005), *Demographics Perspectives on India's Tribes,* New Delhi: Oxford University Press.

Man, Edward Horace (1975), *Dictionary of the Central Nicobarese Language,* London: Sanskaran Prakashan.

Mathur and Kaushal Kumar (1957), *Nicobar Islands,* New Delhi: National Book Trust India.

Mehna, V. H. 1986), *An Investigation into Some Factors Affecting Academic Achievement in Science of Standard IX Students of Greater Bombay,* New Delhi: NCERT.

Michalis, J. U., *et.al.,* (1967), *New Designs for the Elementary School Curriculum,* New York: Mc–Graw-Hill Book Company.

Mishra, M. (2007), *Status of Elementary Education in Tribal Areas of Orissa,* Bhuvaneswar: Department of Tribal, Government of Orissa.

Mukherjee, S. N. (1958), *An Introduction to Indian Education,* Baroda: Acharya Book Depot.

Mullick, S. P. (1983), *Development of Learning Materials for Non-formal Education for Girls in the Age Group of 11-14 Yearsin Rural Areas,* New Delhi: Department of Teaching Aids, NCERT.

Nag, D. S. (1958), *Tribal Economy,* New Delhi: Bharatiya Adimjati Sevak Sangh.

Nair, P. (2007), *Whose Public Action? Analyzing Inter-Sectoral Collaboration for Service Delivery?,* New Delhi: Economic and Social Research Council.

Nambissan, G. (2000), *The Social Context of Learning and the Schooling of Dalit and Tribal Children,* Bangalore: A Collection of Articles.

National Tribal Commission (2008), *Education of Tribal People in India,* New Delhi: National Tribal Commission Report.

Niki, T. B. (1969), *Impact of Education on the Bhils – Cultural Change in the Tribal Life of Madhya Pradesh,* New Delhi: Planning Commission, Government of India.

Noronha, A. 2006), *Education of Tribal Children from Social Mobilization to Poverty Allevation in South Asia.*

Patel, Motibhai M. (1999), *Selected Educational Statistics,* New Delhi: Allied Publishing House.

Phadake, J. K and Shukla, R. G. (1980), *Educational Waste: A Study in Dropouts Among Scheduled Tribe College Students in Vyara,* Vyara: The Institute of Tribal and Rural Development and Research.

Porteus, S.D. (1937), *Primitive Intelligence and Environment,* New York: The Mac Millan.

Portman, M.V. (1899), *A History of our Relations with the Andamanese* (Vol. I and II), Calcutta: Superintendent of Government Printing.

Ratha, S. N. (1986), *A New Thought on Tribal Education*, New Delhi: UGC Seminar on Tribal Education.

Rathaninh (1977), *Sanctural Constraints in Tribal Education*, New Delhi: Sterling Publishers.

Ratnayya, V. (1978), *Structural Constraints in Tribal Education, Regional Study*, New Delhi: Sterling Publishers.

Read, Margarett (1956), *Education and Social Change in Tropical Areas*, Edinburg: Thomas Nelson and Sons.

Reddy, G. P. (1970), *Causes of Wastage in Tribal Education of A.P.*, Andhra Pradesh: Vanyajati.

Rena, Ravinder (2006), *Value-based Education for Human Development — Eritrean Perspective*, USA: Essays in Education.

Rena, Ravinder (2006), *A Handbook on the Eritrean Economy*, Tanzania: New Africa Press.

Renuka Ray Committee Report on *Educational Programmes in Tribal Areas* (1959), New Delhi: Government of India.

Sachidananda (1964), *Tribal Education in India*, Vanyajati, 12(1), pp. 3.6.

Sachidananda (1967), *Socio-Economic Aspects of Tribal Education*, New Delhi: NCERT.

Sarva Shiksha Abhiyan (2002), *Education of Tribal Children in India*, New Delhi: MHRD.

Sathar, Z. A. and Lloyd, C. B. (1994), *Who gets Primary Schooling in Pakistan?*, Pakistan Development Review, 33(2), pp. 103-134.

Sengupta, P. J. Guha (2002), Enrolment, Drop Out and Grade Completion of Girl Children in West Bengal, *Economic and Political Weekly*, 37(17), pp. 121-137.

Shah and Patel (1981), *Social Contexts of Tribal Education in Gujarat*. Ahmedabad: Department of Sociology, Gujarat University.

Shah, A. J. (1979), *A Critical Study of the Programmes of Non-formal Education in Baroda City and Their Impact on the Community*, Unpublished Ph.D. thesis, Education, Baroda: M.S University.

Sharma, B. D. (1975), *Development of Small Tribal Communities*, New Delhi: Ministry of Home Affairs.

Shivastava, L. R. N., *et.al.* (1971), *Identification of Educational Problems of the Saora of Orissa*, New Delhi: NCERT.

Solanki (1973), *Problems of College-going Tribal Students*, Headband: Tribal Research and Training Institute, Gujarat Vidyapeet.

Sudharshan Ratna, M. (2000), *Educational Status of Girls and Women: The Emerging Scenario*, New Delhi: Sage Publications.

Syamlal (1987), *Education among Tribals: Research Project on Tribal Education in Rajasthan*, Jaipur: Print well Publishers.

Tara, Patel (1984), *Development of Education among Tribal Women*, Delhi: Mittal Publications.

Taradutta, D. (2001), *Tribal development in India*, New Delhi: Gyan Publishing House.

Tekie Asehun (2004), *Student Selection and Retention at the University of Asmara*, Eritrea: Centre for Development Studies.

Van Valen and Deobold, B. *Understanding Educational Research – An Introduction*, New York: McGraw-Hill Book Company.

Verma, Mahesh (2006), *Gender, Girls and Women Education*, New Delhi: National Institute of Advanced Studies.

Yosso, Tara J. (2005), *Whose Culture has Capital?*. New Delhi: Discussion of Community Cultural Wealth.

Additional Reading

Bhaskara Rao, Digumarti (1994), *Scientific Aptitude*, New Delhi: Ashish Publishing House. ISBN 81-7024-658-X.

Bhaskara Rao, Digumarti (1995), *Animal Kingdom*, New Delhi: Discovery Publishing House ISBN 81-7141-274-2.

Bhaskara Rao, Digumarti (1995), *Batracology*, New Delhi: Discovery Publishing House ISBN 81-7141-279-3.

Bhaskara Rao, Digumarti (1997), *Scientific Attitude*, New Delhi: Discovery Publishing House. ISBN 81-7141-381-1.

Bhaskara Rao, Digumarti (1996), *Scientific Attitude vis-à-vis Scientific Aptitude,* New Delhi: Discovery Publishing House. ISBN 81-7141-308-0.

Bhaskara Rao, Digumarti (2004), *Scientific Attitude, Scientific Aptitude and Achievement,* New Delhi: Discovery Publishing House. ISBN 81-7141-781-7.

Bhaskara Rao, Digumarti (2004), *Educational Administration,* New Delhi: Discovery Publishing House. ISBN 81-7141-842-2.

Bhaskara Rao, Digumarti (2004), *Issues in School Education,* New Delhi: Discovery Publishing House. ISBN 81-8356-025-3.

Bhaskara Rao, Digumarti, Editor (1996), *Encyclopaedia of Education For All,* 5 Volumes. New Delhi: APH Publishing Corporation. ISBN 81-7024-759-4 (set).

Vol. I Education For All: The World Conference. ISBN 81-7024-760-8.

Vol. II Education For All: The EPA-9 Summit. ISBN 81-7024-761-6.

Vol. II Education For All: Quality Education For All. ISBN 81-7024-762-6.

Vol. IV Education For All: Planning and Monitoring. ISBN 81-7024-763-4.

Vol. V Education For All: The Indian Scenario. ISBN 81-7024-764-0.

Bhaskara Rao, Digumarti, Editor (1999), *International Encyclopaedia of AIDS,* 11 Volumes. New Delhi: Discovery Publishing House. ISBN 81-7141-522-6 (set).

Vol. 1. Introduction to HIV/AIDS. ISBN 81-7141-523-7.

Vol. 2. HIV/AIDS – Issues and Challenges, 2 Parts. ISBN 81-7141-524-5.

Vol. 3. HIV/AIDS – Socio Economic Realities. ISBN 81-7141-524-3.

Vol. 4. HIV/AIDS – Law Ethics and Human Rights, 2 Parts. ISBN 81-7141-526-1.

Vol. 5. AIDS and NGOs. ISBN 81-7141-527-X.

Vol. 6. AIDS and Home Care. ISBN 81-7141-528-8.

Vol. 7. STD Case Management. ISBN 81-7141-529-6.

Vol. 8. HIV/AIDS Prevention and Care – Teaching Modules for Nurses and Midwives. ISBN 81-7141-530-X.

Vol. 9. HIV Prevention Education for Educational Institutions. ISBN 81-7141-531-8.

Vol.10. Instructional Modules for AIDS Education. ISBN 81-7141-532-6.

Vol.11. School Health Education to prevent AIDS and STD – A Package for Curriculum Planners. ISBN 81-7141-533-4.

Bhaskara Rao, Digumarti, Editor (2000), *International Encyclopaedia of Human Rights*, 7 Volumes in 13 Parts, New Delhi: Discovery Publishing House. ISBN 81-7141-567-9 (set).

Vol. 1. International Instruments of Human Rights, 2 Parts. ISBN 81-7141-569-4.

Vol. 2. Regional Instruments of Human Rights. ISBN 81-7141-604-7.

Vol. 3. Human Rights and the United Nations, 2 Parts. ISBN 81-7141-605-5.

Vol. 4. Fact Files of Human Rights, 3 parts. ISBN 81-7141-606-3.

Vol. 5. Study Stories of Human Rights, 3 parts. ISBN 81-7141-607-3.

Vol. 6. International Meetings on Human Rights, 2 Parts. ISBN 81-714-608-X.

Vol. 7. Professional Training in Human Rights. ISBN 81-7141-609-8.

Bhaskara Rao, Digumarti, Editor (2000), *International Encyclopaedia of Science and Technology Education*, 11 Volumes, New Delhi: Discovery Publishing House. ISBN 81-7141-548-2 (set).

Vol. 1. Science and Technology Education. ISBN 81-7141-568-7.

Vol. 2. Science Education in Developing Countries. ISBN 81-7141-569-9.

Vol. 3. Organizational Structure of Science. ISBN 81-7141-570-9.

Vol. 4. Science Education in Asia and the Pacific. ISBN 81-7141-571-7

Vol. 5. Science and Technology Education For All. ISBN 81-7141-572-5.

Vol. 6. Values, Ethics, Talent and Girls in Science and Technology Education. ISBN 81-7141-573-3.

Vol. 7. *Popularization of Science and Technology Education,* ISBN 81-7141-574-1.

Vol. 8. *Science, Power and Society.* ISBN 81-7141-575-X.

Vol. 9. *Information Technology.* ISBN 81-7141-576-8.

Vol.10. *Teacher Training in Science and Technology Education.* ISBN 81-7142-577-6.

Vol.11. Teacher Training in Science and Technology: A Curriculum Framework. ISBN 81-7141-578-4.

Bhaskara Rao, Digumarti, Editor (2000), *Education For All*: Achieving the Goal, 3 Volumes, New Delhi: APH Publishing Corporation. ISBN 81-7648-152-1 (set).

Vol. I The Global Consensus. ISBN 81-7648-155-6.

Vol. II Mid-Decade Review Reports of Regional Seminars. ISBN 81-7648-154-8.

Vol. III Issues and Trends. ISBN 81-7648-155-6.

Bhaskara Rao, Digumarti, Editor (2004), *International Encyclopaedia of Learning to Live Together*, 4 Volumes, New Delhi: Discovery Publishing House. ISBN 81-7141-848-1.

Vol. 1. International Conference on Learning to Live Together.

Vol. 2. Globalization and Living Together.

Vol. 3. Curriculum for Learning to Live Together.

Vol. 4. Science Education for the Contemporary Society.

Bhaskara Rao, Digumarti, Editor (2005), *Encyclopaedia of Education For All*, 3 Volumes. New Delhi: Discovery Publishing House. ISBN 81-7141-647-0 (set).

Bhaskara Rao, Digumarti, Editor (2007), *Encyclopaedia of Teacher Education*, 4 Volumes. New Delhi: Discovery Publishing House. ISBN 81-8356-306-6 (set).

Bhaskara Rao, Digumarti, Editor (2007), *Encyclopaedia of Edeucation for Living Together*, 4 Volumes. New Delhi: Discovery Publishing House. ISBN 81-7141-848-1 (set).

Bhaskara Rao, Digumarti, Editor (1995), *National Policy on Education*, 2 Volumes, New Delhi: Anmol Publications Pvt. Ltd. ISBN 81-7488-323-1.

Bhaskara Rao, Digumarti, Editor (1996), *Global Perceptions on Peace Education*, 3 Volumes, New Delhi: Discovery Publishing House. ISBN 81-7141-319-6.

Bhaskara Rao, Digumarti, Editor (1997), *Education for the 21st Century*, New Delhi: Discovery Publishing House. ISBN 81-7141-389-7.

Bhaskara Rao, Digumarti, Editor (1997), *Reflections on Scientific Attitude*, New Delhi: Discovery Publishing House. ISBN 81-7141-319-6.

Bhaskara Rao, Digumarti, Editor (1997), *Success Story of a Primary Education Project*, New Delhi: APH Publishing Corporation. ISBN 81-7024-850-7.

Bhaskara Rao, Digumarti, Editor (1997), *World Food Summit*, New Delhi: Discovery Publishing House. ISBN 81-7141-386-2.

Bhaskara Rao, Digumarti, Editor (1997), *Care the Child*, 2 Volumes. New Delhi: Discovery Publishing House. ISBN 81-7141-394-3.

Bhaskara Rao, Digumarti, Editor (1998), *Earth Summit*, 2 Volumes. New Delhi: Discovery Publishing House. ISBN 81-7141-435-4.

Bhaskara Rao, Digumarti, Editor (1998), *Adolescence Education*, New Delhi: Discovery Publishing House. ISBN 81-7141-432-X.

Bhaskara Rao, Digumarti, Editor (1998), *Community and School Nutrition Education,* New Delhi: Discovery Publishing House. ISBN 81-7141-435-4.

Bhaskara Rao, Digumarti, Editor (1998), *District Primary Education Programme,* New Delhi: Discovery Publishing House. ISBN 81-7141-396-X.

Bhaskara Rao, Digumarti, Editor (1998), *National Policy on Education: Towards an Enlightened and Humane Society,* New Delhi: Discovery Publishing House. ISBN 81-7141-426-5.

Bhaskara Rao, Digumarti, Editor (1998), *Reforming School Education,* New Delhi: Discovery Publishing House. ISBN 81-7141-403-6.

Bhaskara Rao, Digumarti, Editor (1998), *Teacher Education in India,* New Delhi: Discovery Publishing House. ISBN 81-7141-406-0.

Bhaskara Rao, Digumarti, Editor (1998), *World Summit for Social Development.* New Delhi: Discovery Publishing House. ISBN 81-7141-420-6.

Bhaskara Rao, Digumarti, Editor (2001), *Nuclear Materials: Issues and Concerns,* 2 Volumes, New Delhi: Discovery Publishing House. ISBN 81-7141-611-X.

Bhaskara Rao, Digumarti, Editor (2001), *Distance Education in Different Countries,* New Delhi: APH Publishing Corporation. ISBN 81-7648-229-3.

Bhaskara Rao, Digumarti, Editor (2001), *Decentralised Management of Education: Management of Education in Panchayati Raj and Municipal Bodies,* New Delhi: Discovery Publishing House. ISBN 81-7141-617-9.

Bhaskara Rao, Digumarti, Editor (2001), *Electrochemistry for Environmental Protection,* New Delhi: Discovery Publishing House. ISBN 81-7141-619-5.

Bhaskara Rao, Digumarti, Editor (2001), *Global Educational Studies,* New Delhi: Discovery Publishing House. ISBN 81-7141-616-0.

Bhaskara Rao, Digumarti, Editor (2001), *Global Synthesis of Educational Assessment*, New Delhi: Discovery Publishing House. ISBN 81-7141-613-6.

Bhaskara Rao, Digumarti, Editor (2001), *Jomtein Decade of Education*. New Delhi: Discovery Publishing House. ISBN 81-7141-618-7.

Bhaskara Rao, Digumarti, Editor (2001), *World Conference on Education for All*, New Delhi: AFH Publishing Corporation. ISBN 81-7141-274-9.

Bhaskara Rao, Digumarti, Editor (2001), *World Conference on Higher Education*, New Delhi: Discovery Publishing House. ISBN 81-7141-610-1.

Bhaskara Rao, Digumarti, Editor (2001), *World Conference on Science*, New Delhi: Discovery Publishing House. ISBN 81-7141-612-8.

Bhaskara Rao, Digumarti, Editor (2003), *Inspiring Experiences in Teacher Education*, New Delhi: Discovery Publishing House. ISBN 81-7141-656-X.

Bhaskara Rao, Digumarti, Editor (2003), *International Studies in Education*, 3 Volumes. New Delhi: Discovery Publishing House. ISBN 81-7141-647-0.

Bhaskara Rao, Digumarti, Editor (2003), *Military Conversion: Impact on Science and Technology*, New Delhi: Discovery Publishing House. ISBN 81-7141-578-4.

Bhaskara Rao, Digumarti, Editor (2003), *United Nations Millennium Summit*, New Delhi: Discovery Publishing House. ISBN 81-7141-632-2.

Bhaskara Rao, Digumarti, Editor (2003), *World Assembly on Aging*, New Delhi: Discovery Publishing House. ISBN 81-7141-637-3.

Bhaskara Rao, Digumarti, Editor (2003), *World Conference on Human Rights*, New Delhi: Discovery Publishing House. ISBN 81-7141-661-6.

Bhaskara Rao, Digumarti, Editor (2003), *World Education Forum*, New Delhi: Discovery Publishing House. ISBN 81-7141-639-X.

Bhaskara Rao, Digumarti, Editor (2003), *Education, Employment and Human Resource Development,* New Delhi: Discovery Publishing House. ISBN 81-7141-681-0.

Bhaskara Rao, Digumarti, Editor (2003), *Successful Schooling,* New Delhi: Discovery Publishing House. ISBN 81-7141-677-2.

Bhaskara Rao, Digumarti, Editor (2003), *European Education and Teachers,* New Delhi: Discovery Publishing House. ISBN 81-7141-702-7.

Bhaskara Rao, Digumarti, Editor (2003), *Teachers in a Changing World,* New Delhi: Discovery Publishing House. ISBN 81-7141-694-2.

Bhaskara Rao, Digumarti, Editor (2004), *International Guidelines on Open and Distance Teacher Education,* New Delhi: Discovery Publishing House. ISBN 81-7141-777-9.

Bhaskara Rao, Digumarti, Editor (2004), *Adult Learning in the 21st Century,* New Delhi: Discovery Publishing House. ISBN 81-7141-797-3.

Bhaskara Rao, Digumarti, Editor (2004), *Educational Practices: Research and Recommendations,* New Delhi: Discovery Publishing House. ISBN 81-7141-835-X.

Bhaskara Rao, Digumarti, Editor (2004), *General Secondary Education In the 21st Century,* New Delhi: Discovery Publishing House.

Bhaskara Rao, Digumarti, Editor (2004), *Reforming Secondary Education,* New Delhi: Discovery Publishing House. ISBN 81-7141-843-0.

Bhaskara Rao, Digumarti, Editor (2004), *Human Rights Education,* New Delhi: Discovery Publishing House. ISBN 81-7141-882-1.

Bhaskara Rao, Digumarti, Editor (2004), *United Nations Decade for Human Rights Education,* New Delhi: Discovery Publishing House. ISBN 81-7141-887-2.

Bhaskara Rao, Digumarti, Editor (2004), *Technical and Vocational Education and Training in the 21st Century,* New Delhi: Discovery Publishing House. ISBN 81-7141-984-4.

Bhaskara Rao, Digumarti, Editor (2005), *Encyclopaedia of Education For All*, 3 Volumes, New Delhi: Discovery Publishing House.

Bhaskara Rao, Digumarti, Editor (2011), *Right to Education*, Hyderabad: Neel Kamal Publishers. ISBN 81-7648-470-9. 978-81-8316-284-5.

Bhaskara Rao, Digumarti, Editor (2011), *International Encyclopaedia of Educational Policies*, Hyderabad: Neel Kamal Publishers.

Bhaskara Rao, Digumarti, Editor (2011), *International Encyclopaedia of Educational Practices*, Hyderabad: Neel Kamal Publishers.

Bhaskara Rao, Digumarti, Editor (2012), *Constitution of India*, New Delhi: Discovery Publishing House.

Bhaskara Rao, Digumarti, Editor (2012) *Inclusive Education and Policy Frameworks*, New Delhi: Discovery Publishing House.

Bhaskara Rao, Digumarti and B.S.V Dutt, Editors (2003), *Education: Programmes and Policies*, New Delhi: APH Publishing Corporation. ISBN 81-7648-470-9.

Bhaskara Rao, Digumarti, C.A.P. Swamy and B.S.V. Dutt (1997), *Self-Evaluation in Student Teaching*, New Delhi: Discovery Publishing House. ISBN 81-7141-374-9.

Bhaskara Rao, Digumarti and C. D. Swarna Lattha, Editors (2006), *Encyclopaedia of Biotechnology*, 5 Volumes. New Delhi: Discovery Publishing House. ISBN 81-8356-168-3 (set).

Bhaskara Rao, Digumarti, C. Sridevi and K. Vijaya (1995), *Achievement in Social Studies*, New Delhi: Discovery Publishing House. ISBN 81-7141-281-5.

Bhaskara Rao, Digumarti and D. Naresh Kumar (2004), *School Teacher Effectiveness*, New Delhi: Discovery Publishing House. ISBN 81-7141-78[illegible]-5.

Bhaskara Rao, Digumarti and D. Sridhar (2002), *Job Satisfaction of School Teachers*, New Delhi: Discovery Publishing House. ISBN 81-7141-652-7.

Bhaskara Rao, Digumarti and Digumarti Pushpa Latha, Editors (1998), *International Encyclopaedia of Women*, 5 Volumes, New Delhi: Discovery Publishing House. ISBN 81-7141-410-9 (set).

Vol. 1 Status of World's Women. ISBN 81-7141- 494-X.

Vol. 2 Women, Education and Empowerment. ISBN 81-7141-498-1.

Vol. 3 Women Challenges and Advancement. ISBN 81-7141-497-4.

Vol. 4 Women and Family Health. ISBN 81-7141- 497-4.

Vol. 5 Women and International Action. ISBN 81-7141-498-2.

Bhaskara Rao, Digumarti and Digumarti Pushpa Latha (1994), *Achievement in Biology,* New Delhi: Discovery Publishing House. ISBN 81-7141-264-5.

Bhaskara Rao, Digumarti and Digumarti Pushpa Latha (1995), *Achievement in English,* New Delhi: Discovery Publishing House. ISBN 81-7141-283-1.

Bhaskara Rao, Digumarti and Digumarti Pushpa Latha (1994), *Achievement in Science,* New Delhi: Discovery Publishing House. ISBN 81-7141-280-70.

Bhaskara Rao, Digumarti and Digumarti Pushpa Latha (1995), *Achievement in Mathematics,* New Delhi: Discovery Publishing House. ISBN 81-7141-278-5.

Bhaskara Rao, Digumarti and Digumarti Pushpa Latha (2004), *Education for Women,* New Delhi: Discovery Publishing House. ISBN 81-7141-873-2.

Bhaskara Rao, Digumarti, Digumarti Pushpa Latha and Digumarthi Harshitha, Editors (2001), *Biological Warfare,* New Delhi: Discovery Publishing House. ISBN 81-7141-597-0.

Bhaskara Rao, Digumarti, Digumarti Pushpa Latha and Digumarthi Harshitha, Editors (2001), *Women as Educators,* New Delhi: Discovery Publishing House. ISBN 81-7141-602-0.

Bhaskara Rao, Digumarti and Digumarthi Harshitha (2004), *Adjustment of Adolescents,* New Delhi: APH Publishing House. ISBN 81-7648-836-8.

Bhaskara Rao, Digumarti and Digumarthi Harshitha, Editors (2001), *Education in India,* New Delhi: APH Publishing House. ISBN 81-7648-207-2.

Bhaskara Rao, Digumarti, Digumarti Pushpa Latha and Digumarthi Harshitha, Editors (2001), *Assessing Learning Achievement,* New Delhi: Discovery Publishing House. ISBN 81-7141-601-2.

Bhaskara Rao, Digumarti, Digumarti Pushpa Latha and Digumarthi Harshitha, Editors (2001), *Energy Security,* New Delhi: Discovery Publishing House. ISBN 81-7141-598-9.

Bhaskara Rao, Digumarti, Digumarthi Harshitha and K.R.S. Sambasiva Rao, Editors (1999), *Advanced Biotechnology,* New Delhi: Discovery Publishing House. ISBN 81-7141-516-4.

Bhaskara Rao, Digumarti and K.R.S. Sambasiva Rao, Editors (1996), *Current Trends in Indian Education,* New Delhi: Discovery Publishing House. ISBN 81-7141-311-0

Bhaskara Rao, Digumarti and D. Naresh Kumar (2004), *School Teacher Effectiveness,* New Delhi: Discovery Publishing House. ISBN 81-7141-782-5.

Bhaskara Rao, Digumarti and E. Sreekanth Babu (2004), *Educational Interests of School Students,* New Delhi: Discovery Publishing House. ISBN 81-7141-837-6.

Bhaskara Rao, Digumarti and K. Vijaya (1995), *A Text Book Evaluation,* Ambala Cantt: The Associated Publishers.

Bhaskara Rao, Digumarti and M.A. Fayaz (2004), *Problems of Primary School Drop-outs,* New Delhi: Discovery Publishing House. ISBN 81-7141-834-1.

Bhaskara Rao, Digumarti and N.V.M. Mohana Rao (2002), *Problems of Mentally Handicapped Children,* New Delhi: Discovery Publishing House. ISBN 81-7141-645-4.

Bhaskara Rao, Digumarti and S. Chandra Mohan (2002), *Sports Management,* New Delhi: APH Publishing House. ISBN 81-7648-467-9.

Bhaskara Rao, Digumarti and S.A. Khader (2004), *Problems of Private School Teachers,* New Delhi: Discovery Publishing Corporation. ISBN 81-7141-838-4.

Bhaskara Rao, Digumarti and S.A. Khader (2004), *School Education in India,* New Delhi: Discovery Publishing Corporation. ISBN 81-7141-849-X.

Bhaskara Rao, Digumarti and Sk. Johni Basha (2004), *Teachers' Population Education Awareness,* New Delhi: Discovery Publishing House. ISBN 81-7141-832-5.

Bhaskara Rao, Digumarti, V.V. Rao, V.V. Lakshmi and V.V. Krishna, Editors (1999), *Status and Advancement of Women,* New Delhi: APH Publishing Corporation. ISBN 81-7648-169-6.

Appala Naidu, P. Ch., Author and Digumarti Bhaskara Rao, Editor (2007), *Student Feedback Methods,* New Delhi: Discovery Publishing House.

Babu, P.C., Author and Digumarti Bhaskara Rao, Editor (2004), *Flowers of Wisdom,* New Delhi: Discovery Publishing House. ISBN 81-7141-695-0.

Babu, P.C., Author and Digumarti Bhaskara Rao, Editor (2008), *Worlds of Wisdom,* New Delhi: Discovery Publishing House.

Bujji Babu, K., Author and Digumarti Bhaskara Rao, Editor (2007), *Teaching Aptitude of Primary School Teachers,* New Delhi: Sonali Publications. ISBN 81-8411-083-9.

Amala, P. A. and Anupama, P., Authors and Digumarti Bhaskara Rao, Editor (2004), *History of Education,* New Delhi: Discovery Publishing House. ISBN 81-7141-860-0.

Bhagya Lakshmi, L., Author and Digumarti Bhaskara Rao, Editor (2000), *Reading and Comprehension,* New Delhi: Discovery Publishing House. ISBN 81-7141-543-1.

Bhasha, S.A., Author and Digumarti Bhaskara Rao, Editor (2004), *Methods of Teaching Geography,* New Delhi: Discovery Publishing House. ISBN 81-7141-807-4.

Bhuvaneswara Lakshmi, Gadde, Author and Digumarti Bhaskara Rao, Editor (2000), *Attitude Towards Science,* New Delhi: Discovery Publishing House. ISBN 81-7141-541-6.

Bhuvaneswara Lakshmi, G., Author and Digumarti Bhaskara Rao, Editor (2004), *Methods of Teaching Life Science,* New Delhi: Discovery Publishing House. ISBN 81-7141-804-X.

Bhuvaneswara Lakshmi, G. and K. Subba Rao, Authors and Digumarti Bhaskara Rao, Editor (2004), *Methods of Teaching Biology,* New Delhi: Discovery Publishing House. ISBN 81-7141-914-3.

Chary, K.V.N.B., Author and Digumarti Bhaskara Rao, Editor (2006), *Techniques of Teaching Physics,* New Delhi: Sonali Publications. ISBN 81-8411-046-4.

Chowdary, S.B.J.R. and Naga Raju, Authors and Digumarti Bhaskara Rao, Editor (200[illegible]), *Mastery of Teaching Skills,* New Delhi: Discovery Publishing House.

Dayakara Reddy, V. and Digumarti Bhaskara Rao, Editors (2006), *Value-Oriented Education,* New Delhi: Discovery Publishing House.

Devraj, T.A.S., Author and Digumarti Bhaskara Rao, Editor (1997), *Trace Analysis of Uranium and Thorium,* New Delhi: Discovery Publishing House. ISBN 81-7141-375-7.

Durga Rani, K., Author and Digumarti Bhaskara Rao, Editor (2000), *Educational Aspirations and Scientific Attitudes,* New Delhi: Discovery Publishing House. ISBN 81-7141-555-5.

Durga Prasad, V., Author and Digumarti Bhaskara Rao, Editor (2012), *Problems of Tribal Girl Students,* New Delhi: Discovery Publishing House.

Dutt, B.S.V. and Digumarti Bhaskara Rao (2001), *Empowering Primary Teachers,* New Delhi: Discovery Publishing House. ISBN 81-7141-615-2.

Dutt, B.S.V., Author and Digumarti Bhaskara Rao, Editor (2004), *Comparative Education,* New Delhi: Discovery Publishing House. ISBN 81-7141-912-7.

Ediger, Marlow and Digumarti Bhaskara Rao, Editors (2006), *Encyclopaedia of School Education,* 5 Volumes. New Delhi: Discovery Publishing House. ISBN 81-8356-308-2 (set).

Ediger, Marlow and Digumarti Bhaskara Rao, Editors (2006), *Encyclopaedia of School Administration,* 4 Volumes. New Delhi: Discovery Publishing House. ISBN 81-8356-307-4 (set).

Ediger, Marlow and Digumarti Bhaskara Rao, Editors (2007), *Encyclopaedia of School Curriculum,* 10 Volumes. New Delhi: Discovery Publishing House. ISBN 81-8356-305-8 (set).

Ediger, Marlow and Digumarti Bhaskara Rao, Editors (2007), *Encyclopaedia of Teaching,* 8 Volumes. New Delhi: Discovery Publishing House. ISBN 81-8356-305-8 (set).

Marlow Ediger and Digumarti Bhaskara Rao, Editors (2006), *Encyclopaedia of School Education,* 5 Volumes. New Delhi: Discovery Publishing House. ISBN 81-8356-308-2 (set).

Marlow Ediger and Digumarti Bhaskara Rao, Editors (2006), *Encyclopaedia of School Administration,* 4 Volumes. New Delhi: Discovery Publishing House. ISBN 81-8356-307-4 (set).

Marlow Ediger and Digumarti Bhaskara Rao, Editors (2007), *Encyclopaedia of School Curriculum,* 10 Volumes. New Delhi: Discovery Publishing House. ISBN 81-8356-305-8 (set).

Marlow Ediger and Digumarti Bhaskara Rao, Editors (2007), *Encyclopaedia of Teaching,* 8 Volumes. New Delhi: Discovery Publishing House. ISBN 81-8356-305-8 (set).

Ediger, Marlow and Digumarti Bhaskara Rao (1996), *Science Curriculum,* New Delhi: Discovery Publishing House. ISBN 81-7141-321-8.

Ediger, Marlow and Digumarti Bhaskara Rao (2000), *Teaching Mathematics Successfully.* New Delhi: Discovery Publishing House. ISBN 81-7141-552-0.

Ediger, Marlow and Digumarti Bhaskara Rao (2001), *Teaching Science Successfully,* New Delhi: Discovery Publishing House. ISBN 81-7141-600-4.

Ediger, Marlow and Digumarti Bhaskara Rao (2001), *Teaching Social Studies Successfully.* New Delhi: Discovery Publishing House. ISBN 81-7141-596-2.

Ediger, Marlow and Digumarti Bhaskara Rao (2002), *Philosophy and Curriculum,* New Delhi: Discovery Publishing House. ISBN 81-7141-631-4.

Ediger, Marlow and Digumarti Bhaskara Rao (2002), *Improving School Administration,* New Delhi: Discovery Publishing House. ISBN 81-7141-633-0.

Ediger, Marlow and Digumarti Bhaskara Rao (2002), *Elementary Curriculum,* New Delhi: Discovery Publishing House. ISBN 81-7141-658-6.

Ediger, Marlow and Digumarti Bhaskara Rao (2003), *Language Arts Curriculum,* New Delhi: Discovery Publishing House. ISBN 81-7141-657-8.

Ediger, Marlow and Digumarti Bhaskara Rao (2003), *Psychology and Curriculum,* New Delhi: Discovery Publishing House. ISBN 81-7141-691-8.

Ediger, Marlow and Digumarti Bhaskara Rao (2003), *Teaching Language Arts Successfully,* New Delhi: Discovery Publishing House. ISBN 81-7141-678-0.

Ediger, Marlow and Digumarti Bhaskara Rao (2003), *School Curriculum and Administration,* New Delhi: Discovery Publishing House. ISBN 81-7141-709-4.

Ediger, Marlow and Digumarti Bhaskara Rao (2003), *Teaching Mathematics in Elementary Schools,* New Delhi: Discovery Publishing House. ISBN 81-7141-687-X.

Ediger, Marlow and Digumarti Bhaskara Rao (2003), *Teaching Science in Elementary Schools,* New Delhi: Discovery Publishing House. ISBN 81-7141-698-5.

Ediger, Marlow and Digumarti Bhaskara Rao (2003), *School Curriculum and Administration,* New Delhi: Discovery Publishing House. ISBN 81-7141-709-4.

Ediger, Marlow and Digumarti Bhaskara Rao (2003), *Elementary Curriculum Improvement,* New Delhi: Discovery Publishing House. ISBN 81-7141-740-X.

Ediger, Marlow and Digumarti Bhaskara Rao (2004), *School Organisation,* New Delhi: Discovery Publishing House. ISBN 81-7141-843-0.

Ediger, Marlow and Digumarti Bhaskara Rao (2004), *Relevancy in Elementary Curriculum,* New Delhi: Discovery Publishing House. ISBN 81-7141-845-9.

Ediger, Marlow and Digumarti Bhaskara Rao (2005), *Quality School Education,* New Delhi: Discovery Publishing House. ISBN 81-8356-022-9.

Ediger, Marlow and Digumarti Bhaskara Rao (2006), *Successful School Education,* New Delhi: Discovery Publishing House. ISBN 81-8356-054-7.

Ediger, Marlow and Digumarti Bhaskara Rao (2006), *Successful School Administration,* New Delhi: Discovery Publishing House. ISBN 81-8356-046-6.

Ediger, Marlow and Digumarti Bhaskara Rao (2006), *Issues in School Curruculum,* New Delhi: Discovery Publishing House. ISBN 81-8356-052-0.

Ediger, Marlow and Digumarti Bhaskara Rao (2006), *Community College – Curriculum and Teaching,* New Delhi: Discovery Publishing House. ISBN 81-8356-053-9.

Ediger, Marlow and Digumarti Bhaskara Rao (2006), *Administration of Schools,* New Delhi: Discovery Publishing House. ISBN 81-8356-244-2.

Ediger, Marlow and Digumarti Bhaskara Rao (2006), *Reading Curriculum and Instruction,* New Delhi: Discovery Publishing House. ISBN 81-8356-266-3.

Ediger, Marlow and Digumarti Bhaskara Rao (2006), *Curriculum Organisation,* New Delhi: Discovery Publishing House. ISBN 81-8356-205-1.

Ediger, Marlow and Digumarti Bhaskara Rao (2006), *Curriculum of School Subjects,* New Delhi: Discovery Publishing House. ISBN 81-8356-207-8.

Ediger, Marlow, B.S.V. Dutt and Digumarti Bhaskara Rao (2003), *Teaching English Successfully,* New Delhi: Discovery Publishing House. ISBN 81-7141-707-8.

Ediger, Marlow and Digumarti Bhaskara Rao (2007), *School Science Education*, New Delhi: Discovery Publishing House. ISBN 81-8356-352-X.

Ediger, Marlow and Digumarti Bhaskara Rao (2007), *Language Arts Education*, New Delhi: Discovery Publishing House. ISBN 81-8356-333-3.

Ediger, Marlow and Digumarti Bhaskara Rao (2010), *Effective Schooling*, New Delhi: Discovery Publishing House. ISBN 978-81-8356-613-1.

Ediger, Marlow and Digumarti Bhaskara Rao (2010), *Effective School Curriculum*, New Delhi: Discovery Publishing House. ISBN 978-81-8356-585-1.

Ediger, Marlow and Digumarti Bhaskara Rao (2010), *Essays on Teaching Science*, New Delhi: Discovery Publishing House. ISBN 978-81-8356-882-1.

Ediger, Marlow and Digumarti Bhaskara Rao (2010), *Essays on Teaching Social Studies*, New Delhi: Discovery Publishing House. ISBN 978-81-8356-883-8.

Ediger, Marlow and Digumarti Bhaskara Rao (2010), *Essays on Teaching Reading*, New Delhi: Discovery Publishing House. ISBN 978-81-8356-881-4.

Ediger, Marlow and Digumarti Bhaskara Rao (2011), *Essays on Teaching Mathematics*, New Delhi: Discovery Publishing House. ISBN 978-81-8356-880-7.

Ediger, Marlow and Digumarti Bhaskara Rao (2010), *Essays on Teaching*, New Delhi: Discovery Publishing House.

Ediger, Marlow and Digumarti Bhaskara Rao (2010), *Essays on School Issues*, New Delhi: Discovery Publishing House.

Elizabeth, M.E.S., Author and Digumarti Bhaskara Rao, Editor (2004), *Methods of Teaching English*, New Delhi: Discovery Publishing House. ISBN 81-7141-809-0.

Elizabeth, M.E.S., Author and Digumarti Bhaskara Rao, Editor (2004), *Acquisition of English Vocabulary*, New Delhi: Discovery Publishing House. ISBN 81-8356-075-X.

Fatima, SK. Author and Digumarti Bhaskara Rao, Editor (2007), *Reasoning Ability of School Students,* New Delhi: Discovery Publishing House. ISBN 81-8356-330-9.

Fatima, SK. and Digumarti Bhaskara Rao (2008), *Reasoning Ability of Adolescent Students,* New Delhi: Sonali Publications.

Gopala Krishna, M., Author and Digumarti Bhaskara Rao, Editor (2007), *Techniques of Teaching Physical Education,* New Delhi: Sonali Publications. ISBN 81-8411-044-8.

Gopala Krishna, M., Author and Digumarti Bhaskara Rao, Editor (2007), *Techniques of Teaching Education,* New Delhi: Sonali Publications. ISBN 81-8411-062-6.

Harshitha, Digumarthi, Author and Digumarti Bhaskara Rao, Editor (2004), *Methods of Teaching Information Technology,* New Delhi: Discovery Publishing House. ISBN 81-7141-805-8.

Harshitha, Digumarthi, Author and Digumarti Bhaskara Rao, Editor (2007), *Techniques of Teaching Computer Science,* New Delhi: Sonali Publications. ISBN 81-8411-036-7.

Indira Devi, Author and J. Prasanth Kumar and Digumarti Bhaskara Rao, Editors (2004), *Values in Language Text Books,* New Delhi: APH Publishing Corporation.

Jalaja Kumari, C., Author and Digumarti Bhaskara Rao, Editor (2004), *Methods of Teaching Educational Technology,* New Delhi: Discovery Publishing House. ISBN 81-7141-810-4.

Jalaja Kumari, C., Author and Digumarti Bhaskara Rao, Editor (2007), *Job Satisfaction of Teachers,* New Delhi: Discovery Publishing House. ISBN 81-8356-329-5.

Janardhan Reddy, B., Author and Digumarti Bhaskara Rao, Editor (2006), *Techniques of Teaching Sociology,* New Delhi: Sonali Publications. ISBN 81-8411-042-1.

Jayasree, K., Author and Digumarti Bhaskara Rao, Editor (1999), *Correlates of Socialisation,* New Delhi: Discovery Publishing House. ISBN 81-7141-517-2.

Jayasree, K., Author and Digumarti Bhaskara Rao, Editor (2004), *Methods of Teaching Science,* New Delhi: Discovery Publishing House. ISBN 81-7141-801-5.

John Babu, C., Author and T.J.R. Prasad, G.M. Madhukar and Digumarti Bhaskara Rao, Editors (2004), *Problem Solving in Mathematics,* New Delhi: APH Publishing Corporation. ISBN 81-7648-273-0.

Joseph Raju, B and G.A. Anitha, Authors and Digumarti Bhaskara Rao, Editor (2004), *Population Education* New Delhi: Sonali Publications. ISBN 81-88836-31-3.

Jyosthana, M., Author and Digumarti Bhaskara Rao, Editor (2011), *Achievement Motivation and Achievement in English of School Students,* New Delhi: Discovery Publishing House. ISBN 978-93-5056-002-0.

Lalitha, T., Author and K.S. Prabhakaram, D.S.N. Sastry and Digumarti Bhaskara Rao Editors (2004), *Educational Philosophic Beliefs,* New Delhi: Discovery Publishing House. ISBN 81-7141-765-5.

Krishna, G., Author and Digumarti Bhaskara Rao, Editor (2006), *Techniques of Teaching Physical Education,* New Delhi: Discovery Publishing House. ISBN 81-8411-044-8.

Kumar Raja, G., Author and Digumarti Bhaskara Rao, Editor (2007), *Principles of Primary School,* New Delhi: Sonali Publications. ISBN 81-8411-054-5.

Lakshmi Kumari, V., Author and Digumarti Bhaskara Rao, Editor (2006), *Techniques of Teaching Home Science,* New Delhi: Discovery Publishing House. ISBN 81-8411-048-0.

Madhava, K., Author and Digumarti Bhaskara Rao, Editor (2008), *Personality of Adolescent Students,* New Delhi: Sonali Publications.

Madhu Bala, Jampala, Author and Digumarti Bhaskara Rao, Editor (2004), *Methods of Teaching Exceptional Children,* New Delhi: Discovery Publishing House. ISBN 81-7141-802-3.

Mallikarjuna Reddy, V., Author and Digumarti Bhaskara Rao, Editor (2011), *Teaching Aptitude, Social Adjustment and Job Satisfaction of Science Teachers,* New Delhi: Discovery Publishing House. ISBN 978-93-5056-121-8.

Marja, Talvi and Digumarti Bhaskara Rao, Editors (1996), *Educational Leadership and Social Changes,* New Delhi: Discovery Publishing House. ISBN 81-7141-320-X.

Naga Kumari, U., Author and Digumarti Bhaskara Rao, Editor (2008), *Science Process Skills of School Students,* New Delhi: Sonali Publications.

Nageswara Rao, S. and M. Srihari, Authors and Digumarti Bhaskara Rao, Editor (2004), *Guidance and Counselling,* New Delhi: Discovery Publishing House. ISBN 81-7141-840-6.

Nageswara Rao, S., Author and Digumarti Bhaskara Rao, Editor (2006), *Techniques of Teaching Psychology,* New Delhi: Discovery Publishing House. ISBN 81-8411-040-5.

Naidu., P.Ch. A., Author and Digumarti Bhaskara Rao, Editor (2007), *Fedback Methods and Students Performance,* New Delhi: Discovery Publishing House. 81-8356-284-1.

Nageswara Rao, S. and P. Sridhar, Authors and Digumarti Bhaskara Rao, Editor (2004), *Methods and Techniques of Teaching,* New Delhi: Sonali Publications. ISBN 81-88836-33-8.

Nirmala Jyothi, M., Author and Digumarti Bhaskara Rao, Editor (2003), *Non-detention System in School Education,* New Delhi: Discovery Publishing House. ISBN 81-7141-654-3.

Padma Tulasi, G., Author and Digumarti Bhaskara Rao, Editor (2004), *Methods of Teaching Elementary Science,* New Delhi: Discovery Publishing House. ISBN 81-7141-871-6.

Pala Prasada Rao, V., Author and K. N. Rani and D. Bhaskara Rao, Editors (2004), *India Pakistan: Partition Perspectives in Indo English Novels,* New Delhi: Discovery Publishing House. ISBN 81-7141-871-6.

Pala Prasada Rao, V., Author and D. Bhaskara Rao, Editors (2008), *Functioning of Autonomous Colleges*, New Delhi: Sonali Publications.

Pitchi Reddy, M., Author and Digumarti Bhaskara Rao, Editor (2007), *Techniques of Teaching Social Sciences*, New Delhi: Sonali Publications. ISBN 81-8411-066-X.

Prasad Babu, B., Author and P. Madhu and Digumarti Bhaskara Rao, Editors (2006), *Psychological Adjustment and Well-being*. New Delhi: Discovery Publishing House. ISBN 81-8356-204-3.

Prasad Babu, B., Author and M.V.R. Raju and Digumarti Bhaskara Rao, Editors (2006), *Behavioural Problems of School Children*, New Delhi: Discovery Publishing House. ISBN 81-8356-206-X.

Prabhakaram, K.S., Author and Digumarti Bhaskara Rao, Editors (1998), *Concept Attainment Model in Mathematics Teaching*, New Delhi: Discovery Publishing House. ISBN 81-7141-424-9.

Prasanth Kumar, J., Author and Digumarti Bhaskara Rao, Editor (1998), *Effectiveness of Distance Education System*, New Delhi: Discovery Publishing House. ISBN 81-7141-437-0.

Prasanth Kumar, J., Author and Digumarti Bhaskara Rao, Editor (2004), *Methods of Teaching Civics*, New Delhi: Discovery Publishing House. ISBN 81-7141-806-6.

Prasanth Kumar, J., Author and G. Sundara Rao and Digumarti Bhaskara Rao, Editors (2000), *Open University Student Support Services*, New Delhi: Discovery Publishing House. ISBN 81-7141-550-4.

Raja Kumari, M.A. and D.R.S. Sundari, Authors and Digumarti Bhaskara Rao, Editor (2004), *Special Education*, New Delhi: Discovery Publishing House. ISBN 81-7141-846-5.

Raja Kumari, M.A. and D.R.S. Sundari, Authors and Digumarti Bhaskara Rao, Editor (2004). *Methods of Teaching Educational Psychology*, New Delhi: Discovery Publishing House. ISBN 81-7141-820-1.

Ramatulasamma, K., Author and Digumarti Bhaskara Rao, Editor (2002), *Job Satisfaction of Teacher Educators,* New Delhi: Discovery Publishing House. ISBN 81-7141-655-1.

Rama Krishnaiah, D., Author and Digumarti Bhaskara Rao, Editor (1998), *Job Satisfaction of College Teachers,* New Delhi: Discovery Publishing House. ISBN 81-7141-438-9.

Rama Kumar Ratnam, M.V., Author and Digumarti Bhaskara Rao, Editor (1998), *Dukkha: Suffering in Early Buddhism,* New Delhi: Discovery Publishing House. ISBN 81-7141-653-5.

Rama Krishna Prasad and P. Vide Sagar, Authors and Digumarti Bhaskara Rao, Editor (2004), *Methods of Teaching Physical Education,* New Delhi: Discovery Publishing House. ISBN 81-7141-868-6.

Rama Seshaiah, P. Author and Digumarti Bhaskara Rao, Editor (2004), *Methods of Teaching Home Science,* New Delhi: Discovery Publishing House. ISBN 81-7141-916-X.

Rama Swamy, K., Author and Digumarti Bhaskara Rao, Editor (2007), *Techniques of Teaching Environmental Science,* New Delhi: Sonali Publications. ISBN 81-8411-035-9.

Ramesh, A.R., Author and Digumarti Bhaskara Rao, Editor (2006), *Techniques of Teaching Commerce,* New Delhi: Sonali Publications. ISBN 81-8411-043-X.

Ramesh, Ghanta and Digumarti Bhaskara Rao, Editors (1998), *Environmental Education: Problems and Prospects,* New Delhi: Discovery Publishing House. ISBN 81-7141-423-0.

Ranga Rao, B., Author and Digumarti Bhaskara Rao, Editor (2007), *Techniques of Teaching Economics,* New Delhi: Sonali Publications. ISBN 81-8411-056-1.

Ranga Rao, R., Author and Digumarti Bhaskara Rao, Editor (2004), *Methods of Teacher Teaching,* New Delhi: Discovery Publishing House. ISBN 81-7141-812-0.

Rani, S.S., Author and Digumarti Bhaskara Rao, Editor (2006), *Techniques of Teaching Botany,* New Delhi: Discovery Publishing House. ISBN 81-8411-037-5.

Rathaiah, Lavu and Digumarti Bhaskara Rao, Editors (1996), *International Innovations in Education,* New Delhi: Discovery Publishing House. ISBN 81-7141-359-5.

Rathaiah, Lavu and Digumarti Bhaskara Rao (1997), *Achievement Correlates,* New Delhi: Discovery Publishing House. ISBN 81-7141- 385-4.

Ravi Krishna, M., Author and Digumarti Bhaskara Rao, Editor (2004), *Examination System,* New Delhi: Discovery Publishing House. ISBN 81-7141-824-4.

Ravi Kumar, M., Author and Digumarti Bhaskara Rao, Editor (2004), *Methods of Teaching Computer Science,* New Delhi: Discovery Publishing House. ISBN 81-7141-823-6.

Rudramamba, B., Author and Digumarti Bhaskara Rao, Editor (2003), *Problems of Teaching* New Delhi: APH Publishing Corporation. ISBN 81-7648-462-8.

Rudramamba, B. and V. Lakshmi Kumari, Authors and Digumarti Bhaskara Rao, Editor (2004), *Methods of Teaching Economics,* New Delhi: Discovery Publishing House. ISBN 81-7141-900-3.

Sambasiva Rao, P., Author and Digumarti Bhaskara Rao, Editor (2007), *Techniques of Teaching Psychology,* New Delhi: Sonali Publications. ISBN 81-8411-040-5.

Sanjeeva Rao, P.C., Author and Digumarti Bhaskara Rao, Editor (1996), *A Text Book of Geology,* New Delhi: Discovery Publishing House. ISBN 81-7141-313-7.

Santhanam, T., B. Prasad Babu and S. Sugandhi, Authors and Digumarti Bhaskara Rao, Editor (2007), *Children with Learning Disabilities,* New Delhi: Sonali Publications. ISBN 81-8411-077-4.

Santhanam, T., B. Prasad Babu and S. Sugandhi, Authors and Digumarti Bhaskara Rao, Editor (2008), *Learning Disabilities and Remedial Programmes,* New Delhi: Discovery Publishing House. ISBN 978-81-8356-257-7.

Sarala, M.M.O., Author and Digumarti Bhaskara Rao, Editor (2006), *Techniques of Teaching English,* New Delhi: Sonali Publications. ISBN 81-8411-047-2.

Satya Narayana, G., Author and Digumarti Bhaskara Rao, Editor (2008), *Attitude towards Social Studies and Achievement in Social Studies,* New Delhi: Sonali Publications.

Satya Narayana, V., Author and Digumarti Bhaskara Rao, Editor (2001), *Physical Education, Social Attitudes and Leadership Qualities.* New Delhi: Discovery Publishing House. ISBN 81-7141-593-8.

Satya Narayana, P.V.V. and G. Krishna, Authors and Digumarti Bhaskara Rao, Editor (2004), *Curriculum Development and Management.* New Delhi: Discovery Publishing House. ISBN 81-7141-813-9.

Shamsuddin, SK. and V. Dayakara Reddy, Authors and Digumarti Bhaskara Rao, Editor (2007), *Values and Academic Achievement,* New Delhi: Discovery Publishing House. ISBN 81-8356-283-3.

Singh, Y.C., Author and Digumarti Bhaskara Rao, Editor (2006), *Techniques of Teaching Science,* New Delhi: Sonali Publications. ISBN 81-8411-041-3.

Sirisha Rani, S., Author and Digumarti Bhaskara Rao, Editor (2007), *Techniques of Teaching Botany,* New Delhi: Sonali Publications. ISBN 81-8411-037-5.

Sivaratnam Reddy, M., Author and Digumarti Bhaskara Rao, Editor (2004), *Creativity in College Students,* New Delhi: Discovery Publishing House. ISBN 81-7141-697-7.

Siva Lakshmi, G.V. and G.L. Subbaiah, Authors and Digumarti Bhaskara Rao, Editor (2004), *Methods of Teaching Environmental Science,* New Delhi: Discovery Publishing House. ISBN 81-7141-839-2.

Srinivas, G. and Digumarti Bhaskara Rao (2007), *Anxiety of Prospective Teachers,* New Delhi: Sonali Publications. ISBN 81-8411-084-7.

Srinivas, G. and Digumarti Bhaskara Rao (2011), *Intelligence and Personality of Prospective Teachers,* New Delhi: Discovery Publishing House. 978-93-5056-101-0.

Srinivas, M. and I. Prasada Rao, Authors and Digumarti Bhaskara Rao, Editor (2004), *Methods of Teaching History*, New Delhi: Discovery Publishing House. ISBN 81-7141-803-1.

Srinivas Rao, P., Author and Digumarti Bhaskara Rao, Editor (2007), *Principles of Secondary School*, New Delhi: Sonali Publications. ISBN 81-8411-058-8.

Srinivasulu, K., Author and Digumarti Bhaskara Rao, Editor (2011), *Achievement Motivation and Academic Achievement of Alcoholic and Non-alcoholic Students*, New Delhi: Discovery Publishing House. ISBN 978-93-5056-063-1.

Srinivasulu, Kopperla and Digumarti Bhaskara Rao (2011), *Achievement Motivation, Academic Achievement and Alcoholism*, Saarbrucken, Germany: LAMBERT Academic Publishing GmbH and Co. KG. ISBN 978-3-8465-9296-0.

Srinivasulu Reddy, M. and K.R.S. Sambasiva Rao, Authors and Digumarti Bhaskara Rao, Editor (1999), *A Text Book of Aquaculture*, New Delhi: Discovery Publishing House. ISBN 81-7141-482-6.

Srinivasa Rao, Mandalapu, Author and Digumarti Bhaskara Rao, Editor (2003), *Achievement Motivation and Achievement in Mathematics*, New Delhi: Discovery Publishing House. ISBN 81-7141-674-8.

Srihari, M., Author and Digumarti Bhaskara Rao, Editor (2003), *Values of Prospective Teachers*, New Delhi: Discovery Publishing House. ISBN 81-8356-328-7.

Subba Rao, K., Author and Digumarti Bhaskara Rao, Editor (2007), *School Education Policy*, New Delhi: Discovery Publishing House. ISBN 81-8356-285-X.

Subba Rao, K., Author and Digumarti Bhaskara Rao, Editor (2007), *Education Planning*, New Delhi: Sonali Publications. ISBN 81-8411-053-7.

Subramanyam, N.R., Author and Digumarti Bhaskara Rao, Editor (2011), *Effectiveness of In-service Training Programmes*, New Delhi: Discovery Publishing House. ISBN 978-93-5056-078-5.

Sudhakar Reddy, Y., Author and Digumarti Bhaskara Rao, Editor (2003), *Creativity in Adolescents,* New Delhi: Discovery Publishing House. ISBN 81-7141-659-4.

Sunil Kumar, K. and K. Rama Krishana, Authors and Digumarti Bhaskara Rao, Editor (2004), *Methods of Teaching Chemistry,* New Delhi: Discovery Publishing House. ISBN 81-7141-913-5.

Suneetha, G., Author and Digumarti Bhaskara Rao, Editor (2004), *Environmental Awareness of School Students,* New Delhi: Sonali Publications. ISBN 81-8411-085-5.

Sunita, E. and R. Sambasiva Rao, Authors and Digumarti Bhaskara Rao, Editor (2004), *Methods of Teaching Mathematics,* New Delhi: Discovery Publishing House. ISBN 81-7141-915-1.

Surya Madhava, I., Author and Digumarti Bhaskara Rao, Editor (2006), *Techniques of Teaching Geography,* New Delhi: Discovery Publishing House. ISBN 81-8411-034-0.

Surya Madhava, I., Author and Digumarti Bhaskara Rao, Editor (2007), *Techniques of Teaching Political Science,* New Delhi: Discovery Publishing House. ISBN 81-8411-061-8.

Swamy, K.R., Author and Digumarti Bhaskara Rao, Editor (2006), *Techniques of Teaching Environmental Science,* New Delhi: Discovery Publishing House. ISBN 81-8411-035-9.

Swarna Jyothi, K., Author and Digumarti Bhaskara Rao, Editor (2007), *Educational Research.* New Delhi: Sonali Publications. ISBN 81-8411-063-4.

Swarna Latha, C.D., and Digumarti Bhaskara Rao, Editors (2006), *Encyclopaedia of Biotechnology,* 5 Volumes. New Delhi: Discovery Publishing House. ISBN 81-8356-168-3.

Swarupa Rani, T. and J.R. Priyadarshini, Authors and Digumarti Bhaskara Rao, Editor (2004), *Educational Measurement and Evaluation,* New Delhi: Discovery Publishing House. ISBN 81-7141-859-7.

Vanaja, M., Author and Digumarti Bhaskara Rao, Editor (1999), *Inquiry Training Model,* New Delhi: Discovery Publishing House. ISBN 81-7141-515-6.

Vanaja, M., Author and Digumarti Bhaskara Rao, Editor (2004), *Methods of Teaching Physics,* New Delhi: Discovery Publishing House. ISBN 81-7141-867-8.

Vanaja, M. and N. Sneha Latha, Authors and Digumarti Bhaskara Rao, Editor (2004), *Student Shyness,* New Delhi: APH Publishing Corporation.

Valeri V. Koustiouk, Author and Digumarti Bhaskara Rao, Editor (2002), *A Text Book of Cryogenics,* New Delhi: Discovery Publishing House. ISBN 81-7141-642-X.

Vamsi Krishna, V., Author and Digumarti Bhaskara Rao, Editor (2004), *School Psychology,* New Delhi: Discovery Publishing House. ISBN 81-7141-880-5.

Veena Kumari, Balusu and Digumarti Bhaskara Rao (1996), *Operation Black Board,* New Delhi: APH Publishing Corporation. ISBN 81-7024-711-X.

Veena Kumari, Balusu, Author and Digumarti Bhaskara Rao, Editor (2004), *Methods of Teaching Social Studies,* New Delhi: Discovery Publishing House. ISBN 81-7141-899-6.

Veena Kumari, Balusu, Author and Digumarti Bhaskara Rao, Editor (2000), *Psycho-Social Correlates of Achievement,* New Delhi: Discovery Publishing House. ISBN 81-7141-547-4.

Venkata Rao, B., Author and Digumarti Bhaskara Rao, Editor (2007), *Techniques of Teaching Chemistry,* New Delhi: Sonali Publications. ISBN 81-8411-057-X.

Venkata Rao, P. and Digumarti Bhaskara Rao (1989), *A Text Book of Zoology – Junior Intermediate,* Guntur: Vignan Publishers.

Venkata Rao, P. and Digumarti Bhaskara Rao (1989), *A Text Book of Zoology – Senior Intermediate,* Guntur: Vignan Publishers.

Venkateswara Rao, V., Author and Digumarti Bhaskara Rao, Editor (2004), *Problems of Education,* New Delhi: Discovery Publishing House. ISBN 81-7141-841-4.

Venkateswara Rao, V., V. Vijaya Lakshmi and V. Vamsi Krishna, Authors and Digumarti Bhaskara Rao, Editor (2004),

Education For All, New Delhi: Sonali Publications. ISBN 81-88836-30-3.

Venkateswara Rao, V., V. Vijaya Lakshmi and V. Vamsi Krishna, Authors and Digumarti Bhaskara Rao, Editor (2004), *Education in India,* New Delhi: Sonali Publications. ISBN 81-88836-858-9.

Venkateswara Reddy, L. and Narayana, M. L., Authors and Digumarti Bhaskara Rao, Editor (2004), *Education for Dalits,* New Delhi: Discovery Publishing House. ISBN 81-7141-872-4.

Venkateswara Reddy, L. and Narayana, M. L, Authors and Digumarti Bhaskara Rao, Editor (2004), *Methods of Teaching Rural Sociology,* New Delhi: Discovery Publishing House. ISBN 81-7141-811-2.

Venkateswarlu, K. and S.J. Basha, Authors and Digumarti Bhaskara Rao, Editor (2004), *Methods of Teaching Commerce,* New Delhi: Discovery Publishing House. ISBN 81-7141-808-2.

Venugopala Rao, K., Author and Digumarti Bhaskara Rao, Editor (2000), *Teacher Morale in Secondary Schools,* New Delhi: Discovery Publishing House. ISBN 81-7141-551-2.

Venugopala Rao, K., Author and Digumarti Bhaskara Rao, Editor (2007), *Techniques of Teaching History,* New Delhi: Sonali Publications. ISBN 81-8411-059-6.

Vidya, C., Author and Digumarti Bhaskara Rao, Editor (1996), *A Text Book of Nutrition,* New Delhi: Discovery Publishing House. ISBN 81-7141-309-9.

Vimala, T.D., B. Prasad Babu and Digumarti Bhaskara Rao, Editors (2007), *Stress, Coping and Management,* New Delhi: Sonali Publications. ISBN 81-8411-086-3.

Vijaya Bharathi, D., Author and Digumarti Bhaskara Rao, Editor (2000), *Educational Philosophies of Swami Vivekananda and John Dewey,* New Delhi: APH Publishing House. ISBN 81-7648-309-9.

Vijaya Bharathi, D., Author and Digumarti Bhaskara Rao, Editor (2005), *Educational Philosophy of John Dewey*, New Delhi: Discovery Publishing House. ISBN 81-8356-024-5.

Vijaya Bharathi, D., Author and Digumarti Bhaskara Rao, Editor (2005), *Educational Philosophy of Swami Vivekananda*, New Delhi: Discovery Publishing House. ISBN 81-8356-023-7.

Vijaya Lakshmi, D., Author and Digumarti Bhaskara Rao, Editor (2004), *Basic Education*, New Delhi: Discovery Publishing House. ISBN 81-7141-881-3.

Vijaya Lakshmi, V., Author and Digumarti Bhaskara Rao, Editor (2006), *Techniques of Teaching Music*, New Delhi: Discovery Publishing House. ISBN 81-8411-038-3.

Vijaya Kumar, S.J., Author and Digumarti Bhaskara Rao, Editor (2006), *Techniques of Teaching Mathematics*, New Delhi: Sonali Publications. ISBN 81-8411-039-1.

Visalakshi, V., Author and Digumarti Bhaskara Rao, Editor (2006), *Techniques of Teaching Biology*, New Delhi: Sonali Publications. ISBN 81-8411-045-6.

Visalakshi, V., Author and Digumarti Bhaskara Rao, Editor (2007), *Techniques of Teaching Zoology*, New Delhi: Sonali Publications. ISBN 81-8411-055-3.

Books in Telugu Language

Bhaskara Rao, Digumarti (1986), *Dhrushya Sravana Bodhanapakaranalu* (Audio Visual Teaching Aids), Guntur: Nagarjuna Publishers.

Bhaskara Rao, Digumarti (1993), *Jeevasashtra Bodhana* (Teaching of Biology), Guntur: Nagarjuna Publishers.

Bhaskara Rao, Digumarti (1995), *Vignanasasthra Bodhana* (Teaching of Science), Guntur: Nagarjuna Publishers.

Bhaskara Rao, Digumarti (1991), *Vidya Manovignana Sastram* (Educational Psychology), Guntur: Nagarjuna Publishers.

Bhaskara Rao, Digumarti (1997), *Vidya Manovignana Sastram* (Educational Psychology), Guntur: Creative Press.

Bhaskara Rao, Digumarti (1998), *DSC Study Material*, Guntur: Nagarjuna Publishers.

Bhaskara Rao, Digumarti (1998), *Upadhyayudu Vidya*, (Teacher and Education), Guntur: Nagarjuna Publishers.

Bhaskara Rao, Digumarti (1998), *Vidya Drukpadalu* (Perspectives of Education), Guntur: Nagarjuna Publishers.

Bhaskara Rao, Digumarti (1999), *EdCET Teaching Aptitude*, Guntur: Nagarjuna Publishers.

Bhaskara Rao, Digumarti (2001), *Bharata Samajamulo Upadyayudu Vidhya* (Teacher and Education in Emerging Indian Society), Guntur: Sri Nagarjuna Publishers.

Bhaskara Rao, Digumarti (2001), *Bhoutika Sastra Bodhana Padhatulu* (Methods of Teaching Physical Science), Guntur: Sri Nagarjuna Publishers.

Bhaskara Rao, Digumarti (2001), *Jeeva Sastra Bodhana Padhatulu* (Methods of Teaching Biology), Guntur: Sri Nagarjuna Publishers.

Bhaskara Rao, Digumarti (2001), *Vidya Manovignana Sastram* (Educational Psychology), Guntur: Sri Nagarjuna Publishers.

Bhaskara Rao, Digumarti (2003), *Patasala Yajamanyam/ Paripalana* (School Management and Administration), Guntur: Sri Nagarjuna Publishers.

Bhaskara Rao, Digumarti and M. Srihari (2009), *Vardamana Bharata Desamulo Vidya* (Education in Emerging India), Guntur: Sri Nagarjuna Publishers.

Bhaskara Rao, Digumarti and B. Prasad Babu (2009), *Vidya Manovignana Sastram* (Educational Psychology), Guntur: Sri Nagarjuna Publishers.

Bhaskara Rao, Digumarti and B. Prasad Babu (2009), *Pradhamika Vidya Mariyu Vileena Vidya Dhrukpadhalu* (Perspectives in Primary Education and Inclusive Education), Guntur: Sri Nagarjuna Publishers.

Bhaskara Rao, Digumarti and K. Subba Rao (2009), *Elementary Vidya, Pranalika, Yajamanyam, Upadyaya Kartavyalu*

(Elementary Education, Planning, Management and Teacher Functions), Guntur: Sri Nagarjuna Publishers.

Bhaskara Rao, Digumarti and C. Prasanthi (2009), *Samardya Nirmanamu* (Capacity Building), Guntur: Sri Nagarjuna Publishers.

Bhaskara Rao, Digumarti and A. Jagadish (2009), *Vignansastra Bodhana Padhatulu* (Methods of Teaching Science), Guntur: Sri Nagarjuna Publishers.

Bhaskara Rao, Digumarti, Editor (2010), *Vardamana Bharata Desamulo Vidya – Question Bank* (D.Ed. Education in Emerging India), Guntur: Sri Nagarjuna Publishers.

Bhaskara Rao, Digumarti, Editor (2010), *Vidya Manovignana Sastram – Question Bank* (D.Ed. Educational Psychology), Guntur: Sri Nagarjuna Publishers.

Bhaskara Rao, Digumarti, Editor (2010), *Pradhamika Vidya mariyu Vileena Vidya Dhrukpadhalu – Question Bank* (D.Ed. Perspectives in Primary Education and Inclusive Education), Guntur: Sri Nagarjuna Publishers.

Bhaskara Rao, Digumarti, Editor (2010), *Elementary Vidya Pranalika, Yajamanyam, Upadyaya Kartavyalu – Question Bank* (D.Ed. Elementary Education, Planning, Management and Teacher Functions), Guntur: Sri Nagarjuna Publishers.

Bhaskara Rao, Digumarti, Editor (2010), *Samardya Nirmanamu – Question Bank* (D.Ed. Capacity Building), Guntur: Sri Nagarjuna Publishers.

Bhaskara Rao, Digumarti, Editor (2010), *Ganithasastra Bodhana Padhatulu – Question Bank* (D.Ed. Methods of Teaching Science), Guntur: Sri Nagarjuna Publishers.

Bhaskara Rao, Digumarti, Editor (2010), *Vignansastra Bodhana Padhatulu – Question Bank* (D.Ed. Methods of Teaching Science), Guntur: Sri Nagarjuna Publishers.

Bhaskara Rao, Digumarti, Editor (2010), *Sanghikasastra Bodhana Padhatulu – Question Bank* (D.Ed. Methods of Teaching Social Studies), Guntur: Sri Nagarjuna Publishers.

Bhaskara Rao, Digumarti, Editor (2010), *Telugu Bodhana Padhatulu – Question Bank* (D.Ed. Methods of Teaching Social Studies), Guntur: Sri Nagarjuna Publishers.

Bhaskara Rao, Digumarti, Editor (2010), *Methods of Teaching English – Question Bank.* (D.Ed.) Guntur: Sri Nagarjuna Publishers.

Bhaskara Rao, Digumarti, Editor (2011), *Vidya Adhralu – Question Bank* (B.Ed. Philosophical Foundations of Education), Guntur: Sri Nagarjuna Publishers.

Bhaskara Rao, Digumarti, Editor (2011), *Vidya Manovignana Sastram – Question Bank* (B.Ed. Educational Psychology), Guntur: Sri Nagarjuna Publishers.

Bhaskara Rao, Digumarti, Editor (2011), *Vidya Sanketika Sastrm – Computer Vidya – Question Bank* (B.Ed. Educational Technology and Computer Vidya), Guntur: Sri Nagarjuna Publishers.

Bhaskara Rao, Digumarti, Editor (2011), *School Management – Systems of Education – Question Bank* (B.Ed. School Management and Systems of Education), Guntur: Sri Nagarjuna Publishers.

Bhaskara Rao, Digumarti, Editor (2011), *Personality Development and Communicative English – Question Bank* (B.Ed. Personality Development and Communicative English), Guntur: Sri Nagarjuna Publishers.

Bhaskara Rao, Digumarti, Editor (2011), *Ganithasastra Bodhana Padhatulu – Question Bank* (B.Ed. Methods of Teaching Science), Guntur: Sri Nagarjuna Publishers.

Bhaskara Rao, Digumarti, Editor (2011), *Bhoutikasastra Bodhana Padhatulu – Question Bank* (B.Ed. Methods of Teaching Physical Science), Guntur: Sri Nagarjuna Publishers.

Bhaskara Rao, Digumarti, Editor (2011), *Jeevasastra Bodhana Padhatulu – Question Bank* (B.Ed. Methods of Teaching Biological Science), Guntur: Sri Nagarjuna Publishers.

Bhaskara Rao, Digumarti, Editor (2011), *Sanghikasastra Bodhana Padhatulu – Question Bank* (B.Ed. Methods of Teaching Social Studies), Guntur: Sri Nagarjuna Publishers.

Bhaskara Rao, Digumarti, Editor (2011), *Telugu Bodhana Padhatulu – Question Bank* (B.Ed. Methods of Teaching Social Studies), Guntur: Sri Nagarjuna Publishers.

Bhaskara Rao, Digumarti, Editor (2011), *Methods of Teaching English – Question Bank*. (B.Ed.), Guntur: Sri Nagarjuna Publishers.

Bhaskara Rao, Digumarti, N. Saraja, J. Lalitha and V. Mrunalini, Translators (2008), *Vidya – Samajam (Education - Society). Hyderabad*: Dr. B. R. Ambedkar Open University.

Gopala Krishna, G., A. Rama Krishna, K. Subba Rao and Bhaskara Rao, Digumarti (2004), *Jeevasashtra Bodhana Padhatulu* (Methods of Teaching of Biological Science), Guntur: Sri Nagarjuna Publishers.

Krishna Murthy, V., K.S. Sudheer Reddy and Digumarti Bhaskara Rao (2004), *Vidya Manovignana Sastra Adharalu* (Foundations of Educational Psychology), Guntur: Sri Nagarjuna Publishers.

Lalini, V., V. Dayakara Reddy, M. Srihari and Digumarti Bhaskara Rao (2004), *Vidya Adharalu* (Foundations of Education), Guntur: Sri Nagarjuna Publishers.

Sastry, G.E.P. and G. Satya Narayana, Authors, Bhaskara Rao, Digumarti, Editor (2009), *Sanghikasastra Bodhana Padhatulu* (Methods of Teaching Social Studies), Guntur: Sri Nagarjuna Publishers.

Subba Rao, K.P., P. Ayodhya and Digumarti Bhaskara Rao (2004), *Patasala Yajamanyam – Vidhya Vyavasthalu* (School Management and Systems of Education), Guntur: Sri Nagarjuna Publishers.

Sudhakar, V., B. Ravindra Babu, D.S. Kumar and Digumarti Bhaskara Rao (2004), *Vidya Sanketika Sastram - Computer Vidhya* (Educational Technology and Computer Education), Guntur: Sri Nagarjuna Publishers.

Index

T

U

V

W

FINANCING AGRIBUSINESS
A BIRD'S EYE VIEW

FINANCING AGRIBUSINESS
A BIRD'S EYE VIEW

By

Dr. R. Dayanandan
Associate Professor
College of Business & Economics
Hawassa University
Post Box: 692
Hawassa, SNNPR
ETHIOPIA

DISCOVERY PUBLISHING HOUSE PVT. LTD.
NEW DELHI-110 002

Published by:

Tilak Wasan

DISCOVERY PUBLISHING HOUSE PVT. LTD.

4383/4B, Ansari Road, Darya Ganj

New Delhi-110 002 (India)

Phone : +91-11-23279245, 43596064-65

Fax : +91-11-23253475

E-mail : discoverypublishinghouse@gmail.com

sales@discoverypublishinggroup.com

parul.wasan@gmail.com

web : www.discoverypublishinggroup.com

***First Edition:* 2014**

ISBN: 978-93-5056-458-5

Financing Agribusiness: ***A Bird's Eye View***

© 2014, Author

All rights reserved. No part of this publication should be reproduced, stored in a retrieval system, or transmitted in any form or by any means: electronic, mechanical, photocopying, recording or otherwise, without the prior written permission of the author and the publisher.

This book has been published in good faith that the material provided by authors is original. Every effort is made to ensure accuracy of material, but the publisher and printer will not be held responsible for any inadvertent error(s). In case of any dispute, all legal matters are to be settled under Delhi jurisdiction only.

Printed at:

Aditi Fine Art Press

Delhi

Preface

Agriculture is the main stay of most of the transition countries in the world and contributes the major part of their Gross Domestic Product (GDP). Production and the distribution of agricultural products in a raw nature is the out of date since it does not contribute anything to the producers. Hence every producer/farmer is in the process of thinking about getting more profit in different forms of value addition activities. In the current situation agribusiness has gained more attention of all stake holders including academicians as well as the researchers. Because management of resources is a vital aspect in agricultural production and marketing to enjoy the fruits by both producers and the consumers including the mediators. Unless it is managed properly, the expected benefits/objectives of such activities may not be achieved. Finance is a lifeblood of any activities either production or marketing in the agricultural sector. Also management of finance also crucial to attain the intended purpose.

This book has been designed in such as way so that it will helpful to the different stakeholders in different forms. For business owners, it will be a yardstick to standardizing the manner within which the operation of business related to input and out marketing of agricultural products. Also the business owners can use it as a comprehensive suite of processes as effectively manage time, cost, quality, change, risks and issues for suppliers and customers. Students can learn how to manage the agribusiness efficiently using a formal methodology and taking their learning into the workplace, by adopting this methodology for their professional management activities. The seasoned professional managers will find value in the book as well.

In writing this book, the author has relied heavily upon a large number of sources which have been duly acknowledged and whole – heartedly expresses his gratitude to those publications and their authors. Hope this book will meet the expectations of our readers. It will be greatly appreciated the comments and suggestions of our readers.

— Author

Contents

Abbreviations

AGLEND	:	Agricultural Lending.
AIDA	:	Attention, Interest, Desire, Action.
ARR	:	Accounting Rate of Return.
CDO	:	Collateralized Debt Obligations.
CIRAD	:	Agricultural Research Centre for International.
CLN	:	Credit linked notes.
CPM	:	Critical Path Method.
DCF	:	Discounted cash flow Development.
DPAP	:	Drought Prone Area Programme.
EVA	:	Economic Value Added.
FAO	:	Food and Agriculture Organization.
FDA	:	Food and Drug Administration.
GTZ	:	German Technical Cooperation.
HVAPs	:	High Value Agricultural Products.
HYV	:	High Yield Variety.
ICT	:	Information and Communication Technology.
IFAD	:	International Fund for Agricultural Development.
IFPRI	:	International Food Policy Research Institute.
IMC	:	Integrated Marketing Communications.
INPhO	:	Information Network on Post-harvest Operations.
IPO	:	Initial Public Offerings.
IPR	:	Intellectual Property Rights.
IRR	:	Internal Rate of Return.
MDGs	:	Millennium Development Goals.
MEW	:	Marketing Extension Worker.

MFIs	:	Micro-finance Institutions.
MIS	:	Management Information Systems.
MMDAs	:	Money Market Deposit Accounts.
MNCs	:	Multi-National Companies.
MVA	:	Market Value Added.
NGOs	:	Non-Governmental Organizations.
NOC	:	No Objection Certificate.
NOWC	:	Net Operating Working Capital.
NPV	:	Net Present value.
NSC	:	National Saving Certificate.
NSP	:	New Seed Policy.
OGL	:	Open General License.
OTC	:	Over-the-counter.
PBR	:	Plant Breeder Rights.
PERT	:	Programme Evaluation and Review Technique.
PI	:	Profitability Index.
PLC	:	Product life cycle.
R&D	:	Research and Development.
ROCE	:	Return on capital employed.
ROI	:	Return on investment.
ROSCAs	:	Rotating Saving and Credit Associations.
SHGs	:	Self Help Groups.
SPO	:	Seed Production Organizer.
SRR	:	Seed replacement rate.
SSCs	:	State Seed Corporations.
TNCs	:	Transactional Corporations.
TRIPR	:	Trade Related Intellectual Property Rights.
TVM	:	Time value of money.
UNIDO	:	United Nations Industrial Development Organization.
WTO	:	World Trade Organization.

1

Agribusiness

An Overview

Agribusiness is one of the areas that is attracting the attention of one and all particularly in the wake of W.T.O regime; several initiatives have been taken to tap the opportunities that have been thrown open. Different authors have defined it differently. It is a concept easy to understand but difficult to define. Literally speaking business means bushes. In simple words 'business means the state of being busy'. Broadly, business involves activities connected with the production of wealth. It is an organized and systematized human activity involving and purchase of goods and service with the object of selling them at a profit. Business concerns with buying and selling goods, manufacturing goods or providing services in order to earn profit.

The word agriculture indicates plowing a field, planting seed, harvesting a crop, milking cows, or feeding livestock. Until recently, this was a fairly accurate picture. But todays' agriculture is radically different. The food and fiber system is increasingly being referred to as 'agribusiness'.

Agribusiness is defined be Dr. E.P. Roy as the 'coordinating science of supplying agricultural production inputs and subsequently producing, processing and distributing food and fiber'. Same definition is given by Prof. Davis who coined the term. It is the management of those businesses that buy from or sell to farmers. Agribusiness includes all the firms and people involved in the off farm aspects of agriculture.

Agribusiness includes the entire farm input and output sectors. It is agricultural economics with a special emphasis on the business aspects of agriculture. Agribusiness includes all those business and management action ties performed by firms that provide inputs to the farm sector, produce farm products, and / or process, transport, finance, handle or market farm products. Our modern day definition of agribusiness involves a broader view that encompasses the total food production and distribution system.

THE BUSINESS OF AGRIBUSINESS

The food production system begins with many varied activities from the farm supply sector, which provides a myriad of production inputs and services to the farm, then continues through the marketing, processing and distribution activities necessary to satisfy consumer wants. As the agricultural production process becomes increasingly complex and specialized, the farm supply sector takes an important new dimensions. Also, as their incomes rise, consumers demand more services with respect to the bundle of food products they purchase. As these trends continue, the agribusiness sector becomes increasingly important because it has the responsibility of providing not only the right type and amount of purchased inputs to the farm sector, but also the correct mix of service to products as they move through the food system to the final consumer. Agriculture has evolved into agribusiness and has become a vast and complex system that reaches far beyond the farm to include all those who are involved in bringing food and fiber to consumers.

Agribusiness includes not only those that farm the land, but also the people and firms that provide the inputs [seed, chemicals, credit etc.], process the outputs [milk, grain, meat etc.], manufacture the food products [ice cream, bread, breakfast cereals etc.], and transport and sell the food products to consumers [restaurants, supermarkets].

Agriculture is now-a-days considered to include more than production. Farmers and ranchers rely on the input industries to provide the products and services they need to produce agricultural commodities. Agribusiness system has undergone a rapid transformation as new industries have evolved and traditional farming operations have grown larger and more specialized. The transformation did not happen overnight, but came slowly as a response to a variety of forces. Knowing something about how agribusiness came about makes it easier to understand how this system operates today and how it is likely to change in the future.

Initially agriculture being the major venture it was easy to become a farmer, but productivity was low. Average farmer produced enough food to feed just four people. As a consequence most farmers were nearly totally self-sufficient. They produced most of the inputs they needed for production, such as seed, draft animals, feed and simple farm equipment. Farm families processed the commodities they grew to make their own food and clothing. They consumed or used just about everything they produced. The small amount of output not consumed on the farm was sold for cash. These items were used to feed and clothe the minor portion of the country's population that lived in villages and cities. A few agricultural products made their way into the export market and were sold to buyers in other countries. Farmers found it increasingly profitable to concentrate on production and began to purchase inputs they formerly made themselves. This trend enabled others to build business that focused on meeting the need for inputs used in production agriculture such as seed, fencing, and machinery and so on. These farms involved into the industries that make up the 'agricultural inputs sector'. Input farms are major part of agribusiness and produce variety of technologically based products that account for approximately 75 per cent of all the inputs used in production of agriculture.

At the same time the agriculture input sector was evolving, a similar evaluation was taking place in a commodity processing and food manufacturing moved off the farm. The form of most commodities (wheat, rice, milk, livestock and so on) must be changed to make them more useful and convenient for consumers. For example, consumers would rather buy flour than grind the wheat themselves before backing a cake. They are willing to pay extra for the convenience of buying the processed commodity (flour) instead of the raw agriculture commodity (wheat). During the same period technological advance being made in food preservation method. Until this time the perishable nature of most agriculture commodities meant that they are available only at harvest. Advance in food processing have made it possible to get those commodities all throughout the year. Today even most farm families use purchased food and fiber products rather than doing the processing themselves. The farms that meet the consumers' demand for greater processing and convenience also constitute a major part of agribusiness and are referred to as the processing manufacturing sector. It is apparent that the definition of agriculture had to be expanded to include more than production. Farmers rely on the input industries to provide the products and service they need to produce agricultural commodities. They also rely on community processors, food manufacturers, and ultimately food distributors and retailers to purchase their raw agricultural commodities and to process and deliver them to the consumer for final scale. The food and fiber system is increasingly being referred to as agribusiness. *Davis and Goldberg* first introduced the term agribusiness in 1957. Agribusiness is made up of three sectors:

(i) The agricultural input marketing sector.

(ii) The agricultural production sector.

(iii) The processing, manufacturing sector.

To capture the full meaning of the term 'agribusiness' it is important to visualize these three sectors as interrelated parts of a system in which the success of each part depends heavily on the proper functioning of the other two. So, agribusiness includes all those business and management activities performed by firms that provide inputs to the farm sector, produce farm products, and/or process, transport, finance, handle, or market farm products.

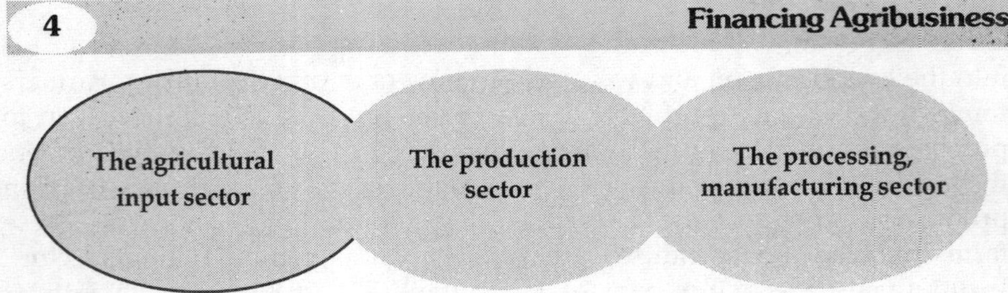

AGRICULTURAL INPUTS MARKETING SECTOR

Agricultural inputs can be categorized into two: *(i)* consumable and *(ii)* capital inputs. The former includes manure and fertilizers, seeds, insecticides/pesticides, diesel oil and electricity. On the other hand, capital input includes tractors, trailers, harvesters and threshers, pump sets, and other implements. Most of the agricultural input markets are at the level of grain market in town and large villages. There are some general aspect of the rural market like underdeveloped markets, illiterate buyers, lack of communication facilities, many languages, vast spread of market, storage, transport problems, seasonality and demand which are applicable to agricultural input markets as well (Gopalaswamy, 1997). However, agricultural input market differ from other product markets in many ways due to the nature of their products, the nature and location of users and the overall environment in which products are being brought and used. Some of the peculiarities of these markets are well discussed in this chapter.

Nature of Demand

From the point of marketing mix concept, the agricultural inputs are between the consumer and the industrial products. The farmers do not use them like consumer product, but are used as per their demand. In this sense, they are derived demand products. They are similar to consumer products, as far as distribution and promotion aspects are concerned as these two are targeted as the farmer level. But so far as product and its price are concerned, they are most likely industrial products as they are bulky, of high cost, and global based. The input is also demanded not individually but as package because one input decides the need for other inputs. This means their demand is complementary to each other. For example, a local and hybrid seeds determine whether to use a fertilizer or a pesticide, in the required quantity and quality. Further, since the product is meant for the production process, its sales are dependent on:

1. The weather in a season.
2. Cropping pattern changes.
3. Nature and health of the crop.
4. Other facilities like government price policy, subsidies, loans and physical facilities for the product.

The demand keeps changing from season to season, month to month and even week to week (Yadav, 1993).

The farmers and other rural buyers are now much open to spending, especially if it helps to raise their levels of income, as now they can see the perceptible change in the lives of those who invent money instead of keeping it as a dead stock. Gone of days of hard work alone, now it is well thought that farming will survive. Therefore the traditional saying in Hindi language that 'Dab ke wah te raj ke khah' (cultivate well and eat well) is later replaced with 'soch ke wah te soch ke khah' (think before cultivating as well as eating). The farmers are quite skeptical about adopting products which are non-traditional and costly. But if they are convinced with the demonstration in their fields, they feel much more comfortable with the products. Therefore, such demonstration have a great role to play in the dissemination of new product and technologies. In agricultural input markets, there are serious problems of imbalance usage due to under or over use of inputs especially chemical inputs, wide disparities in their use or over use across regions and high inefficiency in their usage. These altogether, spoil the economics of input usage and therefore, hurt the market for an input due to its bad image in the term of performance. Credit plays a crucial role in agricultural input markets as most of the time, the farmers are resort to credit purchases of the inputs and intend to repay after the harvest. Therefore, the availability and the cost of the credit for this purpose influences the quantity and the quality of inputs used. Various inputs like seeds, credit and equipments are provided through the rural development schemes of the government. This dampens the open markets as they are at lower rate Also this puts the private channels into difficulty as farmers start comparing the product and price with the government supplied ones.

Promotional Media

Though a lot has changed in the market for inputs, still there are relatively experienced users and influencers who prevail in these markets for various reasons. The opinion makers can be the progressive farmers in relatively less developed areas, the input sellers in all kind of rural product markets, and extension agents in more prosperous situations. Also, sometimes, even if these opinion makers do not have a sound logic to convince the farmers about a product, they use other modes like tying up the product to some other market transaction (Karunakaran, 1993). This is known as interlocking of markets. The retailers play an important role in pushing the products as they hold the faith of the farmers who themselves are not too familiar with the product and its usage. Therefore, the retailers become the ultimate sellers of the product. A good quality product may fail, if it does not get the support from retailers.

Kishan Melas and other rural fairs, which are increasingly becoming important means of marketing, give the farmers an opportunity to do comparative analysis of products and brands. They also bring together opinion makers in one place, who can be contacted and influenced with low cost. The farmers are always in a receptive mood to learn and try new products. The companies can get feedback on products, channels and promotional tools. New sales leads can be generated and new product ideas can be obtained from the farmers in terms of need and local innovations.

Nature of Competition

The Multi-National Companies (MNCs) are placing new demands before the farmers in terms of crop varieties and quality required, if the farmers want to work with them, and make more money out of farming. This is being driven through contract farming, joint ventures, leasing of land, and extension to the loosely contracted farmers in a given area. Also, in some crops, the MNCs are directly competing with the farmers, forcing them to bring agribusiness men who use modern and better inputs. The whole approach to farming is undergoing change with the globalization of rural production processes and privatisation of various systems. The farmers are compelled to think of farming as a business, which needs to compete on its own and still survive. This means that farmers have to be doubly careful in the selection and use of inputs required.

On the other hand, in the input marketing itself, the competition is increasing. New players and the existing ones are adopting new methods and modern equipments to tap the growing market. There is also competition from substitutes like bio-fertilizers and bio-pesticides in fertilizer and pesticide markets respectively. The companies are attempting product bundles and aligning inputs with other product lines like agro-product purchase and credit market. Therefore, competition is to be understood in a more strategic sense of buyers, suppliers, new entrants, substitutes and existing competition.

A FRAMEWORK FOR UNDERSTANDING THE MARKET FOR INPUTS

The experience of developing countries indicates that the growth of input markets is influenced by a large number of price as well as non-price factors. Studies in the wake of explaining the growth and fluctuations of fertilizer consumption in India, China and Sub-Saharan Africa, have indicated the relevance of a more comprehensive framework, which can be used for understanding the market environment for agricultural inputs in developing countries. Based on this, a framework has been developed for understanding the market environment for inputs. The major components are:

1. The Agronomic Potential.
2. The Agro-economic Potential.
3. The Effective Demand.
4. The Actual Consumption.

The market environment can be conceptualized as unfolding, through the developments within and inter-relationship between these components. This framework is depicted in Figure 1.1.

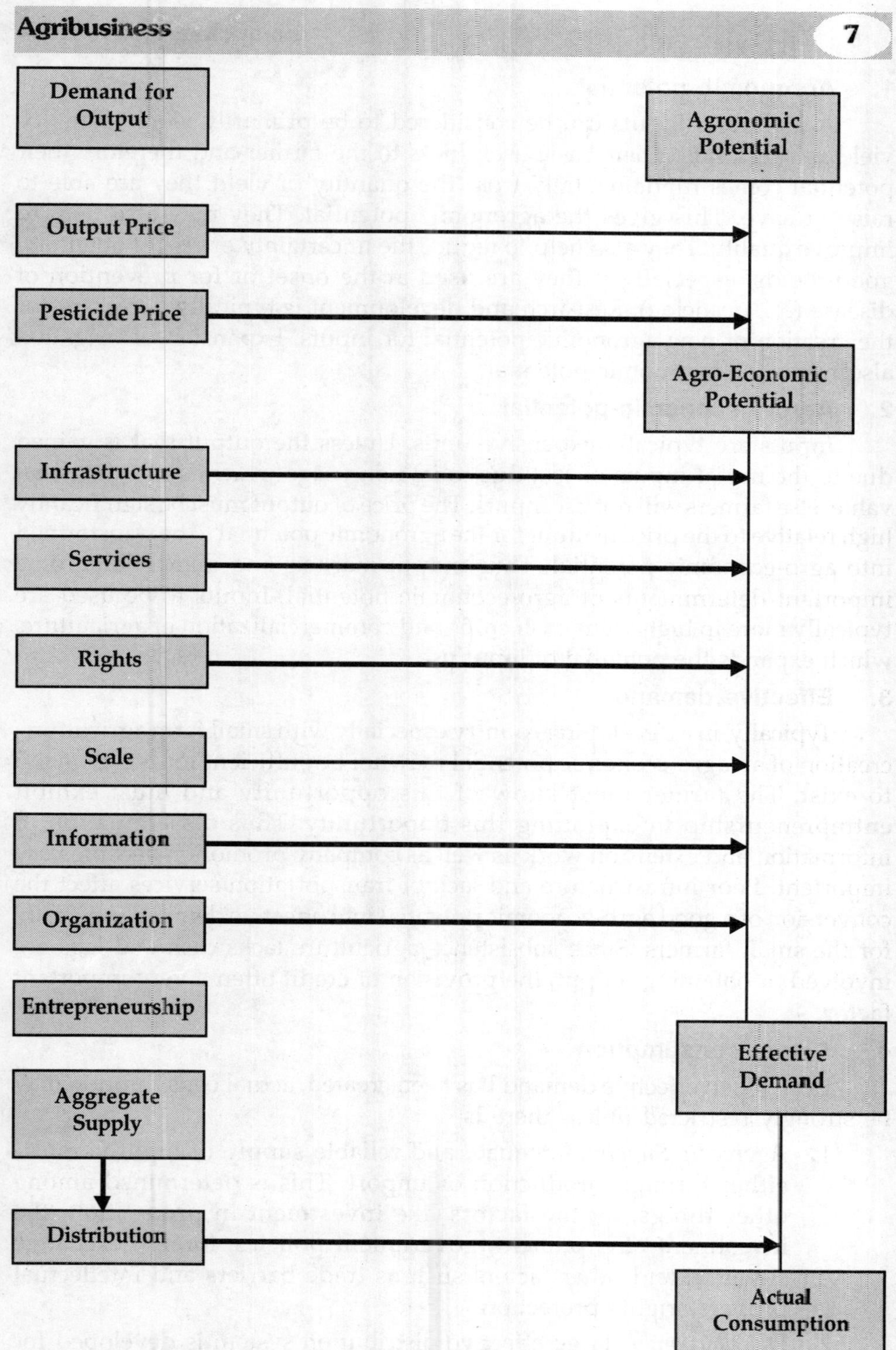

Fig.1.1: Framework for understanding the market environment of inputs

1. Agronomic potential

Agricultural inputs can be considered to be primarily yield saving or yield raising units. Their basic usefulness to the farmer and therefore their potential comes fundamentally from the quantity of yield they are able to raise or save. This gives the agronomic potential. They may also help to improve quality. They also help to reduce the uncertainty or risk of obtaining good yields, especially if they are used at the onset or for prevention of disease (*eg*., pesticide). Research and development is typically necessary for the creation of new agronomic potential for inputs. Expansion of irrigation also raises the agronomic potential.

2. Agro – economic potential

Inputs are typically expensive units. Unless the output that is gained due to the use of inputs or lost due to its non-usage which is of substantial value, else farmers will not use inputs. The price of output must be significantly high relative to the price of input for the agronomic potential to be transformed into agro-economic potential. Thus output markets and demands become important determinants of agro-economic potential. Inputs to be used are typically more in high value cash crops and commercialization of agriculture, which expands the potential of input use.

3. Effective demand

Typically, in a developing country especially with small farm agriculture, creation of an agro-economic potential may not be sufficient for real demand to exist. The farmer must know of this opportunity and must exhibit entrepreneurship in exploiting this opportunity. Thus dissemination of information and extension work as well as company promotion become very important. Poor infrastructure and lack of transportation services affect the conversion of a good agro-economic potential into effective demand especially for the small farmers. Since subsistence agriculture lacks cash and lags are involved in obtaining output, the provision of credit often a very important factor.

4. Actual consumption

Even when effective demand has been created, actual consumption may be strongly restricted unless there is:

1. *Aggregate Supply:* Adequate and reliable supply of input is must-either through production or import. This is determined among other things, by the factors like investment in production, the investment environment, government policies, foreign exchange situation and other factors such as trade barriers and intellectual property rights protection.
2. *Distribution:* A large effective distribution system is developed for catering to small farmers scattered over a large area. This is especially difficult in the early stages when the volumes are small.

Marketing of Seeds

As we all know the agricultural inputs marketing is a vast area and hence the following discussion is confined to only the marketing of seeds, which seems to be important among all the inputs and holds a prime position among those. The commercial seed sector in India grew considerably in the late 1980s and early 1990s both in the private as well as the public sectors. The private sector growth was induced by the policy changes undertaken during the late 1980s. Much of this growth has stemmed from either foreign investments, or from spin off previous companies, with technical and marketing personnel branching off to start their own seed enterprises. For example one seed company alone – Manycohas given birth to at least 8 additional companies. At present there are more than 150 seed firms in India and about 10,000 dealers and distributors of seeds across the country. Following are the major categories of the seed firms operating in India:

- *Seed Firms without R and D:* Private seed enterprises, which only multiply, certified seed of super varieties/hybrids developed by the public sector R and D system. These firms usually purchase their foundation seed suppliers from the government foundation seed agencies (*eg.*, National Seed Corporation and State Universities).
- *Seed Firms with R and D:* Private seed enterprises which have initiated plant breeding research to involve superior hybrids, through their own R and D programmes while still primarily engaged in the multiplication of seeds developed by the public sector. These units obtain their basic building material from public plant breeding stations, state agricultural universities, international agricultural research centres, private seed companies and state sponsored research stations in other countries. Many of these seed companies are already marketing hybrids breed by them. The parental lines of these are not disclosed, resulting in the enterprises monopoly over their sale.
- *Seed Firms with Foreign Collaborations:* Private seed enterprises that have created linkages with Transactional Corporations (TNCs) obtain production and marketing rights of their adaptable hybrids. They maintain parent materials produce and market hybrid seeds. Typically such enterprises also have R and D facilities and are relatively large.
- *Multi National Company Subsidiaries:* Subsidiaries of multinational seed chemical and food companies, which obtain building material from their parent companies, isolate adaptable lines, makes crosses and develop superior hybrids, without disclosing their pedigree.
- *Joint Sector Firms:* Government seed enterprises which primarily play the role of developing seed trade, maintain foundation of seed stocks for sale, and interstate marketing. They also engage in seed production, processing and marketing of HYV seeds. These include National Seed Corporation and various state seed agencies.

The public sector, which accounts for 35-40 per cent of total turnover of seed industry is mostly engaged in production and distribution of seeds of cereals, pulses and oilseed crops. The private sector on the other hand is mainly involved in the business of hybrid seeds of maize, jowar, bajra, cotton, and seeds of high value crops like fruits and vegetables. It accounts for about 60-65 per cent of total turnover of the seed industry. Within the private sector, there are MNCs and large domestic firms, small seed companies and product traders accounting for 50 per cent, 30 per cent and 20 per cent of total private seed business. There are state level associations of seed companies in each state besides one at the national level, to work with government certification agencies and for mutual interaction. Profitability being the important consideration for private sector firms, they provide only those types of seed for which there is effective demand and which are profitable to produce. This means varieties which need to be replaced by formers every season and are popular and with farmers; and also varieties with high multiplication rates and controlled breeding systems (*eg.*, hybrids). Thus, private seed companies deal with a limited number of varieties and seed is good in standard pack sizes and for targeted categories of farmers. These companies also keep changing their markets and products more often than the public sector. The private industry also plays a leading role in the development of planting material through biotechnology and tissue culture. But still only 25 per cent of the cropped area is under hybrid seeds.

Government Policy

There have been significant policy initiatives in the seed sector in the recent past, which entail significant implications for the industry as well as the market. Amendment of the industrial licensing policy in 1987, removed the restrictions that applied to private investment by foreign companies, monopoly houses and large domestic firms resulting in their participation in the Indian seed market.

Liberalization of the seed laws through the New Seed Policy (NSP) 1988, initiated major change in the imports and exports of seeds. The import of vegetable, flower, and fruit seeds has been put under the open general license (OGL). Imports of seeds of wheat and rice, however are not allowed under the New Seed Policy. The import of seeds of oilseeds, pulses and coarse cereals are allowed initially for two years by companies, which have collaborative agreements provided that the foreign supplier agreed to supply the parent lines/nuclear or breeder seeds/seed technology to its Indian clients.

Other incentives for the development and production of new seed varieties, include a huge cut in the import duty on seed equipment used for seed production from 100 per cent to 15 per cent, income tax rebate on R and D expenditure and availability of easier and cheaper financing sources for the organizations involved in the seed research and production. The above policy initiatives has resulted in a boom in the activity of the private sector in the seed industry.

Trade Related Intellectual Property Rights (TRIPR) and Plant Breeder Rights (PBR) are the other major changes in the seed policy and laws. Consequent to this, it is expected that the developer of new varieties and seeds will have greater rights on the process and product developed and will have greater control over the subsequent use of developments. The major and main impact of this will be that, with the increased protection offered to those who develop new seeds, there will be greater incentive for firms to invest in R and D. They will also actively try to develop new seeds either independently or in collaboration with Research Institutions and Agricultural Universities.

Plans of the Government to bring about the ceiling Act to allow firms to hold larger amounts of land for agriculture purposes will also have a bearing on the industry, then as the firms have a larger amount of land dedicated to the multiplication and production of seeds.

With the changes introduced related to IPR and the import restrictions, the farmers are likely to have increased choice and access to high quality seeds of different variety. This will most probably result in an increase in the farm production. Since firms now have greater control over the marketing of the varieties, which are developed by them, the prices of these seeds are likely to rise and the farmer might view this unfavourably. However, if the increase in seed prices is matched by an increase in output or the ultimate returns that the farmer obtains, this is not a cause for worry.

Due to New Economic Policy on opening up and liberalization, and the New Seed Policy along with the Intellectual Property Rights (IPR) related policies, the general public apprehension is that the Indian seed industry will be overrun by imported seeds and dominated by Transactional Corporations with very little chance for domestic firms survive. But this fear does not stand a sound logic, as seeds will be imported only if they result in higher yields and improve the quality of the crop, or are less expensive than the local seed. Further, the imported seeds need to be suited to the various agro-climatic zones of the country, which are quite different from those of the countries from where are quite different from those of the countries from where these seeds are likely to be imported. Taste of the consumers of the agricultural output also acts as a barrier to import the seed. Therefore, even MNCs must be able to adapt and modify their seeds to the local conditions and environment for which they will need to have domestic R and D set-up. To be able to compete with the local industry. Cost will be difficult for the MNCs, if they do not have developed bases in the country. Local companies will be competitive as long as they devote some energy to R and D.

On the seed production front, the Government of India has given approval to the implementation of a pilot scheme on seed crop insurance during 1999-2000. This scheme aims at covering the risk involved in seed production so as to increase the area under breeder, foundation, and certified seed in the country. The seed growers are not coming forward to take up seed production due to the risks involved in various stages of seed production from selection of fields to harvesting, transporting, grading, treating and packing. The seed crops of Tur, Bajra, Cotton, Gram Groundnut, Jowar, Maize, Paddy, Soyabean, Sunflower and Wheat are eligible under the project. The scheme covers all the seed producing entities under government or private control which are involved in the production of notified varieties. This scheme covers of seed crop failure due natural fire, storms, cyclones, landsides, drought, dry spell, excessive rain and large-scale incidence of pests and diseases. The compensation would be 40 per cent of the sum insured, if the crop fails within 11/12 months of sowing and 80 per cent if after that period and till harvest. The minimum area of crop failure should be 0.5 acres. The sum insured would be equivalent to the past 3-5 years average seed yield in the unit area multiplied by the sale price of the seed. The scheme will be implemented by the General Insurance Corporation. This policy if works on sustainable basis is likely to give a major boost to contractual and independent seed production by growers.

Seed Marketing

Marketing of seed is the most important as well as challenging aspect of seed industry, because of the nature of the product. Seed being a living organism, its quality deteriorating faster. Thus its shelf life is limited, it must be marketed in season. Another peculiar feature of seeds is that it requires two to three years lead time to meet the specific requirements *i.e.*, to meet the demand for a particular seed, its production has to be organized at least two years in advance. The changes in the weather, price of the crop, and price of the competing crop may change the prospects of the demand for seed of a particular crop variety at the commencement of sowing season. In times of increase in demand of seed, its supply cannot be increased immediately, whereas a fall in demand would result in carryover of stocks. In fact seed marketing requires working within a whole chain of seed businesses. It includes not only seed production and processing subs-sectors, but also many other agencies like research, quality control and other input services as in any other agricultural chain.

While looking into the marketing aspect of seeds, the following dimension needs careful analysis:

- Product.
- Pricing.
- Distribution.
- Promotion.

Product

Seed is perishable product by nature. Its demand is seasonal and derived. There are also wide fluctuations in its demand, as its demand is the function of various factors like prices of crop under consideration, prices of other crops, climate and replacement rate, and the information about the market. Also it is not possible to create an exclusive distribution network at the retail level, as it is small time and highly seasonal product. This nature of the product results in much specifically at the various stages of the marketing process like production of seeds, procurement, its distribution, seed pricing, and promotion of the product.

Arrangement of Certified Seed Products

Production of quality seeds is carried out in a decentralized manner on individual farms. The certified/truthfully labeled seeds are produced by the contract growers. Here two alternative approaches are in vogue. *Firstly*, growers are selected from a number of villages scattered over a large area, which is the case with many small seed companies and seed corporations. *Secondly*, a few villages are selected for intensive coverage of farmers as is the case with Advent India Ltd. (formerly ITC zoneca) the contract growers, either produce seeds for the enterprise or lease out land to the enterprise. Multinationals like 'Uniliver' and 'Cargill' source certified seeds from India through a network of seed production organizers who pass on the inputs by the company to the contract growers, collect the seeds, conduct tests and give to the multinationals. This is quite common in Andra Pradesh state in cotton, sunflower and jowar seed sectors.

Normally seed enterprises enter into a contract with the growers for production and supply of quality seed of some specified villages. The growers bear all costs including cost of parent/foundation seed, costs of cultivation, quality-monitoring costs, transporting seed to the factory, and wastage losses at the farm, in transit, grading and packaging. They also bear all risks like low germination, reduced yield, poor quality and rejections. They are paid at a pre-agreed price only after the quality of seed is tested and for quantity that passes through those tests. Normally, it takes about 60 days to get the payment.

If the germination of parent seed foundation seed goes down to 70 per cent or lower, the growers are advised to 'plough down' because it will not be economical to pursue the production till end. Plough down can be ordered at subsequent stages in case of severe pests attack or if cross-pollination is not effective. In such cases, the company certainly losses some quantity of quality seeds, but the growers' loss is more in terms of not only costs incurred, but also loss of income from the area. There is no provision of compensation against 'plough down' of the crop. The companies however take the risk of planning 10-20 per cent more areas. Sometimes also give incentive for better germination rate and better quality of seed production. The default rates of contract growers have been low as they are assured market place of grain at least and yields are better than grain crops. There are various ways of obtaining the land facility for contract production of seeds:

(a) *Lease System:* In this system the seed company undertakes the risk of seed production. The land is taken on lease and the company supplies all inputs. The output from the leased land is processed and also packed at the companies' cost. Proagro company is following this system for certified seed production. When a company introduces certain new varieties, the grower may not be willing to undertake the certified seed production as the new varieties are not tested. In those cases, the companies tend to undertake certified seed production through the lease system.

(b) *Collaboration:* This is one more way of ensuring the procurement of certified labeled seeds. Under this arrangement, the seed growers produce certified seeds. Raasi seed is done in a custom processing plant which is near to the production area. The packaged seed is marketed by JK Agrigenetics under its brand name.

(c) *Seed Grower:* Under this agreement, a seed company directly enters into an agreement with the seed grower for procuring the raw seed. National Seed Corporation follows this system. No financial assistance is given to the grower by the Corporation, for his production expenses under this system. This system is also used by the small companies like Ankara and Navbharat and state seed corporations (SSCs) for procuring the seed. Most of the farmers put small acreage under contract, which is ever as lower as 0.25 acres in cotton in the case of small companies as it is labour-intensive production.

(d) *Seed Production Organizer (SPO):* This arrangement is preferred by most of the private seed companies. Most of the companies appoint commission agents called seed production organizers to identify the growers and secure their area commitment for seed production of variety hybrid during the season. They also guide the growers in the proper use of input and sometimes extend credit for seed crop. The minimum commission to be paid to the organizers is decided at the annual meeting conducted between the representatives of the Seed men Association (a body of representatives of various seed companies) and the organizers. The services, financial and non financial, provided by the company to the grower, vary from one company to other and from time to time. The seed production organizers, who undertakes seed production in an area of more than 500 acres, generally employs a sub-organizers under them, so as to facilitate better monitoring and implementation of the programme.

TRADE PRACTICES IN SEED PRODUCTION

There are different trade practices in the seed industry practiced by the different players involved such as the growers, the seed production organizers, and the seed companies. The trade practices are slightly different from one company to the other company and also from one region to the other. These practices are highly depend on the production arrangements followed by the company.

- *Supply of Foundation Seed*: Foundation seed required for the production of certified seeds identity generally supplied to the growers by the seed companies through the seed production organizers or directly under the contracts and contract ground are registered with the seed certification agency as sub-growers. The cost of foundation seed in the case of private companies is deducted while disbursing the payment for the raw seed. However in the case of National Seeds Corporation or State Seeds Corporation foundation seed is supplied on cash and carry basis. Any subsidy given by the government is passed on to the growers.
- *Operational Expenses:* Generally, the grower arranges at his expense all the operations required such as land preparation, sowing, irrigation, intercultural, manuring, plant protection, roughing, detasseling (in case of maize) removing pollen shedders (sorghum and bajra), harvesting, shelling/threshing and any other farm operation connected with the raising of the seed production practices prescribed by the company from time to time. The National and State Seed Corporations, do not supply fertilizers or pesticides to the growers. However some private companies supply pesticides and fertilizers or pesticides to the farmers on credit. This amount and the interest are recovered from the growers at the time of making payment for the raw seed. However, under the lease system of production, as in the case of Proagro Seeds, the entire expenses of production are borne by the company.
- *Financial Inputs:* With a view to meet the bonafide requirements of the grower for inputs and other expenses for seed production, national growers in securing the necessary credit from the co-operative/ commercial banks, nominated by the corporation against terms and conditions laid down by the lending banks. The private seed companies lend money to the growers only when the crop requires very high investment as in the case of cotton seed production. An interest rate of 10-15 per cent is charged on the loan given and the amount is deducted from the payment for raw seeds.
- *Technical Inputs:* The seed production organizer generally gives technical guidance to the seed growers at his own cost. The organizer arranges for required number of technical staff to conduct periodic field inspections at various stages of growth of seed crop. It is the duty of the organizer to ensure completion of the required number of technical staff to conduct periodic field inspections at various stages of growth of seed crop. It is the duty of the organizer to ensure completion of the required number of field inspections by the seed certification staff at

proper growth stages. The organizer arranges for the completion of all formalities and conditions and other work for getting the seed certified, supplies the requisite number of sample bags, slips for packing, packing seals, marking inks etc., at the time of ginning and the cost, there after, is borne by the organizer. The organizer bears the expenses pertaining to the costs of tags, field test charges and all other incidental expenses to be incurred for the purpose of getting seed certified by the State Seed Certification Agency.

- *Transport:* Generally, it is the grower who arranges to transport the raw seed at his own cost, in the gunny bags provided by the company or the seed production organizer after harvest of the crop to the processing plant of the company. However, in some cases, the company provides transportation cost to the grower.
- *Processing Facilities:* The organizer fixes up the processing facilities for seed like the ginning centre (s) having adequate facilities to complete the ginning operations within the given time schedule, specified by the company and agreed by the State Seed Certification Agency. The organizer informs the company about the details of the mechanized processing facilities along with the intake capacity and storage space prior to the processing season. In the case of small companies, growers are giving grinning schedule and they bring the seeds to the ginning factories, which was hired by small companies on job work basis.
- *Packing Material:* The organizer supplies the certified seeds in the standard pack sizes. The company supplies printed cloth bags and truthful labels for the packing of the certified seed at cost. However for transporting the raw seed from the grower's field to the processing plant, gunny bags are supplied by the organizer and the company.
- *Quality Standards:* The seed lots are tested for germination, genetic purity, physical purity, disease incidence and moisture and inert material content etc., at the company's quality control laboratory or at the government seed-testing laboratory. Those lots indicating variation over and above the limits prescribed are subjected to retesting.
- *Conditions for Rejection:* The organizer has to supply only fresh certified seed, certified by the certification agency as per the specifications of the Seed Act 1966. If the seed is rejected at the quality test, the loss is borne mainly by the grower. The seed has to be supplied from the fresh stock and not from the revalidated stock. If the seed is found rain damaged or the container is found to be damaged or torn and unsealed during the transit, the organizer is not entitled for the pavement for such rejected damaged seeds. The rejected seeds can be used for food/ feed or for sale to other agenda for other edible/non-edible purposes.
- *Processing Expenses:* The expenses of processing are borne either by the organizer or by the grower. There is no standard trade practice on this

account. If the organizer bears the processing expenses, then he gets a high commission from the company. In the case of large and medium seed companies, the processing operations is undertaken under the close supervision of the company's representatives.

- *Procurement Price:* The minimum procurement price for the seed crop in most of the stated is decided by the representatives of the Seeds men Association, seed production organizers and the growers. However this rate varies and is dependent on the demand and supply factors to a larger extent and each company may have its own rate. But generally the seed price is higher than the price of the crop output produce in the market.
- *Procurement and the Payments:* The contract growers are to supply the entire product of seeds to the company under a contract at the agreed place and time. Though this is a clause in the contract for penalty for the default, it is rarely implemented due to the practical difficulties. The state soldier and companies pay about 80 per cent of the payments at the time of seed procurement and the remaining 20 per cent seed passes the final quality test.

Seed pricing

The uncertainty in demand for seed and making its price estimate is a complicated exercise. Seeds grown by contract growers for seed corporations and the private sector which meet specified standards attract a premium price over and above the commercial gain price, for the crop which varies between 25 per cent for self pollinated crops like cereals to over 100 per cent for hybrid crops. In the public sector, the NSC is usually retail price setter. There is a Government intervention in pricing of the seed produced by the public sector corporations with the degree of intervention varying from state to state. In some crops like sunflower, retail prices which the farmer pays are double or three times that of the price at which seed company procures from exact growers. The pricing strategies of the private sector are also influenced by the pricing structure followed by the public sector. The final marketing price of the certified seed is the result of number of components as follows:

Input Costs

(a) Same seed price.

(b) Price paid to the seed growers for the raw seed.

(c) Storage processing and costs.

(d) Transportation, distribution, and marketing costs.

Supply and Demand

The total supply available and the total demand generated by the dealers owning to the acreage and credit availability also influence seed price. In case of short supply, the seeds could be sold at a higher price, whereas in case of excess production, the prices have to be realistic and the profits will be reduced. The Indian Seed Industry has not been able to keep pace with the demand over seeds in most crops for several years. It is witnessing the entry of several companies both Indian and foreign. With the introduction of the newer varieties and the increased prospects for exports, the demand for seeds is growing significantly. Supply too is growing, but not at the same pace as there is a lag between the development and introduction of new seeds.

Prices of other farm products and time trend

Time trend and prices of other farm products should be taken into consideration while fixing the price. In case of high price situation, the consumption of seed as a food grain would be reduced. The supply should keep in pace with the demand in terms of quantity, quality, price, place and time.

Some of the seed companies especially MNCs also go for non-price competition wherein they emphasize quality and consumer confidence as their selling points instead of competitive pricing. The higher price is justified in terms of higher yield, farmer confidence and after sales backup.

Distribution system

The private seed companies as well as public sector corporations, market seed through a network of distributors and dealers. At present, public sector markets its product through the following distribution channels.

1. Dealers in private sector.
2. Dealers in co-operative sector.
3. Sale points and depots.
4. Departmental sales.

The major sales of public sector come from the private dealers followed by dealers in co-operative sector and departmental sales respectively. The distributors are appointed for district, which in turn appoint dealers within the district. These distributors and dealers handle other agricultural inputs like fertilizers, pesticides and agricultural machinery. A distributor/stockiest is generally appointed for a region that may consist of one or more states. However, in some areas, the company reserves the right to appoint more than one distributor, depending upon the potential of the state. The dealers are appointed at the district level. There may be more than one dealer depending upon the potential of the district and marketing strategy of the seed agency. Generally, they are appointed on non-exclusive basis, which means the dealers, can deal in products of other companies or even in other commodities. The different channels used for the distribution of seeds are as follows:

- Public/Private – Distributors – Dealers – Retailers – Farmer.
- Public/Private – Co-operative Marketing Federation – Affiliate Primary Societies – Member Farmer.

- Public/private – Agro. Ind. Corp – Block Level Offices – Farmers.
- Agricultural Universities – Farmers.
- Research Institutions – Agricultural Universities – Farmers.

All the above mentioned distribution channels are used for selling all kinds of seeds including food grains, oilseeds, spices, vegetables and fodder crops. Departmental sales include sales of the Department of Agriculture under various heads namely, mini-kits, field demonstration, DPAP and other drives being made for popularizing the modern agricultural practices.

Seed demand is usually seasonal and for a particular seed, it lasts only for 3 to 4 weeks in a season. Hence, the seed forms only a part of the overall business of the dealer in all the agricultural inputs. The retailers combine seed business not only with other agricultural inputs but also with other commodities as well. The distributors, dealers and retailers are paid commission by the companies on sale. Normally 15 to 25 per cent commission is given to distributors who pass 12 to 22 per cent to the dealers while the retailers get 9 to 19 per cent discount on sales. In some cases, the companies directly deal with dealers, who are paid at par with the distributors. The distributor/dealer has to place the order well in advance for the company to get an estimate demand for the seeds from a particular region. The company insists on advance payment at the time of placing an order or full payment at the time of delivery of stocks. However, depending upon the track record of the distributor/dealer, credit is allowed for a maximum of 30 days.

Management of seed distribution

Demand for seeds fluctuates from year to year, even within a season depending on the onset of monsoon and the spread of rainfall during the sowing period. Excess production or scarcity of seeds, is most common in this industry. Further, in the case of seeds, both supply and demand are affected by natural-by-natural factors as a result of which the enterprise has to contend with either excessive stocks or excessive demand. Excessive stocks have to be revalidated in subsequent seasons. This may, however, involve a high rate of rejection due to deterioration in quality. Such losses cannot be borne by the distribution channel. Since in the case of some seeds, shelf life is as short as one season, the cost of excess quantities may have to be borne by the enterprise, In times of scarcity, the temptation to pass the burden onto the consumers would be strong. Effective strategies should be developed keeping in mind, the long-term relationships between the seed enterprise and its consumers.

Seed marketing at the micro level involves, the matching of the farmers needs with timely seed supply. Therefore, adequate supply has to be ensured much ahead of the season. In other words, storage at distribution points that are close to the distributors/dealers has to be ensured. This involves development of sound management information system.

Information on aspects such as:

(i) Availability of seeds for any season.

(ii) Projections of area to be covered by seed verities.

(iii) Expected output prices.

(iv) Behaviour of rainfall.

(v) Adequacy of support system including financing.

(vi) Stocking at different levels.

(vii) Offline information on a weekly basis during the sowing season etc., is critical.

The selection of distribution channel for seeds is not an easy task. Since seeds have a time specified demand, an exclusive channel for seeds is not feasible; seeds have to be sold with other farm outputs, like fertilizers and pesticides. Quick reallocation of stocks may be difficult, if there is an information lag. Effective and continuous communication between the enterprise, the distribution network and farmers is of great significance in this process (Singh and Seetharaman, 1990).

In the event of shortages, dealers begin to charge a very high premium on certain special varieties of seeds, whereas in the event of lower demand, prices are reduced. Decisions pertaining to price are taken in the local market. Seeds are generally sold through a two-tier system, involving the distributor and the dealer. The terms of distribution vary from market to market. All dealings are conducted either, in cash or non secured credit basis. Credit to a dealer is normally extended at the personal risk of the distributor. Dealers sell the seeds to the farmers on cash basis.

The biggest problem in the seed industry is to maintain uniform prices. Seed companies exercise no flexibility over price, as they operate on very small profit margins due to high competition. The distribution channel constantly expects the firm to make available to them, new varieties of seeds and this has become the most important factor in their relationship with the firm. The channel undertakes very limited responsibility for unused and expired date seeds. In the coming years, when the seed market becomes more competitive, the role of distribution channel is going to become more crucial.

Proper storage of seeds

Seeds are the perishable commodity that can bet easily damaged, if the seed handling is not satisfactory at any stage in the overall marketing strategy. Seed marketing being seasonal, will lead to heavy losses, if the unsold stocks are carried over for too long time. The transportation of seeds from production areas to end-users is an immense task and takes considerable time. Successful seed marketing depends on the timely availability of the seeds to the dealers and the users. Transportation of seeds becomes difficult particularly during the rainy season. Therefore, the existence of buffer godowns with proper storage conditions is a must in the end-use areas. The advantages of buffer godown are as follows:

(a) Seeds can be transported during favourable weather conditions, which minimize the risk of seed damages during transit.

(b) Assured timely supply to the dealers.

(c) Seed quality can be tested again after the seed has reached these godowns thus, detecting possible causes of damage during transit. The climate of the location should be dry and cool, since seed storages are better in such areas.

Promotion

The demand for hybrid seeds is largely dormant and has to be awakened and stimulated. Creative use of promotional tools that reach the cultivators is an important way to accomplish this goal. Since the market for hybrid seeds is still small, companies especially MNCs focus on market expansion for hybrids as a generic market promotion strategy, rather than pushing their own particular hybrid brand. For example, Argill orgnises a series of field days and demonstration plots. The company has a team of field assistants who visit farmers and do 'cold selling'. The company also does farmer advocate, wherein, the farmers themselves advocate company's seeds to other farmers who are invited to the field showing uncommonly high yields of branded seeds. It chooses a few exemplary fields at the end of the growing season from its customers' fields and invites hundreds of farmers to these fields, who are not its customers. On the other hand, ITC Zeneca (Advantage India) chooses a few farmers before the growing season and gives the company seeds to plant alongside local varieties. At harvest time, hundreds of farmers are invited to a field day, where the grower narrates his experience of growing the seed to other farmers.

Cargill also has intensive customer contact programme, where Cargill staff sit with a group of farmers under a tree with a flip chart to talk to them. It is also has a farmers' handbook which is published every fortnight in local newspapers during the growing season. This offers farmers practical advice on maximizing the yields they obtain with the hybrid seeds. Some companies like ITC Zeneca also organized inter-village competitions for the best crop where in the victory of one village is attributed to the company seeds.

Promotional media

Seeds form a critical input to ensure higher yield of the crops. Therefore, the farmers involvement is very high at the time of the purchase of the seeds. Here, the advertisements should influence the behaviour of the farmers by encouraging trial, leading to loyalty for the product, and further leading to learn about it. Here, the Dissonance-Attribution hierarchy is used and the advertising objectives to encourage purchase, build conviction and to stimulate awareness.

In seeds, the promotion activities include free samples of the seeds being distributed to the farmers. This is being practiced by both MNCs as well as by local seed companies. This induces trial. Here, the 'seeing as well as doing is believing' attitude is being addressed.

Video shows, exhibition, krishi mela, mobile vans, and wall trolley painting are the most commonly used promotional tools by the seed marketing firms; which give identity and help the farmers in knowing that a particular seed is available. The advertisements in the various media is used to inform, remind and persuade and further positively influence the purchase behaviour of the farmers. With the increasing awareness among the farming community through the habit of watching T.V., many of the firms have resorted to advertise in the electronic media. In a typical village, farmers gather in the house of the T.V., owner and watch the programmes.

Radio is still a major force for farm advertisement in the rural areas due to its easy affordability and convenient size availability. This spot has been highly sought after by the fertilizer companies. Advertising in the radio is highly sought after by the fertilizer companies. Advertising in the radio is a cost-effective way of reaching the farmers. Mass contact through the Field Staff augments the sale to a larger extent. Currently, most of the promotional activities in both the public and the private sector are focusing on television and radio.

Newspaper advertisements can briefly give the advantages of good seeds, price, location of the dealer and variety name. Cinema slides can be developed for local conditions and should emphasize local dealers and seasonal crops. Hoardings are effective for year round publicity and should be placed in important locations like bazaars, bus stands etc. The organization of 'Kisan Melas' by various agricultural universities is effective in reaching the target population in an effective manner. A well-orgnised demonstration would always encourage the farmers to adopt scientific agricultural practices and good quality seeds. This can be done in co-ordination with the available extension agencies.

At the retail point level, the effectiveness of glow signboard, danglers, calendars and stickers can also be explored. Further, dealer incentives in terms of rebates for advance orders and higher sales can be attempted. The advertisements highlight the farmers about the seeds and mainly emphasize on the quality of the output. In the point of purchase material, the handouts/ flyers and the posters show colourful and appealing photographs of the crops. This attacks the effective component of attitude of the farmer.

The handouts give further information about the different varieties available for the same vegetable. More information is available about the resistance of the crop to the various diseases and the exact cropping season. The maturity period and the quality of the output are emphasized in the handouts. There are companies, like Namdhari Seeds, which go on give further information about the agricultural practices, like irrigation requirements and fertilizer requirements etc.

In posters, there is generally no information regarding the agricultural practices that can be followed for better yields. However, the stress is on the freshness and the high quality of the crops. The message execution format used for the posters is 'slice of life' that depicts young girls enjoying fresh fruits in the farms. Testimonial evidence is used as the message execution format, since the ordinary farmer is used to communicate the product benefits to other fellow farmers.

Post-sales service

More emphasis should be placed on educating the farmers and how they can purchase certified seeds and protect themselves from spurious seeds. In addition to this, technical help also should be provided to the farmers and follow up of the complaints about seed quality etc., should be done.

A rather different approach is needed for the marketing of the hybrid seeds, in case of which the farmer needs new seeds each season. The dealers should make market survey periodically, to determine the market potential at least one season in advance.

Farmer Behaviour

It is very essential to understand the buyer behaviour and user behaviour in the product line as it is characterized by many external influences and information asymmetries. The following are some of the major aspects of farmer behaviour in purchase and use of seeds.

1. *Low Replacement Rate:* Seed Replacement Rate (SRR) is very important for a seed firm, because more time the farmer goes for replacement of the seed that he uses, the more will be the demand for that firm's seed. Seed Replacement Rate for certified seeds of a given crop is defined as the ratio of the mount of cultivated land under the certified seeds with respect to the total cultivated area under the crop. This is generally taken as a measure of use for improved seed practices of the farmers. Quality seed is the key input for realizing the productive potential of a crop. As quality practically deteriorates for subsequent generation, the old seed must be replaced with fresh lots of quality seeds. Ideally, the seeds for hybrid should be replaced every year, while for cross-pollinated crops, the seed should be replaced every three years. For self-pollinated crops or non-hybrids, the seed should be replaced every four years. However, the reality is that the seed replacement rate by the farmers is much lower because farmers prefer to use the seed from their own production or from the exchanged seed from the fellow farmers. The reasons for low SRR could be any one or more of the following:

- In some crops, the smaller farmers prefer to use the seeds of their own crop due to various reasons including high price, taste preferences, and non-availability of credit. In crops like cotton, which require to undergo further processing like delimiting for obtaining seeds after the harvesting farmers sell their crops, rather than delimiting on their own, and hence, purchase new seeds every year.
- Sometimes, farmers are not aware of the recommended replacement schedule of the different seeds. As a result they do not go for seed replacement.
- Quality seeds are not easily available at the time when farmers need them.
- The farmers do not attribute the fall in crop yield to the delayed seed replacement.
- The increased use of other inputs or better management practices compensate for the fall in yield due to the low SRR.
- Poor extension.
- Non-availability of credit.

There is an attitude among farmers that the seed alone will do the job of improving productivity. This leads to ignoring the complementary inputs use and therefore, a credibility loss for the seed when good yields are not achieved.

In general, farmers will not go beyond a distance of 30 km to buy the seeds. Hence, the distance becomes a crucial factor in the adoption of quality seeds a choice of variety. Inappropriate timing of sowing of seeds also affects the yield or performance of the seed. Thus, farmers end up believing that new seeds are not really worth all that search and cost.

Credibility of source of seed is important, as the seeds are bought from places or from those outlets with which farmers are familiar or which is generally popular with the people at large. The seeds are purchased largely on cash basis, especially HYVs and only a few days before actual use. Major channels still are fellow farmers and private traders. The reasons for preferring them are quality assurance, timely availability and easy access. The co-operatives are approached only because they provide credit. The promotional media used for making a purchase decision are demonstration, video shows, kisan melas, and dealer advice.

2. *Forecasting:* Demand forecast is absolutely essential in order to estimate the production requirements. This is extremely difficult because of the nature of product. Hence either there is a situation of glut or of short supply. Seed companies do not make some estimates of requirement for the seeds, by considering the relevant information on the individual crops like areas in the previous year, area targeted for the ensuing year, and the expected yield and price of the produce. This exercise is done for each crop at district level. Though this helps in organizing production,

often it goes awry with expected changes in variable like weather in the sowing season. As a result, there is an excessive supply to some centres where demand has fallen in the commencement of the season. On the other hand, supply may be short in some areas, where the demand has increased just before sowing due to some favorable condition.

Forecasting demand and production of seeds are important inputs to production planning. Accurate forecast at an appropriate time involving expenditures does help in avoiding over or under production and maximizing net returns. Normally, the gains from a good forecast are much more than the costs. Short term demand forecasting is useful in efficient management of inventory and distribution of seeds across the areas. It also helps in arranging logistics, working capital and decisions on the payment of comprehension an payment of seeds.

Short-term forecasts are generated primarily through discussions on the basis of feedback obtained from sales force and the distribution channels. The marketing personnel based on the previous years' sales and current crop prospects determine the likely demand for a particular crop. The likely share of the variety in the total demand is estimated later. The resources of each division are assessed for carrying out the production and estimates are revised accordingly. Similarly, information would be generated at various stages of implementation of the production programme for monitoring quality and quantity of seeds.

On the other hand, medium term forecasting helps in arranging parent seeds, foundation seeds, finance for expansion and training of work force, and long-term forecasting in an input in the corporate planning.

The supply of seeds should keep pace with demand in terms of quantity, quality, price, place and time. The factors affecting demand are:

(a) Total cultivated acreage.

(b) Seed rate.

(c) Extension efforts on the introduction of improved techniques.

(d) Current acreage under HYV and seeds sold in the previous year.

(e) Cultivator preference for varieties, package size, quality, and price.

(f) Climate of the area and rainfall.

(g) Crop failure and re-sowing.

(h) Substitution between crops and varieties of seeds.

(i) Irrigation Facilities.

Problems Faced by the Seed Industry

(a)* *Distribution Problems: *(i) Short shelf life of the seeds:* Normally, certified seeds are valid for one season only and they have to be revalidated for use in the next season. The retailers are not equipped to store the seeds for one whole year. *(ii) Unpredictability of the demand:* It is very difficult for the dealers to exactly predict the demand of certified seeds owning to the unpredictability of Nature, changes in the commodity prices and other reasons.

(b) ***Lack of Effective Monitoring Mechanism:*** There is no effective monitoring mechanism for controlling the quality of seeds at the selling points. The dealers even sell those seeds whose samples have failed in the laboratory tests by SSCs. The producing and marketing agencies of seed do not have any control on their production once the product is sold. This is mainly because the monitoring of selling of seeds is neither possible nor economical.

(c) ***Lack of Infrastructure:*** Availability of seeds in time still remains a problem for the farmers. The problem is compounded by poor infrastructure in distant villages, the lack of purchasing power at the time of sowing and the uncertainty of rainfall, on which the sowing is largely dependent.

(d) ***Poor Extension Services:*** The various extension services offered by the Agriculture department leave much to be desired in terms of effectiveness of the programmes offered by them, for popularizing the modern agriculture practices, which includes improved seeds practices. Agricultural supervisors generally are seen active only for showing their targets that are fulfilled, by distributing the minikits and conducting field demonstrations rather than emphasizing on the result oriented approach.

Strategy for a Seed Enterprise

- *Product Differentiation and Brand Image:* A firm, which has to establish itself in the seed market, needs to differentiate its product either in terms of better yield or in terms of providing accessory benefits like pest resistance. Though product differentiation is very difficult in seed industry, some private companies have been innovative and proactive like Mahyco. They developed a variety of pearl millet which is not only high yielding, but it is also resistant to the disease which no other company has been able to offer. Since seeds are prone to fast deterioration, it becomes essential to ensure seeds in the first season itself. The firm should try to minimize the carryover stocks and maximize the sales. Seed is a product where there is hardly any product differentiation possible. Therefore, promoting company's brand name becomes important rather than promoting the product. So, brand image of the company should be the focus in sales management.
- *Monitoring:* To adjust the imbalances in the demand and supply during the season, the firm should continuously monitor variables like weather till the sowing season is over, so as to avoid additional cost and efforts in cross transportation. In short, an efficient information system should be developed which helps to organize production better and market efficient. Perhaps, the Seed Association of India or any such organization can take up this responsibility.

- *Seed Replacement Rate:* Increase in SRR will surely increase the demand for certified seeds and it will also lead to increase in the productivity of different crops. Thus, alleviating the problems faced by the farmers in using certified seeds might help to improve the consumption of certified seeds. To enhance the seed replacement rate, both the public sector and private companies should develop and produce seeds which are not only high yielding varieties, but also require replacement every year. This would encourage the farmers to replace seeds every year and thus increase SRR. To increase the SRR, a firm has to concentrate on evolving newer hybrids which could increase the yield and require 100 per cent replacement or should come up with newer varieties of self pollinated and cross-pollinated crops, that would make the farmer to go for newer seed varieties in the next year, to utilise the newer benefit it offer, rather than using the same variety for next sowing season which they can do without any significant change in the yield.
- *Promotional Activities:* Normally, the SSCs and private firms opt for a blending of both pull and push promotion strategy. They intend to generate the demand from the farmers, for their seed only through pull strategy. By the push effort, each company channelizes its product through the dealers to the farmers.

The mixture of this two-prong strategy will yield the best result. Demonstration is one of the cost-effective tools of reaching the farmers. Demonstration has the electrifying effect on the farmers not only for the new varieties. Moreover it brings out the true picture of the attributes of the seed and thus increases the credibility of the particular variety and of the company.

Types of Skills and Knowledge Utilised in Agribusiness

- Agricultural production and propagation of animals, animal products, plants, plant products, forests and forest products.
- The provision of services associated with agricultural production and the manufacture and distribution of supplies used in agricultural production.
- The design, installation, repair, operation and servicing of machinery and servicing of equipment, and power sources, and the construction of structures used in agricultural production.
- Any activities related to the inspection, processing, and marketing of agricultural products and primary by-products.
- Any aspects of green house, nursery, landscaping, and other ornamental horticultural operations.
- The conservation, propagation, improvement, and utilisation of renewable natural resources.
- The multiple use of forest lands and resources.

We can list out about 950 occupations and 1900 selected industries that require or utilise agribusiness competencies. Thus our definition of agribusiness involves a broader view that encompasses the total food production and distribution system.

Scope of Agribusiness

Agribusiness is a dynamic, challenging area of employment. Many large corporations have consolidated and will continue to consolidate with agribusiness-related companies. Opportunities for employment will increase, especially in the areas of sales and marketing. The input and product sectors offer outstanding employment opportunities. The relative health of the farm sector is closely related to employment in the input sector.

Agribusiness can be taken up as a profession by small entrepreneurs and also by the rich. To solve the problems of unemployment and poverty in the rural areas, one has to promote Agribusiness. Agribusiness course will give the students some guidelines to go by which will be useful in evaluating decisions in the uncertain economic climate that lies ahead.

The study of agribusiness includes understanding the economic and personal skills prospective employees need if they are to be successful in this sector. Many agribusiness management tools are to be understood by the agribusiness managers so that an in-depth study of agribusiness and agribusiness management is essential for individual entrepreneurs as well as for those who work in the co-operative sector.

Agribusiness and rural enterprises of all types have received growing attention as potential sources of increased rural employment and income. Agribusiness and rural enterprises occupy a pivotal intermediate position between farms and consumers and can have powerful and far reaching catalytic effects in accelerating rural development.

Labour intensive, small-scale and relatively efficient enterprise systems exist in most countries and their expansion has favorable impacts on the income and employment of the rural landless and non-farm poor. One of the important potentials of the agribusiness sector is in providing growth possibilities without an equity conflict.

Agribusiness and rural enterprises are used to often refer to small and medium scale rural enterprises located in a non metropolitan areas. Small firms can play an important role in developing economies, although their ability to do so depends on the existence of an adequate environment to support their growth. Most of such firms will be dependent on the demand of the domestic population for their goods, their development requires the development of an expanding agricultural sector. Slow growth in agriculture may restrict the opportunity for new or existing enterprises. The potential contributions which small and medium sized rural enterprises can make to a country's economy include the following:

- Opportunities for rural employment can be increased.
- Offer viable and critical possibility for providing productive workplaces for rural labourers.
- Has the advantage of opening employment opportunities for women who are culturally excluded from agricultural pursuits.
- Contribute to the income and employment of families and small farms.
- Enterprises involved in processing and marketing can be catalytic in allowing small farmers to pursue the high income option.
- The enterprises have the potential to improve income distribution by increasing the number of workers participating in the labour force. They can also provide opportunities for landless families to become entrepreneurs rather than labourers.
- By focusing on areas outside the major metropolitan areas, governments can encourage decentralization of industrial development.
- The agribusiness activity can contribute to growth of overall economy by being efficient users of capital.

Constraints in Agribusiness

- Inadequate planning by the entrepreneurs.
- Inadequate financial position.
- Problems in getting access to credit.
- Inadequate marketing net works.
- Poor quality of the raw materials and products.
- Deficiency of demand of certain commodities.
- Non adoption of techniques for value addition.
- Shortage of raw materials during the off seasons.
- Damage to perishable commodities during storage and transportation.
- Inadequate storage facilities.
- Inadequate efficient transport facilities.
- Poor vision about the possible risk.
- Political domination and interference
- Dominating trade unionism.
- Lack of experience and vision.
- In-group conflicts and rivalry.
- Corruption and malpractices.
- Inadequate training and education.
- Vested interests.
- Lack of perseverance.
- Want of skilled workers.
- High initial cost for shops and showrooms.

- Inadequate support from family members/community.
- Inadequate linkage with rural community organizations, NGOs and Government departments.
- Ineffective leadership and team spirit.
- Poor management.
- Unhealthy competitions in the field.
- Income of the consumers.
- Tastes and habits of the consumers.
- Customers' preferences.
- Adverse social and cultural factors prevailing in the village/region.
- Law and order problems.
- Low credibility of the agribusiness man.
- Rigid rules and regulations of Government.
- Gender issue related problems.

DEMAND AND SUPPLY OF AGRICULTURAL PRODUCTS

Consumers spend everything they earn on goods and services. Consumers never seem to get enough of most things. The consumer behaviour is that human wants are unlimited. Consumers do not buy infinite quantities of everything since they have a limited amount of money income. We assume that consumer, with a given money income will purchase clothing, housing, food and other things that will maximize utility or satisfaction for them. The utility of a product or service is derived from the inherent qualities that cause them to be desired. Two individuals may not obtain the same utility or satisfaction from the consumption of the same amount of a product.

Another noticeable of consumer behaviour is that income is not spent on a single item; a variety of goods and services is purchased. The reason for this behaviour is contained in the law of diminishing utility. This law means that when an individual consumes additional units of a specific commodity, consumption of other goods and services unchanged, the amount of satisfaction derived from each additional unit of that good decreases.

Consumer Choice

The fact that people buy a certain combination of goods with spendable money, and not some other combination, implies that the choice made was more satisfying to the consumer than some other allocation of funds might have been. Because the consumer's income is limited, the consumer is attempting to purchase goods and services that will maximize satisfaction. Once the consumer is in equilibrium, it is possible to determine the quantities of a good purchased. By changing the price of a good, and hence the consumer's budget constraint, additional price – quantity relationship can be found. The price – quantity data can be plotted to derive the individual's demand curve for the product.

Price elasticity of demand is a measure of the responsiveness of quantity demanded to a change in price, ceteris paribus. When the elasticity co-efficient is less than one in absolute value, demand is inelastic; when greater than one in absolute value, demand is elastic, and when price elasticity is equal to one, demand is unitary. If demand for a product is inelastic, price and consumer expenditures vary directly. An increase in price increases consumer spending. A decrease in price decreases consumer expenditure on the product. On the other hand, if demand is elastic, price and consumer expenditure on the product vary inversely.

Income elasticity of demand is a measure of the responsiveness of quantity of a good purchased to changes in income. How products are related can be determined by the cross price elasticity of demand. Commodities with negative cross elastic ties are complementary. Commodities with positive cross elasticity of demand are substitutes.

The seven factors that influence the demand

1. Price of the good.
2. Price of the substitute goods.
3. Price of complementary goods.
4. Income.
5. Population.
6. Tastes and preferences.
7. Seasonality.

Supply

Production is the use of inputs to create an output that has economic value. Inputs to the production process include items such as grain, animals, chemicals, labour, money and anything else that an agribusiness uses to create an output. Output from the production process can be a commodity such as feed, fertilizer, milk or grain. It can also be a product such as ice cream. Services such as financial planning, insurance, market price news etc., are also outputs. The production process is how an agribusiness combines the various inputs to create an output.

The production decisions

When agribusinesses decide to undertake the production of an output, they face four major production decisions.

1. What to produce? What products and services can this business profitably offer?
2. How to produce? What is the most efficient technical combination of inputs to use in producing the output?
3. How much to produce? What is the correct amount of output to produce that will maximize the firm's long run profits?
4. When to produce? What is the correct time to produce the output?

The answers to these production questions rest heavily on the level of demand for the output at various prices. The answers are also influenced by cost factors such as the availability and prices of inputs. Economic efficiency {profit maximization} occurs when the change in the cost (marginal cost) is equal to the change in total revenue.

INFRASTRUCTURE, HANDLING AND STORAGE

The development of a physical distribution system that can efficiently and effectively moves products to the consumer is important in agribusiness. Physical distribution should be viewed from a marketing perspective, not thought of an extension of the production process. Physical distribution is an indispensable part of the marketing process. Although the stated objective of many firms is to minimize physical distribution costs, it is important to keep in mind the most convenient placement of the product for the consumer and thereby maximize the profits of the firm. Physical distribution involves control of inventory levels, selection of transportation modes {*eg*. Rail *vs*. Truck *vs*. Ship}, and location of plants, warehouses, and retail outlets. All the three areas play a part in the overall physical and technical efficiency of the firm and its ability to satisfy the needs of customers.

The physical distribution planning process begins with an examination of the tasks affecting consumer satisfaction that are related to place utility. According to Kotler, these are order processing, warehousing, inventory and transportation.

- *Order Processing:* A computer assisted order processing system can speed up the process so that the consumers can receive their goods quickly. The use of computers can reduce the errors in order transmitted. This can lead to greater consumer satisfaction and service.
- *Warehousing:* The location and design of warehouse can greatly affect the ability of the firm to meet customer's need efficiently. One food distribution firm made a great improvement in warehousing efficiency by having order form printed with products listed in the order in which they are stored on the shelves. This allows the warehouse personnel to pick up orders quickly without backtracking.
- *Inventory:* The maintenance of inventory is expensive. Carrying large inventories guards against stock outs. The objective is to have the right amounts of the right products on hand at all times.
- *Transportation:* Selection of the best mode of transportation should be based on carrier costs and the level of customer satisfaction desired [on time delivery performance of carrier, condition of the goods when they arrive etc.]

SOCIAL AND CULTURAL FACTORS INFLUENCING AGRIBUSINESS

Agribusiness industry is very diverse and complex. It comprises large corporate giants and small proprietorships. It includes the manufacture, distribution, storage, wholesaling, retailing and marketing of varied products, commodities and services. The investor owned corporation is chartered and secures its capital from its investors and shareholders. These shareholders elect directors who represent their interests in company policy. Earnings are distributed back to the shareholders in proportion to their investment. The patron owned co-operative is a special type of business corporation, also chartered and also operating with investor capital. However, the co-operative investors are also the co-operative patron members. Elections are most often based on one man – one vote rather than the number of shares owned. This means that members in the co-operative business have equal rights and power. So, personal, social and cultural variables influence the agribusiness. Some of these are given below.

- Incompatibility of the human and physical resources. Heterophily in the group may be due to ethnic economic and cultural dissimilarities. Language incompatibility can also become a barrier in effective group functioning and promotion of co-operative agribusiness.
- Non-co-operation from elders of the family.
- Religious sentiments may affect adversely.
- Food habits.
- Ethnocentrism.
- High labour charges.
- Trade unionism and strikes.
- Law and order problems.
- Communal disharmony.
- False propaganda and unhealthy competitions.
- Negative attitude of some societies of towards women who conduct agribusiness.
- Inadequate opportunities for women entrepreneurs.
- Inadequate participation of women members.
- Poor educational status of the business man.
- Lack of entrepreneurship and perseverance of the manager and agribusiness men.
- Joint family system.
- Lack of infrastructure and poor economic conditions.
- Non-conducive working conditions.
- Rigid social system.
- Multiplicity of family/kinship/caste rituals/Superstitions {They eat up bulk of what is generated in production}.
- Traditional and conventional attitudes of different ethnic groups. {*eg.* Taboo against selling milk in certain parts of Assam; White leghorn birds in some part of China}.
- Strong political and religious afiliations and fatalism.

RESOURCE UTILISATION AND OPPORTUNITIES IN AGRIBUSINESS

Land, water, biomass and humans are the basic resources for agricultural development. But the actual cultivated area of the country is far from providing the calculated minimum adequate diet for the present population. Under-utilisation of the potential land resources is generally due to limitations imposed by primitive technologies or environmental constraints such as insufficient rainfall, low fertility, infestation by pests and diseases, degradation of land etc. Agricultural production can be enhanced in two ways: bringing more land under cultivation and increasing productivity per unit of land.

Natural resources are those resources provided by nature. They become valuable when the technology of their utilisation and the demand for their products makes use feasible. Some natural resources such as wind and sunlight are available for use on a continuing or flow basis. Use of these resources do not diminish their future availability. Other resources are present only in a fixed quantity. Present indiscriminate use of such resources may diminish the physical amounts remaining for use in feature. Effective watershed management including soil and water conservation has become a crucial need.

The depleting supply of any resource such as land, petroleum, water etc., will cause the price to increase, ceteris paribus, provided the market is permitted to function. With price increases that truly reflect economic conditions surrounding the use of a resource, a number of forces are set in motion.

(a) The higher resource price is reflected in the prices of certain consumer goods, causing consumers to restrict their purchases by shifting to alternate goods.

(b) The economic supply expands as the increased price makes possible the use of lower quality resources.

(c) The search for alternate sources is intensified.

As the supply of land for food and fiber declines, food and fiber prices will increase. Increasing price for food and fiber will be reflected back to land with the price of land also increasing. With increasing scarcity of food products, and consequent unemployment and hunger, agribusiness emerges as the only way of socio-economic development of the small and marginal farmers.

Organizational Forms of Enterprises in the Agribusiness Industry

Agribusiness can be taken up in either one of the four organizational forms:

(i) Individual proprietorship.
(ii) Partnership.
(iii) Corporation – Investor owned.
(iv) Co-operative – Patron owned.

Table 1.1: Comparison of organizational forms of enterprises in the agribusiness industry

Organizational Characteristics	Individual Proprietorship	Partnership	Corporation Investor Owned	Co-operative Patron Owned
1. Management control	The proprietor	The partners	Board of directors	Board of directors
2. Management orientation	The proprietor	The partners	Investors	User members
3. Functions	To buy, produce, or provide good and services for sale	Same as proprietorship	Same as proprietorship	To purchase and Provide supplies and service or market processed commodities
4. Objectives	Profit for the proprietor	Profit for the partners	Profit for the investor stockholders	Savings for the member patrons
5. Users	The public	The public	The public	Member patrons
6. Ownership representation	The proprietor	Legal agreement of associates under law	The investors one vote per share owned	Members have one vote each
7. Legal base	Unincorporated	Legal agreement of associates under law	Incorporated under law	Usually incorporated under special enabling legislation
8. Liability	Assets of the proprietor	Assets of the partners	Assets of the Corporation	Assets of the Co-operative
9. Proceeds recipients	The proprietor	The partner	The stockholders proportionate to ownership	Members – Proportionate to patronage
10. Return on invested capital	Unlimited	Unlimited	Unlimited	Limited by law

Note: 'Unlimited' indicates that even the other assets of the proprietor or partners can be attached in case of liability. Public companies have only limited liability. That means that liability will be limited to the face value of shares.

Some Agribusiness Activities

The subsistence farmer has very particular problems arising from the scarcity of resources and poverty. One of the principal arguments in favor of co-operative organization for agribusiness is that it directly involves the individual farmer in the decision-making process, and so helps to ensure that the facilities provided are relevant to his particular needs and circumstances.

At the same time, just as the individual farmer' success will depend on his physical effort, farming skill, and in which he manages his own resources, so will the business efficiency of any co-operative, or other type of organization of which he may be a member, be highly significant in catering for his needs. Inefficient or badly managed servicing agencies, co-operatives and agribusiness firms are likely to add to the farmer's problems, rather than help to resolve them.

Examples of Small-scale Agro-based and Horticulture-based Industries

Banana production and marketing Jam, jelly, squash production and marketing Vegetable procurement and marketing Fruit juice preparation and sales, Coconut processing and marketing, Cashew processing, Pine apple processing and marketing, Coffee processing and marketing units, Rubber collection and marketing units, Vermi compost units, Banana chips making units, Mushroom production units, Bakery units, Pickle production and distribution units, Vegetable oil production units. Large units possible in the co-operative sector are Bone meal industry, Bio-fertilizer industry, Vegetable oil industry, Insecticide factories Fertilizer factories, Farm implements factory, Plant protection equipments factory, Tea factory etc.

AGRICULTURAL EXTENSION SERVICES

Extension is a professional communication intervention deployed to induce changes in voluntary behaviours with a presumed public or collective utility. Extension is a potential, persuasive educational instrument, when operated efficiently, can bring desirable changes in the knowledge, skill and attitude of the people by stimulating and assisting them in their learning process, self search and self discovery and decision-making and facilitating farmers and the sources of technology generation simultaneously.

There is a felt need in for more effective extension services. In order to develop the socio-economic conditions of the rural poor, many agri-based enterprises should sprout up. Agro-based industries will definitely lead to improvement of the socio-economic conditions of the rural poor.

Extension personnel can take up the noble task of motivating people to start, promote and strengthen agribusiness enterprises, organizing themselves into co-operatives, provide technical guidance in increasing agricultural production, assisting in the selection of the crops to be planted based on the market behaviour, providing market information, train them in processing, storage and value addition.

Considering the economic backwardness of the peasants, the farmers need to take up some agro-based industries as a collective, group effort. The extension worker can help the farmers to form self-help groups, train the members of self-help groups and members of co-operatives and provide the needed market information.

In addition to the public extension service and mass media, various private extension services can operate in the country. They are: community based organizations such as: farmer's organizations, co-operatives and self-help groups, para-extension workers, input suppliers, NGOs and other international agencies. Private extension need not be considered as competition to government extension services. Rather it is complementary. As it is, there is a need of more qualified and competent agribusiness extension workers and agricultural marketing extension workers in the country.

There is a demand for participatory, demand driven extension system by providing farmers with access to linkage mechanisms through they can articulate their problems and needs. A key factor for improving the feedback system is to organize the farmers into functional groups such as self help groups, commodity associations and other types of farmers organizations. Agricultural extension services should play a crucial role in these areas.

Setting up of Small and Medium Enterprises

The development of agribusiness and small-scale industries has been one of the most significant and characteristic features of development. One of the distinctive characteristics of small-scale sector is that, the development of these industries would create broader employment opportunities, assist in entrepreneurship and skills development, and ensure a better use of scarce financial resources and appropriate technology. Furthermore, they can play a main role in the achievement of national economic and socio political objectives. The gestation period is very short and they need smaller amount of capital to start. It also helps in the dissemination of productive capacity unlike the large scale industries which tend to concentrate in a few hands. Establishment of such industries in rural areas and small towns helps to check the influx of population into bigger towns.

Basic Objectives

The basic objectives underlying the development of small and medium scale industries are the increase in the supply of manufactured goods, the promotion of capital information, the development of indigenous entrepreneurial talents and skills and the creation of broader employment opportunities. In addition, they include socio economic goals such as the decentralization and the dispersal of manufacturing activities from the metropolitan to the non-metropolitan and rural areas, the reduction of regional economic imbalances within a country and the diffusion of entrepreneurial and management abilities and skills and technology throughout the country.

In any economy, agribusiness and small-scale industries have a significant role to play. With increasing pace of industrialization and sophistication of the large scale industries, a new orientation is inevitable in the relationship of the small-scale industries with the large and medium enterprises. This relationship calls for integration of the production methods, upgradation of the qualities of production and ability to meet stringent delivery.

Setting up a Small-scale Industry

There are different stages in the setting up of a small-scale industry. They are:

- Selection of industry.
- Arrangement for know-how.
- Selection of location and acquisition of premises.
- Preparation of project report.
- Apply for NOC, registration and power allotment.
- Apply to financial institutions for assistance for fixed assets and working capital inclusive of export finance if warranted.
- Apply to local bodies for NOC and permission.
- Recruit staff (labour).
- Apply for quota of raw materials (if necessary).
- Apply for power connection.
- Place orders for machinery.
- Install machinery.
- Connect machinery.
- Procure raw materials.
- Trial runs.
- Corrective measures.
- Production.
- Sales.
- Sales realization.
- Maintenance of records.
- Standardization of products and Quality.

A small entrepreneur is the chief executive of his unit, its floor supervisor, accounts clerk, purchase manager, salesman, legal and economic adviser, planner and visionary all rolled into one.

Phases

- Project selection phase.
- Information phase.
- Creative phase.

- Evaluation phase.
- Recommendation phase.
- Implementation phase.
- Follow up phase.

An entrepreneur may be an academically qualified person. Even so, he cannot become an entrepreneur unless he is confident of meeting the following essential requirements.

1. The entrepreneur should be fully conversant with the production line. It is not enough that he knows the method of manufacture; he should also know how to operate the machines.
2. He should have adequate shop floor experience to guide the machine operators in setting techniques.
3. He should be familiar with the raw materials he needs, their specifications, how to ensure the quality and where to get them at reasonable prices.
4. He should know how to keep accounts, how to maintain stores, how to prepare the balance sheet etc.
5. He should have knowledge of the marketing channels, distribution net work, agency practices, transport intricacies and the economics of packaging.
6. He should know how to ensure the stipulated quality of his product.
7. He should be well-versed in taxation and other laws governing small-scale industries.
8. He should be willing to bear up with bureaucratic regulations and be functional under any circumstances.
9. He should know how to avail himself of the various benefits available to the SSIs.
10. He should possess expertise, shrewdness, resourcefulness and perseverance in his business dealings.
11. He should have the guts to withstand the high pressure climate in which he has to build his unit.

Steps in the ladder of the entrepreneur (small) one has to climb in a continuous process of industrialization:

1. Analyze yourself and your objectives and also market behaviour.
2. Update with newer ideas.
3. Consult publication and agencies.
4. Discuss with all around you and with officials of the concerned department.
5. Choose a line.
6. Decide on form of ownership sole proprietorship, partnership etc.}
7. Decide whether to purchase a going concern or start a new one.

8. Obtain the project report or prepare it yourself. Have an idea about the possible profit and also all the possible risks.
9. Decide on location and site.
10. Arrange the work shed facilities.
11. Make sure what laws will particularly affect you.
12. Obtain clearance from central and local authorities the SSI registration.
13. Plan finance.
14. Plan sources of machinery.
15. Place order for machinery [may be on hire purchase].
16. Apply for materials.
17. Plan buying.
18. Install machinery.
19. Procure materials.
20. Recruit personnel.
21. Trial run.
22. Decide on pricing policy.
23. Organize marketing.
24. Plan out record keeping.
25. Produce.
26. Sell.
27. Keep up-to-date and ensure effective supervision at all stages of production and marketing.
28. Plough back profits.
29. Diversification.
30. Modernization.
31. Compete with others.
32. Grow bigger.
33. Development.

The requirements for future success of agribusiness

- Planning agricultural production based on market behaviour.
- Greater attention to meeting consumer needs.
- More attention to value addition.
- Assumption that marketing has a central role in the operation of agribusiness firms in order to remain profitable.
- Use of more sophisticated marketing techniques.
- The same level of effort devoted to marketing that has been devoted to production.

Value Addition

To recognise and investigate value-added opportunities and constraints we must first define what we mean by 'value-added'. There are varying definitions, but most include addition of 'value' to a product/good, process or service, with accompanying cost and price increases at various steps (often in different places, by different businesses) along the way.

The 'New Gates' initiative views value-added broadly to include: products and services processed/packaged/marketed in ways especially VALUED by consumers, agriculturalists, other local businesses, and the people and communities of the region where they originate.

To especially benefit rural people and the areas from which agriculture and forest products originate, 'New Gates' stresses good communication and joint-work for the mutual benefit of a region's agriculturalists, businesses, and neighboring communities. It emphasizes locally desired, owned, and managed value-added initiatives which contribute to rural quality of life and economic well-being. Likewise, stewardship of rural-area's natural, human, and other community resources are emphasized.

If thoughtfully pursued, value-added work can contribute to locally-desired diversification of an area's economic and employment base and to its general quality of life. It can be linked with other strategies to promote regional well-being, *eg*., to home-based, retail, and wholesale trade; social/cultural and recreational/natural resource attractions for area residents; heritage tourism for visitors; health, education, transportation, and communications services.

Some 'New Gates' Examples of Value-Added

Many specific examples of value-added efforts fit 'New Gates' definitions. Here are a few different types of value-added examples:

- Local processing, packaging, or marketing which adds value to raw agriculture/forest products.
- Cost-effective new/alternative crops for niche, 'high value' markets (and which might also be locally packaged for added appeal).
- Supplements to agriculture production activity (*eg*., farm/ranch bed and breakfast, farm/ranch working vacations, guided hunting/fishing vacations).
- Partnerships, networks, alliances, co-operatives among producers, small business, and neighboring communities to support value-added (*eg*., business referrals; separate small businesses in an area adding 'step-wise' value to local raw products; business and business-community ventures for joint-marketing, purchasing, 'incubator services', employee training/child care/insurance, pooled capital to encourage business start-up).

- Creative combinations of products/by-products, processing, and markets – for example, locally-unique raw or processed agriculture products (such as speciality beans, popcorn, flower seeds, dried fruits or meat, fiber products) packaged in locally-produced boxes made from by-products of an area lumber mill, marketed via regional retailers and motels when hunters/fisherman or other visitors are present, and/or via a regional catalog of 'value-added' products published on the Internet.

Guides to Recognise and Investigate Value-Added Opportunities and Constraints

Rapid reconnaissance. Work with others in your community/region to conduct a quick broad-gauged scan to gather information on factors especially relevant to value-added.

Invite a wide variety of people, organizations and communities in your region to contribute data, ideas, and opinions (*eg*., producers, processors, retailers, lenders, local government, community leadership, area youths, economic development groups, colleges/universities, state/federal agencies, non-profit groups).

You will need some factual data and information on area resources, strengths, and constraints. Equally important, you will need to search for creative ideas, for example:

- new ideas for adding value to raw products;
- ideas for combinations of products or products and services which might be linked in new or different ways;
- ideas for linking agriculture/forest value-added efforts with other economic activities of the area (*eg*., with tourism, retail trade, cottage industry);
- ideas which capitalize on interests, skills and life ways of people and communities of the area, and which recognise their limitations;
- like wise, ideas which take into account and are respectful of natural/environmental resources of the area…ideas which take into account the infrastructure, services, and social capacities of area communities.

More specifically gather information on:

- Availability of locally-produced raw products, area natural and human resources, and especially those products in the region which might fairly easily have value-added to them locally.
- Aspirations and goals of area producers, businesses, local communities – how might value-added efforts relate to and complement them?
- Local/regional labour force considerations: are there available workers in the region, with required skills and interests to fill the types of new jobs that might be created? Are there times of the year when residents of our region need to supplement their incomes? Would workers need to be attracted from elsewhere?

- Whether there are adequate local/regional resources and infrastructure to support value-added efforts (*eg*., investment capital, transportation, communications, water, waste disposal, housing, schools, health care, other public facilities/services).
- Whether producers and other business people, lenders, citizens/leaders, organizations in the area have interest in working to pursue value-added feasibility studies and potential new ventures.

Focus greatest attention on ideas and potential ventures which build on community and business goals and strengths and which take into account realistic constraints of human, financial, natural/environmental, and community resources of the area. Recognise that efforts which start small, and those of a 'scale' appropriate to the size, interests, and resources of the area often have greater likelihood of long-term success.

Seek assistance from community, business, professional agriculture, finance, and other professionals to further evaluate the value-added ideas which you have decided to pursue first. Discuss your ideas with other teams involved in the 'New Gates' initiative, and with representatives of supporting agencies, colleges, and universities. As needed, encourage/gather resources to commission feasibility studies that take into account enterprise – and community-level costs and benefits of potential value-added actions

EVALUATING THE MARKETPLACE

Competition in the marketplace needs to be carefully evaluated for every new business venture. Even if you have a good idea and product that looks like a natural fit in the existing marketplace, getting into the market is not always easy. For example, in the mid-1930s Southeastern Arizona apple growers tried to penetrate the marketplace with fresh apples in the late summer and early fall at selected supermarket channels. Due to a warmer climate than other major apple producing regions, harvest was early enough so that their fresh apples would be competing with a poorer quality apple that had been stored at least 8 months in controlled atmosphere storage. But the marketplace was virtually impossible for them to penetrate because Washington State warehouses had established a firm stronghold in the market. Washington State had an established reputation as a reliable producer and supplier of apples. Consequently, retailers were very reluctant to switch from buying Washington apples for a relatively small window of their annual supply requirements. Arizona was also an unknown supplier and later found difficulty in delivering a quality and reliable supply. Arizona was not able to obtain reliable supplies and quality from one year to the next with frost, hail, and other production problems. Convincing retailers that you have the ability to deliver a reliable supply of quality goods as a new entrant into the marketplace is often the biggest hurdle to overcome for penetrating an existing market.

When Washington State tried to enter the Japanese market for apples, they found the marketplace there difficult to penetrate even though they possess a world renowned reputation in apple production. The best quality of apples that Washington State had to offer Japan were essentially given an unsatisfactory rating by Japanese consumers. *First*, the Fuji and Gala apples Japan is accustomed to are much sweeter in taste than the traditional Washington Red Delicious. *Second*, Japanese consumers' willingness to pay for fruit in an unblemished form and attractive package is beyond what the average US consumer or retailer would imagine. As global exporter Jim Woodson explained, the Japanese are really buying 'gifts' rather than food with most of their apple, melon, and other fruit purchases.

Persistence is often another key ingredient for bringing new products to fruition. New product ideas are not generally readily accepted, even though they may eventually have broad appeal to consumers. The idea of marketing a 'natural beef', beef grown without any hormones, feed additives, confinement, or vaccinations was conceived in the early 1970s by the Coleman Ranch in Colorado. But when they first contacted potential retail outlets in the Rocky Mountain region no one was interested. Then they headed to Los Angeles and finally found one speciality store that was interested in selling their beef. Growth was almost non-existent for over 15 years and they didn't operate in the black until the mid-1990s. Today Coleman beef products can be found in health food stores nationwide because they were persistent in selling the concept of 'natural beef' to retailers and consumers. Persistence also paid off for them because they identified a product with growth potential and they were able to establish a solid distribution network for their products by proving themselves as a consistent supplier of quality products.

Penetrating into a new market is somewhat like exploring new territory – you never know for sure how the consumer or community is going to respond. Key items or questions that should always be evaluated or addressed are:

- How does my product differ from existing or established products in the marketplace or what is the closest substitute for my product?
- How difficult is my identified market to penetrate?
- Do I have the proper contacts and distribution channels identified and how does my product and idea sell with them?
- What is the growth potential for new customers and related products?
- How do my business venture and future plans fit in with the community?

Community support is becoming more critical since it is not uncommon for local county, city, or state governments to offer financial loans or incentives. Furthermore, the long-term goals of the community need to fit together with your plans or else the two will eventually clash. All of these questions are important to carefully evaluate since it only takes one 'weak link' to keep a new business venture or product from succeeding. Entering a marketplace takes much more than a 'competitive price'. None of the marketing 'failures' at getting into the marketplace above were because someone else had a lower price than they could offer.

BUSINESS/COMMUNITY NETWORKS AND LINKAGES

Community support can be the catalyst for deciding on where a value-added enterprise should be located. After evaluating the production, labour, and community resources that a location has to offer – business support programmes related to financing, planning assistance, and joint marketing efforts need to be explored. Start-up loans are often available for attracting new enterprises to a community. For example, the greenhouse operation in Bonita, Arizona received some of their initial financing through a small business loan. In 1961, a small company named Iowa Beef Processors was organized in Dennison, Iowa, using a Small Business Administration loan for financing. Today IBP is one of the few industry giants in the meat packing business. Other organizing and support systems may include those such as partnerships, multiple enterprise-/employee-/community-owned co-operatives, business incubators, and less formal networks and alliances. In rural areas, sharing access with business-support services such as fax and copy machines, internet connections, employee training, child care, insurance programmes, accounting services, and other related services can greatly decrease the cost of doing business for small rural companies.

Processing Efficiency

The processing-manufacturing sector is dominated by large companies that have grown to capture processing economies available through large scale production. Some of these large companies include Iowa Beef Processors (meat packing), Sunkist (citrus processing), Archer Daniels Midland (grain processing), and Mid-America Dairymen (dairy processing). Finding a niche around the food processing giants is essential since they have the edge on processing efficiency or cost of production.

Volume and regulatory issues play a key role in selecting an affordable processing technology. When starting out, it is always good to be on the conservative side when estimating volume. Every major food processor had its start as a 'small entity' that eventually grew into a large corporation. Not enough can be said for the merits of starting on a small-scale.

Starting small allows you to test your production and processing capabilities, devote more time and learning to quality control, obtain valuable market feedback from initial product sales, secure less financing, and assess the work load before a full-time commitment is made.

Health and regulatory issues also need to be addressed before identifying appropriate processing procedures for food products. Hazard Analysis Critical Control Points need to be identified and monitored to ensure food safety requirements are met and liability risks are minimized. Other requirements to consider are proper labeling, weights and measures, state standards, state workmen's compensation, building safety, zoning, and other regulations. Insurance coverage for product liability, premise liability, employer's liability, and physical damage should all be reviewed and considered.

Opportunities for complimentary sharing of processing facilities should be given in-depth thought and exploration. Because the ownership or fixed costs (*i.e.*, committed costs that don't change with decreasing or increasing output) of processing are generally high, an idle processing facility is costing someone lots of money. A broader base of geographical production with a longer production period is one management practice commonly used to help pay for large processing facility costs. California's source for processing tomatoes moves from South to North so they can keep their processing plants busy for as long a season as possible. If possible, using the same processing facility for products with different harvest windows is most desirable since transportation costs are kept to a minimum.

Securing Input Supplies

Securing an adequate supply of raw materials throughout the year can be a challenge since most raw food products are seasonal in production and perishable in nature. Increasingly, food products are becoming more vertically integrated. That is, companies have moved backward and forward in the marketing channel of converting raw products into products desired by the final consumer. Companies integrate vertically to gain greater control of their final product and earn higher profits. For example, Coleman beef moved their product forward to the final consumer by processing 'natural beef' that they could ship to retailers. Currently, Coleman beef is looking for ranchers that are willing to produce beef under the conditions required to meet their 'natural beef' definition and they are willing to pay a premium. Coleman beef has also made significant networking expenditures for attracting their input supply of 'natural beef'. Few substitutes exist for a face-to-face contact when it comes to developing successful business relationships. These networking costs need to be budgeted in the cost of starting a business venture that has to secure input supplies.

Labour Force Considerations

Securing a labour supply that is skilled, trainable, and cost-effective is one of the most important bricks for building a sound enterprise. Here are a few questions that people contemplating a potential enterprise and people from the larger community will want to consider:

- Might the new firm create safe, adequately-paying jobs which current local residents are interested in and qualified to fill? Will new workers from outside the area also need to be attracted? If so, what types of new workers, and how might current residents, businesses, schools, and government officials work to welcome and integrate them into the community? Is there adequate, affordable housing available for new workers and their families?

- If job training is required for employees of the new firm, will the firm provide the training itself? Would employees and the firm benefit from some training assistance from additional groups (*eg*., Local schools, Community Colleges, Co-operative Extension Educators), and how might this be arranged? Employee morale is very important for achieving high productivity. Economic incentives or a reward structure based on individual or group performance has been recognised as a vital component for success by many large and small enterprises. Small enterprises starting out are generally short on cash so that financial incentives in the form of stock options are offered to key employees. This kind of incentive is beneficial for venture capitalists and employees when quality work turns into higher venture profits. Also, employee benefits are generally a better deal for both employers and employees than wages due to the current tax structure. But certain restrictions apply for how much can be contributed to employee benefits like retirement accounts.

Encouraging employees to better themselves through additional training and education can help boost morale and improve venture productivity. Likewise, access to safe, affordable child-care and transportation can strengthen employees commitment and productivity. Flex hours for talented employees to increase their human capital can be important for keeping employees up-to-date and on top of today's rapidly changing technology.

Financing Availability

Finance, production, and marketing are often referred to as the three fundamental areas that require strong management expertise. Careful financial planning should precede the acquisition of any significant asset or change in business focus. Sales and expenses must be scrutinized in line item detail on at least a monthly basis to assure financial obligations are on target. Cash flow is crucial to wise financial planning and cash or similar current assets on hand should be 1.5 times the level of current liabilities. The amount of collateral required for loans will vary by industry but expect to provide at least 30 to 40 per cent of the equity needed for traditional loan purchases. Five credit factors generally considered are character, capacity for repayment, capital, collateral, and loan conditions. All of these elements relate to one's ability to raise adequate capital.

In the 1930s, a former paper cup salesman named Ray Kroc was impressed with the number of people that the McDonald brothers were packing in to a small drive-in restaurant in California. He negotiated with the two McDonald brothers, who were hoping to become movie stars at the time, to let him franchise outlets nationwide. Although outlets grew slowly at first, McDonald's restaurants can now be found throughout the world. If a franchise fits in with your desired business venture, they can be another source of financing since the parent company will often finance the land and buildings if the franchisee is unable to do so. But franchisees must pay a franchise fee plus royalties on sales to operate at a specific site chosen by the parent company.

If you have virtually no equity to apply towards a business venture, you can try and sell your idea to venture capitalists. Because they are taking essentially all the financial risk for your business ideas, they will require a significant stake in ownership of your venture and will generally require a say in major business decisions. If your business plan can stand up to the scrutiny of venture capitalists it probably has more likelihood of success than if you solicit financing from family members or friends. Although friends and family know your character they are probably not the best evaluators of the business venture you are proposing.

Entrepreneurial/Managerial Ability

Managerial abilities are developed through time and there is no substitute for having a good feel for your enterprise. What are the standard profit margins for your enterprise? How capital intensive and cyclical is the business you are in? What is considered the optimal economic unit? How can one effectively minimize price risk? How can one most effectively use people in your business? All of these questions need to be answered in order to effectively plan and manage. Managerial talent also requires personal skills that are more natural to some than others but must be perfected by everyone. Communicating effectively with business partners, investors, service providers and employees are all needed to make a business operate smoothly and profitably. In short, sound industry knowledge, people skills, and a good handle on business management principles related to finance, marketing, and production are invaluable for making a successful business.

How can the poor benefit from the growing markets for high value agricultural products?

High value crops refer to non-traditional food crops such as vegetables, fruits, flowers, houseplants and foliage, condiments and spices. High value livestock and fishery products include products such as milk, beef, poultry, pork, eggs, and fish that are non-traditional sources of protein. Most High Value Agricultural Products (HVAPs) have higher market values than traditional cereal grains and export crops. A particular feature of HVAPs is that they often do not form part of the customary diet of the local population and are mainly grown for their cash values in domestic and export markets. This review defines HVAP as products with high monetary value with emerging and expanding products markets worldwide. Lack of a standard definition of HVAP and non-traditional export products has made researchers to adopt their own definitions based on their research emphasis. It is acknowledged that the task of linking small-scale farmers to markets is much more challenging (when one deals with HVAPs) compared to traditional export crops.

SOME TIPS FOR A SUCCESSFUL CAREER IN AGRIBUSINESS

There is no one clear path to a successful career in agribusiness. Dedication, hard work, perseverance and loyalty are necessary. Yet, there are some tips that have proved useful.

- *Begin at Grass Roots Level:* Most people begin their professional careers in agribusiness physically handling products and servicing customers. The grass root level experience is invaluable for understanding the fundamentals of agribusiness management.
- *Pay your Dues*: Accept the initiation period during which all new employees must prove themselves to become accepted by their peers.
- *Learn the Power Structure:* In every agribusiness there are individuals who wield far more power than their formal position would suggest. It may be unwise to ignore powerful people in organizations.
- *Make your Boss Look Good*: Nothing can get you more attention and favorable evaluations than making your boss look good.
- *Be a Team Member*: A successful agribusiness operates as a team.
- *Be Visible:* It is important to do something that is clearly your own.
- *Make Suggestions:* As a professional, you have a responsibility to watch for weak areas and suggest improvements.
- *Recognise that Change is Threatening*: Promote change cautiously.
- *Weigh the Cost of Being Right*: Whenever conflicts arise, you must decide whether to push your ideas, and if so, how far.
- *Allow People to Save Face:* Always leave the other person with a way of saving face in situations in which conflict arises.
- *Manage Expectations:* All discontent is relative to expectation. You should be realistic and not overstate what you can do.
- *Ask for Help:* The experienced personnel can help and are often eager to play a parental role and can even be protective.
- *Always Give a Little Extra:* For a fast movement and a rewarding professional career, it pays to do a bit more than expected of you in every aspect of your job.

2

Agribusiness Management

Management can be defined as 'the art of successfully pursuing desired results with the resources available to the organization'. There are two dimensions for good management: the human dimension and the technical dimension. The former is more important. A manager's ability to achieve results through others (both men and women) is the very essence of good management.

Successful managers feel like managers, see themselves as managers, and are ready and willing to play the management role. When successful managers look in the mirror, they see a leader, a person who is willing to accept the responsibility for change and become the catalyst for action. The success – minded manager is comfortable with the managerial role, and accepts responsibility and power as a challenge rather than a curse. The famous educator 'Nicholas Murray Butler' once placed managers in three classes: *(i)* 'the few who make things happen, *(ii)* the many who watch things happen, and *(iii)* the majority who have no idea what has happened'.

Thus the Manager can be defined as that person who provides the organization with leadership and who acts as a catalyst for change. Good managers are most effective in the environment that permits creative change. Such managers live to make things happen. The ineffective manager concentrates on doing things right, rather than on doing the right things. Success as a manager, then, necessitates the ability to understand and be comfortable with the managerial role, to accept the responsibility, and to provide leadership for change.

THE IMPORTANCE OF GOOD MANAGEMENT

Dun and Bradstreet, after studying hundreds of cases, concluded that 88 per cent of all business failures could be traced directly to ineffective management. The manager's concept of the management role, of what managers are and what they do, was the most single most important factor in determining whether managers were effective or ineffective in their roles. Success or failure of any agribusiness rests primarily on its manager's effective or ineffective utilisation of the organization's resources. The ability to manage does not surface as an inborn gift; rather it is a skill that can and must be learned. Although certain management skills and principles can be learned, they must be adapted by each individual to fit the unique situation.

Agribusiness management refers to the application of basic managerial principles to a specific sector of agricultural economy. 'Span of Control', 'Managerial Decentralization' and 'Delegation of Authority' are three well known principles relating to managerial supervision. Employee motivation and managerial entrepreneurship are important factors deciding the success of the manager of the enterprises. The management functions such as planning, organizing, directing, coordinating and control are important as far as the manager is concerned.

ECONOMICS AND THE MANAGER

Agribusiness managers must understand the economic world in which they operate. Not only economic principles are useful in predicting business trends, but those same principles serve as the basis for many management decisions. Professionally trained managers should under gird themselves with basic economics through both formal and informal study.

Economics involves the allocation of scarce resources, that is land, labour, capital and management, to meet the needs of people. The profit motive is used as an incentive that guides business in fulfilling consumer wants in the market place with their money.

Agribusiness managers use many economic principles to make important business decisions. The marginal cost and marginal revenue concept suggests the most profitable level of production. The opportunity cost concept is critical in assessing various decision alternatives. Applying supply and demand principles to agricultural supplies and farm products is basic to almost all agricultural plans.

General Guidelines for Effective Agribusiness Management

Management is defined as "The art of successfully pursuing desired results with the resources available to the organization". The following are some of the general guidelines for effective agribusiness management:

- Managers ability to achieve results through others.
- Providing leadership.

- Acts as a catalyst for change.
- Effective in utilisation of resources.
- Motivates the staff.
- Attending the 5+2 managerial functions (Planning, Organizing, Directing, Coordinating, Controlling, + Communicating+Motivating).
- Accepts responsibilities and power.
- Recognises the difference between what is and what should be.
- If the worker is happy, productivity will follow.

From the above definition the key factors for successful agribusiness management are:

- The first is the man in management. There are two dimensions to good management – the human dimension and the technical dimension, but the former is more important one. A manager's ability to achieve results through others is the very essence of good management. Investment of time and energy in one's subordinates can pay good rewards.
- Art is the second key word, management is an art, it deals largely with people. Everyone can use management principles to foster continuous growth and progress toward managerial potential.

ROLE OF MARKETING IN AGRIBUSINESS

Agribusiness is the largest industry, and marketing is its largest segment. About 80 per cent of those involved in agribusiness are employed in marketing. The role of marketing is:

- Helps to bridge the gap between the needs of the producers and consumers.
- Helps producers to better understand the needs of the consumers so they can do a better job of meeting them.
- Helps producers to decide what to produce and when to produce.

The pre-requisites to an efficient economic system:

1. A free market economy.
2. Prices that reflect the full value of resources.
3. A high degree of interaction between consumers and producers.

The nine marketing functions are:

The exchange functions.....

1. Buying – Ownership separation.
2. Selling – Ownership separation.

The physical functions ......

3. Storage – Time separation.
4. Transportation – Space separation.
5. Processing – Value separation.

The facilitating functions ......

6. Grades and standards – Information separation.
7. Financing – Value separation.
8. Risk taking – Time separation.
9. Market Information – Information separation.

The Four Utilities of Marketing

Another way to describe marketing is to look at the performance of the marketing functions as a way of adding value to products. Middle men add value by performing the nine marketing functions described above in a production process. Marketers or middle men continue to exist because they add value to products that consumers want and are willing to pay extra to receive. Consumers receive satisfaction or utility from using the products. Marketers add the following four types of utility to the products they handle:

(i) Time.

(ii) Place.

(iii) Form.

(iv) Possession.

Marketing management is concerned with marketing decisions within the agribusiness firm. Its object is to develop, execute, and control a strategic marketing plan that will satisfy consumer's needs while generating a profit for the firm.

The movement of farm supplies and services to farmers and the flow of agricultural products from farms to the final consumers occur within the agricultural marketing system. It is a complex system, involving hundreds of thousands of businesses that perform the basic marketing functions of buying, selling, transporting, storing, processing, informing, risk bearing, financing and standardizing agricultural products. Each of these market functions contributes in some way to the final value or utility of the product; that is, it adds form, time, place or possession utility.

Marketing is a costly activity. The cost is measured by the marketing margin, that is, the share of the consumer required to cover the marketing costs. Consumers are demanding more services built into what they buy; therefore, the farmer's share of the consumer is falling. Agricultural marketing is a complex, but efficient system for reflecting consumer wants to the producers.

Market Planning Tools

Managing a marketing programme in agribusiness can be a complex task, particularly in larger firms with many products. Nearly all agribusinesses face seasonal demand that creates the possibility of critical bottlenecks in servicing customers. Unpredictable weather patterns further complicate market planning, and volatile agricultural commodity prices often cause the demand for farm supplies and services to fluctuate. Because of their complexity, agri-marketing programmes require a great deal of planning. Successful managers spend much time in analyzing their market and mapping their strategic plan. Agri-marketing managers not only build a marketing programme from the marketing mix, but they also utilise wide assortment of analytical tools and concepts to assist them in the planning process.

A marketing audit is a thorough and objective examination of a firm's marketing programme. With this market performance and potential for each product are analyzed; distinctive competencies can be recognised; current and future market conditions are reviewed; current marketing programmes are evaluated; execution of the marketing programme is considered; and finally the human resources available and their organization are studied.

Sales forecasting is another highly useful marketing tool that is especially valuable in agribusiness because of the volatility of agricultural products. It usually begins with general economic forecasts and becomes more and more specific as the forecaster moves towards forecasting sales for an individual product or service.

Marketing managers must also analyze competition and monitor their marketing programmes. Formal competitors' strength and weakness analysis is a useful tool that suggests strategic marketing approaches for competing with each competitor. Various marketing research methods provide invaluable information for developing marketing plans. Simple tools, such as pinpointing customers by type or size on a map, provide much information. Customer surveys and personal and group interviews are also popular methods. Marketing managers must synthesize information from a variety of sources to assist them in developing a successful marketing programme.

The strategic management plan must integrate all facets of business activity. *First*, the corporate mission is defined, objectives and goals are established, and a step-by-step strategy for accomplishing these goals is laid out; then the plan is executed through daily activities or tactics. Marketing managers must first carefully analyze the market, identifying various segments or classes of customers who have unique characteristics so that marketing programmes can be adapted to various segments.

The marketing plan has four major decision areas called the marketing mix. Product decisions determine what products or services to offer. Each product has a life cycle, with distinct phases from its introduction to its demise. As products are introduced they move through a systematic adoption and diffusion process that offers the marketing managers regarding important opportunities to market the product.

Pricing decisions are critical to marketing process. Pricing strategies are based on competitive actions, consumer responses, and internal cost considerations. Promotional decisions determine the proper mix of advertising, publicity, selling, and sales support programmes needed to reach sales objectives. Place decisions concentrate on the methods and channels of distribution that will optimize sales and profits. All elements of the marketing mix are critical decision areas for the marketing manager.

Selling is an integral part of enterprise economy. Without adequate sales, a business cannot survive. Selling is the process of helping people to buy. It links the customer to business. It has an educational dimension because it helps customers become aware of the alternatives that can benefit them. Whenever an exchange takes place, both the seller and the buyer expect to benefit.

Professional selling in agriculture seldom means door-to-door superficial contacts. It is often an ongoing long-term personal relationship that is based on a high level of technical ability. It is a highly individual job in which each person is responsible for his or her own performance.

There are many rewards associated with agri-selling. Financially, the selling profession can be especially rewarding. It is also an excellent route for advancement and personal satisfaction. But it is hard work, and it can be discouraging when things do not go well.

There are many levels of agri-selling. Some people sell only to distributors and dealers, while others call on farmers. Still others deal directly with the general public. Each level has its own unique life style, but all utilise professional selling skills that involve close working relationships with customers.

The sales person has a variety of responsibilities in addition to actual selling. Salespeople must monitor the market for information necessary to firm decisions, provide technical support for their customers, handle complaints, collect accounts, maintain good relationships with public institutions in their area, and do a great deal of paper work. But they have a lot of support. Most salespeople receive special training, have technical specialists to call on for help, can utilise firm advertising and promotional programmes as selling aids, and can count on their supervisor to assist them when problems arise.

Selling is a process that can be learned by applying certain principles. Preparation is the first technique or step. Agribusiness people must be knowledgeable about their product, the prospect, and the market. They therefore spend time prospecting for and qualifying new customers and planning a sales-call strategy that will improve their chances for success.

The first few minutes of the sales call are often the most critical because they set the tone for the entire interview. During this period the sales person must build rapport, ask questions to learn more about the customer and arouse interest in the product.

Making the presentation itself is often thought to be the core of the sales call, but it can be done well only if the planning and opening have been well executed. The days, weeks or months following the sale are also a critical part of the sales process. In this follow up period, the customer should be serviced to ensure satisfaction, thereby hopefully creating the possibility of future sales.

The Four Functions of Management and Marketing Management

The management of marketing activities within the firm can be studied within the broad confines of the four management functions: *(i)* planning, *(ii)* organizing, *(iii)* controlling, and *(iv)* directing or implementing. The only difference is that marketing management focuses on understanding customer needs.

- ***Planning:*** The first type of planning affirm must do is heavily related to marketing. It must decide which consumer needs it is going to fill and how it will accomplish this better than anyone else or differently. When this type of planning is done on a company wide basis, it is called strategic planning. Its primary objective is look for market opportunities (unmet consumer needs) that can be filled by the company. Once these needs have been identified, management must determine how the firm can fill them properly. This strategic plan includes a clear definition of:
    1. *The target market* – The relatively homogenous group of consumers whose unmet needs the firm hopes to fulfill efficiently. The market should be as homogeneous as possible.
    2. *How consumers' needs will be better met by this firm* – The competitive edge that will cause consumers to choose this firm's product over someone else's.
- ***Organizing:*** Once the decisions are made about the consumer needs this firm is to fill and how it will be done, a manager's attention should turn to developing an organization to accomplish it, keeping in mind the priority to consumer's purchase satisfaction.
- ***Controlling:*** The management's next task is to establish a procedure to see that the firm is accomplishing what it set out to do. Controlling function depends on developing the feedback mechanisms. Controls can be both internal and external. Internal controls include reports on production levels, inventory levels and so on.
- ***Directing:*** Marketing managers also have a strong interest in the fourth function of management called directing. It is here that all the previous functions are converted into reality and the consumer need is actually met. Directing is also referred to as implementing.

Production management involves a complex network of decisions that affect the production process. Four kinds of production processes (analysis, synthesis, extraction, and fabrication) relate to the number and kind of raw materials or number and kind of end products. Production may be either intermittent or continuous, depending on whether it is handled by function to produce variable outputs or handled as continuous, step-by step process to produce very similar outputs.

Production of agricultural products is hampered by severe problems of seasonality, perishability, bulkiness, and variations in quantity, quality or value.

Risk management is an important consideration in many agribusiness decisions today. In making many capital expenditure decisions, managers must consider the many different economic climates possible in the long run.

Distinctive Features of Agribusiness Management

Management principles are the same for any business. The differences between large and small businesses, between agribusiness and other kinds of businesses, rest in the art of applying basic management principles to the running of the business.

As a professional, the manager might be compared to a physician. The knowledge and principles of medicine are the same, but patients differ in such vital details as age, sex, build, and general health. The physician's skill is to apply general medical principles to the individual patient's unique circumstances. Agribusiness is unique, and requires unique abilities and skills of its managers.

Some of the reasons why agribusiness management differs from other kinds are the following:

1. The tremendous variety in the kinds of businesses in the agribusiness sector; that is, from basic producers to shippers, brokers, wholesalers, processors, packagers, manufacturers, storage firms, transporters, financing institutions, retailers, food chains, restaurants etc.
2. The sheer number of agribusinesses. Literally millions of different businesses have evolved to handle the route from the producer through the retail marketer.
3. The way in which basic agribusiness is built around several million farm producers. These farmers produce hundreds of different food and fiber products. Most agribusiness deal with farmers either directly or indirectly. No other industry is built principally around the basic producer of its raw product.
4. The infinite variety in the size of agribusinesses, from giants to the one-person or one-family organization. Most agribusinesses tend to be small when compared with other business and industrial segments.
5. Agribusinesses are small and compete in a relatively free market in which there are many sellers and fewer buyers and in which the numbers and sizes of agribusinesses do not allow monopoly – like enterprises. Product differentiation is also difficult in most agribusinesses.

6. The traditional philosophy of life exhibited by many agribusiness workers which tends to make agribusinesses more conservative than some other businesses.
7. Agribusiness firms tend to be family – oriented.
8. Agribusinesses tend to be community oriented. Many are located in small towns and rural areas where interpersonal relationships are important and associations are long-term. People know each other.
9. Agribusinesses are likely to be highly seasonal in nature. Because of the intimate relationship and interdependence of agribusiness and farm producers, and because of the nature of planting and harvesting seasons, special problems often arise.
10. Agribusinesses deal with the vagaries of nature.
11. The government programmes and policies have direct impact on agribusinesses. For example, the price of wheat may be influenced by government regulation.

INTEGRATED MARKETING COMMUNICATION STRATEGIES FOR AGRIBUSINESS

During the past several decades, companies around the world have perfected the art of mass marketing – selling highly standardized products to masses of consumers. Modern marketing calls for more than just developing a good product, pricing it attractively, and making it available to target customers. Companies must also communicate with current and prospective consumers, and what they communicate should not be left to chance. All of their communications efforts must be blended into a consistent and coordinated communications programme. Just as good communication is important in building and maintaining any kind of relationship, it is a crucial element in a company's efforts to build customer relationships.

The Changing Communications Environment

Two major factors are changing the face of today's marketing communications. *First*, as mass markets have fragmented, marketers are shifting away from mass marketing. More and more, they are developing focused marketing programmes designed to build closer relationships with customers in more narrowly defined micro-markets.

Second, vast improvements in information technology are speeding the movement toward segmented marketing. Today's information technology helps marketers to keep closer track of customers needs-more information about consumers at the individual and household levels is available than ever before. New technologies also provide new communications avenues for reaching smaller customer segments with more-tailored messages. The shift from mass marketing to segmented marketing has had a dramatic impact on marketing communications. Just as mass marketing gave rise to a new generation of mass-media communications, the shift toward one-to-one marketing is spawning a new generation of more specialized and highly targeted communications efforts.

Given this new communications environment, marketers must rethink the role of various media and promotion mix tools. Mass-media advertising has long dominated the promotion mixes of consumer product companies. However, although television, magazines, and other mass media remain very important, their dominance is now declining. Market fragmentation has resulted in media fragmentation-in an explosion of more-focused media that better match today's targeting strategies. Beyond the traditional mass-media channels, advertisers are making increased use of new, highly targeted media, ranging from highly focused specialty magazines and cable television channels, to CD catalogs and web coupon promotions, to airport kiosks and floor decals in supermarket aisles. In all, companies are doing less *broadcasting* and more narrowcasting.

The Need for Integrated Marketing Communications

In the past, no person or department was responsible for thinking through the communication roles of the various promotion tools and coordinating promotion mix. Today, however, more companies are adopting the concept of integrated marketing communications (IMC). Under this concept, as illustrated in Figure 2.1 the company carefully integrates and coordinates its many communications channels to deliver a clear, consistent, and compelling message about the organization and its products.

As one marketing executive puts it, "IMC builds a strong brand identity in the marketplace by trying together and reinforcing all your images and messages. IMC means that all your corporate messages, positioning and images, and identity are coordinated across all (marketing communications) venues. It means that your Promotional Resource materials say the same thing as your direct-mail campaign, and your advertising has the same 'look and feel' as your website".

IMC calls for recognising all contact points where the consumer may encounter the company, its products and its brands. Each brand contact will deliver a message, whether good, bad, or indifferent. The company must strive to deliver a consistent and positive message at all contact points.

Integrated marketing communications produces better communications consistency and greater sales impact. It places the responsibility in someone's hands-where none existed before to unify the company's image as it is shaped by thousands of company activities. It leads to a total marketing communication strategy aimed at showing how the company and its products can help consumers to solve their problems.

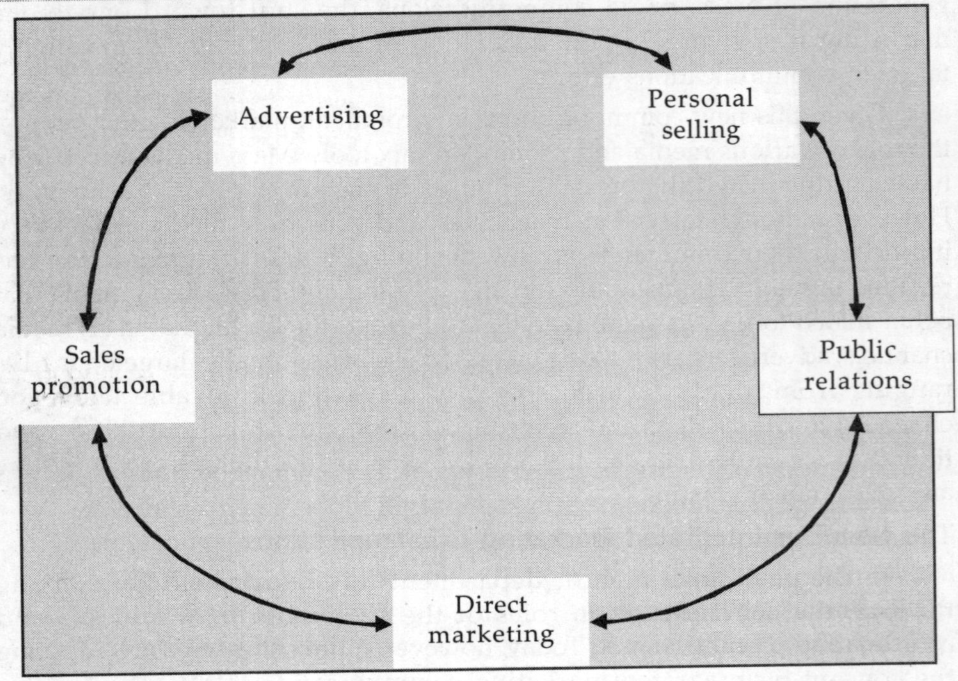

Fig. 2.1. Integrated Marketing Communications

A View of the Communication Process

- Integrated marketing communication involves identifying the target audience and shaping a well-coordinated promotional programme to elicit the desired audience response.
- The communication process should start with an audit of all the potential contacts target customers may have with the company and its brands.
- The marketer needs to assess what influence each of these communications experiences will have at different stages of the buying process. This understanding will help marketers allocate their communication expenses more efficiently and effectively.
- To communicate effectively, marketers need to understand how communication works. Communication involves the nine elements as shown in Figure 2.2.
  - Two of these elements are the major parties in a communication-the sender and the receiver.
  - Another two are the major communication tools – the message and the media.
  - Four more are major communication functions – encoding, decoding, response, and feedback.
  - The last element is noise in the system.

Definitions of the nine elements:

- *Sender:* The party sending the message to another party.
- *Encoding:* The process of putting thought into symbolic form.
- *Message:* The set of symbols that the sender transmits.
- *Media:* The communication channels through which the message moves from sender to receiver.
- *Decoding:* The process by which the receiver assigns meaning to the symbols encoded by the sender.
- *Receiver:* The party receiving the message sent by another party.
- *Response:* The reactions of the receiver after being exposed to the message.
- *Feedback:* The party of the receiver's response communicated back to the sender.
- *Noise:* The unplanned static or distortion during the communication process, which results in the receivers getting a different message than the one the sender sent.

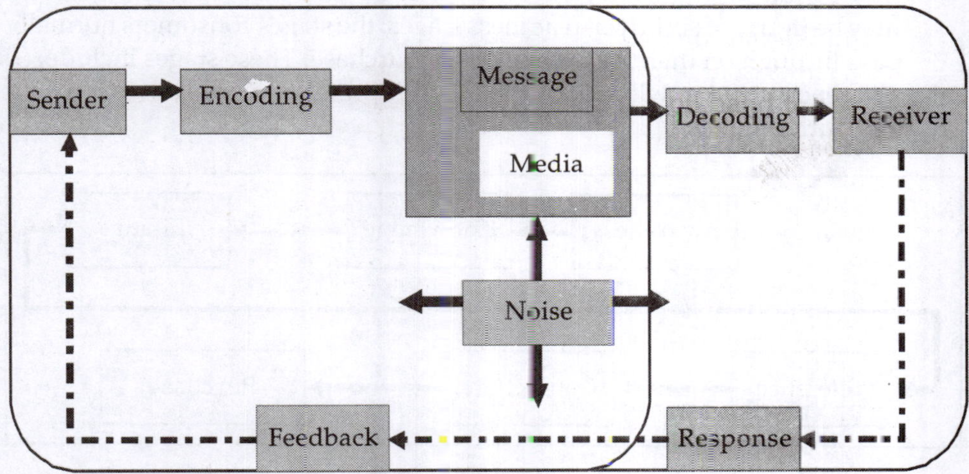

Fig. 2.2. Elements in the Communication Process

For a message to be effective, the sender's encoding process must mesh with the receiver's decoding process. Thus, the best messages consist of words and other symbols that are familiar to the receiver. The more the sender's field of experience overlaps with that of the receiver, the more effective the message is likely to be.

This model points out several key factors in good communication. Senders need to know what audiences they wish to reach and what responses they want. They must be good at encoding messages that take into account how the target audience decodes them. They must send messages through media that reach target audiences, and they must develop feedback channels so that they can assess the audience's response to the message.

Steps in Developing Effective Communication

In developing an effective integrated communications and promotion programme, the marketing communicator must do,

1. ***Identifying the Target Audience:*** A marketing communicator stars with a clear target audience in mind. The audience may be potential buyers or current users, those who make the buying decision or those who influence it. The audience may be individuals, groups, special publics, or the general public. The target audience will heavily affect the communicator's decisions on what will be said, how it will be said, when it will be said, where it will be said, and who will say it.
2. ***Determining the Communication Objectives:*** Once the target audience has been defined, the marketing communicator must decide what response is sought. Of course, in many cases, the final response is purchase. But purchase is the result of a long process of consumer decision-making. The marketing communicator needs to know where the target audience now stands and to what stage it needs to be moved. The target audience may be in any of six buyer-readiness stages, the stages consumers normally pass through on their way to making a purchase. These stages include; *(i)* awareness, *(ii)* knowledge, *(iii)* liking, *(vi)* preference, *(v)* conviction, and *(iv)* purchase.

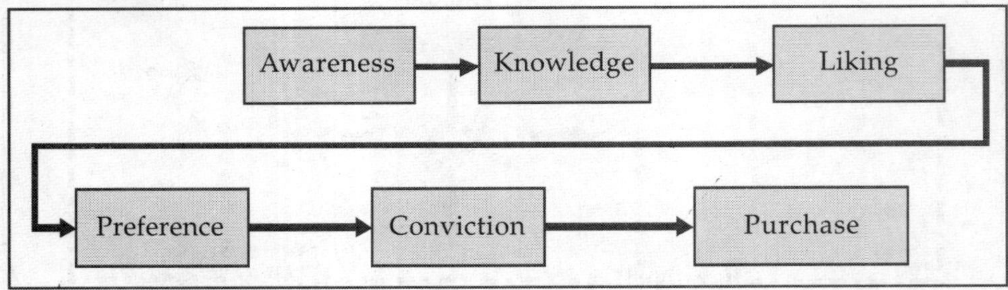

Fig. 2.3: Buyer-readiness Stages

3. ***Designing A Message:*** Having defined the desired audience response, the communicator turns to developing an effective message. Ideally, the message should get attention, hold interest, arouse desire, and obtain action (a framework known as the AIDA model). In putting the message together, the marketing communicator must decide what to say (message content) and how to say it (message structure and format).
    - *Message Content* – The communicator has to figure out an appeal or theme that will produce the desired response. There are three types of appeals: *(i)* rational, *(ii)* emotional, and *(iii)* moral.
        (a) Rational appeals relate to the audience's self-interest. They show that the product will produce the desired benefits.

(b) Emotional appeals attempt to stir up either negative or positive emotions that can motivate purchase. Communicators may use positive emotional appeals such as love, pride, joy, and humor.

(c) Moral appeals are directed to the audience's sense of what is 'right' and 'proper'. They are often used to urge people to support social causes such as a cleaner environment, better race relations, equal rights for women, and aid to the disadvantaged.

- *Message Structure:* The communicator must also decide how to handle three message-structure issues. The first is whether to draw a conclusion or leave it to the audience. The second message-structure issue is whether to present a one-sided argument (mentioning only the product's strengths) or a two-sided argument (touting the product's strengths while also admitting its shortcomings). Usually, a one-sided argument is more effective in sales presentations-except when audiences are highly educated or likely to hear opposing claims, or when the communicator has a negative association to overcome. The third message-structure issue is whether to present the strongest arguments first or last. Presenting them first gets strong attention but may lead to an anticlimactic ending.
- *Message Format:* The marketing communicator also needs a strong format for the message. In a print advertisement, communicator has to decide on the headline, copy, illustration, and color. To attract attention, advertisers can use novelty and contrast; eye-catching pictures and headlines; distinctive formats; message size and position; and color, shape, and movement. If the message is to be carried over the radio, the communicator has to choose words, sounds, and voices. The 'sound' of an announcer promoting banking services should be different from one promoting quality furniture. If the message is to be carried on television or in person, then all these elements plus body language have to be planned. If the message is carried on the product or its package, the communicator has to watch texture, scent, color, size, and shape.

4. ***Choosing Media:*** The communicator now must select channels of communication. There are two broad types of communication channels – personal and non-personal.

- *In Personal Communication Channels* – Two or more people communicate directly with each other. They might communicate face-to-face, over the telephone, through the mail, or even through an internet 'chat'. Word-of-mouth–personal communication about a product between target buyers and neighbors, friends, family members, and associates. Buzz marketing involves cultivating opinion leaders and getting them to spread information about a product or service to others in their communities.

- *Non-personal Communication Channels* – Are media that carry messages without personal contact or feedback. They include major media, atmospheres, and events. Major media includes print media, broadcast media, display media, and online media. Atmospheres are designed environments that create or reinforce the buyer's learning toward buying a product. Events are staged occurrences that communicate messages to target audiences. Non-personal communication affects buyers directly.

5. ***Selecting the Message Source:*** In either personal or non-personal communication, the message's impact on the target audience is also affected by how the audience views the communicator. Messages delivered by highly credible sources are more pervasive.
6. ***Collecting Feedback:*** After sending the message, the communicator must research its effect on the target audience. This involves asking the target audience members whether they remember the message, how many times they saw it, what points they recall, how they felt about the message, and their past and present attitudes toward the product and company. The communicator would also like to measure behaviour resulting from the message-how many people bought a product, talked to others about it, or visited the store.

Setting the Total Promotion Budget and Mix

(a) ***Setting the Total Promotion Budget***: One of the hardest marketing decisions facing a firm is how much to spend on promotion. We look at four common methods used to set the total budget from advertising:

(i) *Affordable method* – Setting the promotion budget at the level management thinks the firm can afford.

(ii) *Percentage-of-sales method* – Setting the promotion budget at a certain percentage of current or forecasted sales or as a percentage of the unit sales price. Or they budget a percentage of the unit sales price. The percentage-of-sales method has advantages. It is simple to use and helps to management think about the relationships between promotion spending, selling price, and profit per unit.

(iii) *Competitive-parity method setting* – The promotion budget to match competitor's outlay. They monitor competitor's advertising or get industry promotion spending estimates from publications or trade associations, and then set their budgets based on the industry average.

(iv) *Objective-and-task method* – It is the most logical budget-setting method. Whereby the company sets its promotion budget based on what it wants to accomplish with promotion. Developing promotion budget by *(a)* defining specific objectives; *(b)* determining the tasks that must be performed to achieve these objectives; and *(c)* estimating the costs of performing these tasks. The sum of these costs is the proposed promotion budget.

(b) ***Setting the Overall Promotion Mix.*** Each promotion tool has unique characteristics and costs. Marketers must understand these characteristics in selecting their mix of tools.

(i) *Advertising* – It can reach masses of geographically dispersed buyers at a low cost per exposure, and it enables the seller to repeat a message many times. Low cost per exposure, large scale advertisement says something positive about the seller's size, popularity and success. Consumers assume as more legitimate. Building up long-term image for the product. Can trigger quick sale.

(ii) *Personal selling* – Is most effective tool at certain stages of the buying process, particularly in building up buyers' preferences, convictions, and actions. It involves personal interaction between two or more people. So each person can observe the other's needs and characteristics and make quick adjustments. Builds long-term relationship.

(iii) *Sales promotion* – Includes a wide assortment of tools-coupons, contests, cents-off-deals, premiums, and others. They have unique qualities, attract consumer attention, offer strong incentives to purchase, and to boost sagging sales. Its shortcoming is short lived.

(iv) *Public relations* – Is very believable-news stories, features, sponsorships, and events seem more real and believable to readers than advertisements do. Message gets to the buyers as 'news' rather than as a sales-directed communication.

(v) *Direct marketing* – Forms are telephone marketing, direct mail, online marketing, and others-they all share four distinct characteristics. Direct marketing is non-personal. The message is normally directed to a specific person. Direct marketing is immediate and customized. It is interactive: It allows a dialogue between the marketing team and the consumer, and messages can be altered depending on the consumer's response.

Promotional Mix Strategy

Marketers can choose from two basic mix strategies....

- *Push Strategy:* A promotion strategy that calls for using the sales force and trade promotion to push the product through channels. The producer promotes the product to wholesalers, the wholesalers promote to retailers, and the retailers promote to consumers.
- *Pull Strategy:* A promotion strategy that calls for spending a lot on advertising and consumer promotion to build up consumer demand. If the strategy is successful, consumers will ask their retailers for the product, the retailers will ask the wholesalers, and the wholesalers will ask the producers.

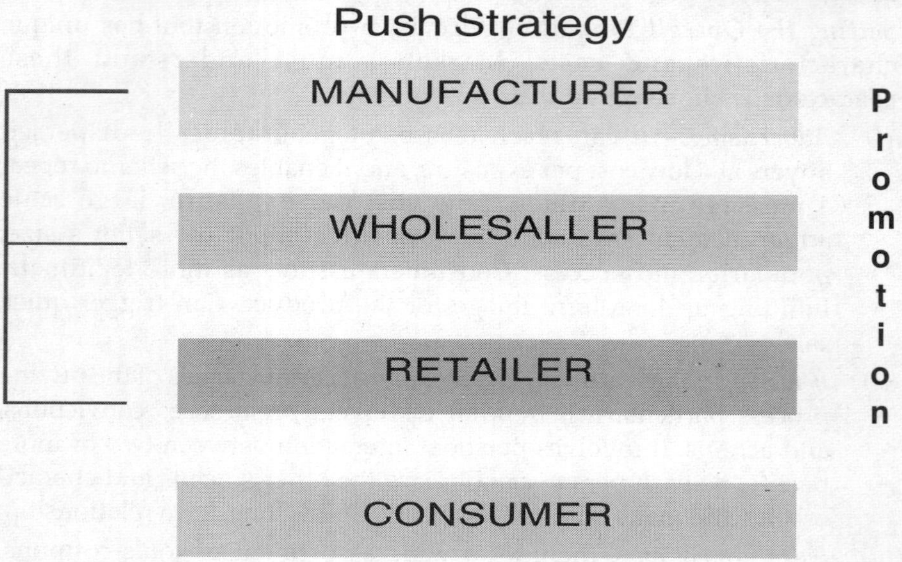

Push Strategy

Source: www.learnmarketing.net

Fig.2.4: Push strategy in promotion

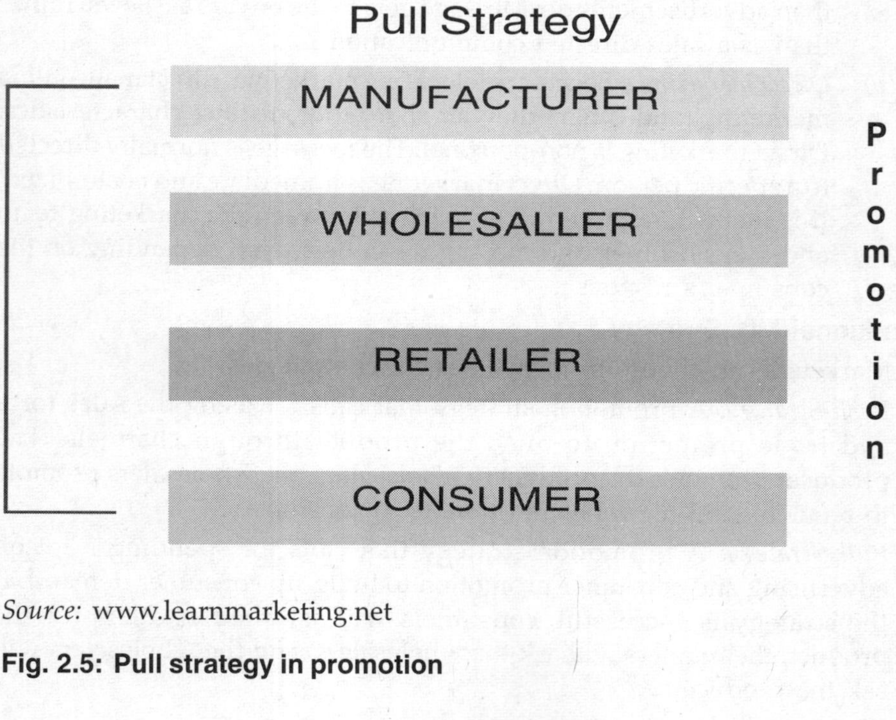

Pull Strategy

Source: www.learnmarketing.net

Fig. 2.5: Pull strategy in promotion

Integrating the Promotion Mix

A checklist for integrating the firm's marketing communications is...

- Analyzing trends-internal and external – that can affect the firm's ability to do business.
- Audit the pockets of communications spending throughout the organization.
- Identify all contact points for the venture and its brands.
- Team up in communications planning.
- Create compatible themes, tones, and quality across all communications media.
- Create performance measures that are shared by all communications elements.
- Appoint a director responsible for the firm's persuasive communications efforts.

Socially Responsible Marketing Communication

In shaping its promotion mix, a firm must be aware of the large body of legal and ethical issues surrounding marketing communications.

- *Advertising and Sales Promotion by Law:* Firms must avoid false or deceptive advertising. Advertisers must not make false claim. Sellers must avoid bait-and-switch advertising that attracts buyers under false pretenses. Firms can use advertising to encourage and promote socially responsible programmes and actions.
- *Personal Selling*: A firm's sales people must follow the rules of 'fair competition'. Most states have enacted deceptive sales acts that spell out what is not allowed.

New Product Development and Value Marketing in Agribusiness

1. ***The New Product:*** A firm has to be good at developing and managing new products. Every product seems to go through a life cycle – it is born, goes through several phase, and eventually dies as newer products come along that better serve consumer needs. This product life cycle presents two major challenges:
    - *First*, because all products eventually decline, a firm must be good at developing new products to replace aging ones (the challenge of new – product development).
    - *Second,* the firm must be good at adapting its marketing strategies in the face of changing tastes, technologies, and competition (the challenge of product life-cycle strategies).
    - We first look at the problem of finding and developing new products and then at the problem of managing them successfully over their life cycles.

- New-product development is the development of original products, improvements, product modifications, and new brands through the firm's own Research and Development efforts.

2. ***New-Product Development Strategy:*** Given the rapid change in consumer tastes, technology, and competition, companies must develop a steady stream of new products and services. A firm can obtain products in two ways:
   - Through acquisition – by buying a whole firm a patent or a license to product someone else's product. .
   - The other is through new product development in the firm's own research-and-development.
     - By new product we mean original products, product improvement, product modifications and new branch that the firm develops through its own research and development efforts.
     - Innovation can be very risky.
     - New products continue to fail at a disturbing rate.

3. ***Do Many New Products Fail?:*** There are several reasons for. Although an idea may be good, the market size may have been over estimated. Perhaps the actual product was not designed as well as it should have been, or was incorrectly positioned in the market priced too high, or advertised poorly. A high level executive might push a favorite idea despite poor marketing research finding. Sometimes the costs of product development are higher than expected, and sometimes competitors fight back harder than expected.

So, firms face a problem – they must develop new products, but the odds weigh heavily against success. In all, to create successful new products, a firm must understand its consumers, markets, and competitors and develop products that deliver superior value to customers. It must carry out strong new-product planning and set up a systematic new-product development process for finding and growing new products.

Major Steps in New Product Development

There are eight major steps in it. *(i)* Idea generation, *(ii)* Screening, *(iii)* Concept development and testing, *(iv)* Marketing strategy, *(v)* Business analysis, *(vi)* Product development, *(vii)* Test marketing, *(viii)* Commercialization.

1. *The Idea Generation:* New product development starts with the idea generation is the systematic search for new product ideas. A firm typically has to generate many ideas in order to find a few good ones. Major sources of new-product ideas include internal, competitors, distributors or suppliers, and others.
2. *Idea Screening:* The purpose of the succeeding stages is to reduce that number. The first stage is idea screening, which helps spot good ideas

and drop poor ones as soon as possible. Product development costs rise greatly in later stages, so the firm wants to go ahead only with the product ideas that will turn into profitable products.

Executives write up new-product ideas on a standard form to be reviewed by a committee, it describes the product, the target market, and the competition. It estimates market size, product price, development time and costs, manufacturing costs, and rate of return and so evaluates and asks different questions.

3. *Concept Development and Testing:* An attractive idea must be developed into a product concept. Information Technology is important to distinguish between a product idea which is an idea for a possible product that the company can see itself offering to the market, a product concept which is a detailed version of the idea stated in meaningful consumer terms, and a product image which is the way consumers perceive an actual or potential product.

Concept testing calls for testing new-product concepts with groups of target consumers. It may be presented to consumers symbolically or physically. So testing new-product concepts with a group of target consumers to find out if the concepts have strong consumer appeal.

4. *Marketing Strategy Development:* Is designing an initial marketing strategy for a new product based on the product concept. The marketing strategy statement consists of three parts.
   - The *first* part describes the target market; the planned product positioning and the sales, market share, and profit goods for the first few years. Thus the target market is younger, well educated, moderate-to-high-income individuals, couples or small families seeking practical, environmentally responsible transportation.
   - The *second* outlines the product's planned price, distribution, and marketing budget for the first year.
   - The *third* describes the planned long-run sales, profit goals, and marketing mix strategy.

5. *Business Analysis:* Once management has decided on its product concept and marketing strategy, it can evaluate the business attractiveness of the proposal. Business analysis involves a review of the sales, costs and profit projections for a new product to find out whether they satisfy the firm's objectives. If they do, the product can move to the product development stage.

6. *Product Development:* So far, for many new-product concepts, the product may have existed only as a word description, a drawing, or perhaps a crude mock-up. If the product concept passes the business test, it moves into product development. Here, R and D or engineering develops the product concept into a physical product. The product development step,

however now calls for a large jump in investment. It will show whether the product idea can be turned into workable product.

7. *Test Marketing:* If the product passes functional and consumer test, the next step is test marketing, the stage at which the product and marketing programme are introduced into more realistic market settings. Test marketing gives the marketing experience with marketing the product and its entire marketing programme – positioning, strategy, advertising, distribution, pricing, branding, packaging and budget levels.

8. *Commercialization*: Test marketing gives management the information needed to make a final decision about whether to launch the new product. If the firm goes ahead with commercialization which is introducing a new product into the market, it will face high costs. The firm may have to build or rent a manufacturing facility. The firm launching a new product must first decide on introducing timing where to launch the new product – in a single location, a region, the national market, or the international market.

Organizing for New-product Development

Many firms organize their new product development process into the orderly sequence of steps, starting with idea generation and ending with commercialization. This is called sequential product development. A new product development approach in which one firm's department works individually to complete its stage of the process before passing the new product along to the next department and stage.

This orderly, step-by-step process can helps bring control to complex and risky projects. But it also can be dangerously slow. In fast-changing, highly competitive markets – such slow-but sure product development can result in product failure, loss in sales and profits, and crumbling market positions. 'Speed to market' and reducing new-product development cycle time have become pressing concerned to firms in all sectors.

In order to get their new-products to market more quickly, many firms are adopting a faster, team-oriented approach called simultaneously product development (team-based or collaborative product development). In it, firm departments work closely together through cross-functional teams, overlapping the steps in the product development process to save time and increase effectiveness. Instead of passing the new product from department to department, the firm assembles a team of people from various departments that stays with the new product from start to finish. Such teams usually included people from the marketing, finance, manufacturing, and legal department.

Top management gives the product development team general strategic direction but no clear cut product idea or work plan. It challenges the team with stiff and seemingly contradiction goals – "turn out carefully planned and superior new products, but do it quickly" and then gives the team whatever freedom and resources it needs to meet the challenge. In the sequential process, a bottle neck at one phase can seriously slow the entire project. In the simultaneous approach, if one functional area hits snags, it works to resolve them while the team moves on. The simultaneous team-based approach does have some limitations.

- Super fast product development can be riskier and more costly than the slower, more orderly sequential approach.
- Moreover, it often creates increased organizational tension and confusion. And the firm must take care that rushing a product faster, but to create them better and faster.

Despite these drawbacks, in rapidly changing industries facing increasing shorter product life cycle, the rewards of fast and flexible product development for exceed the risks. Firms that get new and improved products to the market faster than competitors often gain a big competitive edge. They can respond more quickly to emerging consumer tasks and charge higher prices for more advanced designs. "Whoever gets there first get all the marbles".

Thus, new product success requires more than simply thinking up a few good ideas, turning them into products and finding customers for them. It requires a systematic approach for finding new ways to create valued customer experiences, from generating and screaming new product ideas to creating and rolling out, want satisfying products to customers. More than this, successful new products development requires a total firm commitment.

Product Life Cycle Strategies

After launching the new product, management wants the product to enjoy a long and happy life. Although it does not expect the product to sell forever, the firm wants to earn a decent profit to cover all the effort and risk that went into launching it. Management is aware that each product will have a life cycle, although its exact shape and length is not known in advance. The typical product life cycle (PLC) the course that a product's sales and profit take over its lifetime has 5 distinct stages.

Product development begins when the firm finds and develops a new product idea during product development, sales are zero and the firm's investment costs mount.

- Introduction is a period of slow sales growth as the product is introduced in the market. Profits are nonexistent in this stage because of heavy expenses of product introduction.
- Growth is a period of rapid market acceptance and increasing profits.
- Maturity is a period of slowdown in sales growth because the product has achieved acceptance by most potential buyers. Profits level off or decline because of product against competition.
- Decline is the period when sales fall off and profit drop.

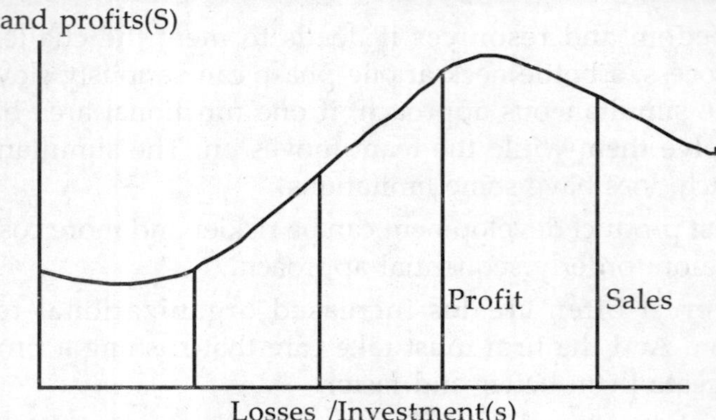

Fig.2.6: Sales and profits over the products' life cycle

REQUISITES FOR SUCCESS OF AGRIBUSINESS

The following are requisites for successful implementation of agribusiness, as Dr. B K. Baruah has put it in 'Agribusiness Management, its Meaning...", obtained from internet.

1. *Clear Objectives:* Determination of objectives is one of the most essential pre-requisite for the success of business. The objectives set forth should be SMART.
2. *Planning:* Planning is a pre-determined line of action. The accomplishment of objectives set, to a great extent, depends upon planning itself.
3. *Sound Organization:* Organization is, such a systematic combination of various related parts for achieving a defined objective in an effective manner.
4. *Research:* Market research enable a business in finding out new methods of production, improving the quality of product and developing new products as per the changing tastes and wants if the consumers.
5. *Finance:* Agribusiness should estimate its financial requirements adequately so that it may keep the business wheel on moving. Therefore, proper arrangements should be made for securing the required finance for the enterprise.
6. *Proper Plant Location, Layout and Size:* The success of agribusiness depends to a great extent on the location. Where it is set up?. Location of the business should be convenient from various points of view such as availability of required infrastructure facilities, availability of inputs like raw materials, skilled labours, nearer to the market etc.
7. *Efficient Management:* One of the reasons for failure of business often attributed to as their poor management or inefficient management. The one man, *i.e.*, the proprietor may not be equally good in all areas of the business. Efficient businessman can make proper use of available resources for achieving the objectives set for the business.

8. *Harmonious Relations with the Workers:* In an agribusiness organization, the farmer operator occupies a distinct place because he/she is the main living factor among all factors of production. In fact, it is the human factor who makes the use of other non-human factors like land, machine, money etc. Therefore, for successful operation of business, there should be cordial and harmonious relations maintained with the workers/ labours to get their full cooperation in achieving business activities.

Managing Agribusiness

The management process is often divided into five traditional functions: planning, organizing, directing, controlling, and coordinating. Planning is determining a course of action to accomplish stated objectives; organizing is fitting people and resources together in the most effective way; directing pertains to supervising and motivating people; the controlling function monitors performance and make adjustments to stay on purpose; and coordinating synchronizes the total effort. Each of these is a necessary ingredient for accomplishing the established objectives. (Downey and Erickson, 1987). Management of agricultural business is unique because agricultural business is extremely seasonal, its products are perishable commodities, and it deals in the local communities where long-term interpersonal relationships are critical.

Therefore, agribusiness managers have to deal with the legal aspects such as land lease agreements; crop/livestock and business insurance; dealing with custom work agreements, etc., which are not easy to manage. Managing agribusiness inventory also require careful planning and adequate experience. Agribusiness inventory is directly related to and that also determine the production and marketing capacities of the firm. Managing agribusiness resources is also a difficult task that agribusiness manager has also to accomplish well. For example, the manager has to see the comparative advantages of renting land versus using own land, owning machinery versus using rented one, using own money versus using borrowed money (opportunity cost), etc.

Decision-making is one of the primary responsibilities of agribusiness managers. Professional managers approach this activity in a systematic way, identifying the problem, summarizing facts, laying out and analyzing alternatives, and taking action. Their analysis often utilises a wide variety of analytic tools to aid their decisions. Computers are useful for calculating and production data, preparing database files and spreadsheets, preparing business records and analysis useful for management decisions. Moreover, electronic media is necessary to access market information through the use of computers. Thus, the use of computers as a decision aid tool for managing agribusiness is also given importance.

Control programmes are the means by which an agribusiness manager coordinates the activities of the business, predicts trends and results, amasses data for planning, set goals, and utilises the lessons of the past experience. Control is achieved by means of basic programmes relating to marketing, production, personnel, and financial records, along with more complex programmes for larger organizations.

Marketing in Agribusiness

The movement of farm supplies and services to farmers and the flow of agricultural products from farms to the final consumer occur within the agricultural marketing system. It is complex system, involving literally hundreds of thousands of businesses that perform the basic marketing functions of buying, selling, transporting, storing, processing, informing, risk bearing, financing, and standardizing agricultural products. Each of these market functions contributes in some way to the final value or utility of the product; that is, it adds form, time, place or possession utility (Downey and Erickson, 1987).

Marketing management is concerned with marketing decisions within the agribusiness firm. Its object is to develop, execute, and control a strategic marketing plan that satisfy customers' needs while generating a profit for the firm.

Market managers must first carefully analyze the market, identifying various segments or classes of customers who have unique characteristics so that marketing programmes can be adapted to major segments.

Planning a marketing strategy requires a variety of techniques and tools to analyze markets and make decisions. Some tools are simple applications of logic, while others are highly sophisticated analytical models.

A marketing audit is a thorough and objective examination of a firm's marketing programme. With it market performance and potential for each product are analyzed; distinctive competencies (*i.e.*, areas of unique strength relative to competition) can be recognised; current and future market conditions are reviewed; current marketing programmes are evaluated; execution of the marketing programme is considered; and finally, the human resources available and their organization are studied.

Sales forecasting is another highly useful marketing tool that is especially valuable in agribusiness because of the volatility of agricultural markets. It usually begins with general economic forecasts and becomes more and more specific as the forecaster moves toward forecasting sales for an individual product or service.

Marketing managers must also analyze competition and monitor their marketing programmes. Formal competitor strengths-and-weakness analysis is a useful tool that suggests strategic marketing approaches for competing with each other competitor.

Various marketing-research methods provide invaluable information for developing marketing plans. Simple tools, such as pinpointing customers by type or size on a map, provide much information. Customer surveys and personal and group interviews are also popular methods. Marketing managers must synthesize information from a variety of sources to assist them in developing a successful marketing programme.

Operating the Agribusiness

Production management involves a complex network of decisions that affect the production process. Production of agricultural products is hampered by severe problems of seasonality, perishability, bulkiness, and variations in quantity and quality, or value. Production involves planning, and must be viewed as a total system involving location, size, and layout of plant; purchasing; inventory control; and production controls. There are several categories that affect each of these decisions, and agribusiness managers are urged to consider all factors and their effect on the total system before making-decision.

Agribusiness production managers who wish to maintain control of their operations will have to forecast trends; order purchases that are in line with these trends; control the amount of inventory on hand to see that it is neither too much, which is costly, nor too little, which can result in loss of sales opportunities; and employ sophisticated scheduling methods and quality controls. Purchasing is an operation that requires skill, knowledge, and honesty in dealing with bids and negotiations from suppliers. Such factors as quantity, quality, price, time, and service are elements of efficient purchasing. The amount of inventory and kind of inventory systems used depend upon an agribusiness's size, complexity, and management sophistication; Programme Evaluation and Review Technique (PERT) and Critical Path Method (CPM) are two highly sophisticated network scheduling models. Managers must periodically inspect outputs to ensure quality and adherence to specifications. The manager who is able to exercise control over these facets of production will have a tightly run operation that stands a good chance of maximizing profits.

Human Resource Management in Agribusiness

Managing human resources is a fundamental responsibility of agribusiness managers. Managers must develop an organizational structure in which the responsibilities, authority, and accountability of individuals are clearly defined. Management must then direct and supervise daily activities, motivating and controlling employees to maximize productivity.

Human resources are the most important asset of any agribusiness. The personnel function of management is concerned with administering the mechanics of employment. The larger the agribusiness, the more formal and complex the process; but the personnel function must be accomplished in any agribusiness. In most agribusiness, the personnel function also includes regular evaluation of employee performance and ensuring continual professional growth through ongoing training and development programmes. Personnel managers are often designated to coordinate the agribusiness's relationship with labour unions. Negotiating union contracts and carrying out contract specifications are difficult but important personnel functions.

Management is a complex process based on the individual characteristics of the leader, the led, and the situation. But there are many approaches and theories that can help the agribusiness manager a great deal. Leadership is challenging task for most agribusiness managers. There are many different styles of leadership, ranging from authoritarian to democratic to free rein. Management theorists have developed many models and theories to explain effective leadership. Transactional analysis is one of the many models for understanding employees and what motivates them. It offers a simple language and framework for discussing various leadership problems.

Financial Management and Control in Agribusiness

Agribusiness managers use a great many economic principles to make important business decisions. The marginal cost-marginal revenue concept suggests the most profitable level of production. The opportunity cost concept is critical in assessing various decision alternatives. And applying supply and demand principles to agricultural supplies and farm products is basic to almost all agribusiness plans. Profit is the focal point of any agribusiness, but it is the net result of many factors, many of which are reflected by financial statements. Agribusiness managers rely on basic financial statements to interpret how the business is doing and to suggest the direction it should take.

Financial management requires the highest degree of specialized know-how in interpreting financial information from a firm's records. Without this know-how, agribusiness manager at any level find it difficult to implement the goals and objectives of the organization. Financial statements provide a wealth of information for a variety of persons and organizations interested in evaluating the agribusiness. Owners, managers, lenders, and government agencies all look at financial statements from a different perspective. Analysis of financial statements is often comparative, over time, against budget, or with similar firms. Ratios show important financial relationships in the business. These ratios must be understood and used carefully or they will be misleading; used properly, they are indicators of strengths and weaknesses in the business.

A balance sheet shows assets, or what the business owns at a certain point. It also shows liabilities, or claims of creditors against those assets, and the value of owners' claims against the assets. Assets always equal liabilities plus net worth; the latter is included because all the assets must be claimed. Both assets and liabilities are broken down into several categories to provide a useful financial picture of the business.

Ratios generally measure profitability, liquidity, solvency, or efficiency. Return on the owners' investment (ROI) is the most fundamental measure of profit. The ROI chart shows the relationship of sales and expenses with assets. Sometimes, graphing financial ratios over time is a highly valuable management tool. Financial analysis is a fundamental management tool for the agribusiness manager. Although it is not a substitute for human judgment, financial analysis gives the manager important insights of decisions.

Financing the agribusiness is a necessary and important management responsibility. Money must be available to finance capital purchases and operate the business in a day-in, day-out basis. There are three primary sources of capital: *(i)* borrowing, *(ii)* funds generated from business operations, and *(iii)* additional investments from owners. Each financing method has pros and cons and must be considered carefully by management.

The most common control programmes are budget and forecasts, or predictions of business inputs and output. One of the most important areas in which development of a strong control programme is credit control, where upward spiraling costs often cause serious financial problems of agribusiness. Two possible solutions are to make the extension of credit, a profit centre or to discount cash sales. In any event, credit programmes should be planned and monitored carefully in order to develop systems for determining a customer's credit worth and for minimizing accounts receivable or outright bad debts.

An exciting and new management technique called management by exception focuses attention on those areas of the agribusiness where problems exist, and makes data easier to produce and understand. The agribusiness manager who incorporates these basic tools for control into the daily activities of the business will stand a good chance of developing and maintaining a profitable enterprise.

Volume-cost analysis is one of the more powerful tools used by agribusiness managers. By separating fixed costs from variable costs, managers can study the impact of a variety of cost and price changes on their profit and determine the amount of business necessary to break even. They can even project the amount of the business necessary to reach a certain profit level.

Another widely used tool involves the concept of the time-value of money. Investment decisions must take into consideration the cost of tying up money investments over periods of time. Discounted cash flow and the net present value of money are methods for evaluating various investment alternatives that are widely used by agribusiness managers.

In sum, agribusiness manager has to be based on sensible planning that takes the inherent uncertainty associated with agricultural production. The management aspects of agribusiness manager has to consider well the seasonality, perishability of agricultural commodities; as well as the interpersonal and traditional relationships of the local communities in to account. Thus, the consideration of all these and the implementation of the managerial functions discussed are the means and conditions necessary for effective agribusiness management.

Post-harvest Technology Management in Agribusiness

Over the past decade, domestic and international food markets have undergone rapid transformation and the global food production and distribution system is changing from a sector dominated by family-based farms and small-scale, relatively independent firms to one of larger, global companies that are more tightly integrated and aligned up and down the food supply chain.

Increasing emphasis on higher value farm products to meet the changing diets of urban consumers has focused renewed attention on post-harvest systems, while unacceptably high losses due to poor handling and lack of appropriate infrastructure have reduced economic benefits to small producers.

Post-harvest activities are an integral part of the food production system, and the aim is to promote best practices for post-harvest handling and management along the entire food supply chain, focusing on a broad spectrum of operations and stakeholders in traditional and modern marketing systems. The ultimate goal of the system is to deliver high quality, safe food to consumers. FAO assists member countries in meeting these goals by:

- Building the technical capacity of farmers, traders and other stakeholders in good post-harvest handling practices in agricultural value chains.
- Developing, consolidating and disseminating information on post-harvest operations through publications and the web-based Information Network on Post-harvest Operations (INPhO).
- Strengthening the capacity of public and private sector organizations to provide appropriate post-harvest services to their clients.
- Providing advice and training on the design and proper management of post-harvest specific infrastructure.

POST-HARVEST MANAGEMENT

Individual Crops

For the purpose of post-harvest management the agricultural commodities can be grouped as follows:

Durables

Durable crops such as cereals, pulses, oilseeds and roots and tubers are staple foods for millions of poor people in developing countries. It is thus important to maintain the quality of these crops along the entire supply chain to ensure that consumers have access to food that is safe and nutritious. However, traditional techniques of grain storage on the farm are not in general very efficient and, as a result, post-harvest losses during storage can be considerable due to insect and rodent attack. Poorly stored grain is also susceptible to contamination with mycotoxins which poses a major health hazard to consumers.

On farm grain storage structure can be modified to meet optimum storage requirements of storage grain. Hence any improved storage structures should aim at overcoming the constraints due to environmental, biological, technological and socio-economic grain loss contributing factors on already existing traditional storage structures. Therefore, an improved storage structures should meet the following desirable features:

- Maintain an even cool and dry storage environment.
- Provide adequate protection from common storage loss agents.
- Offer reasonable protection from thieves.
- Be simple and inexpensive to construct using locally available materials where possible (be economical on unit storage basis).
- Be easy to clean and repair and must not have cracks and crevices that might harbor and or facilitate multiplication of storage pests.
- Be reasonable long lasting.
- Be with flexible capacity and performance.
- It should permit easy inspection.
- It should permit aeration and fumigation where required.

FAO aims to improve traditional technologies and introduce new techniques in the post-harvest handling and storage of agricultural products. One example is the metal silo technology for grain storage on the farm. The silo can be hermetically sealed for fumigation purposes, provide an effective barrier against insects and rodents and allow grain to be stored in good condition for longer periods of time. The structures have been promoted in many countries in Latin America, Africa and Asia and local artisans trained in their fabrication.

However, improved storage structures by themselves are not enough to improve grain quality. Their promotion goes hand in hand with training in good storage practice, store hygiene, proper use of insecticides and adequate drying.

Perishables

The demand for high quality fruits and vegetables to satisfy growing and changing market demand necessitates that all stakeholders in horticultural value chains have a working knowledge and understanding of technical operations that add and create value and which enhance safety and quality of fresh horticultural produce.

A number of resource materials in the form of technical bulletins, brochures and guidelines tailored to addressing technical aspects of post-harvest handling, value creation, safety, quality and cost efficiency in fresh fruit and vegetable chains have been developed.

Herbs and spices

There is a continuing and expanding international demand for herbs, spices and essential oils. Social changes, including food diversification, desire for new flavors, increasing importance of 'ethnic' and processed foods which require condiments and aromatic herbs for their preparation are driving this demand. Many of these species are found only in the tropics and developing countries have a significant opportunity to benefit from this increasing demand. Many of these products can be sold in a dried form or as extracts, which gives them a high value per unit weight. These products could be a profitable source of diversification for small farmers in developing countries.

However, good post-harvest operations are often the limiting factor in the establishment of a profitable production enterprise based around herbs, spices and essential oils in developing countries. In view of the increasing importance of this sector, FAO in collaboration with UNIDO has prepared a guide for extension services and small producers on post-harvest handling and processing of herbs and spices to improve the quality and marketability of these products.

Capacity Building

A key component of FAO's work is building the capacity of farmers, traders and other stakeholders in the agricultural value-chain in post-harvest operations. Collaboration with other organizations to develop training programmes designed to transfer technology, disseminate information and build capacity in post-harvest management. Courses are generally designed as 'training of trainers', where technologists, extension personnel, NGOs, government officials, entrepreneurs and key farmers are trained and then made responsible for training other stakeholders, often small-scale farmers. Examples of such training programmes include:

Metal silos for grain storage at farm level

FAO aims to transfer improved technologies such as the metal silo for the storage of grains on the farm. Traditional techniques of grain storage are not in general very efficient, and as an alternative method of storage, FAO has introduced the metal silo technology. This technique reduces losses and allows grain to be stored for longer periods. The technology has been transferred to many countries in Latin America, Africa and Asia where core groups of local artisans (including women) have been trained on the construction of metal silos.

Horticultural chain management

FAO in collaboration with the Commonwealth Secretariat funded the development of a 'Train the Trainer' programme on Horticultural Chain Management, developed by the University of Pretoria.

Safety management for durable crops in africa

Mycotoxin contamination of grain staples is a major food safety concern in many African countries and a major health hazard for local populations. Following a major mycotoxin outbreak in Kenya in 2004, FAO, in collaboration with the Kenya Ministry of Agriculture, designed a training course for agricultural extension staff on mycotoxin control in the maize supply chain. The training was then replicated in different parts of the country.

Information resources

FAO consolidates and disseminates information on post-harvest technologies to farmers, traders, entrepreneurs and other stakeholders in the agricultural value-chain. This is done through a variety of technical publications, but the flagship resource for post-harvest operations is the Information Network on Post-harvest Operations (INPhO). INPhO is a web based information network developed by FAO in collaboration with GTZ and CIRAD to better address the information needs of developing countries on post-harvest issues and to exchange information and experiences on post-harvest operations.

INPhO includes:

(a) *Virtual library:* The library contains more than 200 full-text documents on a broad range of post-harvest operations. It is continually being updated with new documents from both FAO and collaborating organizations to ensure up-to-date and relevant information.

(b) *Post-harvest compendium:* The compendium contains detailed information on over 30 commodities, including grains, pulses, oilseeds, spices, fruits and vegetables.

(c) *Decision support tools:* To assist entrepreneurs in establishing agro-enterprises, a range of decision support tools has been developed with the intention of contributing to improved preparation and evaluation of agribusiness projects, leading to more sustainable agro-industrial enterprises and enhanced incomes in agribusiness, particularly in developing countries. Agriventure is a software tool that guides users through the entire process of data entry and financial analyses required in the formulation of an agro-industrial investment project. A database of Technical Co-efficients from selected projects has been prepared for raw materials, utilities and other resources necessary for the operation of a food processing company. This will assist users of Agriventure to estimate co-efficients in the preparation of data for their own projects.

(d) *Food processing toolkits:* Four toolkits have been developed covering processing of cereals; fruits and vegetables; oilseeds and roots and tubers. The toolkits are designed for entrepreneurs and development professionals to assist with the preparation of projects on post-harvest processing, and the establishment or improvement of food processing businesses. Each toolkit is a practical package that can be used by small and medium scale food processors to establish or improve a food processing enterprise, primarily in developing countries.

(e) *Global 'cookbook':* The 'cookbook' is a collection of over 800 traditional and modern recipes from around the world.

The Processing-Manufacturing Sector

The processing-manufacturing sector includes all the individuals and firms that process agricultural commodities (for instance, turning wheat in to flour), manufacture food products (turning flour, eggs, and other inputs in to bread), and distribute and retail food products to the final consumer.

The rising cost of labour and changing farmer attitudes toward credit helped to bring about a rapid rise in the use of purchases inputs of the development of a separate agricultural input sector. Changing consumer preferences created opportunities for those firms involved in processing, manufacturing, distributing, and retailing of food and fiber products. The growth of these two sectors and either side of production agriculture requires an expansion of the definition of agriculture to include all three parts: *(i)* the agricultural input sector, *(ii)* the production sector, and *(iii)* the processing-manufacturing sector of what is now called agribusiness.

Future Focus of Post-harvest Technology

The traditional goals of post-harvest technology are to improve handling system with emphasis on post-harvest treatments including storage, packaging and transportation to maintain quality and reduce losses of products between the field and the ultimate destination. The post-harvest technology has increasingly become vital in the supply chain management. The medium and long-term challenges are that post-harvest technology should be more viable to enhance the value chain and to cope with the changing market environments. Following are the new roles of post-harvest technology:

- To meet the demand-driven legality, safety, and quality requirements.
- To provide mechanisms for combating non-tariff trade barriers and market access.
- Post-harvest technology and quality management system integration in supply chain management.
- Shift to appropriate technologies to serve the modern trade stores and global sourcing by multinational retail chain.
- Targeted/focused technologies to meet the challenge of emerging new supplies and the requirement of the new markets.

INFRASTRUCTURE FOR AGRIBUSINESS

For industrial development strategy, infrastructure is a top priority in development strategies, if the intention is to reduce poverty, maximize the positive effects of other investments, and foster broadly distributed economic growth. This is especially true when we consider the existing situation in many of the small holder villages of the developing countries.

Moreover, infrastructure is a pivotal part of the county's development strategy, in part because it is the backbone of rural development strategies, be it education, agriculture, health, and also absence of one or more infrastructure components adversely affects the results of any rural development process.

1. *Roads:* A dramatically improved roads network undoubtedly contributes to enhancing the transport of produced goods to local and regional markets. It opens up isolated and disadvantaged areas and contributes to improved standards of living by substantially reducing travel time and costs and improving travel conditions.
2. *Transport:* Agriculture is best served by consistent high urban, and international demand. This is best brought about by an efficient, high volume, transport and marketing system where the transporting and marketing unit costs are low (Hine and Ellis, 2001).
3. *Storage:* Storage is one of the basic physical functions which take place in agricultural commodity marketing system. Storage of agriculture produces helps to speed up the supplies though out the year and avoid gluts in market and significant price decline during the peak period (IFPRI and IFAD, 2003). In addition, storage plays significant role keeping the quality of some products. One of the methods that minimize post-harvest production losses is the usage of modern storage facilities. Moreover, the existence of modern storage facilities is the prerequisite for the functioning of warehouse receipt system. However, different market participants especially in proximity to production areas have no modern storage facilities.
4. *Market Places:* Market facilities are one of the major components of market development. According to Tracy, equipping a market; improving transport facilities; institutional restructuring, including reducing or reallocating staff; a system for the management of market facilities and information; providing training to market staff and to farmers' groups; introducing quality control standards, and properly enforcing market regulations and equipping with necessary facilities helps to increases market efficiencies by creating good marketing networks.

Therefore, improvement of village markets (and or selecting the rural market centres) is often combined with programmes for general upgrading of post-harvest handling facilities or for access road improvement such as:

- Provide a road side shaded assembly area.
- Allow producers to cool and/or more efficiently prepare their produce for sale and often better access to traders and truckers.
- Allow producer cooperatives to assemble and market larger volume of agriculture produces at more competitive prices.

The location of the village markets/centres should be....

- Close proximity to the main village road so that trucks could reach the market centres.
- Nearby concentration of agricultural products.

5. *Energy:* Adequate supply of quality and adequacy of power facilitate the agribusiness in many ways such as for cold storage, large markets operates during day and nights, also helps the farmers for transportation of goods without any hardships.
6. *Telecommunication:* The task of further developing telecommunications service converge would require considerable investment in terms of technology and know-how point, it is in consideration of this and the importance of ICT for economic development.
7. *Water:* Supplying adequate and clean water to the population improves many of the economics and social dimensions of poverty. It improves the health of the population with concomitant advances in the quality of the life. Moreover, it releases the labour (particularly that of women and female children) used to carry water, which in turn could be used elsewhere, mainly in education for girls. Increase in the availability of water is also essential for crop production, livestock rearing, and electricity (power) generation.

MARKET BASED PLANNING OF AGRICULTURAL PRODUCTION

Production Decisions

In market based planning of agricultural production, before deciding to produce a product the following four production decisions should be addressed:

1. What to produce? What products are highly demanded in the market?
2. How to produce? What is the most technical combination of inputs to use in producing the output?
3. How much to produce? What is the correct amount of output to produce that will maximize the profit of the producer?
4. When to produce? What is the correct time to produce the output *i.e.,* at what time the demand for the output is high?

The answers to these four production questions rest heavily on the level of demand for the output at various prices. But the answers are also heavily influenced by cost factors such as the availability and prices of inputs.

Consumer Buying Behaviour

Before developing their marketing plans, marketers need to study consumer markets and consumer behaviour. In analyzing consumer markets, firms need to research who constitutes the market (occupants), what the market buys (object), why the market buys (objectives), who participates in the buying (organizations), how the market buys (operations), when the market buys (occasions), and where the market buys (outlets). Consumer behaviour is influenced by four factors: cultural, social, personal and psychological factors. Research in to all these factors can provide clues as to how to reach and serve consumers more effectively.

Producing for the Market

Food losses stem both from poor post-harvest handling and from over production. In order to avoid wasteful over production, post-harvest loss reduction activities should begin even before the crop is planted. If there is limited consumer demand for a product (whether sold at the market price or at an official government price) then production should only be under taken if the market has been clearly identified. This, of course, refers primarily to horticultural crops, although there have been cases of governments promoting excessive production of grains, beyond the ability the market system to store and market them.

Advice on Product Planning

Marketing Extension Worker (MEW) should be able to advise farmers on what crop and variety to grow in the coming season and at what time. Even for small farmers, the concept of product planning, *i.e.*, careful selection of the crops to be produced considering marketability is important. The small farmer is often very slow in adapting to changing market situations. He keeps on producing the same traditional crops or handicraft products to which he is accustomed. He should take up lines of production for which the smaller grower has some advantage. He should select activities which require relatively less land but intensive cultivation with high labour inputs and with relatively higher market value. High value cash crops, such as mushrooms, vegetables – especially off-season vegetables – poultry, and piggery, fishery etc., may do much more to raise small farmers' income than cereals.

Market Information

Small farmers need different types of information: forecast of market trends, current prices and market arrival information. Information on market trends and expected price movement is useful in planning production. An expected fall in grain prices, for example, would suggest that a small farmer grows the minimum to meet family requirements, and devotes the balance of his resources to other products. For this purpose, 'market forecast information systems' has been introduced in some countries to assist farmers in planning their production. A marketing extension service will provide such information and field level workers will use it to advise farmers.

Enlightened Marketing

Enlightened marketing is a marketing philosophy holding that a firm's marketing should support the best long run performance of the marketing system.

THE 'SEVEN CORE PRINCIPLES' OF ENLIGHTENED MARKETING

1. *Enlightened Marketing has Integrity:* In order to attract clients successfully, we need to do it with the highest integrity. Clients will be more likely to hire us if they perceive that we are sincere and can be trusted. Marketing with integrity means that we are honest about the strengths and limitations of our services in all aspects of our marketing.
2. *Enlightened Marketing is Authentic:* In order to market with authenticity we need to put our authentic self out there for people to see and experience. Acting authentically illuminates our uniqueness and naturally attracts the clients who feel they can benefit from our individuality and what we distinctly have to offer.
3. *Enlightened Marketing is Passionate:* When we are passionate about marketing and the services that we offer, we will be more motivated to take the steps necessary to build our business effectively. In addition, the enthusiasm that we exude will be part of what draws clients to us and builds our reputation.
4. *Enlightened Marketing has Vision:* Our marketing efforts will be more successful if we have a clear vision for our practice and know how we intend to achieve this vision. Furthermore, the more creative we are with our vision, the more profound and limitless it will be. We need to hold our vision throughout all our marketing activities, while allowing it to evolve and grow.
5. *Enlightened Marketing is Conscious:* To be conscious from the perspective of enlightened marketing means that we are aware of how marketing functions as both an art and a science. We make a conscious effort to learn and experiment with marketing strategies, discovering what works and what doesn't, and modifying our plans accordingly.
6. *Enlightened Marketing Shows Commitment and Dedication:* In order to achieve the results we desire, we must be committed and dedicated to developing our business and making it a priority in our life. To this end, marketing must be taken just as seriously as the service we provide to our clients.
7. *Enlightened Marketing is Unattached to Outcomes:* While it is important to remain committed to our marketing it's equally important that we remain unattached to the outcome of our marketing efforts. Regardless of how much marketing knowledge we have, things do not always go as planned. Patience and persistence are essential.

Making the above seven core principles foundational to our marketing ill enable us to enjoy marketing more, and help ensure us attract the type clients we most enjoy working with. In the end, we will be able to build a ving and highly rewarding private practice.

The Requirements for Future Success of Agribusiness Management

- Planning agricultural production based on market behaviour.
- Greater attention to meeting consumer needs.
- More attention to value addition.
- Assumption by marketing of a more central role in the operation of agribusiness firms in order for them to remain profitable.
- More sophisticated marketing techniques.

3

Credit and Finance in Agribusiness

THE MEANING AND SCOPE OF CREDIT AND FINANCE IN AGRIBUSINESS

The majority of the world's poor live in rural areas. Yet most lack access to the range of financial services they need. Financial institutions seeking to work in rural areas face numerous constraints, such as poor infrastructure, dispersed demand, price and yield risks, and collateral limitations. Moreover, the main products of many micro-finance institutions – short-term working capital loans with frequent expected repayments – may not be well-suited to longer-term agricultural activities, nor the resultant seasonality in the cash flow of rural households.

Not all rural finance is agricultural or micro-finance and not all agricultural finance is rural. Yet, financial service providers offering *rural finance* (financial services used in rural areas by people of all income levels), *micro-finance* (financial services for poor and low-income people), and *agricultural finance* (financing of agriculture-related activities, from production to market) often have overlapping objectives and opportunities. The clients served by micro-finance are often the same clients or households that would benefit from increased rural or agricultural finance.

The financial systems approach in micro and rural finance – which emphasizes a favorable policy environment and institution-building – has improved the overall effectiveness of rural finance interventions. But numerous challenges remain, especially in agricultural finance.

ROLE OF AGRICULTURAL FINANCE IN ECONOMIC DEVELOPMENT

Agriculture is still a leading economic sector, exporter, and source of livelihood in many developing countries, especially for the poor and women. Rural livelihoods are often closely linked to agriculture. Financial services for the rural poor offer the same benefits of risk mitigation and income-smoothing as they do for urban and peri-urban micro-enterprises. Rural finance can also assist households in maintaining food security. Financial savings enable rural households to diversify and complement in-kind savings, while payment services enable them to cost-effectively send and receive money.

Rural development means nothing but the transformation of the subsistence agricultural production to a market oriented agricultural economy. Availability and access to financial resources is one of the key elements to this transition. Financial resource is a very important, if not the most important, factor in economic development.

Shortage of finance is one of the major problems facing small farmers. Farmers need financial resource to buy improved agricultural inputs and farm implements so that they can increase their output and income level and break the cycle of poverty. Farmer's investment in these technologies cannot be real without having in place organizations and systems that are capable of adequately providing rural financial services to farmers. So, the effort to develop agriculture could suffer in the absence of a strong financial base that aims at expanding access to credit for small farmers.

Unfortunately, the state of rural financial markets in developing countries is characterized by inadequate availability of financing for both agricultural and non-agricultural activities. Very few of the rural populations have access to financial services because commercial banks consider lending to small farmers as a risky business and because providing financial services to rural people is considered to be more costly and difficult. Lending to small farmers involves high transaction costs. They lack conventional collateral and the managerial skill and do not keep records.

In a country where agriculture accounts for a major proportion of economic activities and employs a large proportion of the population increased availability of credit to the sector would lead to increased production and growth. Therefore, in order for agriculture to effectively meet the challenge of being an engine of growth credit should be made available and accessible to small farmers in particular.

Need for Financial Service

The financial service needs are broad and may include:

- Short-term credit/working capital – for inputs, cash flow management, income smoothing.
- Term credit – for fixed assets or land acquisition, leasing, inventory build-up.

- Deposit and transfer services including domestic payment services and remittances – for cash flow management, risk mitigation, investment and asset-building.
- Insurance products (health, life, weather).

Working capital is more readily available to rural enterprises than long-term credit or other financial services. It meets seasonal needs for inputs, labour, and production services. When timed correctly, working capital allows use of seed varieties, fertilizer, labour and other inputs that may lead to increased income. Working capital has limitations in that it is short-term financing for immediate needs of an enterprise. Also, very short-term loans (for instance, three months) for agricultural inputs are often too brief to allow repayment from the sale of seasonal crops. Without access to the flexibility of investment capital or other long-term sources of capital, enterprises cannot easily expand or upgrade their business or overcome unforeseen events.

Term funds finance capital improvements such as a new barn, storage facility, equipment or livestock expansion. Investments in these assets help businesses to grow and jump to the next level. Long-term credit is not readily available in rural areas, at least to smaller farms and enterprises.

A well-functioning financial system is one of the key foundations on which sustained economic development can be built. Research suggests that financial sector development plays an independent and causal role in promoting long-run economic growth. More recent evidence has also shown that finance is not only pro-growth, but also pro-poor: Well developed financial systems are associated with more rapid growth in the incomes of the poor, helping them catch up with the rest of the economy as it grows.

Yet, financial development differs sharply around the world. Even at similar levels of income, countries have very different levels of financial development. If finance is a key driver of economic development, what can governments do to promote financial development? Research so far suggests a number of important policy recommendations.

First and foremost, well functioning financial systems need stable macro-economic policies and strong legal and information systems. Making infrastructure improvements a priority is a must.

Second, promoting a contestable financial sector – as characterized by lower entry barriers, fewer regulatory restrictions on bank activities, greater banking freedom – is essential for improving depth, efficiency and access. This means reducing government ownership through careful privatization, and domestic and international liberalization including foreign entry. Opening up is also accompanied by risks however, particularly a higher risk of financial crisis, and therefore needs to be synchronized with improvements in institutional improvements.

Third, governments have an important role to play as regulators. But empirical evidence suggests the best approach to regulation is one which empowers the markets, rather than creating all powerful regulators who may be subject to corruption and political and industry capture. Empowering the market entails enforcing accurate and timely information disclosure and providing the right incentives for market participants to make sure they remain vigilant monitors – for example, through avoiding generous and miss-priced deposit insurance, or forbearance policies that distort risk-taking incentives. Research also questions the wisdom of transplanting First World practice to developing countries. Often regulations considered appropriate in developed economies prove ineffective or counterproductive in weaker institutional settings: Explicit deposit insurance may destabilize the very financial system it is meant to protect, and powerful supervisors may be more prone to corruption and extracting rents. Hence, the importance of institutional factors that need strengthening to support these policies.

Finally, governments have an important role to play in facilitating broad access to financial services, *i.e.*, in expanding the availability of the range of financial services to a broader set of households, firms and sectors in the economy. A sure way of improving access is by making and encouraging infrastructure improvements. Better legal, information, payments systems, distribution and other structures can allow technology to bring down transaction costs.

Promoting competition in the financial sector and allowing foreign institutions will also encourage the private sector to reach the under-served segments and increase the speed with which access-improving technologies are adopted. Consumer protection rules such as anti-discrimination and anti-predatory lending regulations would help, and so would removal of interest ceilings that end up hurting the poor. Governments can also be instrumental in facilitating innovative technologies to improve access through private-public partnerships. Finally, while the general messages will be similar, the priorities and the extent to which financial sector needs improvement in each country will depend on initial conditions, with the reforms being the most challenging for low-income countries.

CAPITAL FOR AGRIBUSINESS

- *Basic Concept of Capital:* The long-term investments we make today will determine the value of our business tomorrow. In order to make long-term investments in new product lines, new equipment and other assets, managers must know the cost of obtaining funds to acquire these assets. The cost associated with different sources of funds is called the cost of capital. *Cost of Capital represents the rate a business must pay for each source of funds – debt, preferred stock, common stock, and retained earnings.* Since we want to maintain existing market values, cost of capital is the minimum acceptable rate of return for long-term investments. If the business earns more than its cost of capital, the market value of the business will increase. Likewise, if returns on long-term investments are below the cost of capital, market values will decline. This leads us to a very fundamental objective within financial management – maximizing values for the owners of the business. Therefore, how we manage capital is extremely important to fulfilling the basic objective of increased shareholder value.

- *The Economics of Capital:* An understanding of economics and capital can also help us understand how we should manage capital within an organization. For example, the total amount of capital available is determined by the total amount of investment. The overall economy has a total capital equal to the sum of all capital goods (assets). Since these goods lose value over time, some level of reinvestment is needed to maintain the asset base at its current size. Additional investments will cause the capital stock of an economy to grow, similar to the assets of a business. The amount invested in the economy is determined by the after tax rate of return on capital. The actual level of investment depends on the willingness of people to invest in assets. People invest based on the returns they expect to receive. The returns to investors must be adjusted for inflation, taxes, depreciation, and risk related to the investment. It is the after tax real rate of return that drives investment.

In general, the after tax rate will remain constant over time due to changes in investment spending. For example, if the rate of return on capital is to increase, there will be an increase in investment spending. As the capital stock expands from increased investment, the rate of return on capital will drop back down. Conversely, when the rate of return on capital is low, there will be a decrease in investment. As capital shrinks, the rate of return on capital rises. Consequently, investment spending will keep rates of return on capital at stable levels. Taxation of capital will increase the cost of capital. In order to supply capital, investors must receive a minimum after tax real rate of return. The users of capital not only pay investors a nominal rate of return, but they also incur the cost of economic depreciation (lost values of capital assets) and related taxes on capital. These total costs represent the cost of capital.

- *Basic Considerations in Managing Capital:* The overall objective is to find an 'optimal' capital structure – the right mix of capital sources (debt and equity) that minimizes the overall cost of capital and maximizes values to the shareholders (owners of the business). When we raise capital, we have two choices – issue debt or issue stock. Debt is represented by bonds which are long-term instruments sold to investors. Stock is the ownership interest of the business and depending upon the rules of incorporation, stockholders will have certain rights. Therefore, we start our understanding of capital management by looking at the advantages and disadvantages of the two sources of capital:

Some Advantages of using Stock:

- No fixed payments are required to investors; dividends are paid only as earnings are available.
- No maturity date on the security, the invested capital does not have to be repaid.
- Improves the credit worthiness of the enterprise.

Some Disadvantages to using Stock are:

- Dilutes the earnings per share to shareholders.
- Issuance costs are higher than debt.
- Issuing more stock can increase the overall cost of capital.
- Dividend payments to shareholders are not tax deductible.

Some Advantages to using Debt

- Interest payments are tax deductible.
- Does not dilute earnings per share or control within the company.
- Cost is fixed; interest and principal do not change.
- Expected returns to investors are usually lower than stock.

Some Disadvantages to using Debt:

- Fixed charges must be paid regardless of available earnings or cash flow.
- Adds more risk to the business.
- Has a maturity date and the capital invested must be repaid to investors.

In addition to understanding the pros and cons of financial securities, we also need to recognise that several conditions will impact how we raise capital. These conditions include:

- *Economic Conditions:* The demand and supply of capital in the marketplace can impact how capital is raised. For example, expectations of inflation will influence the cost that is paid for capital. Higher rates of inflation erode the values of investments and thus, investors will demand higher rates of return.
- *Market Conditions:* The demand for higher rates of return will increase the cost of capital. For example, if we raise capital with a security that is not highly marketable, investors will require higher rates of return for the increased risk.
- *Operating Conditions:* The level of fixed costs used to operate the business needs to be considered. For example, higher fixed costs can result in wider variations to operating income from numerous factors – increased competition, slower economic growth, etc. This is referred to as business risk.
- *Financial Conditions:* The existing levels of outstanding debt will impact how capital will be raised. Higher levels of debt (including preferred stock) can result in wider variations to earnings due to higher fixed

obligations that must be paid (interest to debt holders and fixed dividends to preferred stock holders). This is referred to as financial risk. Not only do we need to look at various conditions, but we need to consider how financing will impact capital structure. Capital structure appears on the right side of the Balance Sheet as liabilities and equity; *i.e.,* the long-term sources of funds to finance assets. Assets appear on the left side of the Balance Sheet. Capital structure is the permanent financing of the business through the use of debt and stock. The total of all liabilities and equity is referred to as Financial Structure.

Therefore, Capital Structure = Financial Structure – Current Liabilities

Finding the right capital structure encompasses numerous considerations – growth rates in sales, risk attitudes of management, liquidity of assets, control position of the enterprise, etc. Finding the right capital structure also involves finding the right amount of financial leverage. Financial leverage is the financing of assets with fixed obligations – debt and preferred stock. The use of financial leverage increases return on equity up to a certain level of operating income. As we use more financial leverage (debt and preferred stock), higher levels of operating income are needed to cover the additional fixed obligations (interest on debt and fixed dividends on preferred stock).

Generally, the use of financial leverage will improve financial performance whenever returns are higher than the costs of obtaining funds. In a perfect world, management would favor more leverage whenever return on capital exceeds the after tax costs of debt. However, higher returns also result in higher risk to the business (risk return trade off). Therefore, the use of financial leverage is a balancing act between higher returns for shareholders *vs*. higher risk to shareholders.

- *Refinancing Risk:* One of the objectives within the financing decision is to match the maturity of liabilities with the life expectancy of assets. This allows liabilities to be self-liquidating. If the maturity of liabilities is less than the life expectancy of assets, then we face refinancing risk since we have to raise new capital to pay off liabilities. If the maturity of liabilities is longer than the life expectancy of assets, then there will be plenty of assets around to pay off debts. However, these surplus assets may not earn enough to increase the market value of the firm.

The mismatching of liabilities with assets can occur if financing is not available. For example, suppose long-term financing is not available, short-term sources of financing may have to be used. Mismatching can also be intentional. For example, suppose we expect long-term interest rates to fall, we may want to finance assets with short-term maturities since we can refinance in a few years at much lower rates.

- *Inflation:* Another factor to consider in the financing decision is inflation. By using debt financing during periods of high inflation, we will repay the debt with dollars that are worth less. As expectations of inflation increase, the rate of borrowing will increase since creditors must be compensated for a loss in value. Since inflation is a major driving force behind interest rates, the financing decision should be cognizant of inflationary trends.

- *Floatation Cost*: Equity sources of capital will cost more than debt sources of capital. One reason is due to higher risk to investors. Whenever investors incur more risk, they demand higher rates of return; *i.e.*, risk return trade off. Additionally, the actual out-of-pocket cost associated with equity financing is higher than debt financing. These costs are referred to as floatation costs. Floatation costs include all costs of issuing the securities, such as bankers' fees, legal fees, filing costs, etc.

Marginal Cost of Capital

A basic consideration within the financing decision is how much money do we need to raise? If we assume that all projects have the same average level of risk, then we can establish an optimal capital budget by plotting the Marginal Cost of Capital. The relationship between cost of capital and required financing is referred to as the Marginal Cost of Capital. The Marginal Cost of Capital Rate is the discount rate used for capital budgeting analysis. Marginal Cost of Capital is calculated as follows:

1. Determine the cost and percentage of financing needed for each source of capital – debt, stock, retained earnings.
2. Calculate breaking points where the weighted average cost of capital begins to increase under different financing plans. The break point can be calculated as: *Maximum Amount of Lowest Source of Capital/Per cent of Financing Provided by this Specific Source of Capital*.
3. Calculate the weighted average cost of capital over the range of financing between the break points.
4. A graph can be used to show the range of cost of capital in relation to total financing. If a project's internal rate of return is greater than the marginal cost of capital, then the project should be accepted.

SOURCES OF FINANCE IN AGRIBUSINESS

Finance is essential for a business's operation, development and expansion. Finance is the core limiting factor for most businesses and therefore it is crucial for businesses to manage their financial resources properly. The main source of credit for many farmers and agribusinesses is other agribusinesses along the value chain including input suppliers, traders, and processors. Moreover, the clients' own savings and credit from financial institutions continues to play a role in agricultural production.

Suppliers of rural and agricultural finance can be broadly categorised as:

- Value Chain Actors: exporters/wholesalers; processors; local traders and processors; producer groups; farmers; and input suppliers.
- Financial Institutions:

- Banks (commercial, agricultural banks, state development banks),
- Non bank financial institutions (commercial MFIs, other non-bank lenders, and leasing companies,
- Not-for-profit MFIs, which tend to work with poorer clients.

- Credit unions and Agricultural Cooperatives.

It is also crucial for businesses to choose the most appropriate source of finance for its several needs as different sources have its own benefits and costs. Sources of finance can be classified based on a number of factors. They can be classified as Internal and External, Short-term and Long-term or Equity and Debt. It would be uncomplicated to classify the sources as internal and external.

(A) Internal Sources of Finance

Internal sources of finance are the funds readily available within the firm/enterprise and consist of:

- Personal savings.
- Retained profits.
- Working capital.
- Sale of fixed assets.

1. Personal savings

This is the amount of personal money an owner, partner or shareholder of a business has at his disposal to do whatever he wants. When a business seeks to borrow the personal money of a shareholder, partner or owner for a business's financial needs, the source of finance is known as personal savings.

Advantages

- The owner would not want collateral to lend money to the business.
- There is no paperwork required.
- The money need not necessarily be paid back to the owner on time.
- Can be interest free or carry a lower rate of interest since the owner provides the loan.

Disadvantages

- Personal savings is not an option where very large amounts of funds are required.
- Since it is an informal agreement, if the owner demands the money back in a short notice it might cause cash flow problems for the business.

2. Retained profits

Retained profits are the undistributed profits of firm. Not all the profits made by a firm are distributed as dividends to its shareholders. The remainder of the profits after all payments are made for a trading year is known as retained profits. This remainder of finance is saved by the business as a back-up in times of financial needs and may be used later for a firm's development or expansion. Retained profits are a very valuable no-cost source of finance.

Advantages

- They need not be paid back since it is the firm's own savings
- There are no interest payments to be made on the usage of retained profits.
- The firm's debt capital does not increase and thus gearing ratio is maintained.
- There are no costs of raising the finance such as issuing costs for ordinary shares.
- The plans of what is to be done with the money need not be revealed to outsiders because they are not involved and therefore privacy can be maintained.

Disadvantages

- There may be opportunity costs involved.
- Retained profits are not available for starting up businesses or for those businesses that have been making losses for a long period.

3. Working capital

Working capital refers to the sum of money that a business uses for its daily activities. Working capital is the difference of current assets and current liabilities (*i.e.* Working capital = Current assets – Current Liabilities). Proper working capital management is also vital as it is also a source of finance for a business.

Advantages

- Since it is an internal source of finance there are no costs involved.
- No repayment is needed.
- External parties cannot influence business decisions.
- Will not increase debt capital of the firm so gearing ratio is maintained.

Disadvantages

- Opportunity costs are involved.
- It is not suitable for long term investments.
- Working capital cannot raise large amounts of funds.
- Total risk is undertaken by the enterprise.
- Using working capital as a source of finance will affect the current ratio of the business.

(i) ***Current Assets:*** Current assets are also known as cash equivalents because they are easily convertible to cash. Current assets consist of Stocks, Debtors, Prepayments, Bank and Cash. These assets are used up, sold or keep changing in the short-run.

- *Stock* – This refers to the stock of goods available to the business for sale at a given time. It is very important to maintain the right amount of stock of goods for a business. If stock levels are too high it means that too much of money is being held up in the form of stock and if stock levels are too low the business will loose possible opportunities of higher sales.
- *Debtors* – Are a business's customers owing money to the business having been bought the business's goods or service on credit. If a business has cash flow problems it can maintain a low level of debtors by encouraging the debtors to pay as early as possible.
- *Prepayments* – These are the expenses paid in advance. The payment being made even before the expense occurs is a prepayment.
- *Bank and Cash* – Bank is the cash held in banks and cash is money held by the business in the form of cash. Having too much of money in the form of cash is also not good for a business since it can use that money to invest and earn a return but however a business should have healthy current ratio (current assets: current liabilities) of 2:1.

(ii) ***Current Liabilities:*** Current liabilities are short-term debts that are in immediate need of settlement. Some examples of current liabilities are creditors, accruals, proposed dividends and tax owing. These obligations have to be paid within a year.

- *Creditors* – Also known as trade creditors are suppliers from whom the business purchased goods on credit. Paying the creditors as late as possible will ease cash flow requirements for a business.
- *Accruals* – Are the expenses owed by the business.
- *Dividends proposed* – Are the dividends payable for the year that is not yet paid.
- *Tax owing* – Is the sum of money owing as tax.

4. Sale of fixed assets

Fixed assets are the assets a firm that do not get consumed in the process of production. Some examples of fixed assets are land and building, machinery, vehicles, fixtures and fittings and equipments etc. Sometimes where the fixed asset is a surplus and is abandoned, it can be sold to raise finance in demanding times for the business. Otherwise businesses may choose to stop offering certain products and sell its fixed assets to raise finance. Selling fixed assets reduces the production capacity of a business affecting a business's return.

Advantages

- Funds are again raised by the business itself and therefore need not be paid back.
- No interest payments are required.

- Large amounts of finance can be raised depending on the fixed asset sold.
- Would be the ideal source of finance if it was for an asset replacement.

Disadvantages

- If the asset is sold then the business would lose opportunities to generate income from it.
- If the business wants to buy a similar asset later on it may cost more than it was sold for.
- If the asset is sold and the money is spent without return then the business is broke.
- The asset may be able to generate more income than the purpose it was sold for.

(B) External Sources of Finance

Sources of finance that are not internal sources are external sources of finance. External sources of finance are from sources that are outside the business. External sources of finance can either be:

- Ownership capital or
- Non-ownership capital

1. Ownership capital

Ownership capital is the money invested in the business by the owners themselves. It can be the capital funding by owners and partners or it can also be share bought by the shareholders of an enterprise. There are mainly two main types of shares. They are *(i)* Ordinary shares *(ii)* Preference shares.

(i) Ordinary shares

Ordinary shares also known as equity shares are a unit of investment in a firm. Ordinary shareholders have the privilege of receiving a part of firm profits via dividends which is based on the value of shares held by the shareholder and the profit made for the year by the firm. They also have the right to vote at general meetings of the firm. Firms can issue ordinary shares in order to raise finance for long-term financial needs.

Advantages

- The amount need not be paid back – it is a permanent source of capital.
- Able to raise large amounts of finance.
- If the firm follows a rational dividend policy it can create huge reserves for its development programme.
- The dividends need to be paid only if the firm makes a profit.
- No collateral is required for issuing shares.
- It will help to reduce gearing ratio

Disadvantages

- Issuing shares is time consuming.
- It incurs issuing costs.
- There are legal and regulatory issues to comply with when issuing shares. Possible chances of takeover where an investor buys more than 50 per cent of the total issued shares value.
- Groups of equity shareholders holding majority of shares can manipulate the control and management of the company.
- May result in over-capitalisation where dividend per share falls.
- Once issued the shares may not be bought back and therefore the capital structure cannot be changed.

(ii) Preference shares

Preference shares are another type of shares. Preference shareholders receive a fixed rate of dividends before the ordinary shareholders are paid. Preference shareholders do not have the right to vote at general meetings of the firm. Preference shares are also an ownership capital source of finance. There are several types of preference shares. Some of them are Cumulative preference share, Redeemable preference share, Participating preference share and Convertible preference share.

- *Cumulative preference shares* – if a firm is in a loss making situation and is unable to pay dividends for one year then the dividend for that year will be paid the next year along with next year's dividends.
- *Redeemable preference shares* – these preference shares can be bought back by the firm at a later date. Normally the date of redemption is usually agreed.
- *Participating preference shares* – give the benefit of additional dividends to its shareholders above the fixed rate of dividends they receive. The additional dividend is usually paid in proportion to ordinary dividends declared.
- *Convertible preference shares* – convertible preference shareholders have the option of converting their preference shares to ordinary shares.

Advantages

- Have no voting rights and thus the management can retain control over the affairs of the firm.
- Preference shareholders need not be paid if the firm makes a loss.
- Even if the firm makes large profits, preference shareholders need to be paid only a fixed rate of interest.
- Has other benefits similar to ordinary share issue such as – no repayment required, large amounts of capital can be raised, permanent source of capital and no collateral required.
- Redeemable preference shares can be redeemed.

Disadvantages

- Even if the firm makes a very small profit it will have to pay the fixed rate of dividend to its preference shareholders.
- Preference shares are usually cumulative and thus twice the amount must be paid the following year if dividends are not paid on the year they need to be paid.
- Taxable income is not reduced by preference dividends unlike debentures where interest paid reduces taxable income.
- Have other drawbacks similar to ordinary share issues such as the cost, time consumption and legal requirements.

2. Non-ownership capital

Unlike ownership capital, non-ownership capital does not allow the lender to participate in profit-sharing or to influence how the business is run. The main obligations of non-ownership capital are to pay back the borrowed sum of money and interest. Different types of non-ownership capital:

- Debentures.
- Bank overdraft.
- Loan.
- Hire-purchase.
- Lease.
- Grants.
- Venture capital.
- Factoring.
- Invoice discounting.

(a) Debentures

Debentures are issued in order to raise debt capital. Debenture holders are not owners but long-term creditors of the firm. Debenture holders receive a fixed rate of interest annually whether the firm makes a profit or loss. Debentures are issued only for a time period and thus the firm must pay the amount back to the debenture holders at the end of the agreed period. Debentures can be secured, unsecured, fixed or floating.

- *Secured debentures* – are debentures that are secured against an asset. They are also called mortgage debentures.
- *Unsecured debentures* – these debentures do not have an asset as collateral.
- *Fixed debentures* – have a fixed rate of interest.
- *Floating debentures* – do not have fixed rate of interest and are not tied to any specific asset.
- *Bearer debentures* – these debentures are easily transferable.

- *Registered debentures* – are not easily transferable and legal procedures have to be followed in case of a transfer.
- *Convertible debentures* – can be converted to stock at the end of the debenture repayment date.

Advantages

- Debenture holders do not have rights to vote at the firm's general meetings.
- Tax benefits – debenture interests are treated as expenses and charged against profits in the profit and loss account.
- Debentures can be redeemed when the firm has surplus funds.

Disadvantages

- Debenture interests have to be paid regardless the firm makes a profit or loss.
- The money borrowed has to be paid back on an agreed date.

(b) Bank overdraft

Bank overdraft is a short term credit facility provided by banks for its current account holders. This facility allows businesses to withdraw more money than their bank account balances hold. Interest has to be paid on the amount overdrawn. Bank overdraft is the ideal source of finance for short-term cash flow problems.

Advantages

- No security is needed for a bank overdraft.
- Ideal for short-term cash flow deficits.
- Easy and quick to arrange.
- Interest is only paid when overdrawn and on the exact amount needed.
- Since overdraft is a short-term debt it is not included in calculating the firm's gearing ratio.

Disadvantages

- There is a limit to the amount that can be overdrawn.
- Interest has to be paid on an overdraft that is calculated on a daily basis and sometimes the bank charges an overdraft facility fee too.
- Overdrafts are meant to cover only short-term financing and are not a permanent or long-term source of finance.
- Interest is calculated on a variable rate and therefore it is difficult to calculate the cost of borrowings.
- Overdrafts can be recalled by the bank at any time if not stated in the agreement.

(c) Loan

Loans are amounts of money borrowed from banks or other financial institutions for large and long-term business projects such as the development or expansion of the business. However loans can be substituted by other alternative sources of finance which are more suitable.

Advantages

- Large amounts can be borrowed.
- Suitable for long-term investments.
- The lender has no say on how the money is spent.
- Need not be paid back for a fixed time period and banks do not withdraw at a short notice.
- Interest rates are lower than for bank overdrafts and are set in advance.

Disadvantages

- Collateral is needed.
- The amount borrowed has to be repaid at the agreed date.
- Interest is charged.
- Loans will affect a company's gearing ratio.

(d) Hire purchase

Hire purchase allows a business to use an asset without paying the full amount to purchase the asset. The hire purchase firm buys the asset on behalf of the business and gives the business the sole usage of the asset. The business on its part must pay monthly payments to the hire purchase firm amounting to the total value of the asset and charges of the hire purchase firm. At the end of the payment period the business has the option of purchasing the asset for a nominal value.

Advantages

- The business gains use of the asset before paying the asset's value in full.
- The payment is made in affordable installments.
- Hire purchase installments are taxable expenditures.
- At the end of the payments, ownership of the asset is transferred to the firm.
- Payments can be made from the asset's usage and return of the asset.

Disadvantages

- Ownership remains with the lender until the last payment is made.
- The asset will cost the firm more than the original value.
- If payments are not made on time the lender has the right to repossess the asset.
- If the asset is required to be replaced due to breakdown or because it is out-dated in which case the payment may still have to be made and the asset replaced.

(e) Lease

In a lease, the leasing firm buys the asset on behalf of the business and the asset is then provided for the business to its use. Unlike a hire purchase, the ownership of the asset remains with the leasing firm. The business pays a rent throughout the leasing period. The leasing firm is known as the lessor and the customer as lessee. Leasing is of two types, namely: 'Finance lease' and 'Operating lease'.

- *Finance Lease* – this is where the lessee's monthly payments add up to at least 90 per cent of the total value of the asset.
- *Operating Lease* – this lease does not run for the full life of the asset and the lessee is not liable for the full value of the asset. The residual risk is taken up by the lessor.

Advantages

- The amount in full need not be paid in order to start using the asset.
- The total cost and the lease period is pre-determined and thus helps with budgeting cash flow.
- In an operating lease, payments are made only for the usage duration of the asset.
- Lease is inflation friendly where the agreed rate is paid even after five years when other costs increase due to inflation.
- It is easier to obtain a lease than a commercial loan.

Disadvantages

- The ownership of the asset remains with the lessor even after payments but however in a finance lease the option is provided to buy the asset at a nominal value.
- In a finance lease the lessee ends up paying more than the value of the asset.
- Lease cannot be terminated whenever at lessee's will.

(f) Grants

Grants are funding given to businesses for programmes or services that benefit the community or public at large. Grants can be given by the government or private firms. For example a grant may be given to open a new factory where unemployment is high.

Advantages

- Grants do not have to be paid back.
- There are no costs involved in obtaining a grant.

Disadvantages

- Grants are given on certain restrictions and laws imposed by the government.
- Not all organizations are eligible for grants.

- Grants are given freely and therefore are very competitive because lots of firms try for the same source of fund.

(g) Venture capital

Venture capital is the capital that is contributed at the initial stages of an uncertain business. The chance of failure of the business is great while there is also a possibility of providing higher than average return for the investor. The investor expects to have some influence over the business.

Advantages

- Venture capitalists invest large sums of money in the business.
- They may also bring a lot of experience and expertise along with the money.
- Since they become owners by investing in the business they have equal interests in the business's success.
- Venture capitalists are only periodical investors wanting to exit the business at some stage.

Disadvantages

- The profits will be shared with the investor.
- Acquiring venture capitals is a lengthy and complex process where a business plan and financial projections must be submitted to the potential venture capitalist.
- As an owner of the business, the venture capitalist may want to influence the strategic decisions and take control of the business.

(h) Factoring

This is where the factoring firm pays a proportion of the sales invoice of the business within a short time-frame to the business. The remainder of the money is paid to the business when the factoring firm receives the money from the business's debtor. The remainder of the money will be paid only after deducting the factoring firm's service charges. Some factoring firms even offer to maintain the sales ledger of the business. Factoring is of two types: Recourse factoring and Non-recourse factoring.

- *Recourse factoring* – In this type of factoring the client firm is liable for bad debts.
- *Non-recourse factoring* – is where the factor takes responsibility for the payment of the debtors. The client firm is not liable if debtors do not pay back. Non-recourse factoring is usually more expensive because of the high risks experienced by the factor.

Advantages

- A large proportion of money is received within a short time-frame.
- The sales ledger of the business can be outsourced to the factor.
- The money collections from debtors are undertaken by the factoring firm.

- Helps a business to have a smooth cash flow operation.
- Non-recourse factoring protects the client firm from bad debts.

Disadvantages

- The business has to pay interests and fees for the factor for its services.
- The cost will be a reduction on the firm's profit margin.
- Lack of privacy since the sales ledger is maintained by the factor.
- Costumers would not like factoring firm collecting debts from them.

(i) Invoice discounting

In invoice discounting, the client firm send out a copy of the invoice to the invoice discounting firm. The client then receives a portion of the invoice value. In contrast to factoring, the client firm collects the money from its debtors. Once the payment is received it is deposited in a bank account controlled by the invoice discounter. The invoice discounter will then pay the remainder of the invoice less any charges to the client.

Advantages

- The client firm receives the money in a short period.
- There is some amount of privacy since the sales ledger is maintained by the client firm and only some invoices are submitted for immediate cash.
- Less costly than factoring since the sales ledger is maintained by the client firm.
- Unlike factoring, customers are not aware of invoice discounting since the debt collection is undertaken by the client firm.

Disadvantages

- Debt should be collected by the client firm itself and thus resources and time are wasted in debt collection.
- Sales ledger has to be maintained by the client firm itself.

The Costs of the Different Sources of Finance

- *Personal savings* – have low costs since they are provided by an owner, partner or shareholder. The owner may charge a rate of interest for the loan provided.
- *Retained profits* – have opportunity cost, that is the money could have been used elsewhere for some other purpose. Otherwise there is no other costs for this source of finance.
- *Working capital* – they do not have any costs other than opportunity cost.
- *Sale of assets* – by selling fixed assets it uses, then the firm's production capacity will diminish. If it sells unused or abandoned fixed assets then only the potential production capacity reduces. Sometimes firms will

have to stop offering certain products or services in order to sell its asset and raise finance. The asset may cost much more than what it sold for if it wants to replace it.

- *Ordinary and Preference shares* – dividends has to be paid out of profits to shareholders as a return for their investment in the business. There are administrative costs occurring from issuing shares like stock exchange listing fee, printing and distribution fee and advertising fee.
- *Debentures* – have to be paid a fixed or floating interest depending on the type of debenture that is issued.
- *Bank overdraft* – interest is a little higher than for bank loans and interest is calculated on a daily basis.
- *Loans* – interest is usually fixed for short-term loans, and long-term loans usually have a variable rate of interest. Interest rates are lower than for bank overdrafts.
- *Hire-purchase* – the business ends up paying more than the original value of the asset for its purchase.
- *Lease* – the ownership of the asset remains with the leasing firm even after the business pays more than 90 per cent of the asset's value but however some leasing firms provide the option of purchase of the asset a nominal value.
- *Grants* – are free and have no financial costs.
- *Venture capital* – the venture capitalist will have some influence over the business and the business will have to share profits with the investor. The investor will want the capital back at a later date.
- *Factoring* – Factors charge a rate of interest of about 1.5 per cent to 3 per cent of the invoice value as finance charges. Interest is calculated on a daily basis. Credit management and administrative fee are also charged and ranges from about 0.75 per cent to 2.5 per cent of turnover
- *Invoice discounting* – Invoice discounting also charges a rate of interest of about the same but its credit management and administrative charges are lower than factors because only finance is provided and sales ledger is not maintained by an invoice discounting firm.

Choosing An Appropriate Source of Finance

There are many sources of finance available to a business. Finance is needed for several purposes and different purposes need sources of finance which are most suitable for them. When choosing an appropriate source of finance some factors have to be considered. The factors that need to be considered when choosing an appropriate source of finance are:

- The amount of money needed.
- The urgency of funds.
- The cost of the source of finance.

- The risk involved.
- The duration of finance.
- The gearing ratio of the business.
- The control of the business.

1. *The amount of money needed:* This is the amount of finance the firm wants to raise. Not all sources of finance provide all amounts of funds. Some sources are not able to raise large amounts of funds whereas others are not flexible enough to put up for the small sum of money the business requires. Therefore it is necessary to identify the amount of money needed by the firm to choose a suitable source of finance. For example borrowing a commercial loan for a small and short-term cash flow problem is unwise because loans may have a minimum amount that can be borrowed, so taking a bank overdraft would be wise where money can be borrowed in small sums and bank overdrafts can be paid back quickly. Therefore the amount of money required is a key factor in choosing a source of finance.
2. *The urgency of funds:* This refers to the amount of time the business can spend on collecting funds. If the business has plenty of time before its financial needs to be met, then it can spend time searching for cheap alternative sources of finance. On the other hand if the business wants the money as soon as possible, then it would have to make some cost sacrifices and accept a source of finance that may even higher cost. The urgency of funds needs to be identified also because certain sources of finance need more time to be raised than other sources of finance. For example issuing shares is a very long and complex process where there are legal requirements and then the potential shareholders have to be informed (advertising) and after all these the money is collected through the process of application and allotment which takes more time.
3. *The cost of the source of finance*: Different sources of finance have different costs as discussed above. It is always more profitable to a business to seek and obtain cheaper sources of finance. Sometimes however the time does not permit firms to look for cheaper sources of funds. Internal sources of finance are always cheaper than external sources of finance.
4. *The risk involved:* The risk involved is the certainty of receiving returns for the lender on the investment made using the finance. In simpler words, it is the sureness of success of the project. If the provider of finance is not confident that the project in which his money is invested is less likely to reap returns then the lender would be reluctant to provide the business with funds. In this case the money can be secured against an asset as collateral which will encourage the lender to lend.
5. *The duration of finance:* This is the time period for which the money is needed. It can be for a short-term (within one year), medium-term

(one to five years) or long-term (five years and more) time period. By identifying the length of requirement of finance the firm can eliminate inappropriate sources of finance and choose a source of finance that is more suitable for the required timeframe.

6. *The gearing ratio of the business:* The gearing ratio plays an important role in the availability of the sources of finance since the gearing ratio shows the ratio of debt capital to the total capital of a business. If a business is high geared, then commercial lenders will be unwilling to give loans because the business is already operating on more loans than equity capital. A high geared firm will have to pay more of its profits as interests on loans and other debt capital. That being the case potential lenders fears the business' ability to be able to cope with more interest payments and debt settlement.
7. *The control of the business:* The existing shareholders of a company would be reluctant to issue shares because this would cause a dilution in control of the business. Issuing shares in public limited companies also gives opportunity of takeovers to outside parties. The same can be said for venture capitalists where the money is invested as equity and being owners the venture capitalists have the right to influence how the business is run. The existing shareholders and owners of a business who would not want any change to arise in the control and ownership of the business would disregard sources of equity finance.

The Impact of Several Sources of Finance on the Financial Statements

Financial statements keep record of a business's trading year (Trading, Profit and Loss Account) and show the financial position of a business as at a date (Balance sheet). Obtaining finance from different sources bring about a change in the financial statements. This portion of the report investigates how each source of finance is recorded and affects the financial statements.

- *Personal savings* – Personal savings when lent to the business are considered as loans. The amount lent will appear as long-term liabilities on the balance sheet. If any interest payments are to be made, they will be recorded in the profit and loss account and charged against profits.
- *Sale of assets* – Sale of assets will reduce the value of fixed assets on the balance sheet. The profit or loss made on the sale of asset will be recorded in the profit and loss account for the year. The depreciation of the asset along with its original price will be removed from the balance sheet.
- *Ordinary shares and preference shares* – The issue of ordinary shares and preference shares increase the value of equity capital in the balance sheet. If the issued shares market price is greater than the nominal value of the share, then share premium is also increased in the balance sheet. The number of shares issued is also displayed in the balance sheet and for preference shares the rate of dividend is also shown. The

dividends paid to the shareholders are recorded in the appropriation account after tax is deducted from net profit.

- *Debentures* – Debentures are a type of debt capital. The value of debentures along with the rate of interest and the repayment date is presented in the equity and liabilities section of the balance sheet. The interest paid on debentures is reduced from profits before tax is charged.
- *Bank overdraft* – This appears in the balance sheet as a current liability since it is a short-term debt and has to be paid back within a year. The interest charges and bank overdraft fee if charged are deducted from the profit and loss account before tax is charged.
- *Loan* – Loans are long-term debts and therefore come under long-term liabilities in a balance sheet. The loan when displayed on a balance sheet will usually contain information about the repayment date and the interest charged on the loan. The interest is charged in the profit and loss account.
- *Venture capital* – This is an amount of money invested in the business as equity capital and thus comes under equity capital in the balance sheet. The return for venture capitalists is a share of profits which is recorded in the appropriation account.
- *Factoring and invoice discounting* – This does not appear in the balance sheet. However the money received from factoring and invoice discounting can show higher balances of cash. The interest charges and fee is recorded in the profit and loss account.

The Information Needs for Different Decision Makers

Different decision makers will want different information about the firm regarding their interests in the business. A long-term lender will always want to know the gearing ratio of a firm while the short-term lender will want to know about the liquidity ratio of the business. The information for different parties is all taken from financial reports, cash flow and financial statements such as the balance sheet and profit and loss account. The manager needs accounting information to take managerial decisions since all functions of the firm are tied to the financial strength of a business. Using the financial statements, the financial stability and profitability of the firm can be analysed and interpreted. Using this information the interested parties make decisions regarding the business. The business's financial statement can be analysed in a number of ways. Some of them are horizontal analysis, vertical analysis, trend analysis and ratio analysis.

1. *Ratio Analysis:* The ratio shows the relationship between two relevant items in the financial statement. The relationship is shown as a ratio or as a percentage. Different ratios calculable on a business's financial statements are:

- Liquidity ratios –
  - Current ratio.
  - Quick ratio/Acid test ratio.
- Working capital ratios –
  - Stock turnover ratio.
  - Average debt collection period.
  - Average credit taken from creditors.
- Profitability ratios –
  - Return on capital employed.
  - Gross profit margin ratio.
  - Profit before interest and tax/sales.
  - Profit after tax/sales.
- Financial stability/Solvency ratio –
  - Financial gearing ratio.
  - Debt/Asset ratio.
  - Interest cover ratio.
- Investment performance ratio
  - Dividend per share.
  - Dividend yield.
  - Earning per share.
  - Price-Earnings ratio.
  - Interest yield.
  - Redemption yield.

Financial Planning

Financial planning affects the terms and conditions on which the business will be able to obtain funding required to establish, maintain and expand the business. Financial planning influences the raw material a business is able to afford, the products it is likely to produce and whether the business will market its product efficiently. It will affect the resources the business is able to acquire to operate and it will be a major determinant of the success of the business.

A financial plan not only help the business to understand what it wants to do but also helps the business understand how to achieve it. A healthy financial plan consists of the following:

- The basic financial statements.
- Ratio analysis.
- Budgets.
- Break-Even analysis.
- Pricing formulas and policies.

- Types and sources of capital available to finance business operations.
- Short and long-term planning considerations necessary to maximize profits.

The business owner/manager who understands these concepts and uses them effectively to control the evolution of the business is practicing sound financial management thereby increasing the likelihood of success.

Of course, banks remain the obvious and most common source of capital. Bank financing can take various forms, including operating loans, term loans, and mortgages secured against equipment and property, as well as leasing on certain types of vehicles and equipment. Lines of credit are also available and can be useful in bridging cyclical operating shortfalls, and offer flexibility to manage cash flows.

Certain criteria are evaluated when granting credit including the nature of the industry, the management team, and financial measures. The lender will consider cash flow projections, current ratio, debt to tangible net worth and, most importantly, the debt servicing capacity of the applicant. The cyclical patterns, and reliance on nature can make ventures seem too risky. New seed technology may sound pretty, but lenders are more attracted to processing plants and the traditional areas of the seed industry.

- *Ventures:* For non-traditional ventures, such as R and D, venture capital funding may be an option. Venture capitalists may receive periodic dividends, but get their big payoff when a firm goes public. Naturally, they are interested in rapidly growing firms in innovative areas.
- *Equity:* Equity partnerships are another option. As a firm evolves, it may be possible to find partners who want to own part of the firm, as with the case with some venture capitalists. Venture capital is a form of equity investment. For most ventures, the transition from debt financing to equity represents the most significant change in their capital structure.

Unlike a debt holder, equity investors actually become a part owner of the venture and receive a return in the form of dividends or capital appreciation of shares because the investment is not secured by any specific assets. In exchange for the greater risk taken by the equity holder, equity investors will demand some concessions, possibly including a higher expected rate of return, a seat on the Board of Directors, and input into the strategic operation of the firm.

- *Initial Public Offerings (IPOs):* Once a firm and its capital requirements have grown beyond the scope of other available financing options, an initial public offering may be in order. IPOs involve selling the shares of a firm for sale on a stock exchange. The shares can be a primary offering intended to raise new capital for the firm or a secondary offering where founders and venture capitalists sell their existing shares to the public to realize the gain from share appreciation.

4

Investment Decision-making in Farm Business

Today's capital expenditure decisions are more critical than ever. Rapid technological advances, shorter product life cycles, and sophisticated competition make investment decisions vital to the success of a firm. Financial managers have the complex task of analyzing capital investment projects. Faced with a range of proposals, they must analyze and recommend which projects the firm should undertake to meet its goals. Making an error could be costly because many capital investment projects involve large expenditures that may have a direct impact on a firm's performance and future direction. This chapter deals with an overview of capital investment decisions, the importance of capital budgeting, applying different capital budgeting decision models to alternative projects to help evaluate and select which projects to undertake.

CAPITAL INVESTMENTS AND CASH FLOW ANALYSIS

Nature of Capital Budgeting

Business firms regularly make decisions involving capital goods purchases such as equipment and structures. Capital goods are business assets with an expected use of more than one year. The fixed asset account on a firm's balance sheet represents its net investment or capital expenditures in capital goods. Capital goods represent a major portion of the total assets of today's firms. Planned future investments in capital goods make up a firm's capital budget. An investment in capital goods requires an outlay of funds by the firm in exchange for expected future benefits over a period greater than one year. The proper goal in making capital investment decisions should be maximization of the long-term market value of the firm. Managers attempt to maximize value by selecting capital investments in which the value created by the project's future cash flows exceeds the required cash outlay. Capital budgeting is the process used to make this decision. Specifically, capital budgeting is the process of planning, analyzing, selecting, and managing capital investments. Capital budgeting may involve other investments besides the long-term investments in capital goods. Many other long-term investments lend themselves to capital budgeting analysis. Such commitments include outlays for advertising campaigns, research and development (R&D), employee education and training programmes, leasing contracts, and mergers and acquisitions. The focus of our treatment of capital budgeting centres on the decision to acquire capital goods, namely fixed assets, used for a firm's operations. However, firms can use similar procedures and processes to analyze various capital expenditures. Capital budgeting analysis also helps analysts to evaluate existing projects and operations and to decide if a firm should continue to fund certain projects.

Importance of Capital Budgeting

Capital budgeting decisions are important to a firm for three major reasons.

1. *Size of Outlay:* Although a tactical investment decision generally involves a relatively small amount of funds, strategic investment decisions may require large sums of money that directly affect the firm's future course of development. Corporate managers continually face the vexing problem of deciding where to commit the firm's resources.
2. *Effect on Future Direction:* The future success of a business largely depends on the investment decisions that corporate managers make today. Investment decisions may result in a major departure from what the firm has been doing in the past. Through making capital investments, firms acquire the long-lived fixed assets that generate the firm's future cash flows and determine its level of profitability. Thus, these decisions greatly influence a firm's ability to achieve its financial objectives.
3. *Difficulty to Reverse:* Capital investment decisions often commit funds for lengthy periods, rendering such decisions difficult or costly to reverse. Therefore, capital investments are not only vital to a firm's development, but also have the capacity to lock in funds for long periods thereby reducing the firm's flexibility. The Disney example below illustrates the importance of capital budgeting.

Capital budgeting decisions are especially critical in small businesses because they often make few capital expenditures and often have little margin for error. Making a poor decision may tie up large amounts of funds for extended periods in fixed assets while generating little, if any, value to the firm. For example, suppose an entrepreneur starts a business to design and produce resumes and buys expensive computer and copying equipment to support this effort. Shortly afterward, less expensive but more efficient equipment appears on the market. Using the expensive existing equipment could put the business at a competitive disadvantage, but selling the equipment could result in a large financial loss. This is a classic example of the conflicts inherent in capital budgeting. Proper capital budgeting analysis is critical to a firm's successful performance because sound capital investment decisions can improve cash flows and lead to higher stock prices. Yet, poor decisions can lead to financial distress and even to bankruptcy. In summary, making the right capital budgeting decisions is essential to achieving the goal of maximizing shareholder wealth.

Capital Budgeting Process

The capital budgeting process is a system of interrelated steps for generating long-term investment proposals; reviewing, analyzing, and selecting from them; and implementing and following up on those selected. This process is dynamic because a firm's changing environment may influence the attractiveness of current or proposed projects. Thus, managers should integrate the capital budgeting process into the firm's broader budgeting and planning cycle. The planning process begins with top management defining the firm's goals. The main goal for capital budgeting is to make investments in long-lived assets that will maximize owners' wealth. Specifically, the firm selects those projects that it believes will maximize the firm's value for its shareholders. Because this goal is difficult to measure, managers often rely on concrete goals such as attaining a specified market share, sales growth, or level of profitability to measure their success. In turn, managers expect that achieving these goals will affect the value of their firm's stock, thereby creating wealth for their shareholders. Promising capital investments make up a capital budget, which is comprised of planned investment projects and a schedule of estimated outlays associated with each project. Management then develops a business strategy, the plan by which the firm expects to achieve its goals in an uncertain environment. A firm's business strategy provides the framework within which it seeks capital investment opportunities and from which major capital budgeting decisions logically flow. Strategic decisions are fundamental but complex decisions because they affect the multiple variables involved in a firm's future operations, products, and services. Strategic decisions include selecting the business lines in which the firm plans to concentrate and identifying competitive guidelines to use in these sectors. Project proposals should be compatible with a firm's business strategy. If not, the firm should reject them. All strategically acceptable project proposals must then survive a financial appraisal and qualitative considerations by weighing the relative value in achieving management's goals. Thus, business strategy employs capital budgeting on a grand scale resulting in strategic asset allocation decisions.

Although no universal consensus exists, one simple way to view capital budgeting is a six stage process.

1. *Identify Project Proposals:* Develop and provide preliminary screening of project proposals.
2. *Estimate Project Cash flows:* Identify and estimate the incremental, after-tax cash flows for a proposed project.
3. *Evaluate Projects:* Determine the financial viability of projects by evaluating the project's incremental after-tax cash flows.
4. *Select Projects:* Choose the projects that best meet the selection criteria.
5. *Implement Project:* Determine the order of implementation, initiate, and track the selected projects.
6. *Perform a Post-Completion Audit:* Periodically compare the actual cash flows for the project to the prior estimates in the capital budgeting proposal.

Failing to complete any stage of the capital budgeting process properly may lead to detrimental capital budgeting decisions. The most challenging phase is estimating project cash flows followed by evaluating and then selecting projects. Figure 4.1 illustrates the relationship between a firm's goals and its business strategy and the capital budgeting process.

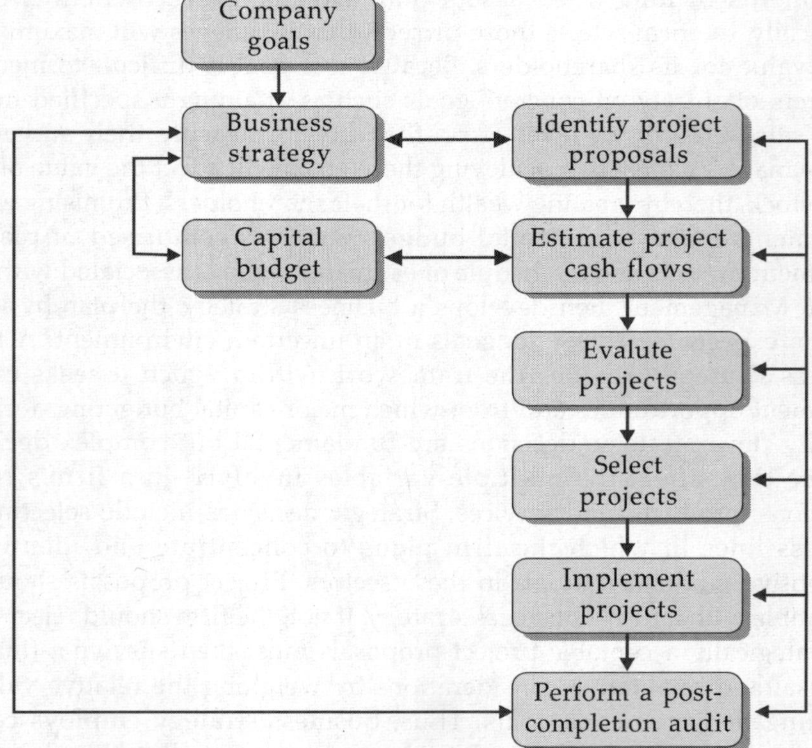

Fig.4.1: An integrated view of the capital budgeting process

Capital Budgeting Stages

Let's take a more detailed look at each of these stages.

1. *Identify Project Proposals:* The first stage of the capital budgeting process is identifying investment opportunities and providing a preliminary screening of project proposals. Ideas for capital investments come from sources both inside and outside the firm – planning committees, research and development groups, employees, outside consultants, and vendors. Under a *top-down approach,* major project proposals start with senior-level managers and information filters down to lower levels. Under a *bottom-up approach,* proposals 'flow up' from the bottom of the organization as various departments or divisions make requests for new capital projects.

Most large and medium-sized firms have formal procedures to generate and analyze new project proposals. Initial ideas undergo preliminary screening to identify those worthy of further development. Developing all ideas into full-fledged capital budgeting proposals would be a time-consuming and waste of firm resources. Consequently, decision makers use their judgment to identify potentially viable projects. Strategic considerations play a vital role in screening projects, especially for those involving large capital outlays.

2. *Estimate Project Cash Flows:* Proposals surviving a preliminary screening usually require further development. Such development involves identifying and estimating a project's expected cash flows. Depending on the type of investment proposal, various units within a firm such as marketing, accounting, and production will ultimately provide this information. Smaller firms, which do not have expertise in all of these areas, often rely on outside consultants to provide such advice, at least for large or important projects. In practice, managers often base cash flows on informed judgment, yet there still exists a large degree of estimation. Estimating future cash flows inevitably involves forecasting errors because managers are dealing with an uncertain future. Expansion projects are often more prone to forecasting errors than are replacement projects, because expanding into new lines of business usually involves greater uncertainty of future revenues and costs. Replacement projects, on the other hand, can rely on historical data to provide reasonable performance parameters. Thus, expansion projects may typically require more effort to obtain reliable cash flow estimates than replacement projects.

3. *Evaluate Projects:* The third stage of the capital budgeting process is evaluating investment opportunities. Improper evaluation can lead to an incorrect decision, despite accurately estimating a project's cash flows. Analysts use many techniques for evaluating capital budgeting projects. The best methods recognise the amount, the time value, and the riskiness of a project's cash flows.

Objective economic criteria should dominate the analysis of capital investments, but subjective judgment may also play a part. Sometimes, qualitative considerations such as the degree of necessity or urgency, the personal preferences of decision makers, governmental regulations or social pressures may be used to complement quantitative measures, or even overrule them. In addition, management may rearrange project priorities strictly based on internal political reasons. Thus, intangible factors are likely to play a role in capital investment decision-making.

4. *Select Projects:* The fourth stage is selecting capital investments. In theory, a firm should accept all projects that have an expected return greater than the required rate of return. Accepting all such projects would add the most value to the firm and thus maximize shareholder wealth. In practice, however, most companies operate under capital rationing at least part of the time. Capital rationing occurs when a firm places an upper limit on its total capital budget. Managers may use capital rationing as a restraint mechanism on the amount and direction of a firm's growth. Capital market conditions, such as the cost and availability of funds, may inherently impose capital rationing. Under capital rationing, a firm may not maximize shareholder wealth because it is unable to accept some profitable projects.
5. *Implement Projects:* Once corporate managers approve a capital investment, they must implement and closely monitor the project. Implementation involves raising capital to finance the projects, authorizing expenditures, and monitoring projects in progress. To ensure that sufficient funds are available when needed, the firm determines the amount and timing of capital investments. Management also monitors projects to avoid delays or cost overruns. If cost overruns occur, managers face three courses of action: complete the project despite its cost, delay implementation and examine the project further, or abandon it.
6. *Perform A Post-completion Audit:* The final stage in the capital budgeting process involves reviewing projects after a specified period. Management conducts a post-completion audit to compare the project's actual costs and benefits to those initially estimated earlier in the process and to decide whether the project's performance warrants its continuance. Because post audits may be costly or impractical, management does not conduct a post-completion audit of all projects. Instead, it often focuses on large capital budgeting projects. Management post audits projects to detect errors in estimating or evaluating a project's cash flows. For example, some project planners may consistently underestimate investment outlays or overstate expected benefits. These optimistic biases may be intentional to make the project appear more attractive or simply result from a lack of experience or difficulty in estimating cash flows. Identifying systematic biases may lead to improved cash flow

estimates and, therefore, to better decision-making in the future. Post-completion audits succeed in holding managers accountable for their estimates and help to reduce systematic biases in future projects.

Capital budgeting *vs.* Current Expenditures

Capital investment projects can be distinguished from current expenditures by two features:

(i) Such projects are relatively large.

(ii) A significant period of time (more than one year) elapses between the investment outlay and the receipt of the benefits..

As a result, most medium-sized and large organizations have developed special procedures and methods for dealing with these decisions. A systematic approach to capital budgeting implies:

(a) The formulation of long-term goals.

(b) The creative search for and identification of new investment opportunities.

(c) Classification of projects and recognition of economically and/or statistically dependent proposals.

(d) The estimation and forecasting of current and future cash flows.

(e) A suitable administrative framework capable of transferring the required information to the decision level.

(f) The controlling of expenditures and careful monitoring of crucial aspects of project execution.

(g) A set of decision rules which can differentiate acceptable from unacceptable alternatives is required.

Estimation of Cash Flows

The term cash flow refers to the actual flow of cash into (cash receipts or savings) and out of (cash payments) a firm during a given period. Reducing a cash outflow results in a savings. This is the same as a cash inflow. For instance, an investment in new equipment or the modernization of existing equipment may reduce operating costs. Although the equipment upgrade is a cash outflow, the reduction in costs results in a cash inflow. If the cash receipts or savings for a given year are greater (less) than the cash payments, cash flow is positive (negative) for that year. Achieving positive cash flow is a key objective for all firms, but is essential to survival for start-ups.

Cash flow and accounting profit (net income) are not necessarily the same due to the presence of certain non-cash expenditures on the firm's income statement. Accrual accounting recognises revenues when earned and expenses when incurred, not when cash associated with those revenues or expenses actually changes hands. Thus, accounting profit includes some cash flows but excludes others. Accounting treats certain items that do not involve a flow of cash as expenses. For example, depreciation is not a cash flow, but it can reduce a firm's tax liability. This explains why profitable start-up companies find themselves in trouble if they do not have substantial positive cash flows to maintain operations. Corporate managers should use cash flows, not accounting profit, because these flows directly affect the firm's ability to pay bills and buy assets. The value of a project depends on the amount, timing, and riskiness of the cash flows of that project. Estimating project cash flows is critical because inaccurate or unreliable data can corrupt the entire capital budgeting process. Accurately forecasting cash flows can be an arduous task. Experience helps identify factors influencing the cash flows of some projects, but historical data may be unavailable on others. Estimating a new project's cash flows involves great uncertainty and may be little more than educated guess work. Therefore, those individuals who prepare cash flow estimates should explicitly state the assumptions underlying their estimates. Corporate managers should thoroughly evaluate and test these assumptions, because faulty assumptions can easily translate into bad investment decisions. The financial staff plays a key role in the cash flow estimation process by coordinating with other departments, maintaining consistency of assumptions, and eliminating biases in the forecasts. Firms use several methods to estimate cash flows. Some firms rely on sophisticated mathematical models and computer simulation. Others use more qualitative methods to forecast cash flows including management's subjective estimates and a survey of expert opinions. Large corporations often combine quantitative and judgmental forecasts to improve their estimates.

When estimating project cash flows, there are three key guidelines to consider:

1. Identify incremental cash flows,
2. Focus on after-tax cash flows, and
3. Postpone considering financing costs.

(i) Identify incremental cash flows

The most important guideline is to consider only those changes in a firm's cash flows that will result if a firm undertakes a project. Specifically, what changes in present and future cash flows are directly attributable to the decision to invest in the project? This requires comparing a firm's cash flow with and without a proposed project. Managers are interested in the additional money the firm will receive in the future for the money they invest today. Therefore, the incremental cash flows generated by a project, not its total cash flows, are what matters for a project's success.

Incremental cash flows are the changes in cash flows that are attributable to the decision to invest in a given project. Cash flows not attributable to a new project are irrelevant to the investment decision-making process. When a firm decides whether to replace an old machine with a new, more efficient one, the relevant cash flows consist of those generated by the new machine less those that would have been retained by keeping the old machine. The decision should hinge on the differences in cash flows between the two machines. Thus, not all of the cash flows received are attributable to the new machine. Favorable incremental net cash flows resulting from making the decision will provide the relevant data needed to make the decision. Although the principle of incremental analysis is a simple idea, applying it in practice is often difficult.

Incremental cash flows occur during all phases of a project's life. Managers often classify such cash flows based on the stage in which they occur. These classifications include the initial cash outlay, the operating cash flows realised during a project's life, and any cash flows resulting from ending a project.

(ii) Focus on after-tax cash flows

The only cash flows relevant to capital budgeting are those generated by a project and still remaining after paying taxes. This is true for all phases of a project's life. Considering a project's untaxed revenues overstates its benefit because the firm cannot invest all these funds in other projects or pay them out to shareholders. Some more common tax provisions influencing cash flows involve depreciation expense as well as gains and losses from the sale of existing fixed assets. The tax effects of selling depreciable assets is discussed in the next part.

(iii) Postpone considering financing costs

A common mistake in estimating cash flows involves the treatment of interest expense and other financial cash flows attributable to financing the project. Financing costs are payments that the firm makes to the parties supplying capital to finance the project. These costs may include interest paid to lenders or dividends paid to shareholders. As a general principle, capital budgeting analyses require separating investment (capital budgeting) and financing decisions. That is, analysts should evaluate a capital budgeting project independently of the source of funds used to finance the project. Analysts should include operating cash flows (cash flows from the project's operating activities) and investment cash flows (cash flows associated with acquiring or disposing of the project's assets) in their estimations, but not financing cash flows (cash flows associated with financing the project). That is, analysts should exclude financing costs from the cash flows used to evaluate projects. As we discuss already, a project's required rate of return reflects financing costs. The process of deducting financing charges as cash flows and then discounting these flows by the required rate of return effectively double-counts these costs. The general rule in capital budgeting is not to deduct financing costs from a project's cash flows.

Other Cash Flow Considerations

The following are other considerations that further complicate estimating cash flows.

- *Net Operating Working Capital:* Adopting a project may require a change in a firm's net operating working capital (NOWC), which is the change in all current assets that do not pay interest less the change in all current liabilities that do not charge interest. For example, a project that entails producing and selling a new product will probably require the firm to increase its inventories and to hold more cash to conduct additional transactions. The firm's accounts receivable are also likely to increase due to rising sales. These increases in current operating assets necessitate cash outlays by the firm. However, the firm would also expect to realise an increase in accrued wages and taxes and an increase in accounts payable due to the firm's acquisition of more raw materials on trade credit. These increases in current liabilities may help the firm finance some of the increase in current assets. The excess of the increase in current operating assets over the increase in current operating liabilities represents a net cash outflow in NOWC for the firm. If a new project increases NOWC, this increase causes a net cash outflow. Assuming this increase in NOWC must occur before the project can begin or early in its first year, it can be included as part of the project's initial cash outlay. In actuality, changes in NOWC can occur any time during a project's life. Expansion projects normally require increases in NOWC, but replacement projects often require little or no change in NOWC.

At the end of a project, the firm may recover the accumulated NOWC invested during the life of the project. Recovering NOWC results from selling remaining inventory, collecting outstanding accounts receivables, and drawing down any increases in cash balances caused by the project. This recovery of NOWC represents a one-time cash inflow in the final year of the project's life. In this situation, current operating assets and current operating liabilities may return to their pre-project levels. In other situations, a firm may be unable to recapture its full investment in accumulated NOWC because the firm cannot sell all inventories or collect all accounts receivable. The recapture of NOWC has no tax effects because the firm makes NOWC investments using after-tax cash.

- *Sunk Costs:* A sunk cost is an outlay incurred before making an investment decision and represents an historical cost. Past expenditures on a project should not influence the decision whether to undertake, continue, or end a project because they are not incremental cash flows. Instead, decision makers should base their decision on future costs and benefits. Sunk costs are irrelevant because the decision to adopt or reject the proposed project will not result in any change in the project's cash flows related to these costs. The firm has already incurred the sunk cost with or without the project. Because these sunk costs are irrevocable and have no bearing on a new project, they are not incremental cash flows. Thus, sunk costs are not part of the evaluation process.

- *Example for Sunk Costs:* A Food Processing Company is considering whether to introduce a new drug. During the past 5 years, the company invested $20 million in research and development (R&D) to create a new beverage product. Researchers report that the product in its current form is unlikely to gain approval of the Food and Drug Administration (FDA) because it has some negative side effects. Corporate managers must now decide whether to incur the additional costs needed to gain FDA approval and to bring the new product to market. Analysts estimate that the potential market for the new drug is immense with potential sales of $50-75 million a year. Should the company include the $20 million R and D expense in evaluating the project's incremental cash flows?
- *Solution:* The firm should exclude the R and D costs because it has already spent the $20 million. Because these costs are irreversible, corporate managers should make the investment decision independently of the sunk costs. The only relevant data are the future costs and benefits of undertaking the project.

Opportunity Costs

Estimating project cash flows requires considering both direct outlays and opportunity costs. An opportunity cost is the most valuable alternative use of a resource or an asset that the firm gives up by accepting a project. By using the asset or resource in the proposed project, the firm forgoes the opportunity to employ the asset in its alternative use. The cash flows that the firm forgoes represent an opportunity cost to the proposed project. Opportunity costs can be difficult to estimate, but they are important to recognise when estimating the relevant cash flows for analyzing a project.

- *Example for Opportunity Costs:* Suppose Wal-Mart Stores, Inc., a major retailer, is considering a project proposal that requires storing additional merchandise. The firm now has excess storage capacity suitable for the new proposal. If Wal-Mart does not use the storage capacity for the new project, it could rent the space for $250,000 a year. Should Wal-Mart attach a cost to this storage space if corporate managers decided to go ahead with the new project?
- *Solution:* Analysts should charge the after-tax loss of revenue against the new project because it entails an opportunity cost or a loss of alternative income for using the storage space instead of renting it. Thus, if Wal-Mart's combined federal and state tax rate were 40 per cent, the $150,000 [$250,000 (1 –0.40)] per year opportunity cost reduces the firm's annual cash inflow by this amount. If the firm cannot rent the unused storage space to outsiders or put it to another productive use, the opportunity cost of using the excess storage capacity is zero. Therefore, analysts should not assign a storage cost to the new project.

Allocated Overhead

For internal reporting purposes, accountants often allocate existing overhead, such as general and administrative expenses, to each unit or division that undertakes a project. However, if the firm's current overhead will remain unchanged by accepting a project, the firm should exclude this allocated overhead from the project's cash flows in the capital budgeting analysis. Here, overhead is an existing (fixed) cost, not an incremental cost. Managers should recognise only an increase in overhead that will result from accepting the project, such as hiring a new accountant, as part of a project's cash flows.

Side Effects

Adopting and implementing new projects may have important side effects because they affect the cash flows of other products or divisions. Project planners should consider these potential side effects, or externalities, in the capital budgeting analysis for the project. Side effects are complements if they enhance the cash flows of existing assets and substitutes if the effect is negative.

- *Example for Side Effects:* Suppose KB Nutrition Company plans to introduce a new product that would compete directly with some of the other health fitness products it sells. The firm's analysts expect that accepting the new product will reduce sales of existing products and, therefore, the cash flows, by $1 million each year over the next 5 years. Should the company consider this reduction in cash flow when making the decision about the new product?
- *Solution:* Yes, the lost cash flow from the lost sales is an incremental cash flow attributable to the proposed project. Therefore, analysts should incorporate this erosion in cash flows called *cannibalization* in estimating the new product's cash flows.

Cash Flow Components

The cash flows of any project can include three basic components. Each component represents incremental, after-tax cash flows after netting any inflows and outflows of cash.

1. Initial investment.
2. Operating cash flows.
3. Terminal cash flows.

Project planners typically can forecast the initial investment more accurately than they can forecast the other components because the initial investment estimates involve forthcoming cash flows that are more predictable than other future cash flows. Operating cash inflows during the project's life are more difficult to forecast accurately because economic, marketing, production, and other factors may cause such inflows to change. These cash flows typically vary from year to year as revenues, operating expenses, and depreciation expense change.

Estimating the terminal cash flow can be especially difficult because it may require projecting cash flows many years in the future. These cash-flow components form two types of cash-flow patterns. A *conventional (normal) cash flow pattern* is a time series of incoming and outgoing cash flows that has only one change in direction or sign. For example, a project may require one or more net cash outflows (–), such as –$100,000 in Year 0, followed by a stream of cash inflows (+), such as $50,000 each for the next 3 years. Conversely, an *unconventional cash flow pattern* in a project is a series of cash flows having more than one sign change. For example, the pattern – + + + +, – + + + + has three sign changes. In this chapter, we limit our discussion to capital budgeting projects with conventional cash flow patterns.

Format for Calculating the Initial Investment

	Purchase price of a new asset (*e.g.*, land, buildings, and equipment).
+	Expenses associated with placing the asset in service.
+	Opportunity cost of any existing assets employed in the project.
+	Initial net operating working capital (NOWC) required.
–	Proceeds from selling an existing asset.
+/–	Tax effects from selling an existing asset.
=	Initial Investment.

(i) Initial investment

The initial investment is the after-tax net cash outlay required at the beginning of an investment project. For simplicity, we often assume that the initial investment occurs immediately ($t = 0$) when the inflows and outflows of cash making up the initial investment occur over a period less than a year. If the initial investment period is less than a year, this assumption is unlikely to have an adverse impact on a project's evaluation. If the period is more than a year, the analyst should estimate the capital outlay amount each year and account for the time value of money of these cash outlays in the initial investment.

The initial cash outflows generally include the cost of any land, buildings, and equipment required to undertake the project. The firm should also include any other costs associated with placing any assets into service such as delivery fees, setup expenses, and testing expenses, and any related initial increase in net operating working capital. In addition, including the opportunity cost of any assets already owned that would be employed in the project may be necessary. Although there are no tax effects associated with a change in NOWC, taxes may affect other costs. For example, training costs are tax-deductible expenses. Thus, the analyst should multiply such costs by one minus the firm's marginal tax rate ($1 - T$) to get the after-tax cash flow.

For replacement projects, where the proposal involves replacing an existing asset with a new asset, the estimated net proceeds from selling the old asset represent a cash inflow that partially offsets the initial cash outlays. The tax impact of selling a depreciable asset may increase (decrease) a firm's tax liability, which adds to (reduces) the initial outlay. The tax implications from selling a depreciable asset depend on the relationship between the selling price and the book value of the old asset.

(ii) Operating cash flows

Operating cash flows are the expected after-tax net cash flows that result from any changes in operating revenue and associated expenses over a project's life. These cash flows normally vary from year to year due to changing revenues, expenses, and depreciation. Although operating cash flows occur throughout the year, analysts often estimate them over annual intervals. In many instances, however, analysts must adjust the cash flows to reflect the actual timing of the cash inflows and outflows. In our examples, we assume that operating cash flows occur at the end of each year. This also serves as a conservative assumption because cash flows received at the end of a year are not worth as much as those received during a year because of the time value of money. Forecasting a project's operating cash flows begins with a proforma (projected) income statement. For an expansion project, the estimates of revenues and expenses are incremental to the results the firm would achieve if the project were not to be accepted. Forecasting the operating results for a replacement project requires analysts to estimate incremental revenues and expenses as follows:

- *Incremental revenue* is equal to the expected revenue from the new project assets minus the revenue generated by keeping the existing assets in operation.
- *Incremental operating expense* is equal to the expected operating expense incurred with the new project assets minus the revenue generated by keeping the existing assets in operation.
- *Incremental depreciation* is equal to the depreciation expense associated with the new project assets minus the depreciation expense that remains for the existing (old) assets. If the firm replaces the existing assets, it would forgo the remaining depreciation expense on these assets.

The issue of depreciation requires special attention. As a non-cash expense, depreciation represents cash that never left the firm. As a rule, depreciation generates a cash flow due to its positive effect (reduction) on taxes paid. Because depreciation expense reduces taxable income, this also reduces the tax outflow, effectively resulting in a cash inflow. The decrease in the tax liability due to the depreciation charge is called the *depreciation tax shield*. This tax shield equals the depreciation amount times the tax rate. Theoretically, the depreciation expense plus the tax shield is the total amount to be added back to net income. As stated, the depreciation expense must be reversed because it is a non-cash book entry not affecting the firm's cash flows. The cash flows must also reflect depreciation's related tax benefits.

Although there may be other non-cash charges against income, such as amortization and depletion expenses, depreciation expense is the most common non-cash charge.

Format for Calculating Operating Cash Flows

Operating revenues.
– Operating expenses.
– Depreciation.
Taxable income.
– Income taxes.
Net income.
\+ Depreciation.
– Increase in net operating working capital (NOWC)
Operating cash flow.

Computing Operating Cash Flows

Calculating net income requires subtracting the incremental operating expenses, income taxes, and depreciation from incremental revenues. As noted earlier, financing costs are excluded in the process of calculating operating cash flows, but are considered in the evaluation stage of the capital budgeting process. Because depreciation does not represent an actual expenditure of cash in computing a firm's profit, depreciation is added back to net income to get operating cash flows. The firm incurs a cash outlay when it buys a fixed asset and this cash outlay is part of the initial investment. To consider an annual depreciation expense as a cash outlay would double count investment costs. Except for ignoring financing costs, this format for estimating a project's cash flows follows a basic income statement approach. The analyst then derives the project cash flow from the project net income by adding back depreciation and subtracting (adding) any increases (decreases) in net operating working capital. Equation 4.1 shows the formula for calculating the changes in operating cash flows using the above format. All incremental cash flows are 'with the project' minus 'without the project'. With a replacement decision, for example, the change in cash flow is the cash flow if the firm acquires a new asset less the cash flow if the firm does not. Rearranging the terms in Equation 4.1 and applying some basic algebra allows us to develop another useful format for calculating operating cash flows.

$$\Delta\text{Operating cash flows} = (\Delta R - \Delta OC - \Delta D)(1 - T)\ \Delta D$$
$$= [(R_{new} - R_{old}) - (OC_{new} - OC_{old}) - (D_{new} - D_{old})]\,(1 - T) \ldots \text{Equation (4.1)}$$

Where Δ is the Greek symbol delta meaning 'change in' or 'incremental'; ΔR is the change in revenues ($R_{new} - R_{old}$); ΔOC is the change in operating costs ($OC_{new} - OC_{old}$); ΔD is the change in depreciation ($D_{new} - D_{old}$); and T is the marginal tax rate (%).

Another approach explicitly recognises that depreciation is a non-cash charge and not part of the cash outflows. However, this method recognises that depreciation has an indirect influence on the tax expense of firm. Equation 4.2 defines operating cash flows as the after-tax incremental net income plus the incremental depreciation tax shield, *TΔD*. For Equations 4.1 and 4.2, we assume that the firm neither defers its tax liabilities, paying them when they are due, nor has any changes in NOWC.

$$\Delta\text{Operating cash flows} = (\Delta R - \Delta OC)(1 - T) + T\Delta D$$
$$= [(R_{new} - R_{old}) - (OC_{new} - OC_{old})](1-T) + T(D_{new} - D_{old}) \cdots \text{ Equation (4.2)}$$

Determining the changes in operating cash flows using Equation 4.2 offers several advantages. *First,* this approach requires fewer computations than the previous income statement format. *Second,* Equation 4.2 highlights the effect that depreciation has on operating cash flows. Specifically, we see directly how a higher depreciation amount for a given year yields a higher operating cash flow for that year. This result is not as obvious in the income statement approach.

- *Example for Computing Incremental Operating Cash Flows:* A firm plans to replace an old machine with a new, more efficient one, which has greater production capacity. An analyst estimates that adopting the new machine will result in the following revenues, operating costs, and depreciation. For simplicity, assume that the changes in revenues, expenses, and depreciation are the same each year and that the marginal tax rate is 34 per cent.

	With new machine	With old machine	Incremental change
Sales revenue *(R)*	$110,000	$100,000	$10,000
Operating costs *(OC)*	55,000	60,000	–5,000
Depreciation *(D)*	15,000	14,000	1,000

The operating costs of the new machine are lower than the old machine. The lower incremental operating costs result in an operating savings, which in turn increases cash inflows. Using Equation 4.2, the change in the operating cash flows is:

$$\Delta\text{Operating cash flows} = (\Delta R - \Delta OC)(1 - T) + t\Delta D$$
$$= [\$10{,}000\ \text{"}\ (-\$5{,}000)](1 - 0.34) + (0.34)(1{,}000)$$
$$= \$9{,}900 + \$340 = \$10{,}240$$

(iii) Terminal cash flows

Because capital budgeting projects have a finite life, the terminal cash flow is the cash flow associated with ending a project. A set of terminal cash flows occurs in the project's final year, along with a set of operating cash flows for that year. In the final year of an expansion project, a firm may receive cash inflows from two major sources. The first source is the release of any accumulated NOWC necessary to operate the project through the sale of inventory, collection of accounts receivable, or freeing up of cash invested in the project. The second source is the sale of any capital assets (an asset's actual value as opposed to estimated salvage value) needed to support the project. Any taxes on the sale of the asset are calculated after subtracting removal costs because removal costs are an operating expense. The tax effects of the sale of an asset depend on the price received, its original cost, and the current book value (cost less accumulated depreciation).

Format for Calculating Terminal Cash Flows

	Salvage value
–	Cost of removing assets and shutting down
	Salvage value before taxes
+/–	Tax effects on disposal of an asset
	Net salvage value
+	Recovery of NOWC
=	Terminal Cash Flow

The firm usually recovers all additions to NOWC that have occurred during the project's life, not simply the initial increase in NOWC. Recaptured NOWC is added to the final period's after-tax cash flow to compute the terminal cash flows. As a practical matter, financial managers generally assume the firm will liquidate current assets at book value. In such cases, the disposal of NOWC has no taxation implications So far, we have examined many guidelines involved in estimating cash flows. The following checklist covers some of the more important guidelines.

- Use incremental cash flows of a project, not accounting profit.
- Adjust for changes in NOWC, opportunity costs, and side effects.
- Use future cash flow and ignore sunk costs.
- Exclude interest and other financial flows to avoid double-counting.
- Exclude any allocation of existing overhead.
- Include depreciation tax-shield benefits in cash flow calculations.
- Add back salvage value adjusted for removal costs and taxes in expansion decisions.

CAPITAL BUDGETING AND CAPITAL BUDGETING TECHNIQUES

Previous section discussed about how to estimate the cash flows of a project and illustrated time value of money concepts needed for project evaluation. This section discusses how to use these elements to conduct investment analysis.

Capital budgeting is about investment in fixed assets. In addition, another type of investment could be in working capital, which will be discussed later. Fixed assets are the part of long-term assets in the balance sheet and working capital is net position of current assets and current liabilities on the balance sheet.

We need to understand why capital budgeting is so important and why do we have to invest in fixed assets? The answer is simple; the equipment or machinery and other fixed assets depreciate over a period, they lose their productivity and get obsolete after sometime. These assets need to be replaced with new assets. This replacement involves investment in fixed assets. Moreover, if a company intends to start a new project, Capital Budgeting techniques are employed to assess the financial viability of the project. Suppose, for instance, a company wants to introduce a new soap and launching of the new product demands changes in the manufacturing process, the company will have to purchase new equipment in the form of fixed assets. Capital budgeting is a technique used to evaluate the value of investment and projects in fixed assets. It is also used to assess the working capital requirements. Combined together it helps the company management to decide whether the new venture should be taken up or not.

The biggest challenge in capital budgeting is to keep finding the valuable projects, *i.e.*, projects that may add to the value of the firm. You must be familiar with the basic objective of financial management by now, which is to maximize shareholders' wealth. This is possible only by investing in the projects, which have positive net present value, which in effect will increase the shareholders' wealth. Most of the developed companies operate in an efficient market environment. We will discuss efficient markets at length after studying the concept of risk akin to financial decisions. However, to give an idea, *efficient markets* can be described as highly competitive markets where good business ideas are taken up immediately.

When evaluating potential capital investments, managers should consider four key questions.

1. Are the projects independent or mutually exclusive?
2. Are the projects of the same size, cash flow pattern, and life?
3. Are the projects subject to capital rationing?
4. Are the projects of the same risk?

When conducting project analysis, decision makers should understand the assumptions made, the techniques used, and the real meaning of the results. The best decision models should help management to achieve the goal of shareholder wealth maximization. That is, a firm should primarily undertake a capital investment if it creates value for the owners.

To simplify the presentation, following assumptions can be made:

- Financial decision makers are economically rational in that they are risk-averse wealth maximizers.
- All projects have the same level of risk to the firm as a whole.
- The firm's cost of capital is constant over time and unaffected by the amount of funds invested in capital projects.

- No resource constraints exist – that is the firm can accept all profitable projects.

PROJECT CLASSIFICATIONS AND ANALYSIS

Before managers can apply decision rules, they need to be able to distinguish between independent and mutually exclusive projects. *Independent projects* are those in which the acceptance or rejection of one project does not prevent the acceptance or rejection of other projects under consideration. That is, implementing independent projects is unrelated to each other. Analysts can evaluate the effects of an independent project on a firm's value without having to consider its effect on other investment opportunities. *Mutually exclusive projects* are those in which the acceptance of one project precludes the acceptance of the others.

These projects can take any of the following forms:

- New project.
- Expansion project.
- Modernization/Replacement.
- Research and development.
- Exploration.
- Other/social responsibility – Pollution control etc.

Capital Budgeting *vs.* Current Expenditures

A capital investment project can be distinguished from current expenditures by two features: *(i)* Such projects are relatively large, *(ii)* A significant period of time (more than one year) elapses between the investment outlay and the receipt of the benefits.

As a result, most medium-sized and large organizations have developed special procedures and methods for dealing with these decisions. A systematic approach to capital budgeting implies:

(a) The formulation of long-term goals.

(b) The creative search for and identification of new investment opportunities.

(c) Classification of projects and recognition of economically and/or statistically dependent proposals.

(d) The estimation and forecasting of current and future cash flows

(e) A suitable administrative framework capable of transferring the required information to the decision level.

(f) The controlling of expenditures and careful monitoring of crucial aspects of project execution.

(g) A set of decision rules which can differentiate acceptable from unacceptable alternatives is required.

The last point (g) is crucial and this is the subject of later sections of the chapter.

The Classification of Investment Projects

(a) By project size

Small projects may be approved by departmental managers. More careful analysis and Board of Directors' approval is needed for large projects.

(b) By type of benefit to the firm

- an increase in cash flow;
- a decrease in risk;
- an indirect benefit (showers for workers, etc).

(c) By degree of dependence

- Mutually exclusive projects (can execute project A or B, but not both)
- Complementary projects: taking project A increases the cash flow of project B.
- Substitute projects: taking project A decreases the cash flow of project B.

(d) By degree of statistical dependence

- Positive dependence.
- Negative dependence.
- Statistical independence.

(e) By type of cash flow

- Conventional cash flow: only one change in the cash flow sign *e.g.* –/++++ or +/——, etc.
- Non-conventional cash flows: more than one change in the cash flow sign, *e.g.* +/–/+++ or –/+/–/++++, etc.

Relevant Costs

These are costs that are relevant with respect to a particular decision. A relevant cost for a particular decision is one that changes if an alternative course of action is taken. Relevant costs are also called differential costs. Making correct decisions is one of the most important tasks of a successful manager. Every decision involves a choice between at least two alternatives. The decision process may be complicated by volumes of data, irrelevant data, incomplete information, an unlimited array of alternatives, etc. The role of the managerial accountant in this process is often that of a gatherer and summarizer of relevant information rather than the ultimate decision maker.

The costs and benefits of the alternatives need to be compared and contrasted before making a decision. The decision should be based only on relevant information. Relevant information includes the predicted future costs and revenues that differ among the alternatives. Any cost or benefit that does not differ between alternatives is irrelevant and can be ignored in a decision. All future revenues and/or costs that do not differ between the alternatives are irrelevant. Sunk costs (costs already irrevocably incurred) are always irrelevant since they will be the same for any alternative. To identify which costs are relevant in a particular situation, take this three step approach:

1. Eliminate sunk costs and committed costs.
2. Eliminate costs and benefits that do not differ between alternatives.
3. Compare the remaining costs and benefits that do differ between alternatives to make the proper decision.
4. Take care of opportunity cost.

TECHNIQUES OF CAPITAL BUDGETING

Capital budgeting is a mathematical concept in the sense that we have to use different quantitative investments criteria to evaluate whether an opportunity is worth investing in or not. Some of these techniques of capital budgeting are separated in to two methods traditional and discounted cash flow; All these methods evaluate projects based on cash flows.

The Traditional Techniques

(i) Payback period

In this technique, we try to figure out how long it would take to recover the invested capital through positive cash flows of the business. The time it takes the cash inflows from a capital investment project to equal the cash outflows, usually expressed in years. When deciding between two or more competing projects, the usual decision is to accept the one with the shortest payback.

Payback is often used as a 'first screening method'. By this, we mean that when a capital investment project is being considered, the first question to ask is: 'How long will it take to pay back its cost?' The firm might have a target payback, and so it would reject a capital project unless its payback period is less than a certain number of years.

Example 1:

Years	0	1	2	3	4	5
Project A	1,000,000	250,000	250,000	250,000	250,000	250,000

For a project with equal annual receipts:

$$PP = \frac{I_o}{C_t}$$

$$= \frac{\$1,000,000}{\$250,000}$$

$$= 4 \text{ years}$$

Example 2:

Years	0	1	2	3	4
Project B	- 10,000	5,000	2,500	4,000	1,000

Payback period lies between year 2 and year 3. Sum of money recovered by the end of the second year

= $7,500, *i.e.* ($5,000 + $2,500)

Sum of money to be recovered by end of 3rd year

= $10,000 - $7,500

= $2,500

$$\text{Payback period} = \left(2 + \frac{\$2,500}{\$4,000}\right) \textit{years}$$

= 2.625 years

For example, an initial investment of $200,000 is required to start a cofe business; $10,000 per month are expected to be earned for the first year, and $20,000 would be earned every month in the second year. Now according to the aforementioned assumptions, in the first year, we earn $10, 000 per month, which make $120,000 for the year (twelve months). Since we had invested $200,000 initially of which $120,000 have been recovered in the first year, we are still $80, 000 short of recovering our initial investment. In the second year, we would be earning $20,000 per month, so the remaining $80,000 can be recovered in the next four months. We can say that the initial invested capital can be recovered in 16 months, or the payback period for this investment is 16 months. The shorter the payback period of a project, the more an investor would be willing to invest his money in the project.

- *Disadvantages of the Payback Method:* While the payback period is a simple and straightforward method for analyzing a capital budgeting proposal, it has certain limitations. It is to be noticed that we have not used any interest rate while making calculation.
  - It ignores the timing of cash flows within the payback period, the cash flows after the end of payback period and therefore the total project return.
  - It ignores the time value of money. This means that it does not take into account the fact that $1 today is worth more than $1 in one year's time. An investor who has $1 today can either consume it immediately or alternatively can invest it at the prevailing interest rate, say 30 per cent, to get a return of $1.30 in a year's time.
  - It is unable to distinguish between projects with the same payback period.
  - It may lead to excessive investment in short-term projects.

- *Advantages of the Payback Method:* Payback can be important; Long pay-back means capital tied up and high investment risk. The method also has the advantage that it involves a quick, simple calculation and an easily understood concept.

(ii) Accounting rate of return (ARR)

The ARR method also called the return on capital employed (ROCE) or the return on investment (ROI), method of appraising a capital project is to estimate the accounting rate of return that the project should yield. If it exceeds a target rate of return, the project will be undertaken. The concept of accounting rate of return loosely defined, as there are a number of ratios that can be used to analyze return on investment. However, in capital budgeting it implies the annual average cash flow a business is making as a percentage of investment. In other words, it is an average percentage of investment recovered in cash every year. The formula for return on investment is as follows:

$$ROI = (\Sigma CF/n) / IO$$

Dividing the average annual cash flow by the initial investment, we can calculate the return on investment.

Example: Taking the same example of a café, the initial investment of \$200,000, \$10,000 per month profit in the 1st year, \$20,000 per month profit for the second year, we can easily calculate the ROI.

ROI= ((120,000+240,000)/2)/200,000= 0.90 = 90 per cent

Where, \$ 120,000 = cash flow for 1st year at \$ 10,000 per month

\$ 240,000 = cash flow for the 2nd year at \$ 20,000 per month.

n = 2 years

Return on Investment is also very easy to calculate, but like payback period, it does not take into account the time value of money concept. A high ROI ratio is considered better and 90 per cent is a very good rate of return but before deciding whether or not this project should be taken up, we should compare this project with the alternative opportunities on hand. It is also important to take into consideration the prevailing rate of inflation in the country so that the returns could be adjusted accordingly.

Disadvantages

- It does not take account of the timing of the profits from an investment.
- It implicitly assumes stable cash receipts over time.
- It is based on accounting profits and not cash flows. Accounting profits are subject to a number of different accounting treatments.
- It is a relative measure rather than an absolute measure and hence takes no account of the size of the investment.
- It takes no account of the length of the project.
- It ignores the time value of money.

The Payback and ARR Methods in Practice

Despite the limitations of the payback method, it is the method most widely used in practice. There are a number of reasons for this:

- It is a particularly useful approach for ranking projects where a firm faces liquidity constraints and requires fast repayment of investments.
- It is appropriate in situations where risky investments are made in uncertain markets that are subject to fast design and product changes or where future cash flows are particularly difficult to predict.
- The method is often used in conjunction with NPV or IRR method and acts as a first screening device to identify projects which are worthy of further investigation.
- It is easily understood by all levels of management.
- It provides an important summary method: how quickly will the initial investment be recouped?

Discounted Cash Flow (DCF) Method

Discounted cash flow (DCF) techniques considers the time value of money. Managers seek projects in which the present value of expected future cash flows exceeds the amount of the invested funds. Only the NPV, PI, IRR, and DPP methods recognise both the time value of money and also consider cash flows over the entire useful life of an investment. Although these five techniques for evaluating cash flows always give the same accept-reject decision for independent projects, they can give conflicting rankings for mutually exclusive decisions.

(i) Net present value (NPV)

NPV is the most important criteria for evaluating a capital budgeting proposal. NPV is a mathematical tool which uses the discounting process, something that we have found missing in the aforementioned capital budgeting techniques. Net Present Value is defined as the value today of the *Future Incremental After-tax Net Cash Flows* less the initial investment. The formula for calculating NPV is as follows:

Formula:

NPV = -Io + CFt /(1+i)t = -Io + CF1/(1+i) + CF2/(1+i) 2 + CF' /(1+i) 3 +..

$$NPV = -Io + \sum CFt / (1+i)^t$$

Where, CFt=cash flows occurring in different time periods

-Io = Initial cash outflow

i = discount /interest rate

t = year in which the cash flow takes place

Initial cash outflow, being an outflow, is always expressed as a negative figure. NPV is considered one of the most popular capital budgeting criteria. The disadvantage with the NPV is that it is difficult to calculate since these calculations are based on too many estimates. In order to calculate the NPV we need to forecast the future cash flows and sales; the discount factor is also an estimate. If the NPV of a project is more than zero, it should be accepted. If two or more projects under contemplation, then the one with the higher NPV, should be accepted. When a firm invests in projects with positive NPV, they raise the shareholders' wealth or firm's value. This would also increase the market value added and the economic value added for the firm.

Example: Taking the same example of a café, an initial investment of \$200,000, \$10,000 per month profit in the 1st year in \$20,000 per month profit for the second year. However, for the calculation of the NPV we would be requiring another important input – the discount rate. Assume the discount rate is 10 per cent. Ten per cent is what we at least expect to earn from the business. This is the rate of return, which we can get by simply putting our money with a bank. If the business cannot yield more than 10 per cent, then it is pointless to take unnecessary headache of setting up a business and running it, since ten per cent can be earned with a no-sweat-effort of placing the money with a bank.

Where, CFt=cash flows occurring in different time periods, *i.e.*, \$120,000 in the first year and \$240,000 in the second year.

-Io = Initial cash outflow = -200,000

i = discount /interest rate = 10 per cent

t = 2 years

Putting in the values in the formula

$$NPV = -Io+\sum CF/i$$

$$= -\ 200{,}000+120{,}000/(1+0.10) + 240{,}000(1+0.10)^2$$

$$= -\ 200{,}000 + 109{,}091 + 198{,}347$$

$$=+\ \$\ 107438$$

At the end of 2nd year, the NPV is +ve, we can also solve this example by monthly compounding if we want to have a more precise answer. The cash flows at the end of the first year and second year will have to be brought back to the present.

The present value of the cash flows occurring at the end of the first year can be calculated by dividing the cash flows by 1 plus discount factor as under.

$$120000/(1+0.10) = 109{,}091$$

The cash flow occurring at the end of the second year can be calculated by dividing the cash flow by one plus discount factor squared.

$$240{,}000/(1+0.10)2 = 198{,}347$$

$$NPV = -\ 2000000+120000/(1+0.10)+240000/(1+0.10)^2$$

$$= -\ 200000+109091+198347$$

$= + \$107438$ at the end of second year NPV is +ve

In other words, according to our cash flow forecast and required return, two years of running this business is worth $107,438 in cash to us today.

NPV - in brief: It is important to understand the NPV equation and to calculate NPV as reliably as possible. It is very difficult to calculate because different inputs used in Net Present Value equation are based upon a forecast, which may or may not be accurate (*e.g.*, future cash flows and sales). Similarly, when we talk about the life of the project, again we are estimating the duration of the project. We also have to choose subjectively the discount rates to be used, including cost of capital, opportunity cost and required rate of return in the calculation of Net Present Value. We shall discuss how to choose the interest rate then we would talk about risk. In NPV the idea is to bring back each cash flow to the present and then to add or subtract them on present time. The project or investment, which is offering the highest NPV, gets the highest rank.

Importance of NPV in Terms of Objectives of Financial Management

The objective of FM is to maximize the shareholders wealth. Now, there is a direct link between shareholder wealth maximization and NPV. It is mentioned earlier that the value of an asset is determined by the future cash flows it generates. We used these future cash flows and discount them to present and we call that the NPV. Hence, there is a direct link between NPV and future cash flows. When the management of the company invest in the +ve NPV projects, they increase the economic value added (E.V.A) and they also increase market value added (M.V.A). It should be clear by now that when company invest in +ve NPV projects they brings in value to the firm. Increase in the value of the firm implies increase in shareholders' wealth.

Example: Let us suppose that we invest $ 100,000 in a Savings Certificate. After 1 Year we will receive a coupon payment (or profit) of $ 12,000 and we also reclaim our initial investment (principal).

Solution Step 1: Identify the Variables: Io = $ 100,000 CF1=$ 12,000 Life = n=1year Required Rate of Return = i =10 per cent (assumed), Annual compounding. CF I1 = $ 100,000. Here, we assume that i=10 because which is the opportunity cost as we can place that money in a bank and can earn 10 per cent. Do not forget that we get back our principal investment after 1 Year. This is a positive cash flow and must be discounted back to the present just like any other future cash flow.

Step 2: Solve the NPV Equation

$$
\begin{aligned}
\text{NPV} &= -\ \text{Io} + \text{CF1} / (1+ i) + \text{CF I1} / (1+ i) \\
&= -\ 100{,}000 + 12{,}000/ (1+0.10) + 100{,}000/ (1+0.10) \\
&= -\ 100{,}000 + 10{,}909 + 90{,}909 \\
&= +\ \$\ 1{,}818 \text{ NPV positive so investment acceptable}
\end{aligned}
$$

Note: PV = NPV + Io = 1,818 + 100,000 = $101,818

(ii) Profitability index

It is quite similar to the NPV in terms of concept and calculation. Profitability index may be defined as the ratio of the present value of future cash flows to the initial investment. It is a relationship between the PV of all the future cash flows and the initial investment. This relationship is expressed as a number calculated by dividing the PV of all cash flows by initial investment. The profitability index can be calculated using the following formula.

$$PI = \frac{PV}{I_o}$$

That means:

$$PI = [\Sigma\, CFt\ /\ (1+ i)^{t}]/\ IO$$

Decision rule:

PI > 1; accept the project
PI < 1; reject the project
If NPV = 0, we have:
NPV = PV - Io = 0
PV = Io

Dividing both sides by Io we get:

$$\frac{PV}{I_o} > 1$$

PI of 1.2 means that the project's profitability is 20 per cent.

Example:

	PV of CF	I_o	PI
Project A	100	50	2.0
Project B	1,500	1,000	1.5

Decision: Choose option B because it maximizes the firm's profitability by $1,500. Those projects with a profitability index ratio of more than one (PI ≥ 1.0) are considered acceptable. Here it is important to mention that those projects, which are ranked as acceptable using the NPV method, would also be acceptable on the profitability index criteria.

Example: The profitability index for the café example can be calculated as under.

$$PI = [120{,}000]/\ (1+ 0.1) + [240{,}000\ /\ (1+ 0.1)^2]/200{,}000$$
$$= (109{,}091 + 198{,}347)\ /\ 200{,}000 = 1.54$$
$$PI = 1.54 > 1.0$$

Therefore, the project is acceptable. Notice that we have taken into consideration the annualized return.

Disadvantage of PI: Like IRR it is a percentage and therefore ignores the scale of investment.

The NPV method is preferred over the PI method. This is because PI greater than 1 implies that the Net Present Value of the project is positive. Secondly, NPV clearly states whether to undertake or reject a project or not and return a dollar value by which the economic contribution is made to value of firm. This is not the case with PI which only expresses the relative profitability of projects being considered.

(iii) Internal rate of return (IRR)

IRR is a widely used and an important measure, which is more common in practice than the NPV. It is popular with the managers because it gives a very simple answer in the form of annual percentage and we can compare it to the inflation rate, cost of capital or financing or to the certain financial accounting ratios. The formula uses trial and error method. IRR, unlike NPV that is expressed in dollar amounts, is always quoted in terms of percentage, which makes it comparable to the other market interest rates or the inflation rate. IRR calculation involves the same equation that we have earlier used for the calculation of NPV.

The only difference is that while calculating IRR, we would set the value of NPV equal to zero and then solve the equation for the value if 'i'. In other words, the value of 'i', at which the net present value of the project equals zero would be considered as the internal rate of return of the project. It is important to remember that unlike NPV calculation, the value of IRR is constant in every year for the life of the project. While working out the NPV, we can change the discount rate for every single, but for IRR we would come up with a rate that is constant and fixed for every single year in the life of the project. Another simplistic explanation of IRR can be that it is the break-even rate of return. In other words, at this rate of return, we would be able to recover the initial investment in project's lifetime. RR is calculated by a trial and error method or iteration. Finding the value of an unknown variable may involve solving of higher degree polynomial equations and the easiest way to go about it is to use trial and error method. In a trial-and-error method, we tryout a value of 'i', and see if the equation comes to the value of zero; if it does not, try another value, even if the second value does not bring the equation down to zero and so on. The higher the IRR, the better it is considered, however, which value of the IRR can be considered as acceptable is difficult to measure.

Another important distinction needs to clarification here is that the internal rate of return is different from the discounting rate that we use in the calculation of the NPV. In the NPV formula, we used the discount rate as the required rate of return that we expected the project to generate. In case of IRR, we used the existing cash flows to find the forecasted return. These two different interpretations of 'i' should be kept in mind while calculating NPV and IRR.

The formula is similar to NPV

$NPV = 0 = -Io + CFt / (1+IRR)^t = -Io + CF1/(1+IRR) + CF2/(1+IRR)^2 + \ldots$

The value of i where NPV is zero is the value of IRR.

We can calculate the IRR for the café project in the following manner. Using the same formula of NPV, we can put the values in the formula

$$NPV = -IO + CF1/(1+IRR) + CF2/(1+IRR)^2$$
$$= 0 = -200{,}000 + 120{,}000/(1+0.1) + 240{,}000/(1+0.1)^2$$

Solving the equation assuming IRR to be 10 per cent, we have obtained a figure of 107,483, which was calculated as our NPV for the café project. However, in order to bring the NPV down to zero, we need to apply a higher rate as an assumed IRR. If we assume IRR to be 50 per cent the equation can be solved as follows:

$$NPV = -IO + CF1/(1+IRR) + CF2/(1+IRR)^2$$
$$= 0 = -200{,}000 + 120{,}000/(1+0.5) + 240{,}000/(1+0.5)^2$$

The calculation gives us a figure of -13,333, which is lesser than zero. In order to bring the value equal to zero we would use a rate lesser than 50 per cent. Trying out various IRR rates, we can finally reach a rate of 43.6 per cent at which the value of NPV would come down to -48 which is close to zero. If we try out IRR with more decimal places, we can bring the value of NPV equal to zero. However, with approximation, 43.6 per cent is the actual IRR of the project.

IRR in brief: IRR represents the Break-even Return on Investment, but the important thing to remember is the difference between IRR and NPV. When you are ranking different projects the ranking we get from NPV may be different from the ranking we get from IRR, because, there is a major difference of interpretation of i between NPV and IRR.

The difference is that in the case of NPV; we are externally specifying the discount rate based on required rate of return. In NPV calculations, we need to have an idea of our opportunity cost for the capital and we use it as 'i'. As mentioned earlier that rate given by the banks on account is considered as opportunity cost of our capital and we will invest in any project, which earns more than the rate offered by a bank. However in IRR, *'i'* is derived from the cash flow pattern of the project. Remember that in IRR project, we do not externally specify the interest rate but we calculated it from the cash flows. Therefore, in the IRR it is what we called forecasted rate of return or an intrinsic rate of return. This is an important difference to keep in mind between NPV and IRR.

Example: Consider the Same Savings Certificate example for IRR calculation. The only difference is that this time, we will not assume any value for 'i' as we had done in the NPV calculation. We set the NPV = 0 and solve the equation for 'i' (or IRR).

NPV = 0 = -Io + [CF1 / (1+IRR)] + [CFI1 / (1+IRR)]

We add $12,000 and $10,000 as both appearing at the same time.

0 = -100,000 + [(CF1 + CFI1) / (1+IRR)]

0 = -100,000 + [(12,000+100,000) / (1+IRR)]

IRR = (112,000 / 100,000) - 1

(No need for trial and error because you have one variable and one unknown)

= 1.12 - 1.00 = 0.12 = 12 per cent per annum

Now, one very important thing, which we need to consider when we are evaluating an investment proposal, is to look at NPV and to see how it changes as we change the discount rate. This is known as NPV Profile (See Fig. 4.2). Logically, when we increase the discount rate, the denominator becomes larger and the net present value becomes smaller. What we find as a result is a downward sloping line. The point where the NPV is zero would be the IRR for the project.

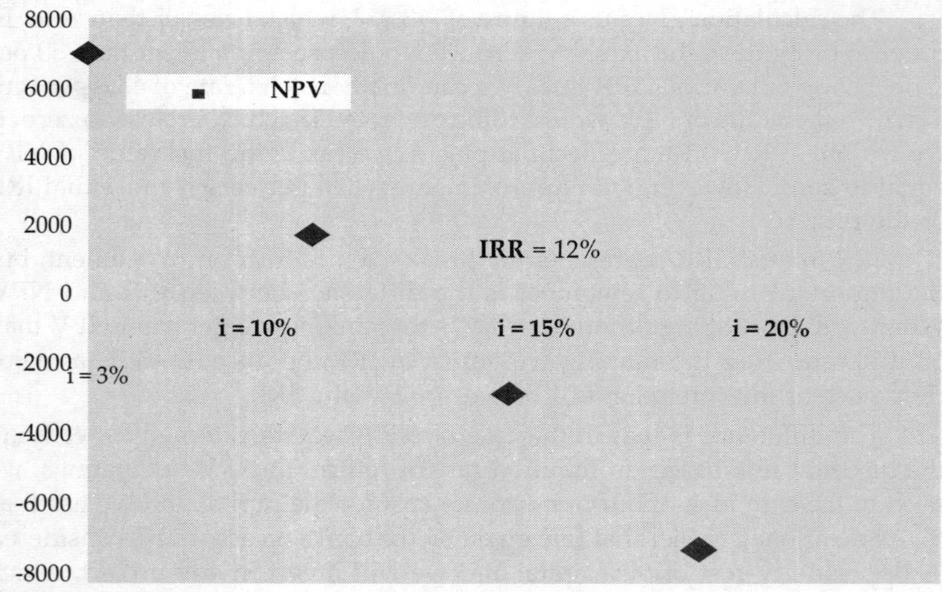

Fig.4.2: Graphical IRR estimation using 'NPV PROFILE'

Using a low and a high value for 'i', plot two points on the graph and extend the NPV line. Where the line cuts the horizontal X-axis would be reflect the value of the IRR.

Use this Graphical Technique When:

1. The investment or project life is longer than 2 years.
2. Graphical technique very useful in IRR calculations as there are polynomial equations that are time consuming to solve algebraically in terms of 'i'.

3. Comparing the NPV's of 2 or more investments, to study how sensitive the NPV's of the different investments are to the discount rate 'i'.

Ranking Two Different Investments: Which Investment is better?

Let us rank two Mutually Exclusive and Independent Investments using NPV and IRR criteria.

1. *Mutually Exclusive* – means that we can invest in ONE of the investment choices and having chosen one we cannot choose another.
2. *Independent* – implies that the cash flows of the two investments are not linked to each other.

Example: Let us consider two investment opportunities. One Investment is the Savings Certificate (which we described earlier) and the second investment is a Bank Deposit of $100,000 at 10 per cent interest compounded annually for two years.

NPV and IRR Numerical - Comparing the 2 Investments.

Since we have calculated the NPV and IRR for the Savings Certificate, we would calculate the NPV and IRR only for the Bank deposit rate.

Bank Deposit Example

$$FV = PV\ (1+i)^n = 100{,}000 \times (1.10)^2 = 121{,}000$$

$$\begin{aligned} NPV &= -100{,}000 + 10{,}000/(1.1) + 11{,}000/(1.1)^2 + 100{,}000/(1.1)^2 \\ &= -100{,}000 + 9{,}090 + 9090.9 + 82645 \\ &= +\$\ 826 \end{aligned}$$

IRR: $NPV = 0 = -100{,}000 + 10{,}000/(1+IRR) + 111{,}000/(1+IRR)^2$ ... by trial and error IRR = 10.5 per cent

Compare the Investment 1 (Savings Certificate) to Investment 2 (Bank Deposit):

NPV of Savings Certificate (i=10%) has + $1,818 and IRR=12 per cent

NPV of Bank Deposit (i= 10%) has + $826 and IRR=10.5 per cent

Savings Certificate appears to be a better investment because it offers both a higher NPV and a higher IRR.

Net Present Value vs. Internal Rate of Return: Independent vs. dependent projects

NPV and IRR methods are closely related because:

(i) both are time-adjusted measures of profitability; and

(ii) their mathematical formulae are almost identical.

So, which method leads to an optimal decision: IRR or NPV?

(a) NPV vs. IRR: Independent projects

Selecting one project does not preclude the choosing of the other. With conventional cash flows (-|+|+) no conflict in decision arises; in this case both NPV and IRR lead to the same accept/reject decisions. Mathematical proof: for a project to be acceptable, the NPV must be positive, *i.e.*

$$\sum_{t-1}^{n} \frac{C_t}{(I+k)^t} - I_o > 0 or \sum_{t-1}^{n} \frac{C_t}{(I+k)^t} - I_o > I_o$$

Similarly for the same project to be acceptable:

$$\sum_{t-1}^{n} \frac{C_i}{(I+R)} = I_o$$

Where R is the IRR.

Since the numerators C_t are identical and positive in both instances:

- Implicitly/intuitively R must be greater than k (R > k);
- If NPV = 0 then R = k: the firm is indifferent to such a project;
- Hence, IRR and NPV lead to the same decision in this case.

Example: Agritex is considering building either a one-storey (Project A) or five-storey (Project B) block of offices on a prime site. The following information is available:

Assume k = 10 per cent, which project should Agritex undertake?

$$NPV_A = \frac{\$11,500}{1.1} - \$9,500$$

$$= \$954.55$$

$$NPV_B = \frac{\$18,000}{1.1} - \$15,000$$

$$= \$1363.64$$

Both projects are of one-year duration:

IRRA:

$$\frac{\$11,500}{1 + R_A} = \$9,5000$$

$$\$11,500 = \$9,500 (1 + RA)$$

$$\frac{\$11,500}{\$9,500} = 1 + R_A$$

$$R_A = \frac{\$11,500}{\$9,500} - 1$$

$$= 1.21-1$$

Therefore IRRA = 21 per cent

IRRB:

$$\frac{\$18,000}{1 + R_B} = \$15,000$$

$$\$18,000 = \$15,000 (1 + RB)$$

$$R_B = \frac{\$ 18,000}{\$ 15,000} - 1$$

$$= 1.2-1$$

Therefore IRRB = 20 per cent

Decision:

Assuming that k = 10 per cent, both projects are acceptable because:

NPVA and NPVB are both positive

IRRA > k and IRRB > k

Which project is a 'better option' for Agritex?

If we use the NPV method:

NPVB ($1,363.64) > NPVA ($954.55): Agritex should choose Project B.

If we use the IRR method:

IRRA (21%) > IRRB (20%): Agritex should choose Project A.

5

Lending Procedure in the Farm Business

Lending to farmers is particularly challenging. It has been a concern of governments for a long-time as they recognise the importance of agricultural development in their economies. Banks, however, are vary of dealing with small farmers as they perceive this to be high risk and likely to reduce the quality of their loan portfolio. Newer micro-finance institutions, anxious to extend their activities in rural areas, also worry about how to lend safely to the farmers.

Types/Classification of Credit

Agricultural Credit

Banks lend to farmers for a variety of purposes, including:

(i) short-term credit to cover operating expenses;

(ii) intermediate credit for investment in farm equipment and real estate improvements;

(iii) long-term credit for acquisition of farm real estate and construction financing; and

(iv) debt repayment and refinancing. Commercial banks are the largest source of agricultural credit, followed by the Farm Credit Banks.

Evaluating Credit Capacity

Objective

To remind bank officials regarding the key factors in loan analysis – character, capacity, capital, collateral and conditions – and see how an initial screening process and loan application form contribute to providing this information.

(a) The initial screening

All financial institutions should have a mission statement that sets out the purpose and objectives of the business. An agricultural bank, for example, quite clearly is targeting farmers and other businesses operating in agricultural sector. Many micro-finance service providers are targeting extremely poor or excluded groups for their core business. Most organizations wish to survive and continue their operations. Surviving in the business of providing financial services means mobilizing funds, lending out funds, recovering those funds and charging sufficient interest to cover the costs of doing this. Lending money is a risk – banks might not get it back. So it is essential to try and make sure to get it back through client selection, careful loan appraisal, asking for security or guarantees, building loyalty and so on. Using a mix of all of these has meant that even lending to very small scale entrepreneurs with limited assets is possible. It requires an initial investment of time, which is costly but less costly than making loans that cannot be repaid. The mix of activities typical of farm based households make collecting information on them particularly time-consuming, so an institution wishing to concentrate on this target audience can prepare a list of basic criteria that will rule someone in or out of a chance of getting a loan immediately. That way staff time will not be wasted gathering detailed information only to find that person does not qualify for a loan due to some basic criterion not being met. AGLEND exemplifies an institution which intends to target farmers with some minimum commercial potential, which in their view will ensure repayment of loans. They do not have a social mandate to reach, for example, extremely poor or landless families. So they have a list of criteria which can be reviewed within 5-10 minutes that will determine whether or not a potential applicant meets their basic eligibility criteria for a loan. These eligibility criteria are highly context specific and any lending institution must carefully consider what criteria it will include in such a list, in order not to exclude potentially good clients or fulfill the institution's mission statement. There are three core criteria that AGLEND consider:

(i) *Previous loans from AGLEND:* AGLEND back office staff review whether the farmer interested in obtaining a loan already has a credit track record with AGLEND. This information is automatically checked in the computer system by entering the name and ID number of the farmer. If the person has accumulated more than 30 days overdue on the previous loans, access to future loans is denied and the loan request is turned down immediately.

(ii) *Previous or current loans with other lending institutions:* In the absence of a credit reference bureau in the country, AGLEND and other rural financial intermediaries have agreed to circulate lists with overdue borrowers that are updated on a monthly basis. Whenever a farmer contacts AGLEND and presents a loan request, these lists are checked to find out whether the person has unpaid loans or has a loan that is currently overdue. If people are listed as overdue borrowers, AGLEND immediately refuses their loan requests.

(iii) Borrower characteristics: As a final step, AGLEND staff check whether the potential borrower complies with specified eligibility criteria. These criteria may be region or even branch specific. For example Table 5.1 deals with the checklist shows that AGLEND wishes to screen out some client groups that are considered a high risk to serve. If any of the questions is answered with 'no', the screening process can be stopped and the client informed that he/she is not eligible. In addition, the AGLEND staff carrying out screening interviews, sometimes develop a 'gut-feeling' about a client's probable credit worthiness. If there are indications that the loan applicant is hiding information or telling lies, the officer can stop the interview and tell the person that he/she is not eligible. In order to prevent the information being collected several times, *e.g.*, during the screening interview, when the loan application is filled out, and during the field visit, the various forms used for these different purposes can be inter-linked in a database. If this is done, all the information that is collected during the screening interview will automatically appear in the loan application form.

Table 5.1: Checklist can be used to screen the applicants

		Yes	No
1.	*Minimum age:* Older than 21 years	[]	[]
2.	*Location of the farm:* Potential borrower from districts other than Magambe and Sobiri	[]	[]
3.	*Crops eligible for lending:* What is the main crop or livestock production?———— Potential borrower produces crops other than: flowers, fruits.	[]	[]
4.	*Length of time that the farmer is carrying out his/her main economic activity:* Minimum track record of at least 2 years.	[]	[]
5.	*Farm property:* Farmer owns his land and can provide adequate proof	[]	[]
6.	*Farm size:* Minimum 1.5 ha. in Caron and Pramot	[]	[]
7.	*Mix of income sources:*		
	Potatoes or coffee as main crop: Minimum 3 different income sources	[]	[]
	Maize as main crop: Minimum 4 different income sources, at least one off-farm activity	[]	[]

(b) The loan application

Once the eligibility of a potential client has been established, they can proceed to make an application for a loan. Financial institutions like AGLEND usually have application forms which may need to be filled out by the staff together with the loan applicant. Loan application forms should contain much of the information a loan officer needs to plan a visit to the applicant's business and carry out the loan appraisal at a later stage. It is essential to consider the key factors (5 Cs) for successful loan analysis: character, capacity, capital, collateral and conditions. All these factors matter but for micro entrepreneurs like small farmers, the first two – character and capacity – are the most important. Here is a list of questions that can help to provide information on each of these key factors:

Character: Personal integrity of the business owner(s) and family:

- How is the business managed?
- Are they honest and trustworthy?
- What is the physical and mental health of the person(s) running the business?
- Have they repaid bills and previous loans on time?
- Do they have family problems (alcohol, frivolous spending, etc.)?
- What is the innovation and creativity of the business in creating new business and growth opportunities?

Capacity: Ability of the business to repay the loan:

- What does the business plan indicate about income and profitability of the business?
- Can the business generate enough cash to make the loan payments with interest, including a margin of security?
- When can the loan be repaid?
- What are the family needs?
- What are the effects of seasonal fluctuation and production and price variations?
- How does the business compare to others within the same sector?

Capital: Money invested in the business:

- What money and assets are invested in the business?
- What is family contribution to the business?

Collateral: Backup sources of repayment for the loan:

- Are the personal guarantees of the group or persons trustworthy?
- Are the assets of the business and personal guarantees adequate to cover the loan if necessary?

Conditions: Key economic factors that impact on the ability to repay the loan:

- Is there an adequate and stable market to sustain the business?

- Are the loan terms (lengths, interest rate, etc.) adequate for repayment capacity of the loans?
- What are the price and production risks?
- What are the general market trends of the sector?

Now let us look at the details of AGLEND's application form and how they start to gather the information they need. There are six sections:

(i) Personal and family data.
(ii) Economic activities.
(iii) Previous and current loans.
(iv) Details of the proposed loan.
(v) References.
(vi) Declaration.

1. *Personal and Family Data*: In order to be able to visit the client, the home address needs to be documented. As official street names are lacking in rural areas, AGLEND staff often add a little drawing on the back of the sheet and take note of reference points in order to be able to locate the loan applicant's home more easily.

<table>
<tr><td>Name: ( ) Male ( ) Female ❷
Civil Status: ( )Married ( )Single ( )Widowed ( )Divorced ( )Other</td><td>ID Number
Birthday / /</td></tr>
<tr><td>Home locality: Street and House No
Community: ❶
Reference points:
For how long have you been living there: — years</td><td>District
Province</td></tr>
<tr><td>Name of wife or husband: ❷</td><td>ID Number</td></tr>
<tr><td colspan="2">No of household members: ——
No of Children: —— ❸ Ages: / / / /
No of other departments: —— Ages: / / / /
No of household members who generate income: Regularly —— Irregulatiy ——</td></tr>
</table>

It is important to know the civil status of the loan applicant and to find out more about his/her family background. So the loan applicant should provide information about the name and age of the spouse as well as about the time they have lived together. This will give an impression about the stability of the family and will also help to involve the partner in the credit process. AGLEND, for example, require spouses to co-sign loan contracts in order to ensure that they know about the loan obligation and feel responsible for it.

Knowing about the overall family situation is important to ensure that the loan officer appreciates the need to analyze the monthly family budget requirements in-depth during the field visit. The number of children and other dependents, who do not generate income, clearly has an influence on household expenditure. While young children lead to school expenses, older children may contribute significantly to household income and help to diversify the family income sources.

2. *Economic Activities*: Another important part of a loan application form is the section on the economic activities carried out by the farm household. This information helps to build a risk profile for the farm household, particularly when analysed together with the family structure and land situation. It also allows the loan officer to obtain insights into the variety of income sources and if they produce a continuous and reliable cash-flow or not. The number of years of professional experience for each economic activity gives an indication of the production skills in the farm household. The variety of crops that are under cultivation, for example, provides an indication about how well the farmer manages crop rotation systems and how well the different crops complement each other. When we analyse this information in the light of the location and size of the plots, we will have the possibility to project very roughly the expected yield of the farm household.

Primary activities in agriculture and livestock management carried out by household members: ❹	Agriculture	Years of experience	Livestock	Years of experiecne
	________	________	________	________
	________	________	________	________
	________	________	________	________
Other economic activities carried out by household members: ❹			Regularly	Irregularly
	________________		________	________
	________________		________	________
	________________		________	________
No of plots ———	Size: / / / / ❺			
Location of plots: ❺			District Province	
Community:				
Reference points:				

Because in rural areas the location of the area under cultivation is not always in the same place as the home, it is important to get a very clear and detailed description of the location of the plot. These descriptions are especially important for planning the field trip. In addition, the exact location of all properties is also important in order to know about the land property situation in legal terms as well as in terms of land quality. A classification of the borrower in legal terms regarding land titles and possible disputes over them can be based on this information. Also, later in the appraisal process, estimations of yields can be cross-checked against the known quality of the cultivated land used by the farmer. Finally, the information about the number of plots that are cultivated, which size they have and where they are precisely located provides further insights into the production strategy of the farm household and the associated cost-income structure and risks. For example, very small plots do only allow manual production, requiring a lot of labours. The existence of several very small plots that are spread over a larger area might contribute to mitigate climate risks but increase transportation costs.

3. *Previous and Current Loans*: It is to remember that AGLEND screens out borrowers with unpaid loans during the screening process prior to filling out the loan application. However, additional information is required to obtain further insights into the complete credit history of the loan applicants.

Obtaining information about previous loans shows how familiar the loan applicant is with borrowing money. The name of the lending institution or person might provide an insight into the potential creditworthiness of the loan applicants. Previous loans from a highly subsidized programme might give warning of tax repayment morale. Information on current loans is particularly interesting as it shows the current level of indebtedness and how much of the current income is already absorbed by servicing other loans.

Did you borrow in the past:	YES / /	NO / /
If yes? where did you borrow in the past?	______________	❻
Do you currently have a loan to repay?	YES / /	NO / /
If yes? Who is the person or institution you own money to?	______________	❼
What was the original loan amount? ______	How much is the remaining balance to repay? ______	When is the loan envisaged to be fully repaid? ______

4. *Details of the Proposed Loan*: Information about the applicant's preferences regarding the proposed loan gives AGLEND the opportunity to tailor

the loan to customer needs. The desired disbursement date, for example, is particularly important for agricultural production as a delay in planting crops can result in significant income losses due to the reduced yield. At the same time, the information provided in this section indicates how realistic the borrower is as regards his financial needs, the term required to repay and the repayment schedule. It gives a clear indication how well a loan applicant knows and manages his cash-flow. In addition, this section of the application can show whether borrowers are interested in a partnership with AGLEND that is frank and honest or whether they are distorting the facts. In many cases, for example, borrowers overestimate their loan amounts and required repayment period. However, once the loan applicant describes in more detail what he or she needs the loan for, AGLEND is in a better position to assess the loan amount and term structure in the light of the actual needs.

Amount applied for:	______________	Term applied for:	______________
Activities to be financed with the loan:	______________ ______________ ______________		
Desired date of disbursement ______________	Desired repayment plan:	Monthly / / Bimonthly / / Quarrely / / / /	Irregular / / one final payment / /

5. *References*: Each loan applicant must name at least two reference persons who can provide further information to AGLEND. If loan applicants refuse to provide this information, AGLEND turns down the loan application immediately as it suggests a degree of moral hazard.

Reference persons:	Address and telephone number:
______________	______________
______________	______________
______________	______________

6. *Declaration*: Once the loan application is filled out, AGLEND asks the loan applicants to sign two statements:

> 1. *Self-Declaration:* I herewith state that all the information that i provided is correct and true and provided in good faith. I am aware that any untrue information will result in the immediate refusal of this loan application and exclude me from accessing any future loans.
> 2. *Authorization:* I herewith allow AGLEND to obtain information about previous and current loans form any financial institution, lending organization of individual lender i have borrowed from. I also authorise AGLEND to contact the persons indicated in the reference section of the application form and use any other source of information deemed necessary to process this loan application.

These statements show that AGLEND is very strict as regards customer transparency. Before visiting the loan applicant at his/her home or fields, the loan officer to which the loan application is assigned, should carry out several cross-checks to review the information that has been provided. This can be considered a *third screening mechanism* that should prevent a costly field visit taking place with borrowers that have little or no credit worthiness.

ECONOMIC FEASIBILITY TEST OF A CREDIT PROPOSAL

Loan Appraisal

Objective

To look in detail at the analysis of repayment capacity and how to appraise information collected about an applicant's character, capital and collateral position. The process of cash flow and balance sheet analysis is examined and key interpretation ratios are introduced. As already explained in the previous section, the key elements of loan appraisal are an assessment of the applicant's:

- *Repayment capacity,* which can be done through cash flow analysis.
- *Character* or personal creditworthiness.
- *Capital and collateral,* which can be determined through a balance sheet.

Cash flow analysis

All the income and expenditure information that has been collected during the field trip is now consolidated in a cash flow projection. The exact period of the projection depends on the envisaged loan term. In agricultural households, one year projections are common because they encompass the majority of crop growing seasons. Loan projections beyond 12 months are very uncertain so it is recommended that cash-flow projections are renewed annually for medium and long-term loans. A typical layout for a cash flow projection can be found in Table 5.2. The instructions are quite simple – write down all the money coming in each month and all the money going out and find the difference between them. This gives the monthly balance or net cash flow. It may be positive or negative. Positive balances can be regarded as net income or surpluses which can be saved provided all the household expenses have been taken into account in the plan. Cumulative net income is cumulative savings from which loan repayments can be made. Information can be grouped together by economic activity, *e.g.*, crop type or product categories, *e.g.*, fertilizer, pesticides, machinery costs. All the facts that were assembled regarding weather impacts, price trends, market conditions, management capacity, risk reduction, etc., should be taken into account when deciding on what figures to put in the cash flow budget. As a general rule it is best to be conservative with estimates especially for new or expanded enterprises. Remember the quality of loan portfolio and the health of financial institution are going to depend on the quality of cash-flow projections and assessment of each applicant's repayment capacity. It is essential for a sound data from the field, good judgement and accurate arithmetic. A cash flow can be prepared first without including any loan assumption or the proposed amount can be included from the beginning.

Once a cash-flow projection has been prepared for all the economic activities of all household members, and all the family expenditure has been incorporated, it needs to be assessed in relation to the loan proposal The most commonly used indicators for doing this are:

- the accumulated repayment capacity; and
- net cash flow after loan repayment or 'free net cash flow'.

In other words, this indicator is calculated by adding up all the monthly balances during the envisaged loan term and comparing this figure to the total amount to be repaid (including both principal and interest). Since the cumulative net cash flow needs to be higher than the total repayment obligation which the applicant would have towards the lender, this indicator must be above 1.

Since it is advisable to have a substantial security cushion for unforeseen events, it is recommended that the ratio should be at least 2:1. Needless to say, the higher the benchmark is set for this ratio, the more conservative is the lender's risk-taking approach. AGLEND applies an accumulated repayment capacity indicator of 2, which means that the borrower would be able to pay back twice the loan amount (plus interest) with the accumulated cash flow generated during the loan period. Let us look at how the Arland family would perform in terms of this indicator in relation to a loan of $1,000 repayable at the end of one year.

Table 5.2: The accumulated repayment capacity indicator

Money Coming in	**Month:**	**Month:**	**Month:**	**Month:**	**Month:**	**Month:**	**Month**
Sales of:							
Wages							
Remittances							
Loans (*e.g.*, from AGLEND)							
Other sources:							
Total (A)							
Money Going out							
Farm/business inputs:							
Capital equipment:							
Household expenses							
Other expenses							
Existing debt repayments							
Total (B)							
Monthly Net Cash Flow (A-B)							
Cumulative Net Cash Flow							C
Section for loan officer use							
Loan repayment plan		← – – – –	– – – –	– – – –	D	– – – –	– – →
Revised Monthly NCF							
Revised Cumulative NCF							

$$\frac{\text{Comulative Net Cash Flow over Loan Period (c)}}{\text{Total Loan Repayment plus Interest (D)}} > 2$$

Table 5.3: Accumulated repayment capacity

Crespo Loan Application		Net Cash Flow before Loan Repayment ($)	
	$	First quarter	600
Loan amount	1,000	Second quarter	1,050
Interest charged at		Third quarter	600
2% flat per month	240	Fourth quarter	550
Total	**1,240**	**Total for 12 months**	**2,800**

Accumulated Repayment Capacity = $2,800 / $1,240 USD = 2.26

Clearly, the Arland family net cash flow would allow them to repay the required loan amount of $1,000 plus interest more than 2 times. The figure is 0.26 points higher than the required benchmark of 2. These ratios may also be expressed as percentages, *e.g.*, the benchmark is 200 per cent and the Arland accumulated repayment capacity is 226 per cent. As we can see, the accumulated repayment capacity is a very simple and straight forward indicator which can be calculated quickly once a cash flow has been prepared. However, it has one major shortcoming: it does not show whether the applicant will be able to cover every individual repayment installment. Due to seasonal variations in agricultural activity, the net cash flow of a farm household generally varies from month to month. Between planting and harvest periods there is always a period of reduced cash availability that has to be bridged by the applicant. Loan repayments, if required by the lender during this period, may not be at the top of the borrower's priority list for using scarce cash. AGLEND's current loan product has to be repaid in equal monthly installments. Consequently, their clients have to ensure that each month's net cash flow is sufficiently high to cover the monthly repayment of capital and interest. This where the second indicator: net cash flow after loan repayment can be useful. It can be calculated montly or at the end of the loan period if repayment is due in one final lump sum.

Table 5.4: Monthly and lum sum repayment calculation

Monthly Net Cash Flow (A-B)						
Cumulative Net Cash Flow						
Section for Loan Officer use						
Loan Repayment Plan	×	×	×	×	×	Y
Revised Monthly NCF						
Revised Cumulative NCF						

Monthly calculation = $\overline{X}$ One repayment calculation = $\overline{Y}$

× represents monthly repayment instalments and Y represents payment in a lumps sum.

A 'free net cash flow' indicator must be positive. A figure greater than 0.5 indicates that after all consumption, economic activity-related expenses and loan repayments have been met, the applicant would still have money left that is equal to more than 50 per cent of the loan installment (including interest payments). The existence of such a security cushion over the entire loan term provides the borrower with resources to cover unforeseen expenditures, expenditures that are higher than initially planned or decreased income. The assumption is that the existence of a security cushion will consistently decrease loan default risk. AGLEND require the 'free net cash flow' ratio to be above 0.5. Let us turn again to the Arland family. Will they have sufficient free net cash flow after loan repayment to pass this hurdle in AGLEND's loan assessment? Here is a summary of figures from their cash flow projection.

Table 5.6: Summary of cash flow projection

Months	Monthly Net Cash Flow (A)	AGLENDS Loan Repayment Instalments (B)	Net Cash Flow after Repayment A-B=C	Free Net Cash Flow C/B
1.	165	103.33	61.67	0.59
2.	220	103.33	116.67	1.12
3.	215	103.33	111.67	1.08
4.	200	103.33	96.67	0.93
5.	250	103.33	146.67	1.41
6.	600	103.33	496.67	4.80
7.	200	103.33	96.67	0.93
8.	185	103.33	81.67	0.79
9.	215	103.33	111.67	1.08
10.	160	103.33	56.67	0.57
11.	190	103.33	86.67	0.83
12.	200	103.33	96.67	0.93

We can see that in every month the free net cash flow is always greater than 0.5 or 50 per cent of the monthly repayment installment. It suggests that the Arland family have sufficient reserves to cope with unexpected events. However, accumulated repayment capacity is more important than monthly free net cash flow. As many farm households have a highly variable income and expense structure, loan products which require equal repayment installments are not really appropriate. Ideally, a more flexible repayment schedule is required. A number of variations are possible:

- Monthly interest payments combined with lump-sum repayment of the capital at the end.

- Various irregular payments of interest and capital.
- The entire loan amount plus interest paid at loan maturity.

In these instances the monthly free net cash-flow will not be of much help. However, the accumulated repayment capacity ratio will be very critical to decide whether a loan should be approved or not. In addition, the free net cash-flow must be positive in all those months where payments are planned.

Sensitivity analysis

In order to find out how a cash flow might be affected by adverse factors, the loan assessment may include a sensitivity analysis. The objective is to know whether adverse circumstances would undermine the repayment capacity to such a degree that the loan repayment will be at risk.

Factors to be considered in the sensitivity analysis of cash-flow projections could include:

- Reduced yields due to bad weather conditions, diseases or pests;
- Delays in payments, *e.g.*, delays in payments for crops after harvest;
- Lower than expected sale prices;
- Higher input costs;
- Additional labour costs, *e.g.*, replacing a sick family member with hired labour.

The cash flow indicators should be carefully assessed regarding their sensitivity to possible changes. In this way, a specific risk profile for the individual loan can be constructed. Financial institutions need clear policies which state what level of tolerance in relation to cash flow indicators is acceptable. For example, it could be stated that the monthly free net cash flow should not fall below zero more than three times within a year for even worst case scenarios. It is important not to take too simplistic an approach to sensitivity analysis, by just recalculating numbers in a mechanical fashion. We learned earlier how farmers use different risk mitigation techniques to keep their vulnerability to risks at a reasonable level. When analysing a cash-flow, these risk mitigating techniques must be taken into account as part of the risk profile of a farm household. Here are some examples:

1. *Diversification of Income Sources:* Prudent farmers tackle income insecurity by diversifying income sources. Potential losses in one agricultural activity may be offset by other agricultural or non-agricultural income-generating activities. Many farmers have off-farm activities, such as wage-based seasonal labour at other farms, work for large agri-business enterprises or the production of handicrafts. Family members may carry out exclusively non-agricultural activities, such as running a small grocery shop or working in the nearby town for a wage. Relatives may also regularly send payments from distant places, or even from abroad.

Many farmers try to quickly diversify their sources of income under a crisis scenario, particularly by selling their labour to others.

2. *Liquidation of Assets:* The majority of farmers have savings in-kind. One of the most popular forms of saving is buying livestock. So confronted with an emergency, many farmers sell a oxen or a goat to obtain funds.
3. *Family Safety Networks:* In many countries, informal safety networks exist within extended families or clans. If one person has a problem, family support is mobilised. In many cases however, this support structure is not without cost. Farm households must constantly contribute to maintain it. When festivities take place, cash contributions from all invitees are expected. However, if a person has lent to others, he obtains the right to gain immediate access to money when he needs it. Understanding how these informal networks work is helpful in determining whether a borrower is likely to be able to mobilize money at short notice from within his extended family to repay.

Character assessment

The information obtained during the field visit, the results of the careful review of the client history and the cross-checking with other information sources must now be combined in a final assessment of the personal credit worthiness of the loan applicant. A structured way of carrying out such a character assessment is the introduction of a simple rating system like this one used in AGLEND.

Table 5.7: Character rating system

		Excellent	Fairly Good	Sub-Optimal	Bad
(a)	Open disclosure of required information				
(b)	Reputation within the community				
(c)	Good credit history with AGLEND and other lending institutions				

(a) *Disclosure of required information:* Clients should demonstrate that they are interested in a relationship of mutual trust with AGLEND. A proxy for this is the client's openness to share account statements, receipts and other documents with the loan officer as well as show him available assets and even cash.

(b) *Reputation within the community:* AGLEND loan officers inquire whether the potential borrower has a reputation of being honest and hard-working. A proxy for 'word of mouth' information on reputation within the community is whether the loan applicant has held public positions and or played a role at public functions. For example, if the loan applicant was elected to be the treasurer of the local village committee, this tells us that the villagers trust him.

(c) *Good credit history:* A borrower who has never failed in previous loan repayments is less likely to default in the future as opposed to somebody who has had repayment problems in the past. Consequently, the credit history of a loan applicant discloses important information about his behaviour and repayment culture. In the case of AGLEND, an evaluation of any of the above mentioned three character assessment categories as 'bad' will result in the immediate rejection of the loan appraisal. This loan application is not even further assessed and is not presented to the credit committee. If any of the three assessment categories receives a 'sub-optimal' status, the loan officers will need to detail in writing and during the credit committee as to why the loan should still be considered. AGLEND supervisors make regular checks during credit committee meetings and on-site with the applicants to ensure that the rating is not used in a lax manner.

Capital

As the next step of the loan appraisal, a brief analysis of the balance sheet should be carried out to assess the applicant's capital position. It is not as critical as the cash flow projection but we can gain some useful insights into a business, even that of a small farmer, from a balance sheet. Here is a reminder of the balance sheet layout (Table 5.8), followed by examples of things we could look out for:

(i) *Large amounts of cash* – especially outside harvest time – should trigger a closer investigation as to why this available cash has not been invested and where it is coming from. Comparably low amounts of cash after harvest combined with a lack of investment in visible household or farm assets on the other side will also signal a potential problem. A close analysis should then be carried out by the loan officer.

(ii) *The existence of savings* – in a deposit account indicates that the loan applicant does not consume or invest all his/her income but rather sets a certain amount aside. On the one hand, this could be a sign of thriftiness and creating a safety reserve for rainy days. On the other hand, it could mean that there are little investment opportunities and there is a lack of entrepreneurial initiative. It would therefore be very important to scrutinize the reasons for savings.

(iii) *The value of the existing agricultural stocks* – supplies or harvested crops – provides insights into how successful the farm business is. Very low stocks prior to the start of the agricultural season can indicate the farm's dependence on external funds to keep on running. In contrast, large quantities of stored crops show that the farmer is able to postpone selling crops until prices are more favourable.

Table 5.8: Balance sheet layout

Assets	Value	Liabilities/Equity	Value
Cash in hand		Accounts payable/Short-term [7]	
Cash in bank or Co-operative Account [2]		Account payable/Long-term	
Inventory/Agricultural [3]		Loans	
Investory/Trade		Leasing Contract	
Investory/Other economic activities		Household Liabilities	
Accounts receivable/short-term [4]		Other Liabilities	
Accounts receivable/Long-term [4]		AGLAND Loan	
Machinery and equipment [5]		Total Liabilities [8] (B)	
Household assets		Equity [9] (C) (= A-B)	
Plant and/or Building [5]			
Other assets			
Total Assets [6] (A)		**Total Liabilities Plus Equity**	

(iv) *Accounts receivable* (debtors) – is an important figure as they can cause severe liquidity problems if they are not received on the due date.

(v) *The composition of fixed assets* – reveals key information about production methods. In addition, the figures indicate how modern the equipment is and whether the farm household is able to maintain its machinery.

(vi) *The amount of total assets* – indicates how successful the household has been and how much wealth it has accumulated over the years. This figure is particularly interesting when farm households with similar family and production patterns are compared.

(vii) *Accounts payable* (creditors) – indicate that the potential borrower already has obligations with other funding sources. This means that there will be cash outflows in the future that must be taken into account.

(viii) *Level of indebtedness* – expressing liabilities as a percentage of total assets indicates what proportion of the farm's assets has been financed through borrowing.

$$\frac{\text{Total Liabilities (B)}}{\text{Total Assets (A)}} \times 100$$

A low ratio, *e.g.* 20 or 30 per cent indicates that a farm household was able to purchase and accumulate most of its assets with own resources. In many country contexts, over-indebtedness is a serious problem for micro enterprises and farm households. Therefore, it is recommended that agricultural lenders check the level of indebtedness before and after the proposed loan as part of the loan appraisal. It may be wise to set a maximum level, *e.g.* 50 per cent.

(xi) *Equity* – percentage is the mirror image of the level of indebtedness. It is the equity or owner's capital expressed as a percentage of total assets.

$$\frac{\text{Equity (C)}}{\text{Total Assets (A)}} \times 100$$

Obviously it gives the same message as the indebtedness ratio and instead of a maximum we would set a minimum of 50 per cent for this ratio. AGLEND includes the requested loan amount including interest that will be accrued over the projected loan period in the total liabilities when calculating the level of indebtedness. On the asset side, however, AGLEND does not include the planned investment.

This very conservative approach enables the loan officer to assess the application on the assumption that the AGLEND loan is either completely diverted to non-economic activity related consumption purposes or that the activity fails completely. As a benchmark, AGLEND has decided that the indebtedness ratio should be below 50 per cent. In other words, more than half of the total assets should be financed by the applicant's own funds while less than half should be financed on credit.

The definition of a benchmark for the indebtedness ratio needs to be done with great care. An educated guess is often made during the initial phase of an agricultural lending programme. If possible, research should be carried out to analyse the indebtedness ratios of a substantial number of past loans at the time of granting the loan and relate these to actual loan performance. This process should be repeated at intervals in order to amend the benchmark to reflect actual default risk. While the inclusion of the requested loan into the calculation of the indebtedness ratio ensures that the analysis concentrates on the situation after the loan has been taken, the conservative approach of not including the assets to be financed by the loan may not be followed by every agricultural lender. Thus its important is to state clearly whether the financed assets are included or not – and if they are included, how they have been valued. One option may be to include the loan on both the liability and assets side, *i.e.*, increasing both by the same amount. Another option may be to deduct a security cushion from the loan amount on the asset side in order to cater for losses of value and potential deviation of funds. No matter which path is chosen in this context, it is most important to define and test out a clear benchmark to reduce default risk through over-indebtedness. Let's have a look at the balance sheet that the AGLEND loan officer constructed for the Arland family.

So they are able to meet the AGLEND benchmark of a maximum indebtedness ratio of 50 per cent, if they get the loan to buy the land they want.

Table 5.9: Balance sheet of arland family

Assets	($)	Liabilities and Equity	($)
Cash on hand	5	Accounts payable	100
Deposit in Co-operative	5	AGLAND Loan	1,000
Agricultural stocks	765		
Accounts receivable	1,425	Equity	1,500
Fixed assets (machines)	250		
Household good	150		
Total	**2,600**	**Total**	**2,600**

What is the indebtedness ratio?

it is $\frac{\$1,100}{\$2,600} \times 100$ Which equals 42.3%

Collateral

Another purpose of examining the asset and liability structure in the balance sheet is to identify appropriate collateral. Compared to the repayment capacity that is the *sine qua non* in lending, collateral is only of second priority. AGLEND considers collateral primarily as a repayment incentive, putting pressure on the borrower to repay in a timely fashion. They have defined the following conditions for any asset that they would accept as collateral:

(i) *Importance to the borrower:* The asset must be of high personal value to the borrower. He/she must be psychologically hurt if the asset were to be taken away by AGLEND.

(ii) *Value:* The asset must be known to have a value that is sufficient to cover the loan amount, interest for the entire loan term and a possible penalty charge. The minimum value of the asset(s) must be 1.35 of the loan amount.

(iii) *Marketability:* The asset must be easy to sell. Transfer of property rights should take place at little cost and with little formalities. In addition, the assets must be free from liability of third parties.

According to these three factors, the economic value of the collateral is only one side of the story. It is even more important that the borrower feels attached to the asset and that losing it would cause him/her considerable – even though psychological – damage. Against this background, AGLEND accepts a wide range of collateral, including household goods like: TV sets or bicycles, personal guarantors, livestock and land. In the majority of cases, a combination of collateral items is used.

In order to avoid lengthy legal procedures, AGLEND asks the borrowers to sign a document agreeing to hand over ownership of certain assets to AGLEND at the moment of signing the loan contract. With this document, AGLEND becomes the owner of these assets during the entire loan period. AGLEND allows the borrower to continue using these assets but is allowed to remove them at any time, if the loan becomes overdue. This allows AGLEND to immediately enforce repayment without a court decision.

LOAN TERMS AND REPAYMENT SCHEDULE

Loan Approval and Follow-up

Objective

To examine in detail the steps that follow: *(i)* loan appraisal, *(ii)* including the approval process, *(iii)* setting loan terms and conditions, *(vi)* loan disbursement and *(v)* loan monitoring.

There are different strategies that a financial institution can follow in each of these phases but the general principles outlined here are widely applicable. After a loan officer has carried out a loan appraisal, the application has to be prepared for approval and, finally disbursement. Decision-making mechanisms vary from institution to institution and often depend on the loan amount and loan term proposed. However, in all cases at least one additional person gets involved in order to respect the 'four-eyes' principle of internal control. Let us now have a closer look at the various steps that follow loan appraisal.

The loan file

As a first step, the loan officer prepares a loan file in accordance with a pre-defined structure. It is useful to have a standard checklist of the information and documents that are needed for a complete loan file. A second list of people, who should sign off when each step of the loan approval process is completed, can provide a useful tool to monitor and manage loan processing time. Many institutions have defined benchmarks for the maximum time a loan should take from the time of application to approval and disbursement. The loan file should include a summary sheet of the loan appraisal, containing key information on the borrower and the loan in a very concise form. This can be an important tool for the credit decision committee to quickly grasp the profile of the proposed loan. AGLEND's summary sheet includes the following five key aspects:

(a) brief description of the economic activities of the farm household (main crops, livestock etc.);

(b) brief risk profile of the farm household and details of risk-mitigating strategies that are used;

(c) characteristics of the loan applied for and the recommendation from the loan officer;

(d) financial indicators:

  (i) Accumulated repayment capacity indicator,

  (ii) Free net cash-flow indicator,

  (iii) Indebtedness ratio,

(e) Rating results as regards personal creditworthiness.

AGLEND's loan officers must present the results of their loan assessment, with a clear statement of the pros and cons and a clear recommendation to the credit committee. A signature by the loan officer under the loan recommendation will increase the level of responsibility. With this signature the loan officer confirms that he/she has carried out an in-depth evaluation of the client's repayment capacity and willingness and has collected sufficient information to come to the recommendation.

Loan terms and conditions

A very important part of preparing the loan file that will be presented is determining the most appropriate loan terms and conditions. Repayment schedules must be in line with the cash-flow patterns of the farmer. Repayments can only be made when the farm household has cash on hand. Thus, it does not make sense to schedule repayment installments for periods when there is a liquidity shortage, *e.g.*, prior to harvest. Depending on the household situation, different options exist for appropriate repayment plans in agricultural households:

(i) Equal (monthly) installments of loan principal and interest.

(ii) Regular monthly interest payments and a bulk payment of loan principal at maturity.

(iii) Regular monthly interest payments and irregular intermediate loan principal payments when cash is available.

Credit for seasonal crops is generally repaid after harvest (between 4-9 months). If family income from other sources is regularly flowing in, at least small payments can be made on a monthly basis. This is often the case with farm households that sell milk on a daily basis or are engaged in vegetable or chicken production, which have short production cycles.

Let us have a look at AGLEND's approach. We know from Arland that AGLEND's loan product requires monthly repayment of principal together with interest payments. This is manageable for farmers like the Arland family who have various income sources and, consequently, a reasonably regular flow of income. However, there are farm households with other production patterns that find equal installments difficult. AGLEND has decided to test more flexible repayment plans, which means moving away from their original loan product of equal monthly installments. Arland has heard about this new possibility and told his brother Carlos about it. Carlos wants start a cattle finishing enterprise. He proposes to buy young cattle, fatten them and sell them at a much higher price after 6 months. He thinks he would need a loan of about $500 to get started. An AGLEND loan officer visits Carlos and prepares the following cash-flow projection. He discovers that Carlos keeps pigs and chickens and that he gets income each month from the sale of eggs. The family income is increased by the wages Carlos's daughter earns in the local shop and the wages that his son gets from occasional work for a machinery contractor. After preparing the cash flow he is able to work out the repayment schedule and then reassess the cash flow indicators that were explained in the appraisal process.

Let us look at the figures he produces for the first six months of Carlos's business, including the proposed cattle fattening enterprise. He builds in an assumption that Carlos gets a loan of $500 as he says he does not have any cash savings he can use.

Table 5.10: Cash flow for carlos for next six months

Money Coming in	Month 1	Month 2	Month 3	Month 4	Month 5	Month 6
Sales of:						
Finished cattle						1000
Pigs			360			
Eggs	40	30	20	20	20	60
Non-farm income	50	60	60	70	70	20
Loans (*e.g.*, from Aglend)	500					
Total (A)	590	90	440	90	90	1080
Money Going out						
Farm/business inputs:						
Purchase of weaned calves	500					
Fodder and salt	45	40	50	35	35	35
Pig and chicken feed			120			
Household expenses	40	40	70	50	50	50
Total (B)	585	80	240	85	85	85
Monthly Net Cash Flow (A – B)	5	10	200	5	5	955
Cumulative net cash flow	5	15	215	220	225	1220
Section for loan officer use						
Loan repayment plan						
Revised monthly NCF						
Revised cumulative NCF						

Here are the loan officer's repayment calculations:

We can see that he believes that Carlos can repay part of the principal in month 3 because of his expected sale of pigs that month. He concludes that the loan can be cleared in two installments: $180 in month 3 which includes $30 of interest and the balance in month 6. There is not enough cash surplus in months 1, 2, 4 and 5 for regular monthly payments, not even regular interest payments. However, the loan seems to be viable as the accumulated total cash-flow during the 6 months is sufficiently high. Here is the effect on the cash flow when the loan officer returns to that to enter in his repayment calculations:

Table 5.11: Repayment calculation

	Month 1	Month 2	Month 3	Month 4	Month 5	Month 6
Proposed instalment			-180			-371
Principal			-150			-350
Interest			-30			-21
Outstanding balance	500	500	500	350	350	350
Interest at 2 per cent p.m.	10	10	10	7	7	7
Cumulative interest	10	20	30	7	14	21

Table 5.12: Effect of cash flow

Monthly Net Cash Flow (A-B)	**5**	**10**	**200**	**5**	**5**	**995**
Cumulative Net Cash Flow	5	15	215	220	225	1220
Section for Loan Officer use						
Loan repayment plan			180			371
Revised Monthly NCF	**5**	**10**	**20**	**5**	**5**	**624**
Revised Cumulative NCF	**5**	**15**	**354**	**40**	**45**	**669**

Every farm household has a unique combination of economic activities and a unique cash flow. It makes sense, therefore, for AGLEND to make their repayment conditions more flexible to match loan terms with each farm's income and expenditures better. For farmers whose main crops are perennial (*e.g.*, coffee, coconut, grapes, etc.), annual payments may be the most appropriate. However, AGLEND is very reluctant to operate with bulk payments. They have decided to demand some intermediate payments, even in the case of perennial crop producers, for various reasons:

(a) Most of the farmers with perennial crops tend to make all their payments when the crop matures, so many people and other lenders may 'compete' for the available cash.

(b) More frequent payments serve as a 'reminder' to borrowers that they have an obligation with a lending institution. This disciplinary effect is obviously greater with regular payments, *e.g.*, monthly installments. However, if this cannot be done, then intermediate, irregular payments should be required, just as proposed for Carlos.

(c) Capturing cash whenever there is cash available at the farm household reduces the risk that cash 'disappears'. AGLEND wishes to avoid large

sums of cash 'burning' in the hands of the borrowers and being spent for purposes that may damage loan repayment.

(d) If borrowers fail to meet intermediate installments, this is an early-warning sign for AGLEND that they may have recovery problems with a client.

Table 5.13: Format to identify repayment problem

Monthly Net Cash Flow (A-B)					
Cumulitive Net Cash Flow					
Selection for Loan Officer use					
Loan repayment plan					
Revised Monthly NCF					
Revsied Cumulative NCF					

Every farm household has a unique combination of economic activities and a unique cash flow. It makes sense, therefore, for AGLEND to make their repayment conditions more flexible to match loan terms with each farm's income and expenditures better. For farmers whose main crops are perennial (*e.g.*, coffee, coconut, grapes, etc.) annual payments may be the most appropriate. However, AGLEND is very reluctant to operate with bulk payments. They have decided to demand some intermediate payments, even in the case of perennial crop producers, for various reasons:

(a) Most of the farmers with perennial crops tend to make all their payments when the crop matures, so many people and other lenders may 'compete' for the available cash.

(b) More frequent payments serve as a 'reminder' to borrowers that they have an obligation with a lending institution. This disciplinary effect is obviously greater with regular payments, *e.g.*, monthly installments. However, if this cannot be done, then intermediate, irregular payments should be required, just as proposed for Carlos.

(c) Capturing cash whenever there is cash available at the farm household reduces the risk that cash 'disappears'. AGLEND wishes to avoid large sums of cash 'burning' in the hands of the borrowers and being spent for purposes that may damage loan repayment.

(d) If borrowers fail to meet intermediate installments, this is an early-warning sign for AGLEND that they may have recovery problems with a client.

Lending decision

Lending decisions are normally taken by a credit committee. Decision-making should be decentralized, *i.e.*, take place as close to the relevant customers and loan officers as possible. This is essential if large distances exist between branches and district, regional or head offices. Another reason for decentralizing credit decision-making is that a good loan decision depends on having good knowledge of the specific economic situation of the client group, the agricultural activities and the regional context.

A credit committee should consist of at least one person in addition to the loan officer. Loan officers should not vote on the credit committee but should rather present the information and provide a clear recommendation for loan approval or rejection. How does this work in practice? Loan officers present a summary of the loan request and their appraisal report, before making their recommendation. Committee members listen to the explanation about the proposal and then are given the opportunity to ask questions of the loan officer regarding the details of the client's economic situation, the market situation and any other relevant issues. Decisions in the credit committee are made on a consensus basis. The credit committee is expected to examine the appraisal and the recommendation made by the loan officer closely. If any doubts exist about the information gathered or the results of the loan appraisal, the credit committee can postpone their decision at this point in time and ask the loan officer to collect additional information. If insufficient collateral or collateral substitutes have been proposed, the loan officer can be sent back to identify additional collateral. In agricultural lending, a fast decision-making process is crucial, since the timing of disbursements is critical to the farmer's production success. Therefore, loan files must be particularly well prepared to avoid the need for additional information.

Decentralized decision-making requires that clear thresholds for loan decisions should be set at branch, district, regional and head office levels. Thresholds specifying the restrictions in relation to loan amounts and loan terms are the most useful. At regional and headquarter levels, it may be difficult for loan officers to participate personally in the credit committee meetings. They may be represented by their branch managers who will have to introduce the loan proposal to the credit committee, based on discussions he has had with the loan officer. This can mean there is less background information available on the applicants during credit committee discussions. It is because requests for larger or long-term loans normally have to be approved at central offices that they take longer to get approved.

Disbursement procedures

Once the loan decision has been made, clients should be informed immediately. Since farmers generally live far away from the central office, it is important to let them know the date on which the application will be presented to the credit committee, and when a decision can be expected. Reducing useless travel time for loan applicants is good client service and reduces the transaction costs of the borrower. There are various methods that can be used for loan disbursement:

- *Cash disbursement:* Many lending institutions disburse loans in cash. They either do this themselves through their own cashiers or by handing out a cheque that can be cashed at a partner-bank.
- *Money transfer to supplier:* Some organizations prefer to transfer the approved loan amount directly to suppliers. This can increase the level of control over how the loan amount is being spent. Although this may be interpreted as a signal of mistrust, there are also advantages attached to this system: *Firstly*, farmers might not want to travel with large amounts of cash because of the risk of money getting stolen. *Secondly*, it removes the temptation for the farmer to spend larger amounts of money, *e.g.*, for investment goods, in a different way. *Thirdly*, financial institutions can establish partnerships with large agricultural suppliers. Either the lending institution can notify the suppliers regularly about the approved credit limits of clients, so that the farmer can go there directly and make his purchases or clients can be given coupons to use as cash in specific shops. In many cases, these partnerships allow farmers to buy supplies at preferential rates. Fourthly, interest calculation will only start to be calculated on the day when the purchase at the supplier is made or the coupons are actually cashed. This is an obvious advantage compared to the system when cash is directly disbursed to the farmer who might not spend it immediately. In this case, he must already bear the costs for the loan without having obtained any benefit from it as yet.
- *Supplying inputs in-kind:* This method was common in the 1970's and 1980's. Many agricultural lending institutions bought agricultural inputs and then disbursed them as credit in kind. In-kind loans, however, have the severe disadvantage that the lender becomes directly connected to the economic success of the investment. If the investment fails, farmers are then more likely to refuse to repay. Whatever disbursement method is chosen, however, it is imperative that the loan is available to the farmer at the moment when it is needed. Late disbursement can undermine the entire investment, put the income flows at risk and, hence, endanger the loan repayment. The cash flow budget should indicate clearly when disbursement is required.

Loan monitoring

The success or failure of any financial institution is closely tied to the quality of its loan portfolio and its loan monitoring system. The assessment of repayment capacity and the creditworthiness of an applicant provides the basis for good loan decisions and thus, portfolio quality. Good loans may turn bad however. In agricultural lending, there are particular risks as we have mentioned and thus careful monitoring to avoid default is crucial. A monitoring system provides the information needed to oversee loan portfolio quality at any given time, identifying potential problems at the earliest moment possible. There are some key requirements for an appropriate monitoring system for agricultural loans:

(a) Open communication between the lender and the borrower is essential for effective loan monitoring. Some borrowers do not like to tell the lender about problems they may face in repaying the loan. The establishment of open communication can help ensure that problems are communicated as soon as they arise. If a clear policy on handling problem loans exists and is known to the borrower, powerful incentives may be given to borrowers to provide lenders with early warning signals when they have to go through difficult times.

(b) Loan files must contain all the documents (loan application, loan assessment, collateral records, memos, loan agreement, etc.), which provide a loan officer and other interested parties with a complete historical and ongoing record of the relationship between the lender and the borrower. These files are the backbone of a loan monitoring system.

(c) Computerisation should be introduced, if it is not already in place. Although in principle loan tracking can be done manually, this will be difficult beyond a certain number of borrowers with highly individual repayment schedules and loan terms. An obvious advantage of computerized loan monitoring system is that reports can be generated automatically. As a speedy response to loan default is vital for maintaining a sound loan portfolio, automation can help to identify problem loans at a very early stage, allowing for immediate corrective action. Various strategies can be employed to monitor loan performance. Let's look at the methods that AGLEND use to identify potential repayment problems as early as possible:

  (i) ***Periodic direct monitoring of clients:*** Generally, an agricultural lending institution should stay in touch with their clients through the loan officers. The loan officer can capitalize on the relationship established during the field visit, the appraisal process, and possibly through earlier business contacts. This is not only prudent loan monitoring practice, it is also good customer relations. However, monitoring a loan by personal contact is costly and raises the institution's operating expenses.

- ***Client visits:*** The most effective way to obtain information about the current performance of a borrower is to visit the farm. This gives an opportunity to uncover organizational and operational problems and discuss the current risk management strategies employed by the client. On-site visits should be timed to coincide with crucial moments in the borrower's agricultural production cycle, *e.g.*, when crops are germinating, when fertilizers are being applied or just before harvest. Pre-harvest visits are particularly useful to assess repayment potential and make the farmer *feel monitored* in his/her repayment performance. Client visits, however, require a lot of time and, hence, represent a significant cost burden for the lending institution. There are other less costly techniques.

(ii) ***Indirect monitoring of clients:*** *Attending local markets, cattle auctions, agricultural fairs:* These occasions bring together a large number of farmers. Many farmers, for example, regularly travel to the local and regional markets to sell their produce. There might be monthly livestock auctions and occasional agricultural fairs. AGLEND's loan officers have a chance to meet many of their clients in one single spot! They can observe how well a client's business is going from marketing activities and, by talking to other farmers, AGLEND loan officers may pick up a lot of additional information about the customer.

- *Meetings with extension officers:* In many countries, farm households are assisted by public extension service programmes. Extension workers visit farmers to help them improve their yields and marketing efforts. AGLEND loan officers regularly meet with the staff of the extension programmes to obtain information about particular clients. In addition, they learn about any specific risks that threaten certain regions or farmers, *e.g.*, a village hit by a particular pest or water shortage problems in a region.
- *Meetings with veterinary officers:* Another good information source can be veterinary officers who assist in livestock management. They are aware which farmers vaccinate their cattle and which do not. They also know which farmers have problems with sick cattle or have recently lost a calf for example. This information is helpful to identify potential problem loans at an early stage.
- *Contacts with agricultural input suppliers, traders, slaughter houses, etc.:* Agricultural input suppliers, wholesalers, traders, slaughter houses, irrigation associations and marketing co-operatives also form part of a larger information network. Maintaining contact with them, attending meetings and so on, is just another way that timely information about problems that individual farmers or groups of farmers may face and which might undermine repayment performance, can be obtained.
- *Other client records in the financial institution:* For those lending institutions that also offer other financial services, other monitoring devices can be used. A lot, for example, can be learned from a borrower's current account or savings passbook. If such accounts exist, an occasional check of the account movements can provide indicative information to the loan officer about the level of repayment capacity.

(iii) *Monitoring actual loan repayment performance:* For those loan borrowers who are in frequent contact with the lending institution because they pay monthly loan installments, close monitoring of repayment performance may be sufficient. Accurate and up-to-date information forms the basis for comparing planned versus actual repayments. Appropriate management information systems (MIS) need to be in place in order to provide loan officers with the required information on their outstanding loan portfolio. If there is no fully integrated and computerized MIS in place, spreadsheets and manually prepared reports have to substitute for automated print-outs. Whether created manually or automatically, some essential reports are required daily by the loan officers.

This is the set of reports that are regularly produced for each AGLEND loan officer:

1. Loan portfolio review.
2. Due payment report.
3. Past-due payment report.
4. Loan portfolio at risk report.

Let's have a look at these reports in some detail.

(i) *Loan portfolio review:* This report includes basic client and loan information, as well as the currently outstanding loan amount.

Table 5.14: Loan portfolio review

Client Name	Client No.	Loan Details				Current Outstanding Balance	
		Date	Amount	Term	Repayment Frequency	Capital	Interest

(ii) *Due payment report:* This report indicates which clients' payments will fall due in the near future. AGLEND produce these reports for the coming two weeks. The report also indicates the main purpose of the loan to assist loan officers in deciding whether a monitoring action such as a client visit is necessary. The loan officer will try to build such visits into his route planning for field visits to new applicants in order to minimise time and transport costs.

(iii) *Past-due payment report:* Once payments are overdue, the loan officer is informed automatically by the system so that immediate action can be taken to collect the outstanding payment. AGLEND's loan policy clearly states the action the loan officer is required to take.

Table 5.15: Due payment report

Client Name	Client No.	Date of Next Due Payment	Loan Purpose	Main Economic Activity of Client	Observation/ Action Needed

Table 5.16: Past-due report

Client Name	Client No.	Loan Balance	Amount in Arrears	No. of Payments in Arrears	No. of Days Overdue	Date of Last Payment

(iii) *Loan portfolio at risk report:* In order to provide an overview of all the loans with repayment problems, an additional report is created by AGLEND which summarises past-due loans according to the number of days in arrears.

Table 5.17: Individual loans at risk

Client Name	Client No.	Outstanding loan balance at risk (USD)			
		1-30 Days	31-90 Days	91-180 Days	> 180 Days
Total					

These reports provide AGLEND loan officers with all the information they need to monitor and follow-up their clients and ensure repayment.

This is an example of a revised repayment plan in which interest is now being paid monthly and the installment of principal in month 3 has been reduced to $100, leaving an outstanding balance of $400 for the remaining months.

Table 5.18: Revised repayment plan

Section for Loan Officer use						
Loan repayment plan	10	10	110	8	8	408
Revised Monthly NCF	**8**	**13**	**103**	**10**	**10**	**600**
Revised Comulative NCF	**8**	**21**	**124**	**134**	**144**	**744**

The Loan Officer

The knowledge, skills, experience and personality of the loan officer are the key to success in agricultural lending. Good loan officers are the 'engines' that drive financial institutions. Loan officers should be in charge of the full loan cycle, *i.e.,* they should be responsible for a loan all the way from the initial client visit until it is completely recovered. This has several advantages:

The loan officer is accountable for his/her own loan portfolio. If a loan becomes overdue, the loan officer who recommended or approved it carries the responsibility. He/she cannot blame others for being responsible for a bad loan and cannot delegate problem loans to other staff members.

Loan officers are the 'human face' of the financial institution. They should establish a personal relationship with each borrower, which is particularly important for rural people. Confidence and mutual trust can only be established on a personal basis. The loan officer's personal knowledge of clients is also important as credit decisions are not only taken on the basis of 'hard facts', but also the officer's judgement of repayment willingness and management capacity.

As already noted, rural lenders rarely have access to credit reference systems – or if they do, these systems give little or incomplete information about farmers' credit histories. Therefore, the loan officer who builds up an 'institutional memory' of clients is particularly important in rural contexts.

In addition, a track-record of background information on the specific characteristics of farming activities in a branch area can be built up with the support of the loan officers. So, to be effective, agricultural loan officers need some quite specific skills, knowledge and personal qualities. For obvious reasons, the details of loan officer job profiles vary from institution to institution and from regional context to regional context. However, let's look at an example of how one institution specified what it expected of its agricultural loan officers:

1. Loan officers must be ready and willing to spend the majority of their time outside the office, working in the field. They should be able to cope with uncomfortable working conditions in a rural environment.
2. Loan officers must have good communication skills. Since little to no written documentation is available in farm households, key information

must be obtained by talking to people. Therefore, the ability to speak the local language or dialect is crucial. Loan officers must also be good listeners and able to detect inconsistencies.

3. Loan officers must be able to make sound judgements and find it easy to take decisions.

4. A basic knowledge of agricultural production is required. Practical experience is more important than theoretical knowledge. Thus a university degree in agricultural economics is not essential unless combined with experience of working on farms.

5. Loan officers must be willing to work flexible hours. Farmers are used to starting work very early in the morning and rural markets often take place on weekends, so loan officers will have to ensure their work plans fit the time frames of rural life.

6. Loan officers must have basic accounting skills and be able to carry out calculations quickly when they start. However, experience with loan appraisal, including cash flow projections and balance sheets, will be built up on the job.

7. Loan officers should have a motorcycle driving licence, as most clients cannot be reached by public transport or walking. It is quite a challenge to be an agricultural loan officer!

6

The Challenges of Agricultural Lending

COST AND RISK SPECIFIC TO AGRICULTURAL LENDING

Agricultural lenders who serve small farmers face high financial transaction costs when granting small loans. High lending risks are suggested by the frequent inability of small farmer-borrowers to provide acceptable forms of loan collateral. In this chapter special attention is given to the challenges that agricultural lenders face in managing their financial transaction costs and risks.

- *Dispersed Clients:* Low population density coupled with dispersed location of rural clients make the provision of formal financial services costly. From the lender's perspective, the long distances between communities and the inadequate rural transportation facilities in many developing countries increase the costs of loan appraisal, loan monitoring and enforcement of loan repayments. The use of mobile loan officers and/or branch offices can be effective in lowering transaction costs. But mobile facilities may be subject to security risks if bank staff are required to transport money. The establishment of a rural branch network reduces the security risks, but branches are costly to maintain and to supervise.

Financial transaction costs of institutional credit can also be high for rural borrowers. This results from the high opportunity costs of lost working time. A borrower may have to pay several visits to the bank branch office to conclude cumbersome loan application procedures which require a long time for processing. Clients often have to spend much time and money to obtain the required documents and to find loan guarantors. For very small loans, these costs can significantly increase the effective lending interest rate. While the decentralization of field operations has been effective in reducing the transaction costs in some countries their success depends on the local environment, infrastructure conditions and the management skills of the financial institution.

- *Seasonality and Loan Term Structure:* The seasonal nature of agricultural production and the relative long gestation periods before crops can be harvested and sold have direct implications for the financial transaction costs of the lender. Agricultural loans are normally larger and are required for longer periods. Matching assets and liabilities is more difficult than for non-farm activities.

UNIQUE FEATURES OF AGRICULTURAL LENDING

1. Lending Activities in a Politically Sensitive Environment

- Agriculture is a politically sensitive sector.
- State interventions often occur in rural financial markets.

2. Risks Associated with Agricultural Lending

- Similar economic activities of borrowers generate covariant risks due to market and price fluctuations, yield uncertainties, changes in domestic and international policies.
- State interventions (*e.g.*, waiver of loan over dues).
- Low loan repayment discipline in externally-funded credit schemes.

3. High Financial Transaction Costs for Lenders and Borrowers

- Long distances to serve a dispersed rural clientele.
- Poorly developed transportation and communication infrastructure.
- Little knowledge about heterogeneous farm households.
- Expensive management and supervision of rural bank branch networks.
- High additional costs for borrowers: opportunity costs (*e.g.*, lost working time), transport costs, bribes, fees.

4. Specific Credit Demand

- The provision of long-term credit can lead to matching problems between assets (loans) and liabilities (funding sources).
- Reduced turnover of agricultural loan portfolio over the year.
- Seasonality in agricultural credit demand.

5. Lack of Required Loan Collateral

- Small farmers have few physical assets (*e.g.*, land).
- Farmers and especially poor rural women have difficulties in clearly demonstrating their legal ownership of assets.
- Legal contract enforcement problems arise even when collateral is available.

6. **Farm Households are Integrated Production and Consumption Units**
   - Demand for loans depends on the self-financing potential, access to savings deposit facilities and risk management ability of borrowers.
   - The money borrowed funds can be used in the farm household for consumption, education, social insurance, production and investment purposes.

Agricultural credit is also often repaid in 'lumpy' installments. These are one or two loan repayments rather than regular weekly or monthly installments common in micro-credit. This irregular pattern implies more difficult monitoring of repayment capacity and willingness. Moreover, an uneven distribution of the agricultural lending operations over the year increases the fixed costs of personnel. The earnings from lending may not be sufficient to cover these costs. Liquidity requirements in periods of high seasonal loan demand also increase the price of loanable funds. In times of low demand, excess liquidity needs to be invested in low or non-earning assets. This will increase the opportunity costs of these funds.

- *Heterogeneity of Farming:* The diversity in farm and non-farm income-generating activities of rural households requires better knowledge of the farm household financial situation. Loan officers have more information than may be needed in the case of urban lending. This can extend the bank staff time (and expenses) needed for loan appraisal. It may also require the setting of individual loan repayment terms. It is likely to increase the costs of training agricultural loan officers.

RISK ASSOCIATED WITH AGRICULTURAL LENDING

Financial Institutions Face Four Major Risks:

1. *Credit or Loan Default Risk:* Refers borrowers who are unable or unwilling to repay the loan principal and to service the interest rate charges.
2. *Liquidity Risk* – occurs when a bank is not able to meet its cash requirements. Mismatching the term of loan assets and liabilities (sources of loanable funds) exposes banks to high liquidity risks.
3. *Interest Rate Risk:* Risk that a loan will decline in value as interest rates change.
4. *Foreign Exchange Risk:* Defines exposure to changes in exchange rates which affect international borrowings denominated in foreign currency.

Agricultural risks in the broadest sense can be discussed as the follows:

Risks

(i) *Moral hazard:* In any lender-borrower relationship, there is a general problem of moral hazard that is the result of specific personal characteristics and decisions of each individual borrower. In this regard, farmers do not differ from any other borrower group in terms of information, incentives, monitoring and enforcement problems associated with the lending process.

Firstly, it is obvious that the lender does not have the same information as the borrower. The latter knows exactly what his/her own management capacity is and how the loan will be used. The lender does not know the potential borrower to such an extent. In rural financial markets, information about low income loan applicants is particularly difficult to obtain. *Secondly*, even if the loan applicant frankly shares all relevant information for the credit decision, his/her future actions cannot be fully predicted. Therefore, it is crucial for financial institutions to apply incentives so that borrowers behave in such a way that repayment is assured. *Thirdly*, the farmer may decide to change his/her economic behaviour, invest the money elsewhere or simply move to another part of the country. Many subsidised agricultural credit programmes tried to manage this risk by imposing very costly regular monitoring of the borrower. Finding cost efficient methods of monitoring borrowers is a particular challenge in agricultural lending. However, there are other risks beyond the general behavioural risks of a borrower. This second category of loan loss risks is associated with the agricultural sector or agricultural production. It refers to factors external to the farmer's repayment attitude.

(ii) *Farming is a Risky Business:* Crops may fail, weather influences the productivity and sale prices fluctuate and are difficult to predict when the crops are planted. If productivity is lower than expected, farmers may not be able to repay loans. These risks and many other aspects of agricultural risk will need to be identified, measured and actively managed in order to stop lending institutions turning away from this clientele. Let's look at the various external risk categories that need to be taken into account in agricultural lending.

- *Production and yield risk:* Agricultural yields are generally uncertain, as natural hazards such as the weather, pests and diseases and other production calamities impact on farm output. Even slight changes in weather conditions – less rain than usual – can seriously impact on farm production. Pests and diseases may spread quickly, leading to a loss of part or all of the crop's produce. The soil quality of the plots as well as their location also significantly influence productivity and yield risk.

Experienced farmers know the specific risk profiles for their agricultural products and try to manage these risks. Strategies applied by many small farmers include diversification of products to outweigh the risk of losing all production. Many small farmers can be considered as risk-averse, *i.e.*, not venturing into new crops in which they are, as yet, inexperienced. Weather impact is managed through various approaches. For example, irrigation systems may limit the risk of drought. Greenhouse production – among other benefits – can limit the risk of frost damage and increase overall productivity significantly. On the other side, however, modern farm technologies can also increase the risk exposure of a farmer if they are poorly managed. Approaches to the management of the risk of pests and diseases include the use of insecticides or other chemical products. Animal illness and mortality can likewise be managed through vaccination and strict hygiene precautions. Contacting agricultural extension services or veterinarians for advice may also complement the farmer's personal knowledge and experience in production and yield risk.

For all these risk management techniques, the experience of the small farmer is the core requirement for good results. The risk of inappropriate management is part of production risk. Accordingly, prudent lending decisions need to be based on an assessment of the management capacity of the farmer. Seasonality of agricultural production provides an additional risk. People invest work in the present for a return in the form of a harvest several months in the future. If a harvest is insufficient to see people through to the next one, they are weakened by malnutrition and in extreme situations can die from starvation. A particular feature of the seasonality risk is the fact that if in a given season part of or the full harvest is lost, new planting often has to wait until the start of the following season. In addition, funds for investing in agricultural inputs for a new production cycle may not be available. Satisfying the repayments scheduled for a current seasonal loan may become impossible, if other sources of income cannot be mobilized.

- *Price and market risk:* Price uncertainty due to market fluctuations is particularly significant where market information is lacking or scanty, or where markets are imperfect – features which are prevalent in many developing countries. The relatively long period of time between planting a crop or starting livestock activities and the realisation of farm output implies that market prices may change from what has been projected. This problem is particularly relevant for longer term agricultural activities, such as perennial tree crops like cocoa or coffee, as several years lie between planting and first harvest. Price fluctuations may be particularly severe in export markets. Over-production, however, may also considerably influence domestic market prices. In many countries, price uncertainty has increased with liberalisation of agricultural marketing. As opposed to the earlier system of parastatal marketing boards with fixed prices, agricultural prices today fluctuate freely in many countries. Private buyers rarely fix a blanket-buying price prior to harvest, even though inter-linked transactions for specific crops have become more common. These arrangements almost always involve the setting of a fixed price or a range of prices prior to planting. Market risk also includes the potential losses involved in marketing agricultural produce. Transportation is a major challenge in many rural areas. Substantial losses may also occur due to a lack of appropriate storage facilities. Lower quality of badly stored produce usually reduces prices.

- *Lack of diversification:* Price and market risk, as well as production and yield risk, is higher for farmers concentrating on a single crop or livestock activity. Accordingly, many farmers apply risk diversification techniques alongside risk mitigation techniques to reduce these risks. Complementing market-oriented production with subsistence farming is one particular safety-net arrangement, which provides survival measures if yield, production, price and market risks diminish the profits made. Small farmers' annual incomes often depend to a large extent on one main crop. This is particularly challenging if harvests are no more frequent than semi-annually. The situation becomes even more difficult if the farmer's plot is very small. Accordingly, an alternative strategy for diversification is the generation of additional income between seasons by engaging in off-farm activities. This can be essential for farmers that are engaged in high-risk agricultural production, *e.g.*, facing a continuous threat of droughts or floods. While diversification of agricultural production is a commonly applied technique, the resulting effect on reducing income insecurity is often insufficient. Small farmers have a long history of going through bad years when cash income comes close to zero, and good years, in which only a small surplus is generated. As income risks directly affect the potential performance of an agricultural loan, the lack of sufficient diversification and risk mitigation remains a major challenge for agricultural lending.

(iii) *Politicians May Add to the Risk*: Political interference in agricultural markets is a common feature to be found in many developing countries. Price intervention is popular for example, as low food prices are in the interest of urban consumers. Abolishing price ceilings for basic food products in former socialist states led to severe social unrest. Accordingly, stabilising these prices has been a common feature of political interventions in many countries. On the other hand, fixed prices for agricultural produce are also frequently used by governments to ensure a certain level of income for small farmers. Changes in policy and state interventions can have a severely damaging impact on rural financial markets. Agricultural lending has, in fact, a long-standing history of political intervention and distortion, which has significantly contributed to the lack of interest from commercial banks in lending to farmers. Promising debt cancellation is a common feature of populist political campaigns and is enormously damaging to financial service providers. Even well-intentioned credit programmes for specific target groups and regions can also substantially distort prudent agricultural lending activities.

(iv) *What about Collateral?*: If a borrower does not repay on time, a lender must enforce the loan payment. In traditional bank lending, collateral is used to compensate for the potential loan loss. Traditional collateral, however, is rarely available from small farmers. Also, legal procedures to use collateral are often cumbersome and costly. Designing enforcement in an efficient way is another challenge to control loan loss risk in agricultural lending. Small farmers rarely possess land titles which can be used as loan collateral by banks. Land is the most accepted asset for use as loan collateral, because it cannot be removed but can generally be transferred at a specific market price. Small farmers' land, however, may have a very limited value if there is no land market. Land registration is often imperfect in developing countries, so land titles may be unavailable or costly to obtain.

The Costs

Lending to small farmers can be a costly business. Clients are often widely dispersed, and long distances have to be travelled by loan officers and/or customers. Providing small loans is also more costly than lending large amounts, as the costs of loan appraisal, monitoring and follow up do not decrease with the size of the loan. Lending costs are mainly fixed costs. The key factors in determining lending costs are the need to collect detailed information about the potential borrower and to be able to do close monitoring. Information is vital in assessing and managing risk. Good client information can serve as a partial substitute for lack of real collateral and as a means to counter moral hazard. However, in rural settings it is often particularly difficult to obtain good information.

Let's have a closer look at some of the factors influencing agricultural lending costs:

(i) *Lack of Credit History Information:* There is a general absence of credit history information as few financial institutions offer the possibility for rural people to generate track-records with them. Also there is an absence of credit reference bureaus in rural areas to store information on borrowers. Beginning a relationship between the agricultural lender and a client, therefore, is particularly costly and involves substantial 'start-up' information costs. The lender must capture at first-hand key information from the borrower, which requires time and experienced staff. After establishing a track record with the agricultural lender, the information costs diminish. In order to achieve these economies of long-term relationship, the financial service provider must have an appropriate client information system and a comprehensive database which tracks customer performance and their economic activity profiles.

(ii) *Lack of Farm Records:* Small farmers usually have a low level of formal education and are not used to keeping documents or filling in record books. Consequently, the loan appraisal must often be based on information obtained by interviewing the potential borrower.

(iii) *Individuality of Farm Households:* The heterogeneity of production conditions and the unique combination of farm and non-farm economic activities of each farm household, calls for a thorough, highly individual approach to loan appraisal. This tailor-made approach to rural finance, catering for the complexity of farm households by employing specific loan appraisal techniques, product design and repayment schedules, is rather cost-intensive.

(iv) *Farmers' Sensitivity to Client Transaction Costs:* Small farmers are particularly sensitive to client transaction costs such as travelling to bank offices. Particularly in peak agricultural seasons, for example during the planting and harvesting period, they face a heavy workload, which makes it difficult for them to spend time and money on visiting financial institutions. Successful agricultural lenders therefore often offer door-step services and visit clients at their homes and in their fields. Consequently, agricultural loan officers travel extensively. This implies high costs for transport, staff and other additional incidental costs such as accident insurance. Other rural financial intermediaries try to get closer to the customer by maintaining an extensive branch network. Establishing sales outlets in rural areas can lower the transaction costs for the borrowers, but increase administrative costs for the financial intermediary. Balancing both cost sides is a major challenge.

(v) *Seasonality of Agricultural Production:* Agricultural production cycles mean that the agricultural lending business is highly seasonal. Given the fact that seasonal agricultural activities are very time-sensitive, loan appraisals must be carried out within a short period of time and timely loan disbursements must be ensured. Consequently, agricultural lenders must adjust their institutional capability to these changes in workload during the year. There might be a need for additional, temporary staff in financial institutions during peak periods while in other months a reduced workload in agricultural lending must be off-set by other lending activities. Cost-effective staff planning is therefore a challenging endeavour.

(vi) *Cost Reducing Strategies:* Given these complex risk structures and high administrative costs, efficiency is essential in agricultural lending. Thus, implementing streamlined policies, procedures and tools is a must. However, standardisation of lending procedures has to be balanced by the need to match the requirements of a diverse farmer clientele and the variety of economic activities within each farm household. The following list summarises various approaches that help to reduce administrative costs in agricultural lending while maintaining a healthy loan portfolio:

- Decentralisation of lending decisions to branch staff and loan officers.
- Delegation of parts of the loan appraisal, disbursement and monitoring procedures to intermediary organizations that are in close contact with the borrowers, *e.g.*, community groups/associations, business development centres, etc.

- Definition of borrower eligibility criteria which will assist in eliminating applicants who will be unable or unwilling to repay at the earliest possible stage of the loan appraisal process.
- Using a standard loan appraisal form with standard assessment indicators, which may be computerized.
- Reducing transport costs by using motorcycles.
- Applying appropriate route-planning to avoid excessive travelling.
- Using incentive systems for loan officers and branch staff to stimulate operational efficiency.

FACTORS AFFECTING THE COST OF CREDIT

Decisions as to whether to spend or not to spend, whether to borrow (or lend) now or to postpone borrowing (or lending) for six or nine months, whether to buy securities today or hold cash for the present, whether borrowing or lending should be short term or long-term, are all decisions influenced by current and expected interest rates. Interest rates are at the centre of the key issues in understanding the economics of financial markets. But what are the factors affecting interest rates and what exact role do interest rates play within the financial system?

- *Interest Rates:* Interest is the amount paid by a borrower to a lender in exchange for the use of the lender's money for a certain period of time. Money is a scarce resource. There is a limited amount of it, and it has value for everyone. Interest represents the cost of money – what a borrower pays in order to rent money for a certain period of time. Interest rates help to determine the allocation of money because, as with other goods in the economy, the demand for money is influenced by its cost. Interest does more than determine the allocation of money; it provides income to lenders. Interest is a cost paid by borrowers that enables lenders to provide an efficient lending service and to generate a reasonable profit. For micro-enterprise credit institutions, interest income determines whether the institution is dependent on donor funds or able to maintain itself with its own earned income.

For entrepreneurs who borrow, interest rates provide a 'hurdle rate' over which investments must pass to be a valid use of scarce resources. If it costs an entrepreneur 9 per cent to borrow $1,000 for a year, then the investment must earn more than $1,090 to be potentially worthwhile. Investments that earn 9 per cent or less are inefficient uses of scarce financial resources. In short, interest rates on loans are critical to borrowers, lenders, and the economy as a whole. The establishment of appropriate interest rates is crucial for the effective operation and financial management of micro-enterprise finance institutions.

INTEREST RATES FROM TWO PERSPECTIVES

1. *The Borrower's Perspective:* Financial Costs are the interest and fees that borrowers pay to lenders in order to use the money for a specific period of time. Transaction costs are indirect costs incurred to obtain loans. Because transaction costs do not benefit either the lender or the borrower, lenders should minimize them to the greatest extent possible. When a borrower approaches a lender for a loan, he is confronted with two different types of costs. The most obvious cost is the actual cost of the money, including the interest to be paid for the use of the loan, and the fees paid to the lender for processing and disbursing the loan. These costs are the financial costs of the loan.

The borrower must also pay transaction costs. Transaction costs are indirect costs incurred to obtain loans. They include bus fares to the lender's place of business, the cost of obtaining documents (like financial statements) required for the loan, the cost of the time spent by the borrower fulfilling the requirements for the loan, and any other costs related to acquiring the loan. Transaction costs also include costs due to inefficiencies in lender delivery systems, such as missed investment opportunities because of delays in loan disbursement; the extra time spent processing a loan because the lending institution misplaces a document, and others. Transaction costs are often greater than the financial costs if lenders are inefficient in their loan approval or disbursal process.

Financial and transaction costs represent the total borrowing costs of a loan. Because transaction costs do not benefit either the lender or the borrower, lenders should minimize them to the greatest extent possible. Financial costs, on the other hand, provide income to the lender in the form of interest and fees. Lenders that minimize transaction costs make it easier for their borrowers to afford higher financial costs. Financial costs should be established carefully by the lending institution in order to generate the income that the institution needs for survival and growth.

Given a fixed level of transaction costs, what level of financial costs can micro-entrepreneurs afford to pay? How much in interest and fees can micro-entrepreneurs pay and still benefit from borrowing money? These are controversial questions, and the source of continual debate in the micro-enterprise credit field. The response depends on the profitability of the enterprises in question.

A financial analysis of micro-enterprises will usually show the activities to be quite profitable, enabling the entrepreneurs to pay financial costs equivalent to or higher than 'commercial' rates and still benefit from the loans. In some cases, however, when the level of profitability is extremely low, financial costs near commercial levels may represent an unbearable burden for certain activities. In such cases, loans may be an inappropriate intervention, and alternative mechanisms to promote economic development should be investigated.

2. *The Lender's Perspective:* There are three basic costs that lending institutions must cover with their income: the financial cost of the funds in their portfolio, known as the cost of funds, the cost of maintaining a loan loss reserve so that the portfolio does not decapitalize when loans are defaulted, and other operating costs that include the salaries of staff, rent, and other operating expenses.

To be self-sufficient, a financial institution must cover the above costs with income generated by financial services. For micro-enterprise credit institutions, interest charged on loans and fees associated with lending are the primary sources of earned income. The loan portfolio (funds lent to borrowers and funds on deposit available to be lent) produces a gross rate of return, or yield, which is the interest and fee income divided by the average portfolio. Self-sufficient lending institutions have a rate of return high enough to cover all of their costs, and keep the value of their funds from deteriorating because of the effects of inflation.

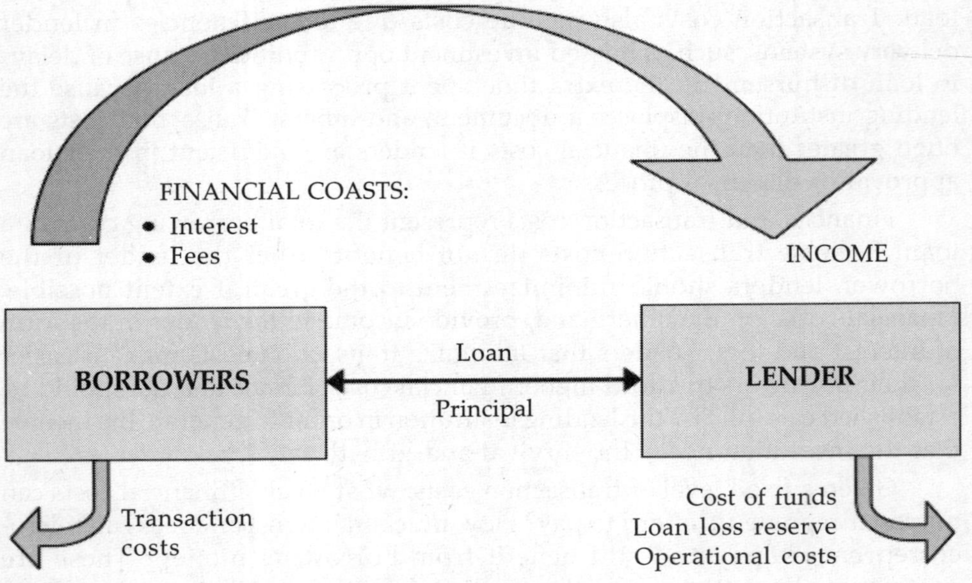

Fig. 6.1: Cash flow of lending transactions

The figure 6.1 shows the flow of cash for borrowers and lenders during a loan transaction. What the borrower pays in financial costs becomes the lender's income, which is used to pay for expenses. What the borrower pays in transaction costs is lost to both the borrower and the lender. The loan principal goes back and forth between the borrower and the lender.

Functions of Interest Rates

Interest rates serve a number of significant functions. *First,* they provide investors with a guide for allocating funds among investment opportunities.

As funds are directed into projects that have higher expected rates of return (risk and other factors being taken into account), the funds are optimally allocated from the viewpoint of both consumer and investor, since the highest returns normally prevail where effective consumer demand is strongest. Unless an investment opportunity promises a return high enough to pay the market rate of interest, it does not justify the required capital outlay. The money market, by channeling funds into projects that have an expected return in excess of the interest rate, provides a valuable service to investors, borrowers, and society as a whole. The interest rate also provides a measure of the relative advantage of current consumption compared to saving. By adjusting the available market rate for expected inflation and taxes, an individual can determine the real amount of additional future consumption that can be obtained by postponing current consumption. Similarly, interest rates help businessmen to decide among alternative production methods. Suppose a product can be made either solely with labour or with a combination of labour and machinery. By calculating the capital cost of the machine (the interest rate times the amount invested in the machine), the expected labour-plus-capital cost can be compared with the labour-alone cost to determine the least expensive means of production.

DETERMINATION OF INTEREST RATES, DEMAND AND SUPPLY OF FUNDS

- *Interest Rates:* Interest rates are prices. Unlike other prices they are usually expressed as percentages of the amount borrowed or lent. But, like other prices, they are determined by supply and demand. Interest rates depend on the supply of and the demand for loanable funds. The sources of the supply of funds are savings, reductions in the demand for money and increases in the supply of money. The sources of the demand for funds are investment demands, consumption demands (for spending on consumer goods) and increases in the demand for money.
- *The Supply of Funds:* Saving, which is the main source of supply of loanable funds, arises in all sectors of the economy and may take many forms. Personal saving, *i.e.*, the excess of personal income over consumption spending, may consist, *inter alia*, of contributions to pension funds, the repayment of mortgage loans, deposits with mutual funds or banks, or the purchase of securities.

Business saving comprises retained profits and, most important, depreciation charges. What is not reinvested in the business is usually held in a liquid form or used to reduce bank loans. The government may also contribute to saving in the economy by raising more in taxes than it needs for its own current expenditure; any surplus goes to offset part of the public sector's own investment. It is important to distinguish between the potential and the actual supply of loanable funds. The reason for this is that households and businesses having savings may not be willing to make these funds available to borrowers. Money is having a store of value. Households and businesses may not want to offer either their current savings or any of their accumulated savings to borrowers. On the contrary they may choose to add a portion of their current savings to their accumulated balances. Having made choices as to how to divide their incomes and receipts between spending and saving, households and businesses must then decide on the specific form in which to hold their savings. The basic choice is between money in the form of either idle cash or bank accounts on the one hand, and securities of some sort on the other. Idle cash and bank accounts are highly liquid assets; securities acquired from borrowers are somewhat less liquid but generally yield a better rate of return. That part of savings (current or accumulated) which households and businesses want to hold as securities flows into the money market as the supply of loanable funds. That part of savings which households and businesses want to hold as cash obviously does not. This division depends upon the liquidity preferences of households and businesses (*i.e.*, their preference to hold cash rather than spend it). More specifically, there are three main reasons why households and businesses prefer to hold cash rather than securities.

1. There is a *transaction motive* for holding money rather than securities. Households and businesses both need a stock of cash on hand to make ordinary day-to-day purchases. Households, for example, usually receive a sizeable chunk of income every week, or every month. Disbursements, on the other hand, occur more or less evenly over time. This means that households have an average money balance of some size bridging the gap between paydays. And it is simply more convenient to have one's assets in their most liquid form, that is, as idle cash balances or bank accounts, than in the form of securities. Furthermore, there are costs (brokerage fees) in transferring cash into securities and back again.
2. There is a *precautionary motive* for holding money. Households and businesses may hold cash balances to meet any rainy day contingencies that might arise. Particularly relevant are those risks which one cannot protect oneself against by purchasing insurance policies, *e.g.*, prolonged illness, unemployment, and so forth.
3. There is a *speculative motive* for holding money. At any time, there is a certain rate of interest that households and businesses, as potential suppliers of loanable funds, consider to be about 'normal'. If the rate of interest is currently low, *i.e.*, 'below normal', households and businesses may withhold a part of their savings that would otherwise flow into the money market as a part of the supply of loanable funds. They hold more money and fewer securities than they normally would. Why? Because they expect that the current below-normal interest rate will probably rise in the future. Conversely, if the current interest rate is unusually high, *i.e.*, 'above normal', households and businesses will

choose to hold less money and more securities to take advantage of high current interest rates as opposed to the lower normal rate expected to prevail again in the future.

The supply of loanable funds is critically influenced by the level of interest rates, *i.e.*, higher interest (real) rates will induce households and businesses (but obviously not necessarily governments) to be less liquid. At relatively high interest rates, households and firms will prefer to hold their assets in the form of interest-bearing securities rather than as non-interest bearing current accounts and idle cash balances. The supply of loanable funds depends on:

(i) *The Rate of Interest:* A high rate of interest encourages savers to place their funds in financial institutions and the supply of loanable funds increases.

(ii) *The Amount of Savings:* Some countries, such as Japan and India are very thrifty. This increases the amount of funds available for borrowers.

(iii) *A Budget Surplus:* This occurs when the government spends less than its revenue. In these conditions the government has a surplus that it can lend to the private sector.

(iv) *International Factors:* When foreigners buy assets in another country they are lending to those domestic residents. Low interest rates overseas encourage funds to flow from the low interest rate country into the countries with higher interest rates increasing the supply of funds available to borrowers in the high interest rate country (and vice versa).

The supply curve for loanable funds is upward sloping, *i.e.*, higher interest rates increase the supply available, and vice versa.

- *The Demand for Funds:* Now let us turn to the demand for funds. Again this can be by private individuals, enterprises or governments. Private individuals borrow in order to increase their current level of consumption either for housing, automobiles, holidays or whatever. Enterprises borrow to pay for factories, plant and equipment. Finally, Governments borrow to pay for current and capital spending (*e.g.*, on schools, roads etc. which they cannot finance from taxation).

  The demand for borrowed funds depends on:

(i) *The Rate of Interest:* When it becomes more expensive to borrow (*i.e.*, when the interest rate rises) demand from the private sector falls (and vice versa).

(ii) *The Level of Income:* The higher the level of income, the more individuals and businesses want to borrow. For example, if investment is to increase, firms will in general require outside finance. Similarly, consumers borrow money to buy durable goods, washing machines, white goods, etc. More generally when incomes rise, individuals increase borrowing for all purposes (houses, automobiles, etc.), and firms need more working capital.

(iii) *The Government Finances:* In most countries governments are major borrowers of funds. This is known as the fiscal deficit or budget deficit (total government expenditure minus tax revenue).

(iv) *International Factors:* When foreigners buy domestic assets they are lending to domestic residents of the country concerned. Low overseas interest rates encourage domestic borrowers to borrow these overseas funds, increasing the supply of funds available to domestic borrowers (and vice versa).

The demand curve for loanable funds is clearly downward sloping, *i.e.*, lower interest rates raise the demand for funds. Businessmen will find it profitable to purchase larger amounts of capital goods when the price of loanable funds declines. Similarly, lower interest rates may encourage some increases in consumer and government borrowing. (In practice it is 'real' interest rates which are relevant.)

How are Interest Rates Determined?

In equilibrium the interaction between the demand for loanable funds and the supply of loanable funds will determine the interest rate. Elementary economic analysis tells us that if the demand rises *(i)* or the supply falls *(ii)* then the interest rate rises. Similarly if the demand falls *(iii)* or if the supply rises *(iv)* then interest rates will fall. This is illustrated in Figure 6.2. The effect on the interest rate of any shift in demand or supply will depend on the elasticities of both supply and demand. Following a change in demand, the less elastic (more elastic) is the supply curve the greater (less) will be the change in interest rates.

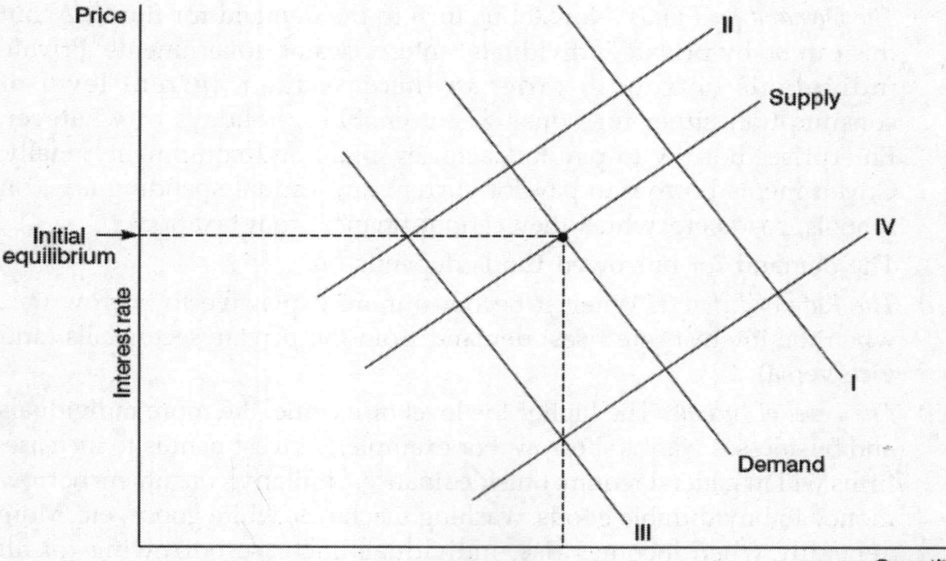

Fig. 6.2: Determination of interest rates

Following a change in supply, the less elastic is the demand curve the greater will be the effect on interest rates and vice versa. How can changes in the supply of funds and demand for funds change interest rates? If there is more saving (relative to demand) by businessmen and consumers, this will bring down interest rates. What happens if there is an increase in the supply of money? This adds to the savings in the capital market. To see how this can occur suppose that instead of raising new funds through the stock market companies borrow from their banks, and the banks increase the supply of money (remember bank loans create bank deposits which are in themselves the most important component of the money supply). Because companies are borrowing from the banks this will increase security prices (due to a lower demand) and the rate of interest on securities will fall correspondingly as companies can now raise funds more cheaply.

INTERNATIONAL FACTORS AFFECTING INTEREST RATES

Given the importance of international factors in affecting interest rates it is worth explaining, in some detail, the mechanics whereby overseas interest rates affect domestic interest rates The speed of the impact of international factors depends on official exchange rate policy. If a country has a fixed exchange rate (*i.e.*, the government is committed to official intervention in order to keep the rate fixed) and the currency is weak (*i.e.*, it is being heavily sold on the foreign exchange market), the government may be induced to raise official interest rates. The objective is to make it more attractive for overseas holders of the currency to hold it and to make it less attractive for domestic holders to transfer it overseas. If a country has a fixed and strong exchange rate there may be pressure for the authorities to lower the interest rate. As funds flow into the currency the authorities, being forced to increase the domestic money supply to keep the exchange rate fixed will, in an attempt to reduce the inflows, reduce domestic interest rates. Under floating exchange rates the effects of capital flows on interest rates occur very quickly. With a weak currency investors will speedily reduce their holdings thereby driving up interest rates, *e.g.*, by selling bonds. Similarly investors will be keen to acquire liabilities in that currency since, if the exchange rate change occurs and is larger than the extra borrowing cost the investor can repay (say his bank loan) and make a profit. The combination of an increase in the supply of loanable funds and a decrease in the demand for loanable funds drives down interest rates.

The effect of international factors also depends on the size of the home economy and how developed the domestic financial system is. For a small economy a given foreign inflow of funds is likely to represent a relatively high proportion of the total capital market. The impact is likely to be bigger therefore in a country with limited facilities for foreign investors, for example, because the capital market is undeveloped or exchange controls are in operation.

THE CONCEPT OF TIME VALUE OF MONEY

Money has time value. We know this intuitively because most of us would prefer to receive $1,000 today than 1 year or 5 years from today. By receiving it today, we can invest the money and expect to have an even greater sum in the future. The same reasoning suggests us, not unlike Wimpie, should prefer to pay money we owe later than sooner. Thus, the value of money depends on the time when it is paid or received. Many important financial decisions of a firm involve cash flows at various points in time. Financial managers should consider how time affects the value of these cash flows. For example, when a firm issues bonds to investors, managers should compare the value of future cash payments owed to the bondholders in exchange for the cash received today. Similarly, when making capital investments, managers need to compare the value of expected cash flows in the future to the present cash outlay needed to undertake the investment. In both cases, financial managers must understand how the value of cash flows varies at different points in time. This section deals with the mathematics of the time value of money. Specifically, the mathematical relationships for determining the future value of a present cash amount and the present value of a specified future cash amount. These future and present value relationships are extended to incorporate multiple cash flows that are equal and periodic (annuities) and multiple cash flows that are not. Also shows how to determine the implied interest rate.

CENTRAL CONCEPTS IN FINANCE

An old saying is that 'A bird in the hand is worth two in the bush'. In a way, this expression refers to the time value of birds. That is, having a single bird in the hand today is worth more than the chance of catching two birds in the future. The bird-in-hand expression reflects two central concepts in finance: the risk return trade-off and the time value of money.

- *Risk-return Trade off:* Investors will take on additional risk only if they anticipate higher return.
- *Time Value of Money:* A dollar available today is worth more than a dollar available at a future date. This is because a dollar today can be invested to earn a return. Thus, investors require compensation for both risk bearing and the time value of money (TVM). These two principles lie at the heart of the financial decision-making concepts discussed in this section.

The notion that money has time value associated with it is intuitively appealing. Investors prefer to receive money earlier than later because they can expect to earn a positive rate of return on invested money. Knowledge of time value of money concepts is essential to an understanding of many topics in finance. In fact, most financial decisions at both the personal and business levels involve cash flows at different points in time. Common users of time value of money concepts include corporate financial managers, securities analysts, portfolio managers, bankers, and investors. Here are a few examples.

- When firms issue bonds to investors in the capital markets, they should compare the value of future cash payments to the bondholders in exchange for the cash received from them today. Analysts and investors use time value of money concepts to value many financial securities.
- Managers who make capital investments in long-lived fixed assets should compare the value of expected future cash flows to the present cash outlay needed to undertake the investment. In all cases, financial managers, analysts, and investors must understand how the value of cash flows varies at different points in time.

In economics, the idea that money has time value is referred to as the opportunity cost of sacrificing the earning potential of a current dollar. Stated differently, an opportunity cost is what funds could earn on an alternative investment of equal risk. A basic principle of investment decisions is that an investment is acceptable only if it earns at least its opportunity cost (risk-adjusted required rate of return).

FUTURE VALUE OF A PRESENT AMOUNT

Some one investing a sum of money today at a given interest rate for a given period of time would expect to have a larger sum of money at that future date. We can determine that future amount using the future value of a present amount formula. We define *future value* as the value of a present amount at a future date after applying compound interest over a specified period. The amount invested today is the *present value*.

Equation 6.1 shows how to compute the future value of a present amount:

$$FV = PV\,(1 + r)^{n} \qquad \text{.................... (6.1)}$$

Where *FV* is the future value of an amount *n* periods from now; *PV* is the present value of an amount – it represents the amount invested today; *r* is the rate of return or interest rate per period; and *n* is the compounding term or interval, which is the number of periods between the *PV* and the *FV*. Thus, future value calculations answer the question: How much will an investment be worth at a specific time in the future, compounded at a specific rate of interest? Future value is a *compounded value* because of compounding of interest. Another common name for future value is *terminal value*. Example 6.1 illustrates how to compute the future value of a present amount using Equation 6.1.

Example 6.1: Future Value of a Single Amount

An investor has the opportunity to earn an 8 per cent annual interest rate for the next 15 years. Assuming an investment of $5,000, how much will the investor have 15 years from today?

Solution: This problem requires computing a future value, given a present value of $5,000, an annual interest rate of 8 per cent, and a compounding term of 15 years. Substituting into Equation 6.1 we get:

$$FV = PV\,(1 + r)^{n}$$

$$FV = \$5{,}000(1.08)^{15} = \$15{,}860.85$$

Effects of Interest Rates and Compounding Terms on Future Values

The level of the interest rate (r) and the length of the compounding term (n) affect future values. Specifically, future values increase as the compound interest rate increases and/or the compounding term becomes longer. As illustrated in Example 6.2 below, substantial increases in future values can result from small changes in interest rates, especially when the compounding term is long.

Example 6.2: Effect of Interest Rates on Future Values

Ananya is considering two long-term investment options for an inheritance of $50,000 she has recently received. Under Option A, she expects an annual return of 10 per cent for the next 30 years; under Option B, she expects an annual return of 12 per cent over the same period. What are the expected future values of these two plans 30 years from today when she retires?

$$\text{Option A: } FV = \$50{,}000(1.10)^{30} = \$872{,}470.11$$

$$\text{Option B: } FV = \$50{,}000(1.12)^{30} = \$1{,}497{,}996.11$$

Solution: This example shows that a relatively small difference in interest rates results in a substantial difference in the future values 30 years later. The future value under Option B is about 72 per cent higher than Option A. This substantial difference in future value amounts explains young investors, who have long investment horizons for their retirement savings, are often encouraged to seek the higher expected returns from long-term growth equity investments.

TIME DIAGRAMS

Using a time diagram is helpful to illustrate the timing of cash flows, especially for situations involving cash flows at different points in time that are not equal. For Example 6.1, our time diagram would look like this:

Compounding of Interest

Interest earned and paid in future years depends not only on the initial amount, but also on any interest earned that has not been withdrawn from the investment account. Thus, with compounding, interest is earned on interest, and the future value amount will increase geometrically over time, not linearly.

To illustrate, assume an investment of $100 today at 10 per cent per year. One year from today, the future value grows to $110, computed as [$100 +

(0.10) ($100)]. Assuming no interest is withdrawn, the investor will earn interest on $110 during the second year and receive a year-end interest payment of $11.00. The future value at the end of the second year will be $121.00, computed as [$110 + 0.10) ($110)]. Assuming that no interest is withdrawn, the investor will earn $12.10 during the third year and will have a future value of $133.10 at the end of three years, computed as: [$121+(0.10) ($121)]. Table 6.1 summarizes these interest and future value amounts.

Table 6.1: Future value of $100 at an interest rate of 10 per cent

Year	Future Value of $100 Investment at 10 Per cent	Interest Earned
1.	$110.00	$10
2.	$121.00	$11
3.	$133.10	$12.10

By compounding rates annually, the interest is earned throughout the year, but it is paid at the end of the year. As just discussed, the first interest payment of $10 on the $100 initial investment would be paid at the end of the first year. If the investor withdrew the principal before the year-end interest payment date, the investor would not receive any partial interest payment. The second interest payment of $11 would be paid at the end of the second year, and the third interest payment of $12.10 would be paid at the end of the third year. Thus, no partial intra-year interest payments are made under annual compounding. Later in this chapter, we examine situations where interest is compounded more frequently than once per year. Writing the future value equation (Equation 6.1) with subscripts on the *FV* and *PV* terms is sometimes helpful. For a present value invested at time *t*, the equation for a future value *n* periods from time *t* may be written:

$$FV_n = PV_t (1 + r)^n$$

For example, suppose an investor expects to receive a sum of money 3 years from today and plans to immediately invest the funds in a savings account at a fixed interest rate for 5 years. We can write the future value equation to show the timing of the cash flows:

$$FV_8 = PV_3 (1 + r)^5$$

Where *PV*3 is the amount to be invested 3 years from now and *FV*8 is the future value 5 years later (8 years from today).

Future Value of Multiple Amounts

When multiple present values need to be compounded to obtain a future value, these compounded future value amounts can be summed together. For example, if an investment provides a cash flow of $100 in year 0, $250 in year 1, and $475 in year 2, the future value in year 3 could be computed by summing the future value of each. Assuming an annual interest rate of 10 per cent, we get:

$$FV3 = PV0(1 + r)^3 + PV1(1 + r)^2 + PV2(1 + r)^1$$

$$FV3 = \$100(1.10)^3 + \$250(1.10)^2 + \$475(1.10)^1 = \$958.10$$

Thus, future value of present amount calculations are additive. Of course, these calculations get tedious when we have many present value amounts. If the present value amounts are equal and periodic, they constitute what is called an annuity and the future value calculation is simplified.

Present Value of a Future Amount

Financial managers are often more interested in determining the present value of a future amount. To solve for the present value of a future amount, we solve equation 6.1 for the present value amount:

$$PV = FV\left[\frac{1}{(1 + r)^n}\right] \quad (6.2a)$$

This equation is also often written as:

$$PV = \frac{1}{(1 + r)^n} \quad (6.2a)$$

The calculation of the present value of a future amount is illustrated in Example 6.3.

Example 6.3: Present Value of a Single Amount

The Hobbs Corporation must make a final payment of $20 million to its bondholders 5 years from today to retire the bond issue. At an interest rate of 6 per cent, what is the present value of the $20 million payment?

Solution: This problem calls for computing a present value, given a future value of $20 million, an annual interest rate of 6 per cent, and a term of 5 years.

The time diagram for our example is illustrated as follows:

We can solve for the present value using Equation 6.2.

$$PV = FV\left[\frac{1}{(1 + r)^n}\right]$$

$$PV = \$20{,}000{,}000\left[\frac{1}{(1.06)^3}\right] = \$14{,}945{,}163.46$$

How should we interpret this present value amount? The $14,945,163.46 present value amount (today) is financially equivalent to $20 million five years from today at an annual interest rate of 6 per cent. Assuming no preference for spending the money today or 5 years from now, an individual would be indifferent between receiving $14,945,163.46 today or $20 million five years from today at an annual interest rate of 6 per cent. Suppose the borrower and lender decide to settle this future liability today. If they both agree that 6 per cent is the appropriate annual interest rate over the next 5 years, a $14,945,163.46 payment would be the appropriate (present value) payment today.

The process of computing the present value of a future amount is called *discounting*. The interest rate used to compute the present value is called the *discount rate,* but may also be referred to as the opportunity cost, required rate of return, and the cost of capital. Regardless of the term used, it represents the compound rate of return that an investor can earn on an investment. In Example 6.3, we would say that $14,945,163.46 is the discounted value of a $20 million payment 5 years from now at a discount rate of 6 per cent. Time value of money analysis is often referred to as *discounted cash flow analysis*. Present values decrease as the discount rate increases. Thus, *present values are inversely related to interest rates*. The logic is simple. Suppose a person needs to have $50,000 five years from today and wants to invest money today to meet that goal. The higher the interest rate, the lower the (present value) amount needed to be invested today. This inverse relationship is an important concept that we will return to several times in this book, especially when we discuss valuing securities issued by firms and capital investment projects that firms adopt.

Present Value of Multiple Future Cash Flows

The present value of multiple future value amounts can be computed by simply summing the present value of each individual future value amount. The following example illustrates the important property that present values are additive.

Example 6.4: Present Value of Uneven Amounts

The ATS Company expects to receive the following payments from one of its delinquent customers: $500 one year from today, $800 two years from today, and $950 three years from today. At an interest rate of 8 per cent, what is the present value of these future value payment amounts?

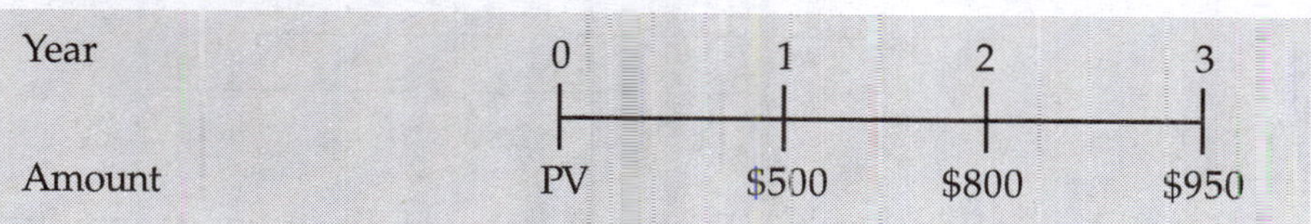

Solution: We obtained the present value of this stream of uneven amounts as follows:

$$PV_0 = FV_1 \left[\frac{1}{(1+r)^1}\right] + FV_2 \left[\frac{1}{(1+r)^2}\right] + FV_3 \left[\frac{1}{(1+r)^3}\right]$$

$$PV = \$500 \left[\frac{1}{(1.08)^1}\right] + \$800 \left[\frac{1}{(1.08)^2}\right] + \$950 \left[\frac{1}{(1+r)^2}\right] = \$1{,}902.97$$

While computing the present value of multiple future value amounts is straightforward, the computations become tedious and time consuming as the number of cash flows increases. When the multiple future value amounts are equal and periodic, they constitute what is called an annuity. Present value of annuity calculations are discussed in the next section. When the amounts are uneven (not equal or periodic), follow the steps in the example above.

Future Value of an Annuity

An annuity is a series of equal and periodic cash flows. For example, if someone deposits $2,000 at the end of each year for 20 years into an IRA account for retirement years, these 20 payments represent a 20-year annuity of $2,000 per year. We could compute the future value of these annuity payments by applying Equation 6.1 twenty times and summing the individual results. We can simplify our work by using the future value of an annuity formula. The future value of an annuity is computed as:

$$FV = PMT \left[\frac{(1+r)^n - 1}{r}\right] \qquad \text{..............(6.3)}$$

Future value of an annuity calculations are used to compute the future compounded value of a series of equal, periodic payments. Let us see how to solve for the future value of an ordinary annuity in which payments occur at the end of each period in Example 6.5 below.

Example 6.5: Future Value of an Ordinary Annuity

Suppose John decides to save $2,000 at the end of each year for the next 10 years. If John can earn 8 per cent per year on his invested funds, what will be the future value of the investment 10 years from today?

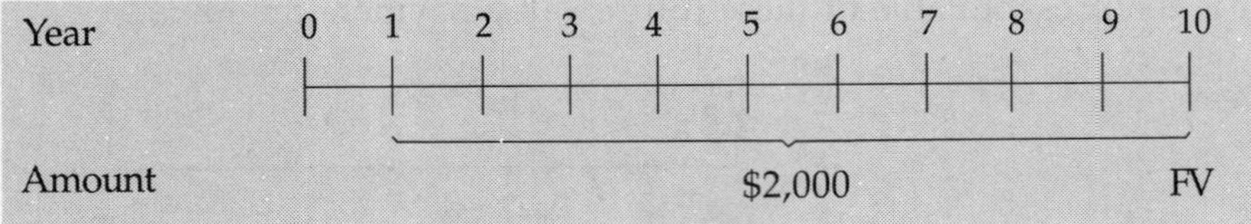

Solution: Using Equation 6.3, the future value of the ordinary annuity is:

$$FV = \$2{,}000 \left[\frac{(1.08)^{10} - 1}{0.08}\right] = \$\ 28{,}973.12$$

In Example 6.5, we also could have treated the 10 cash flows of $2,000 each as separate present values, computed the future value of each, and summed them to get the future value. Computing the future value of 10 separate terms and summing is more work than using the future value of an annuity formula. Two rules or conventions must be observed when solving for the future value of an annuity.

- The value for n is the number of payments in the annuity.
- When using the future value of an annuity formula, the future value is obtained at the time of the last annuity payment.

This convention follows from the derivation of the future value of an annuity formula. To determine the future value at some later date requires the adjustment illustrated in Example 6.6 below:

Example 6.6: Future Value of an Annuity Due

If an investor invests $2,000 at the beginning of each year (beginning today) for the next 5 years, how much will he have 5 years from now if he can earn 10 per cent per year on his investment?

Solution: The time diagram looks like this:

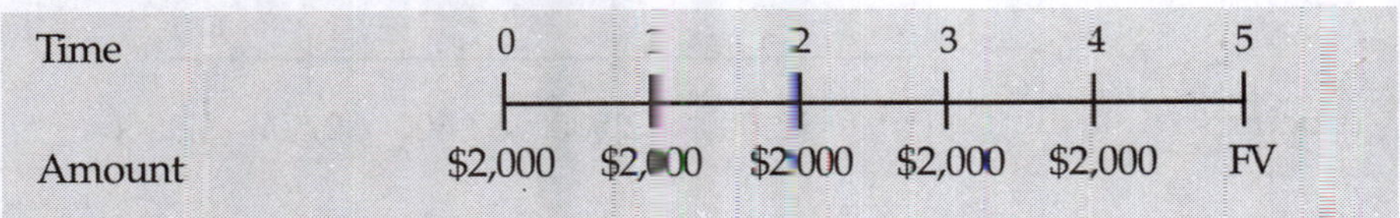

Using Equation 6.3, we obtain the future value at the time of the last payment, which is year 4:

$$FV = \$2{,}000 \left[\frac{(1.10)^5 - 1}{0.10}\right] = \$12{,}210.20$$

Since we want the future value 1 year later, we need to compound this intermediate amount for 1 year:

$$FV5 = PV4(1 - r)^1$$

$$FV = \$12{,}210.20\ (1.10)^1 = \$13{,}431.22$$

Alternatively, we could have combined these two steps into a single step.

$$FV = \$2{,}000 \left[\frac{(1.10)^5 - 1}{0.10}\right] (1.10)^1 = \$13{,}431.22$$

Present Value of an Annuity

When computing the present value of an annuity, we need to distinguish between two types of annuities: ordinary annuities and annuities due. An ordinary annuity is an annuity characterized by amounts that occur at the end of each compounding period. This is the most common type of annuity. For example, a series of $1,000 payments at the end of each year for the next

5 years represent a 5-year ordinary annuity of $1,000. An annuity due is a type of annuity where payments or receipts occur at the beginning of each period. The present value of an ordinary annuity can be computed as:

$$PV = PMT\left[\frac{1-\frac{1}{(1+r)^n}}{r}\right]$$

Where *PMT* is the annuity amount, and *n* is the number of payments or receipts in the annuity.

Example 6.7: Present Value of an Ordinary Annuity

Tastee Foods has five payments of $2,500 remaining on a loan. These payments will occur at the end of each of the next 5 years. At an annual interest rate of 6 per cent, what is the present value of these loan payments?

Solution: Given an annuity amount of $2,500 each year for 5 years and an annual interest rate of 6 per cent, we need to compute the present value of the loan.

The time diagram for our loan can be depicted as follows:

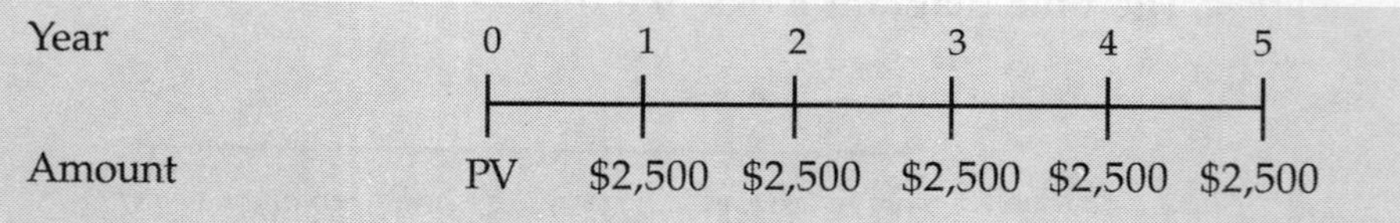

We use the present value of an ordinary annuity formula, Equation 6.4:

$$PV = PMT\left[\frac{1-\frac{1}{(1+r)^n}}{r}\right] \quad \text{........................(6.4)}$$

Substituting $PMT = \$2{,}500$, $r = 0.06$, and $n = 5$, we get:

$$PV = \$2{,}500\left[\frac{1-\frac{1}{(1.06)^5}}{0.06}\right] = \$10{,}530.91$$

Remember two important points when solving for the present value of an ordinary annuity.

- The value for *n* is the number of payments or receipts in the annuity. This definition for *n* differs from its definition when solving future value and present value calculations using Equations 6.1 and 6.2. When compounding or discounting with Equations 6.1 or 6.2, *n* refers to the compounding or discounting interval of time. This point will be clear by reviewing Examples 6.1 and 6.3. Contrast this with Example 6.7 where we used the number of payments in the annuity as our value for *n*.
- When using the present value of an annuity formula, the present value is obtained one period before the annuity begins. This convention

follows from the derivation of the present value of an ordinary annuity formula. End-of-year annuity payments and the present value at time 0 are often referred to as an ordinary annuity. Thus, with an ordinary annuity, we have end-of-year payments with a time diagram as shown below, and the present value is obtained one period before where the annuity starts.

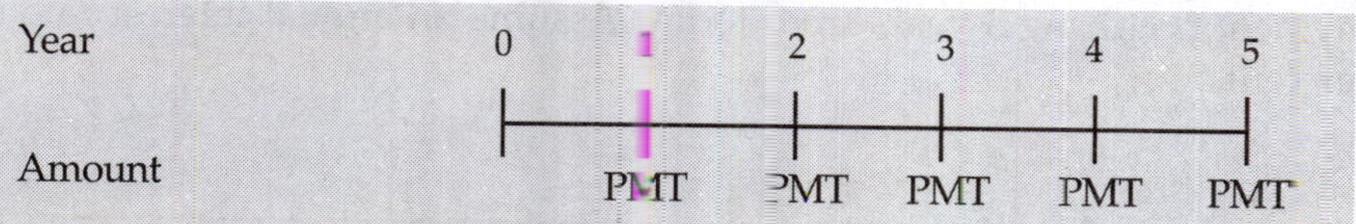

What happens if we need to compute a present value when the payments do not conform to those in the figure above? An adjustment must be made. This is illustrated as two such adjustments in Examples 6.8 and 6.9.

Example 6.8: Present Value of an Annuity Due

Using the data in Example 6.7, let's compute the present value of the five loan payments assuming beginning of year payments, with the first payment occurring today.

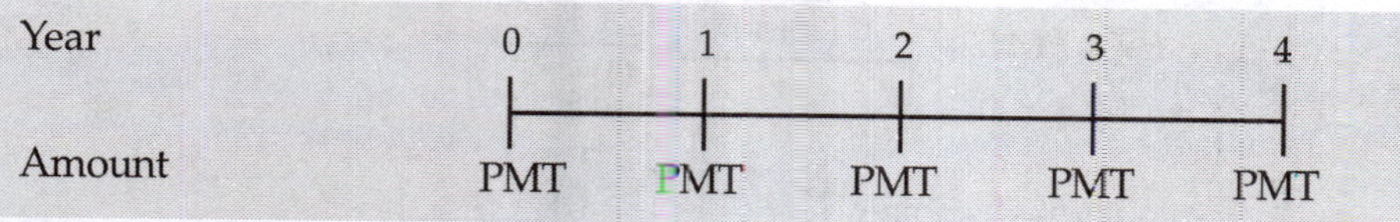

Solution: We can begin by computing the present value of the five payments in the annuity:

$$PV = \$2,500 \left[\frac{1-\frac{1}{(1.06)^5}}{0.06}\right] = \$10,530.91$$

Of course, we get the same result as in Example 6.7. But since the first payment in the annuity occurs today, the present value obtained at time period $t = 1$. To calculate the present value at time 0, we need to take the future value of this present amount for 1 year:

$$FV0 = PV1(1+r)^1$$

$$FV = \$10,530.91(1.06)^1 = \$11,162.76$$

If we combine these two steps, the present value of an annuity with beginning of year payments that begin today can be computed:

$$PV = PMT \left[\frac{1-\frac{1}{(1+r)^n}}{r}\right] = (1+r)$$

This annuity scheme with beginning of year payments is called an annuity due. Example 6.9, illustrates a similar adjustment needed when computing the present value of an annuity when the payments begin in the second period or later.

Example 6.9: Present Value of an Annuity Due – Extended

Compute the present value of five payments of $2,500 with the first payment occurring 5 years from today. Assume an annual interest rate of 6 per cent.

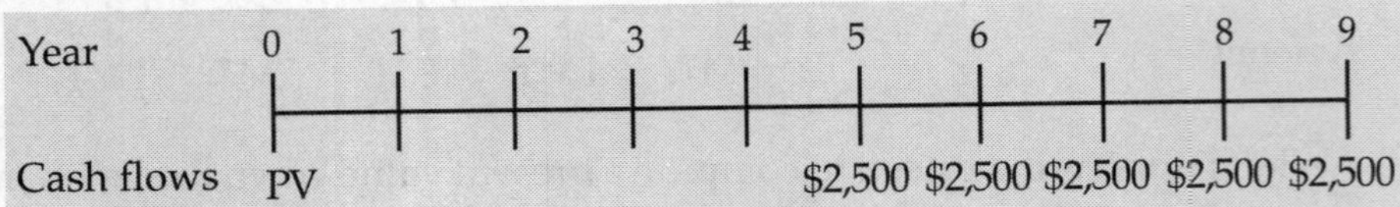

Solution: When we compute the present value of the five payments, we get a 'present value' in year 4 (one period before where the annuity starts). This present value amount is still a future value with respect to time 0. Thus, we must discount this amount for 4 years by taking the present value of this 'future amount' for 4 years. If we combine these two steps, we get:

$$PV = PMT \left[\frac{1-\frac{1}{(1+r)^n}}{r}\right]\left[\frac{1}{(1+r)^n}\right]$$

$$PV = \$2{,}500 \left[\frac{1-\frac{1}{(1.06)^5}}{0.06}\right]\left[\frac{1}{(1.06)^4}\right] = \$8{,}341047$$

Computes the 'PV in year 4' of the five payments in the annuity

Discounts the 'PV in year 4' back to year 0

Present Value of a Perpetuity

A perpetuity is an annuity with an infinite life. The present value of a perpetuity is computed by dividing the perpetuity payment by the discount rate:

$$PV_{perpetuity} = \frac{PMT}{r}$$

Example 6.10: Present Value of a Perpetuity

An investment will pay $10 per year in perpetuity. At an annual interest rate of 12 per cent, what is the present value of the investment?

Solution: Using Equation 4.5, the present value this perpetuity is:

$$PV = \frac{\$10}{0.12} = \$83.33$$

We can determine the value of non callable preferred stock, which pays a constant dividend and has no expiration date, by calculating the present value of the perpetuity payments. We can also use Equation 6.5 to solve for the amount that can be withdrawn in perpetuity from a present value at a given interest rate, fixed indefinitely. For example, suppose someone deposits $10,000 into an account that promises to pay 8 per cent per year forever. The individual could withdraw $800 per year in perpetuity (forever) from this account:

$$PMT = r\,(PV)$$

$$PMT = 0.08\,(\$10,000) = \$800.00$$

Compounding Frequencies

When introduce the time value of money formulas in Equations 6.1, it is defined the interest rate as the interest rate *per period* and defined *n* as the *number of periods*. Since all of the examples so far have assumed annual compounding, the interest rate was on a per year basis (compounded annually) and *n* was the number of years. In many instances, interest is compounded more frequently than once per year. For example, banks often compound interest on a daily basis on savings accounts. Solving a problem where interest is compounded more frequently than once a year involves adjusting the interest rate and number of periods to the appropriate compounding basis. Example 6.11 illustrates these adjustments.

Example 6.11: Future Value with Different Compounding Frequencies

Suppose an investor deposits $1,000 into an account that earns 6 per cent per year. What will be the future value 5 years from today if interest is compounded semi-annually, quarterly, and monthly?

Solution: With interest compounded semi-annually, we need to determine the interest rate per semi-annual period and the number of semi-annual periods.

$$r = 6 \text{ per cent}/2 = 3 \text{ per cent per semi-annual period}$$

$$n = 2x5 = 10 \text{ semi-annual periods}$$

Use these values in Equation 6.1.

$$FV = PV\,(1 + r)^n$$

$$FV = \$1,000(1.03)^{10} = \$1,343.92$$

With annual compounding, our future value would have been $1,338.23. As expected, increasing the compounding frequency to a semi-annual basis increases the future value. With semi-annual compounding, we receive our first interest payment sooner than under annual compounding, and we begin earning interest on interest sooner and more frequently during the term of the investment. What happens if interest is compounded quarterly? Now we need to determine the interest rate per quarter (three-month period) and the number of quarterly periods.

r = 6 per cent/4 = 1.5 per cent per quarter

n = 4x5 = 20 quarters

The future value is calculated as:

$$FV = \$1{,}000(1.015)^{20} = \$1{,}346.86$$

Finally, what happens if interest is compounded monthly? The interest rate would be 0.5 per cent per month (6%/12) and n would be 60 months (12x5). The future value is calculated as:

$$FV = 1{,}000(1.005)\ 60 = \$1{,}348.85$$

The future value increases by compounding more frequently. The adjustments for compounding frequency can be incorporated directly into the future value of a present amount formula as follows:

$$FV = PV\left[1+\frac{r}{m}\right]^{mn} \qquad \text{..............(6.6)}$$

Where *r* is the interest rate per year; *n* is the number of years; and *m* is the number of compounding periods per year. Equation 6.6 is consistent with Equation 6.1 except that we divide the annual interest rate by the number of periods per year (*m*), and multiply the number of years by *m*. These are the same adjustments illustrated in Example 6.11.

Continuous Compounding

Another situation to consider is one where interest is continuously compounded. With continuous compounding, the value for *m* in Equation 6.6 is infinity (∞). Elementary calculus and the concept of limits (beyond the scope of our analysis) can be used to evaluate Equation 6.6 when *m* is infinite; the equation becomes:

$$FV = PV\, e^{rn} \qquad \text{..............(6.7)}$$

Where *r* is the stated annual interest rate; *n* is the number of years in the investment horizon; and e is the base of natural logarithm, approximately equal to 2.71828.

Example 6.12 Future Value with Continuous Compounding

Let's go back to our previous example where an investor deposited $1,000 for 5 years at 6 per cent and compute the future value under continuous compounding.

Solution: Using Equation 6.7, the future value using continuous compounding is:

$$FV = \$1{,}000e^{(0.06)(5)} = \$1{,}349.86$$

Note that the future value with continuous compounding is larger than in the annual, semi-annual, quarterly, or monthly compounding cases. Continuous compounding provides the highest future value for a given annual rate of interest because the interest is compounded every infinite decimal part of a second.

Nominal and Effective Interest Rates

Financial institutions typically quote interest rates as *nominal annual interest rates* that ignore compounding effects. For example, a local bank may quote an annual interest rate of 6 per cent per year on loans that require monthly payments. With monthly compounding, the bank charges 0.5 per cent per month on loans quoted at 6 per cent. With compounding of interest 6 per cent a year is not equal to 0.5 per cent a month. Thus, the stated 6 per cent annual rate does not represent the effective annual interest rate the bank is actually charging. The formula for the effective annual interest rate follows:

$$r_{eff} = \left[1 + \frac{r_{nom}}{m}\right]^{m} - 1 \qquad \text{.......................(6.8)}$$

Where r_{eff} is the effective annual interest rate; r_{nom} is the nominal interest rate, and m is the number of compounding periods per year. The variable m is the number of times per year interest is compounded (for semi-annual compounding, $m = 2$ and for monthly compounding, $m = 12$).

Example 6.13: Effective Annual Interest Rate

The situation just described calls for monthly compounding assuming a 6 per cent nominal interest rate. What is the effective annual rate?

Solution: Using Equation 6.8, the effective annual interest rate would be 6.17 per cent.

$$r_{eff} = \left[1 + \frac{0.06}{12}\right]^{12} - 1 = 0.0617 = 6.17\%$$

Solving for an Unknown Interest Rate

A common time value of money application involves solving for an unknown interest rate that is implied by a given set of cash flows. For example, suppose a financial manager invested $1 million 1 year ago, and today it is worth $1.1 million. Making a quick mental calculation reveals that the manager earned a 10 per cent rate of return on the investment: The 10 per cent rate is implied from the present value ($1 million) and the future value ($1.1 million) amounts. Most problems that involve solving for an unknown interest rate require an iterative (trial and error) approach. As a result, financial calculators or computer spreadsheets become the most efficient method for solving for unknown interest rates. How to solve for unknown interest rates can be illustrated in Examples 6.14 and 6.15.

Example 6.14: Solving for the Implied Annual Interest Rate

An equipment supplier allows a firm to finance the purchase of $100,000 of equipment with a $15,000 down payment followed by five annual year-end payments of $22,000. What is the implied annual interest rate of the equipment purchase?

Solution: The firm has financed the equipment by borrowing \$85,000 and promising to repay the loan with payments of \$22,000 at the end of each year for 5 years.

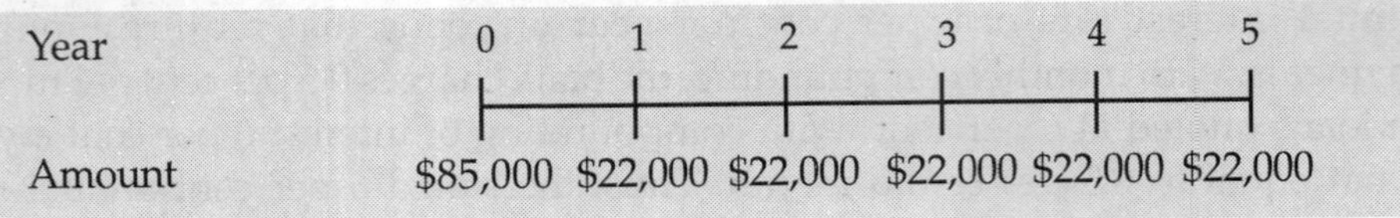

We need to solve for the discount rate that makes the present value of the \$22,000 annuity equal to \$85,000:

$$\$85{,}000 = \$22{,}000\left[\frac{1-\frac{1}{(1+r)^5}}{r}\right]$$

Example 6.15: Solving for the Implied Interest Rate – Extended

An equipment supplier allows a firm to finance the purchase of \$575,000 of equipment with a \$150,000 down payment followed by ten annual (year-end) payments of \$45,000, which are followed by ten annual (year-end) payments of \$52,500. What is the annual interest rate implied by the supplier's financing of the equipment purchase?

Solution: The firm finances the equipment by borrowing \$425,000 from the equipment supplier and repaying the loan with payments of \$45,000 at the end of each year for 10 years followed by payments of \$52,500 at the end of each year for years 11-20.

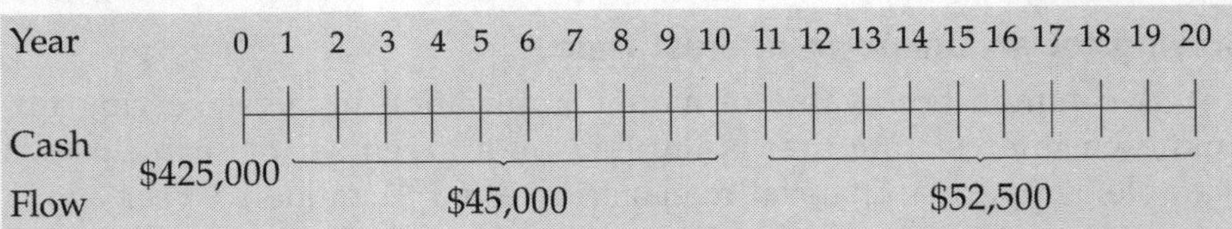

The time value of money equation that makes \$425,000 the present value of the two annuities is written below:

$$\$425{,}000 = \$45{,}000\left[\frac{1-\frac{1}{(1+r)^{10}}}{r}\right] + \$52{,}500\left[\frac{1-\frac{1}{(1+r)^{10}}}{r}\right]\left[\frac{1}{(1+r)^{10}}\right]$$

Solving for unknown interest rates is among the most common time value of money applications. Examples include solving for the expected yield-to-maturity for a corporate bond, and the internal rate of return for a capital investment project, discussed in Chapter 7. Investors often determine the interest rate that equates the present value of expected future amount with the market price of a security to identify the expected return on that investment.

7

Financial Institutions and Instruments in Agribusiness

Financial institutions deal with various financial activities associated with bonds, debentures, stocks, loans, risk diversification, insurance, hedging, retirement planning, investment, portfolio management, and many other types of related functions. With the help of their functions, the financial institutions transfer money or funds to various tiers of economy and thus play a significant role in acting upon the domestic and the international economic scenario. For carrying out their business operations, financial institutions implement different types of economic models. They assist their clients and investors to maximize their profits by rendering appropriate guidance. Financial institutions also impart a wide range of educational programmes to educate the investors on the fundamentals of investment and also regarding the valuation of stock, bonds, assets, foreign exchanges, and commodities. So this chapter aims to generate a broad understanding of the structure and operation of financial markets and the role of different institutions in modern financial systems. The chapter introduces the basic theories and principles of financial markets and instruments which will support agribusiness.

FINANCIAL INSTITUTIONS

Financial institutions can be both private and public in nature. The most common forms of financial institutions can be categorised broadly into the following types:

1. Banks

Perhaps the most common of all financial institutions is the bank. Banks provide the most simplistic of financial services used by a majority of consumers. Checking and savings accounts are staples of most banks, along with relatively safe investment opportunities such as Certificates of Deposit. Banks also offer services such as different types of loans and mortgages for qualified individuals and businesses. For many people, the local bank is the first and possibly only financial institution they will ever do business with.

2. Credit Unions

The credit unions are the co-operative financial institutions that are owned by the members of the union. The major difference between the credit unions and banks is that the credit unions are owned by the members unlike banks. The policies of credit unions are governed by a volunteer Board of Directors that is elected by and from the membership itself. This board of directors also decides on the interest rates to be charged. According to the regulation of credit unions, only the members of the credit union are eligible to deposit money in the union or borrow money from the union. The credit unions are always committed and dedicated to the members and ensure to improve the financial status of the members. The size of the credit unions may vary in a large manner.

The credit unions are generally non-profit organizations. The credit union can also be termed as profit enterprise dedicated to earn profit for its members. The profits earned by the union are received by the members in the forms of dividends. The dividends are paid on savings that are taxed as ordinary income. Usually credit unions have a lower cost of funds than the commercial banks. The credit unions also offer several financial services like banks, but the terminology used here are different from the banks. The credit unions offer the services of share accounts, share draft accounts, share term certificates, credit cards and online banking services. Depending on the financial structure of the country, the functionality of credit unions may vary in different countries.

3. Stock Brokerage Firms

The stock brokerage firms are those entities that are responsible for helping the investors put their money in the stock market. However, the stock brokerage firms are also useful in many other ways, especially for the investors. The stock brokerage firms help their clients, the investors, by providing them with accurate information regarding the workings of a stock market. The stock brokerage firms are useful as they can help the investors get the maximum return from their investments in the stock market. There are primarily two types of stock brokerage firms, based on their mode of operation – the online stock brokerage firms and the off line stock brokerage firms. The off line stock brokerage firms are the traditional stock brokerage firms. The online stock brokerage firms are those, who offer their services through the Internet.

The online stock brokerages are the predominant form of stock brokerages at present. This has happened owing to the coming of Internet and its increasing influence on the world of today. The online stock brokerage firms are regarded as being extremely popular with the investors, by virtue of, the quality of the services, provided by them. The services of the online stock brokerage firms save the investor a lot of money and time, which may be invested in other purposes. It is always easy for the investors to gather information on the online stock brokerage firms and their services, as information on them are always found on the Internet.

4. Asset Management Companies

Asset management companies provide investors with more diversification and investing options than they would have by themselves and attain their investment goals by proper management of assets. There are a large number of asset management firms operating all over the world. These asset management firms are famous for providing professional financial services to the corporations and finance companies on the management of their assets.

The top asset management firms of the world offer professional management services for managing the shares and bonds of their clients. The clients of the asset management firms may be insurance companies, corporations, pension funds or individual investors. The primary goal behind the service of the asset management firms is to help the investors attain their investment goals by proper management of assets. Services like wealth management and portfolio management are also offered by the asset management firms to their clients. Asset management is nothing but the investment management of collective investments of the companies. The asset management firms recruit proficient and knowledgeable investment managers to take the financial decisions.

The investment managers are responsible for managing the assets of the companies and funds in the most feasible way so that the investment ensures maximum profit on a given condition. For a fee, the asset management firm provides more diversification, liquidity, and professional management consulting service than is normally available to individual investors. The diversification of portfolio is done by investing in such securities which are inversely correlated to each other. They collect money from investors by way of floating various mutual fund schemes.

The asset management firms also offer asset management services to the companies in order to maximize the return of the company. It can also be an account at a financial institution that includes services like checking services, debit cards, credit cards, and margin loans and also brokerage services. It has been seen that the services offered by the top asset management firms are for high net-worth clients. The process of asset management includes keeping the records of assets of the companies. The asset management system is believed to have evolved from the maintenance management systems. The main principle of maintenance management is to use work orders for the predictive and preventive maintenance.

5. Savings and Loan Institutions

These also offer many of the services provided by banks and credit unions. In some cases, the mortgages and loans offered by these financial institutions may come with better interest rates than banks or credit unions in the area. While most savings and loans are governed by the same rules, regulations, and protection offered by other banking institutions, there are some countries around the world where the scope of the savings and loan is more limited than other options.

Several different types of financial institutions focus on investing activities for individuals and businesses. These include private lenders, mortgage companies, loan companies, and retirement fund management corporations. Often, these types of institutions work with and through banks and similar organizations in order to conduct business on behalf of their clients. As with other types of financial services, these types of institutions function under the laws that regulate finances within the nation of origin.

With the advent of Internet commerce, many financial institutions function partially or exclusively online. There are online banks that allow consumers to create and manage savings accounts, money market holdings, and even conduct stock and bond transactions.

TYPES OF RURAL FINANCIAL INSTITUTIONS

The following are the rural lenders that can be found in developing countries. The range of rural and agricultural lenders is far more limited than in urban financial markets. This results from the unique features of agricultural production, finance and the history of financial sector development.

1. Formal Lenders

- Agricultural development banks.
- Rural branches of commercial banks.
- Co-operative banks.
- Rural banks/community banks.

2. Semi-formal Lenders

- Credit unions.
- Co-operatives.
- Village or semi-formal community banks.
- NGOs.

3. Informal Lenders

- Relatives and friends.
- Moneylenders.
- Rotating savings and credit associations.

4. Inter-linked Credit Arrangements

- Input suppliers/crop buyers.
- Processing industries.

Institutional Innovation

It does not necessarily mean to create a new institutional type at the international level (as the pioneers of the co-operative movement did), but includes the adaptation of an existing institutional type to the constraints and potentials of a certain client group in a specific local environment. The many different types of MFIs can be distinguished by two criteria their legal status and their lending technology. With respect to their legal status, one can distinguish credit projects, credit unions, village banks, and private-for-profit micro-banks.

1. Credit projects

Credit projects are implemented by a supporting organization (state development agency or a non-government organization (NGO)) and are limited in time. Usually as part of or linked to a larger (integrated) rural development programme, the rationale of the credit project is to finance critical inputs of so-called project beneficiaries. Issues of financial sustainability usually receive little or no consideration at all: interest rates are often subsidized, repayment is low, and overhead high. These give-and-forgive credit projects undermine systematic, long-term efforts to strengthen the financial system. The practice of *revolving credit funds* features similar weaknesses. As credit projects and revolving credit funds lack vision for institution-building, they will not be discussed further.

2. Credit unions

These are owned and controlled by their members and function according to democratic rules (if not disturbed by the central or local government as is the case in many developing countries, or by cronyism among members) Profits are reinvested, or shared among members. Credit unions – especially larger ones with remunerated staff and professional management – are focused on profit, but the co-operative origins and the member-based governance structure also feature equity concerns for weaker members. The one-person, one-vote rule is a clear expression of the co-operative spirit of self-help and care for weaker members in the co-operative movement. Credit unions are registered under a country's co-operative law or are included as a special category in the banking law, but may lack effective external supervision or authorizing legislation. The unions form regional and national networks that enable them to transfer excess liquidity. Credit unions are a viable institutional type for rural micro-finance: They can draw on one hundred and fifty years of experience in rural and urban areas, and are in fact the number one provider of micro-finance. The major comparative advantages of credit unions lie in their ability to service large numbers of depositors, and use these savings to provide a diversified range of loans to individual members.

3. Village banks

These banks are semi-formal, member-based institutions that are mostly promoted by international NGOs. Members own the village bank, but ownership is not formally registered. Members can decide on interest rates for internally generated savings deposits and on-lending their internal account, and usually feature high interest rates on loans and savings deposits compared to going rates in the commercial banking sector. The banks serve a poorer clientele compared to credit unions, and have a high share of female members. Village banks are promoted with the ultimate objective of reducing poverty. Emphasis is therefore on depth of outreach and impact on poverty reduction, and NGOs often provide complementary services such as education or business training to enhance impact.

A village bank is less complex in structure and administration than a credit union, thus enabling less educated members to manage the bank. However, start-up costs for formation and training are believed to be relatively high and are externally financed by the supporting NGO and its donors. The main form of credit guarantee relies on social pressure. One of the major comparative advantages of village banks – especially for rural areas – is that they can operate as member-governed, autonomous institutions, and thus are highly flexible in determining rules of admission and the level of savings and loan interest rates adapted to local socio-economic conditions. The expectation is that the village banks accumulate and retain sufficient equity capital to become self-reliant.

However, this objective of financial sustainability has for the most part not been achieved. Village banks have shown great strength in reaching poorer clientele, but not in reaching financial sustainability most likely because they chose more disadvantaged locations and clientele initially. A major disadvantage of a village bank is that – unless they are linked with a bank, credit union or federation of village banks, their savings and loan portfolio is constrained and influenced by the local village economy, including the threat of covariant risk. Because of the small size of a village bank (30-50 members), it is unclear whether they have significant comparative advantage over informal community-based institutions in financial intermediation and pooling of risks, other than the access to donor-funded external capital for on-lending to the local rural economy. From a financial systems perspective, the long-term sustainability and outreach of village banks hinges upon their ability to integrate into the formal financial system. They need to establish linkages with banks or credit unions for refinancing and for earning return on otherwise seasonally idle funds as this seems to be their long-run competitive advantage compared to informal institutions. Federations of village banks may also serve these intermediation functions across villages and rural areas. If they choose this way to achieve market integration, they will come close to co-operative models.

4. Member-based institutions

Being member-based institutions, credit unions and village banks have some common characteristics and strengths. These include building institutions that can empower communities as a whole and create social capital, their lower-cost in-depth information for example on low-income or illiterate clients, and the flexibility (at least in principle) to adjust interest rates and other terms for savings and credit products to location-specific demand schedules. All these points are highly relevant for extending finance to heterogeneous rural areas and clientele groups. For being sustainable in rural and agricultural finance, it is critical that credit unions and village banks have mechanisms in place to deposit excess liquidity or call in loans through a linkage with banks, or a second-tier or even national-level federation. Covariant risks and seasonality constitute clear limits to expansion and threats to survival for local stand-alone institutions.

5. Linkage type

This alternative retail group-based model builds on pre-existing informal self-help groups (SHGs), such as Rotating Saving and Credit Associations (ROSCAs). Its major advantage is that group formation costs were already born by the members. Like other member-based institutions, the 'linkage model' seeks to combine the strengths of existing informal systems (client proximity, flexibility, social capital, reaching poorer clients) with the strengths of the formal system (*e.g.*, risk pooling, term transformation, provision of long-term investment loans, financial intermediation across regions and sectors). The main principles are:

- *Participation:* Members of a SHGs enter into a group contract with a bank that provides savings and credit services to the group. An intermediary NGO may provide complementary services, such as training or certification of creditworthiness of groups.
- *Responsibilities/profit Sharing:* The bank, sometimes assisted by an NGO, provides the services. The SHGs may organize internal member-managed savings accounts, such as is the case with ROSCAs.
- *Structure:* The SHG is linked to the bank through a group contract. Individual members of the SHG do not have any links with the bank.

OTHER RURAL FINANCIAL INSTITUTIONS

Each of the above MFI-types shows comparative advantages and disadvantages. Let us turn now to state-owned development banks, commercial banks, and other providers of rural and agricultural finance.

Development Banks

Focus on medium and long-term financing of larger rural and agricultural projects (with a high content of public goods, or high impact on economic growth that the private sector for one or the other reason fails to finance). Some of them focus on particular economic sectors. Due to their development objectives, they can and do support micro-finance networks and apex institutions, and provide refinancing to member-based financial institutions, such as rural village banks.

The equity investment can be critically considered a transfer of public funds to private owners, and if the primary (or even declared secondary) objective is not depth of outreach or impact on poverty reduction; it is difficult to justify these public investments on equity grounds as well. However, they can be justified provided that these micro banks constitute critical elements in the rural financial system (for example serving agro-industry and rural SMEs, and as second-tier institutions serving credit unions and village banks).

- *Downscaling Commercial Banks* aims at inducing commercial banks – through technical assistance and staff training for example funded by public funds – to enter into the neglected upper and lower middle market. However, recent experiences by IPC with this approach highlighted many obstacles, These obstacles are likely to be higher for banks entering into rural and agricultural finance because staff is not skilled in financially assessing investments in crop and livestock production and may cherish big-bank investment culture.

Micro Banks for Whole-sale Traders, Agro-processors and Larger Larmers

Many present-day rural financial institutions effectively screen out this relatively wealthy group either directly by setting targeting criteria or indirectly by offering financial products of little relevance to this clientele, which demand larger short-term credit lines as well as long-term investment credit. Larger traders and farmers as well as agribusiness processors are an equally neglected clientele that have critical functions to fulfill in agricultural development and therefore rural poverty reduction. Micro banks aiming at this clientele in rural areas could have considerable potential compared to credit unions, as these types of clientele are too wealthy for credit unions.

- *Contract Farming:* In so-called *bottleneck* markets, agribusiness firms play a viable role in rural finance and technology transfer through contract farming. Bottleneck markets exist because of the specific characteristics of some crops and animal produce (milk) that give a high likelihood to the processor that the farmer will not sell her or his produce in another competing marketing channel. Before agricultural liberalization, there were many politically created bottlenecks through which crops were sold. After liberalization, the array of potential crops shrank tremendously, and competition in the processing sector rose even for classical plantation crops such as palm oil. Contract farming can reduce the risks of processors and farmers, enhance provision of technology, inputs, and loans to farmers, and increase the quality and quantity of produce for processing. These intrinsic risks and other advantages could be better exploited in repeating, long-term contracts, and agribusiness firms may be able to borrow against these contracts from commercial banks. It appears that contract farming is a viable, but under-exploited and under-researched commercial option for agricultural finance in developing and transitioning countries.

TYPES OF FINANCIAL SERVICES

Financial services encompass a variety of businesses that deal with money management. These include many different kinds of organizations such as banks, investment companies, credit card companies, insurance companies and even government programmes. Financial services can also refer to the services and products that money management organizations offer to the public.

Banks are one kind of financial services organizations. Banks generally function by providing a sheltered and secure place for people to store their money. Usually, banks will invest their clients' stored money for the bank's gain, while paying a small amount of interest to those who keep their money in savings or checking accounts.

Banks often provide a variety of financial services, including the issuance of loans, mortgages, checks, and credit cards. Some banks are known as private banks and offer services only to those who have a high net worth. Generally, private banks will offer a broader range of services to their clients than other banks.

Investment services, another type of financial service, generally deals with helping individuals and other entities invest their money in stocks, shares or funds. These services usually offer financial products for investors to buy, such as mutual funds. Usually, money invested with an investment service is managed by the service for the gain of the individual investor or a group of investors. Additionally, they may render professional advice to investors in exchange for payment.

Insurance brokers or agents are companies or individuals that are hired to find appropriate insurance plans for their clients. Insurance providers offer plans which are designed to defer liability for the risk of loss from one entity to another in exchange for a predetermined amount. This makes the second entity, typically an insurance provider, liable for any losses accrued by the first entity, typically an individual or enterprise. Thus, a person will pay a health insurance provider, for example, a recurring fee so that the provider will be responsible for the payment of medical bills should that person fall sick or injured.

Credit card companies are also financial services companies which provide lines of credit to consumers in exchange for interest paid on the money consumers borrow when they charge a purchase to the card. The card company pays for the purchase, but it does so by essentially issuing a high-interest loan to the purchaser.

FINANCIAL INSTRUMENTS

Financial instruments are legal documents that embody monetary value. There are a number of different types of documents that are properly identified as a financial instrument. Under the broad heading of a financial instrument, some would be classified as cash instruments or derivative instruments.

When most people think in terms of a financial instrument, they tend to identify what is commonly known as a cash instrument. This type of financial instrument is simply those documents that are recognised as cash that can be utilised for various transactions. Currency is the most easily identified of all cash instruments, although such documents as checks or funds transfers from bank accounts would also be understood to be a financial instrument of this type.

Derivative instruments are another example of the financial instrument. This classification would include such instruments as futures, options, and swaps. Some analysts also prefer to include stocks, bonds, and currency futures within this category as well, while others tend to think of these instruments as cash equivalents, since it is possible to settle debts by transferring ownership of stocks and bonds. In broad terms, a derivative instrument is some type of contract that has value based on the current status of the underlying assets. Other types of documents are often understood to function as a financial instrument. In the world or real estate funding, the mortgage qualifies as a financial instrument. A commercial paper or stock index also meets the basic definition. Bills of exchange are usually recognised as a financial instrument as well.

A financial instrument may be a hard copy document, or exist as a virtual document. Currency and checks would represent physical documents that represent specific monetary values and are freely used for transactions. Funds transfers between bank accounts would be an example of a virtual financial instrument. In like manner, stocks and bonds may exist as hard copies or as virtual records that assign rights and privileges to a specific investor.

MAIN CHARACTERISTICS AND RISKS OF FINANCIAL INSTRUMENTS

The purpose of the information contained in the present section is to give a brief outline of the main characteristics and risks associated to financial instruments.

Basic Risks

These risks apply to any type of investment. However, depending on the relevant financial instrument, one or several of the risks described here below may apply cumulatively, therefore entailing an overall increase in the level of risk incurred by the investor.

- *Economic Risk:* Changes in the activity of a market economy always influence prices of financial instruments and exchange rates. Prices are fluctuating more or less according to the downward or growth trends of the economic activity. The duration and scope of the economic downward or growth trends are variable, as are the repercussions of those variations on the different sectors of the economy. In addition, the economic cycles may vary depending on the different countries. Failure to take these factors into account as well as a mistaken analysis of the development of the economy when taking an investment decision may lead to losses. In particular, one must take into account the impact of the economic trends on the evolution of investment prices. Depending, *inter alia*, of economic trends, good past performance of a financial instrument is no guarantee of good future performance of the same investment. Price losses, entailing losses to the investor, are always possible. Therefore, an investor must at all times ensure that his investments are appropriate in view of the economic situation and, if necessary, make necessary changes in his portfolio.

- *Risk of Inflation:* Losses in value of a currency may cause financial damage to an investor in relation to investments made by the latter. In this context, such a loss in value may have an influence on the actual value of the existing patrimony of the investor as well as the actual yield that ought to be realised through this patrimony. One should thus take into account actual yields, *i.e.,* the difference between the nominal interest rate and the inflation rate for fixed-rate products. Therefore, when the inflation rate exceeds the yield generated by the financial instruments (gains in capital and interests) this will lead to a loss in the value of the capital actually invested.
- *Country Risk and Transfer Risk:* It may happen that a foreign debtor, although solvent, be unable to pay interest or repay his debts upon maturity or even completely defaults on his debts due to the unavailability of the foreign currency or to currency exchange controls triggered, for instance, by economic, political or social instability in the relevant country. The ensuing unavailability of the foreign currency or currency exchange controls may indeed lead to defaults on payments for the investors. Concerning financial instruments issued in a foreign currency, the investor risks to receive payments in a currency which turns out not to be convertible anymore because of exchange controls. Moreover, even in the absence of any crisis, state intervention in some economic sectors (*e.g.,* nationalization) may have an influence on the value of investors' assets. In certain extreme cases, investors' assets can even be confiscated or frozen by local authorities or investors' rights can be restricted. As a matter of principle, there is no means to hedge against such risks. However, country ratings published in the financial press can be a useful guide for investors from that point of view. Finally, more generally, instability in the political and/or economic and/or social situation of certain countries may lead to quick price fluctuations.

- *Exchange Rate Risk:* Since currency exchange rates fluctuate, there is an exchange rate risk whenever financial instruments are held in a foreign currency. Depending on exchange rates, the same investment may generate profits or entail losses. Moreover, since the activities of companies are, to a greater or lesser extent, related to exchange rates, fluctuations in these latter rates are likely to have an impact on the price of the financial instruments they issue. Material elements affecting the exchange rate of currencies are in particular the inflation rate of a country, the gap between domestic interest rates and foreign rates as well as between domestic and foreign productivities, the assessment of economic activity forecasts, the political situation in the world and the safety of investments in general. Additionally, psychological events, such as lack of confidence in political leaders, may weaken the exchange rate of a domestic currency.
- *Liquidity Risk:* The possibility for an investor to sell financial instruments at any time at market prices is described as liquidity. Therefore, insufficient liquidity of the market may prevent an investor from selling off financial instruments at market prices. Fundamentally, a distinction has to be made between a lack of liquidity caused by market offer and demand and a lack of liquidity due to the characteristics of the financial instrument or market practices. A lack of liquidity due to market offer and demand arises when the offer or the demand for one financial instrument at a certain price is nonexistent or extremely low. Under those circumstances, purchase or sell orders may either not be carried out immediately, and/or only partly (partial execution) and/or at unfavorable conditions. In addition, higher transaction costs may apply. A lack of liquidity due to the inherent characteristics of the financial instrument or to market practice may occur, for example, because of a lengthy transcription procedure for a transaction on registered shares, long performance delays because of market practices or other limitations of trade, short-term liquidity needs that cannot be covered quickly enough by the sale of the financial instruments or long locking periods before being entitled to execute a transaction, in particular for alternative investment funds.
- *Psychological Risk:* Irrational factors may affect the overall evolution of prices, such as for example tendencies, opinions, rumors which may cause important drops in prices, although the financial situation and future perspectives of the relevant companies have not evolved unfavorably.
- *Credit Risk:* Credit-financed purchases of financial instruments contain several additional risks. On the one hand, additional collateral may be required – sometimes at very short notice – in case the credit limit guaranteed is exceeded due to the evolution of the price of the collateral.

If the investor turns out to be unable to provide such collateral, the bank may be forced to sell deposited financial instruments at an unfavorable moment. On the other hand, the loss suffered due to an adverse evolution of the price of a financial instrument may exceed the initial investment amount. Fluctuations of prices of the financial instruments constituting the collateral may influence the capacity to repay loans in a negative way. One needs to be aware that, as a consequence of the leverage effect entailed by the purchase of credit-financed financial instruments, the sensitivity to price fluctuations of those investments will be proportionally more important with the consequence that chances of gains increase, as do the risks of losses. The risks entailed by such purchases rise according to the importance of the leverage.

- *Interest Rate Risk:* Generally speaking, fluctuations in interest rates, whether short-term or long-term rates, may have substantial adverse consequences on the prices of financial instruments.
- *Risk of Insolvency of the Issuer or of the Clearing and Settlement System:* In case of insolvency of the issuer of financial instruments or of the clearing and settlement system on which those instruments are negotiated, an investor may loss part or all the money he has invested.
- *Additional Risks on Emerging Markets:* Emerging markets are the markets of the countries in which the percentage share of income per inhabitant is considered as average or low by the World Bank. More practically, this concept encompasses markets established in countries which are characterized by a certain degree of political instability, relatively unpredictable financial markets and economic growth patterns, a financial market which is still at the development stage and a weak economy. This concept of emerging markets encompasses a large number of markets established in South America, Eastern Europe and certain Asian countries. Generally speaking, on these markets, the risks identified above are enhanced. Indeed, political or economic changes (*e.g.*, inflation, exchange rate) will have more influence on investments' prices in emerging markets than in other countries. Likewise, emerging markets usually react more deeply and durably in case of natural disaster or war. Moreover, emerging markets often have less elaborated rules for clearance and settlement of transactions with the consequence that processing errors or default in delivery of instruments are more likely to occur. Finally, regulatory supervision over these markets and rules to protect investors are often weak
- *Information Risk:* It is the risk of poor investment decisions arising from a lack of information, incomplete information or inaccurate information. This may be due in turn to the use by the investor of unreliable sources, the misinterpretation of originally accurate information by the latter or can be due to communication errors.

- *Transmission Risk:* When placing an order, the investor must provide certain details necessary for its execution by the bank (financial instrument, type of order, volume, execution date, etc). The more precise the order placed is, the smaller the risk of transmission error is.
- *Risks Pertaining to Transaction Costs:* The bank as well as other domestic or foreign-based parties may be involved in the execution of an order (*e.g.,* brokers), in which case the fees and commissions of these persons will be passed on to the investor. An investment becomes profitable only once all these costs have been covered.

SPECIFIC INVESTMENT RISKS

Term Deposits

These are cash deposits remunerated at a fixed maturity date and rate, determined in advance.

Characteristics

- *Yield*: payment of interests,
- *Duration:* short-term (up to 4 years), medium-term (4-8 years) or long-term (more than 8 years),
- *Interests*: Interests depend on the terms and conditions of the deposit; *e.g.,* fixed interest for the entire duration or variable interest often linked to financial market rates.

Advantages

Depending on market conditions, these products may provide a higher return than other fixed-income products.

Risks

These products are mainly subject to the risks of inflation, exchange and interest rate and of insolvency of the counterparty, as described under 1 above.

Bonds

A bond is a certificate or evidence of a debt on which the issuing company or governmental body promises to pay the bondholders a specified amount of interest for a specified length of time, and to repay the loan on the expiration date. A bond may be in bearer or registered form. At issuance, the par value of one bond represents a fraction of the total amount of the loan. The interest payments on bonds may be either fixed or variable. The duration of the loan as well as the terms and conditions of repayment are determined in advance. Certain structured products may take the form of a bond and the purchaser of a bond (the creditor) has a claim against the issuer (the debtor).

Characteristics

- *Yield*: Interest payments, possible increases in value (difference between the purchase/issuance price and the sale/redemption price),

- *Duration*: Short-term (up to 4 years), medium-term (4-8 years) or long-term (more than 8 years),
- *Currency:* National currency of the investor or foreign currency. It can be provided that repayment of capital and interest payments can be made in different currencies. In such a case, an option can be associated to the bond in order to limit the exchange rate risk,
- *Form:* Individual documents with specific nominal values (which can be delivered to the investor) or collectively represented by a global certificate, which is deposited with a custodian bank,
- *Issue Price:* At par (100% of the nominal value), *below par* (the issue price is lower than the nominal value) or *above par* (the issue price is higher than the nominal value),
- *Place of Issuance:* It can be the domestic market of the investor or also a foreign market,
- *Repayment*:
    - *scheduled repayment:* unless otherwise provided for or unless the issuer becomes insolvent, the loans are repaid either on the maturity date, or through annual installments (generally after a lock-in period), or at different dates determined by drawing lots (generally after a lock-in period);
    - *unscheduled repayment:* the issuer may reserve the right to repay at a date he will determine, at his own discretion, at a later stage;
- *Interests*: Interests depend on the terms and conditions of the loan; *e.g.*, fixed interest for the entire duration or variable interest often linked to financial market rates. In this latter case, a minimum and/or maximum rate can be provided;
- *Particular Features (e.g., relations between the issuer and the investor)*: set out in the terms and conditions of issue of the relevant bond.

Advantages

Depending on market conditions, these products may provide a higher return than other fixed-income products.

Risks

(a) *Insolvency risk:* The issuer risks to become temporarily or permanently insolvent, entailing his incapacity to pay back interests and/or the principal amount of the loan. The solvency of an issuer may change depending on the evolution of certain factors during the life of the bond. This may be due in particular to the general evolution of the economy, changes related to the enterprise, the economic sector of the issuer and/or the relevant country as well as political changes entailing substantial economic consequences. This risk is more or less important depending on whether the bonds are issued by a governmental body or a private institution. This risk is also related to the nationality of the issuing governmental body or the type or sector of activity of the private institution which issued the bonds (credit institution, industrial undertaking, etc.), as well as, more generally, the creditworthiness of the latter. This risk is more limited if the bonds are collateralized. However, in such a case, the additional protection granted to the investor will have to be assessed on the basis of the status and creditworthiness of the guarantor. From that point of view, it should be noted that, as a matter of principle, bonds issued by entities which are considered as safe generally offer lower returns. However, the risk of total loss of the investment is correlatively lower. The deterioration of the issuer's creditworthiness does equally influence in a negative manner the price of the relevant financial instruments.

(b) *Interest rate risk:* The uncertainty concerning the evolution of interest rates entails that the purchaser of a fixed-rate financial instrument bears the risk of a decrease in the price of such financial instrument in case of a rise in interest rates. The sensitivity of the bonds to fluctuations in interest rates depends in particular on the period remaining until maturity of the bond and the level of nominal interest rates.

(c) *Anticipated refunding risk:* The issuer of a bond may include a provision allowing him to repay earlier the bondholder in case for instance of a decrease in interest rates in the markets. Such an early repayment can have an impact on the yield expected by the investor.

(d) *Risks specific to bonds redeemable by drawing lots:* The maturity date of bonds that are redeemable by lot is difficult to determine so that unexpected changes may take place in the yield of such bonds.

(e) *Risks related to the country of issue:* If the bond is issued on a foreign market, it will in principle be governed by the law of the country of issue. The investor must thus inquire about the possible impact of the applicability of this foreign law on his rights.

(f) *Risks of specific kinds of bonds:* Concerning some kinds of bonds, additional risks may exist: *e.g.*, floating rate notes, reverse floating rate notes, zero coupon bonds, and bonds in a foreign currency, convertible bonds, index or option-linked bonds, subordinated bonds etc. For those types of bonds, the investor should make inquiries about the risks described in the issuance prospectus and not purchase such financial instruments before being certain to master all risks. The developments here below only aim at providing a brief outline on the additional risks incurred by the investor in relation to specific bonds.

Floating Rate Bonds

Floating rate bonds can take several forms, such as for instance:

- *Floor floater bonds,* which are variable-interest bonds which pay a minimum level of interest. Therefore, in the event that the sum of the reference rate and the spread falls below this level, the investor will receive payment of interests at least at the minimum rate determined in advance. Conversely, for cap floater bonds, the rate of interest paid to the investor is limited to a maximum amount determined in advance. For these bonds, it is not possible to anticipate, as of their issue, the actual yield of the investment since the latter vary according to the fluctuations of market rates.

- For certain *variable-interest bonds*, it can be provided that the interest rate moves in the opposite direction to market rates (*i.e.,* reverse floating rate bonds). For these medium or long-term bonds, the interest rate payable to the investor is calculated according to the difference between a fixed rate of interest and a reference rate. This means that the investor's interest income rises when the reference rate falls. The price of these bonds is usually subject to higher market fluctuations than the fixed-rate bonds having the same maturity;
- There are also *convertible floating rate bonds* which give the investor or the issuer (depending on the terms and conditions of the bonds) the right to convert the note into a normal fixed-interest bond. If the issuer reserves this right, the actual yield of the bond may be lower than that contemplated by the investor.

Zero Bonds

Zero bonds do not have interest coupons attached. Instead of periodic payments of interests, the investor receives the difference between the redemption price and the issue price (in addition to the repayment of the principal amount). Such bonds are usually issued at a discount to their nominal value, and redeemed on maturity *at par*. The size of the discount granted to the investor depends on the maturity of the bond, the borrower's creditworthiness and prevailing market interest rates. Hence, such bonds offer investors a fixed lump-sum payment at a future date if the bond is held until maturity (which may have various tax implications depending on the countries). On the contrary, if the bond is sold before maturity, the investor will only receive payment of the sale price of the bonds. Therefore, if market interest rates decrease, the price of these bonds falls more sharply than for other bonds with the same maturity and credit rating. Moreover, in case of foreign currency denominated zero bonds, there is also an increased exchange rate risk because interest payments are not made on a regular basis over the life of the bond but there is only payment of a lump sum at a future date determined in advance.

Combined-interest Bonds or Step-up Bonds

For combined-interest bonds or step-up bonds, the investor does not receive interest payments at a single, fixed rate over the entire life of the bond. However, such bonds are similar to fixed-rate bonds in so far as the interest rate is determined in advance and does not depend on fluctuations in market rates. Instead, the rate of interest only changes during the term of the bond, following a pattern agreed at the time of issue. Indeed, with combined-interest bonds, it is agreed that there will be no coupon for the first years of the life of the bond but an above-average coupon will be paid to the investor for the remaining years. With step-up bonds, a relatively low coupon is paid initially, and a very high one is paid to the investor for the following years. These bonds are usually issued and redeemed *at par*.

Phased Interest Rate Bonds

These bonds are actually a hybrid of fixed and variable interest notes. They usually have a maturity of 10 years, and pay a fixed coupon for the first years. Afterwards, during a period of several years, the investor will receive interests calculated on the basis of a variable interest rate in line with market rates. For the last years of the life of the bond, the bond reverts to paying a fixed rate of interest to the investor.

Index-linked Bonds

For these bonds, the redemption amount and/or interest payments are determined on the basis of the level of an index or of a managed account determined in advance – at redemption or on the interest payment date – and thus are not fixed. These bonds are often zero bonds. Such bonds are usually issued in two 'tranches': bull bonds (bonds which appreciate in value if the index rises) and bear bonds (bonds which appreciate in value if the index falls). The investor runs the risk of price losses if the value of the index falls (bull bonds) or if the value of the index rises (bear bonds).

Subordinated Bonds

For these bonds, investors ought to inquire about the ranking of the debenture compared to other debentures of the issuer since, in case of a bankruptcy of the issuer, those bonds will only be reimbursed after repayment of all higher ranked creditors (preferential and *pari passu* bonds). However, generally, the better the position of the creditor in case of insolvency is, the lower the return of the bond will be.

Convertible/warrant Bonds

In this case, the investor is granted the right to exchange the bonds, at a specific time or within a specific period, for shares in the issuer at a ratio determined in advance. There is usually a minimum lock-in period during which an investor cannot exercise his right of conversion. In case the right of conversion is not exercised, the bonds remain fixed-interest notes, repayable *at par* on maturity. Because they offer a conversion right, such bonds usually offer a lower interest rate than ordinary bonds. The price of these bonds is essentially determined by the price of the underlying shares. Indeed, if the price of the shares drops, the price of the bonds falls as well. Therefore, the risk of price losses is higher than for bonds without conversion rights (but usually lower than the risk of price losses associated to a direct investment in the relevant shares). There are also bonds which give the investor the right to subscribe for shares, in addition to the bond and not as an alternative. This subscription right is certificated by a warrant which is detachable from the bond. This warrant can be traded separately. The shares in the issuer can be purchased by the investor on surrender of the warrant, on terms agreed in advance. The investor continues, in addition hereto, to hold the bond until maturity. As for bonds with conversion rights, the periodic interest payments are usually relatively low. Moreover, the price of such bonds, with the warrant attached, will equally track the price of the underlying shares. If the bonds are without the warrant attached, they amount to traditional bonds and, therefore, their price is mainly determined by market rates. Certain special forms of the bonds described in the preceding paragraph give the holder of the warrant the right to buy or sell another bond determined in advance at a fixed price.

Shares

A share is a certificate evidencing the rights of the shareholder, to whom it is granted, in a company/firm. Share may take bearer or registered form. One share of stock represents a fraction of the share capital of a corporation.

Characteristics

- *Yield*: Dividend payments and increases in value of the financial instrument are possible;
- *Shareholder's rights*: Financial and ownership rights; those rights are determined by the law and the articles of incorporation of the issuing company;
- *Transferability*: Unless otherwise provided by law, the transfer of bearer shares does not, as a matter of principle, require any formalities, as opposed to the transfer of registered shares which is often subject to limitations.

Advantages

In principle, the investor has voting rights and shares the profits of the company. He may equally obtain higher returns than for investments in term deposits or bonds.

Risks

(a) *Entrepreneurial risk:* A share purchaser is not a creditor of the company, but makes a capital contribution and, as such, becomes a co-owner of the enterprise. Consequently, he is participating in the development of the enterprise as well as in the related opportunities and risks, which may entail unexpected fluctuations in the value of such investment. An extreme situation would consist in the bankruptcy of the issuing firm, which would have as a consequence the complete loss of the invested amount.

(b) *Price fluctuation risk:* Share prices may undergo unforeseeable price fluctuations causing risks of losses. Increases and decreases in prices in the short, medium and long-term alternate without it being possible to determine the duration of those cycles. As a matter of principle, the general market risk must be distinguished from the specific risk attached to the firm itself. Both risks influence the evolution of share prices.

(c) *Dividend risk:* The dividend of a share mainly depends on the profit realised by the issuing firm. Therefore, in case of low profits or even losses, it may happen that dividend payments are reduced or that no payments are made.

Bonus Certificates

Bonus certificates represent patrimonial rights as defined in the terms and conditions of issue of those bonds.

Characteristics

In general, they come in the form of par value debt instruments that entitle their holder to a part of the profit of the firm. As a matter of principle, fixed or variable distribution bonus certificates must be distinguished from bonus certificates with option or conversion right.

Risks

(a) *Absence of distribution or reduction of repayment:* In case of losses by the issuing firm, interest payments may be halted if no minimal interest payment has been provided for. In addition, the repayment of the principal amount may be reduced.

(b) *Issuer risk:* The bankruptcy of the issuer entails the complete loss of the invested funds.

Investment Funds

An investment fund is a company or an organized joint ownership which is collecting funds from a certain number of investors and which is engaged in reinvesting those funds according to the principle of risk spreading and to make its stockholders or members benefit from the results of its asset management.

Characteristics

- *Open-ended funds*: In an open-ended fund, the number of shares/units and, consequently, of participants cannot, in principle, be determined. The mutual fund may issue new shares/units or redeem existing shares/units. Towards investors, the mutual fund is obliged to redeem shares/units, at its own expenses, at the agreed redemption price and in line with the contractual provisions;
- *Closed-ended funds*: In a closed-ended fund, the issue of shares/units is limited to a number determined in advance. As opposed to open-ended funds, the redemption of the shares/units by the fund is not mandatory. Shares/units may only be sold to third parties or, in some cases, on the market. The price of the shares units depends on market offer and demand.

Advantages

The holder of shares/units receives part of the income of the fund. As a result of the diversification of the underlying investments made by the fund, the chances of profits increase or, at least, the risks of losses are limited. For the investments made by the fund, the latter usually benefits from better market conditions (in particular for costs) than the conditions which would apply to the investor if he invested directly in the same products.

Risks

(a) *Management risk:* Since the yield of investments made by a fund depends, among other factors, on the capacities of the managers and on the quality of their decisions, errors in the management of the fund may lead to losses or loss of profits.

(b) *Risk of a drop in share/unit prices:* Investment fund shares/units bear the risk of a drop in their prices, this drop reflecting the decrease in value of the financial instruments or currencies that compose the asset portfolio of the fund, any other things remaining equal. The higher the diversification of the investments made by the fund is, the lower at least theoretically, the risks of losses are. Conversely, risks are more important if the fund makes more specialized and less diversified investments. It is therefore important to pay attention to the general and specific risks attached to financial instruments and currencies contained in the fund's portfolio. The investor must inquire about the risks specific to each fund by consulting, among others, the relevant prospectus.

Derivatives

Derivatives are financial instruments the value of which varies according to the value of an underlying asset; the underlying asset may be the price of a share, a market index, an interest rate, a currency, and the price of raw materials or even another derivative. Concerning derivatives, a distinction must be made in particular between:

- *Option Transactions:* Which give to one of the parties the right, but not the obligation, to enter into a transaction. One party (the seller of the option) is irrevocably bound to perform while the other one (the purchaser of the option) is free to exercise the option or not.
- *Forward Transactions:* Where the parties enter into a transaction which will have to be performed at a specified date in the future. In a forward transaction, parties bind themselves irrevocably to perform the transaction concluded between them at the specified date. Transactions on such products trigger higher risks of losses and can even lead to the total loss of the invested funds. Since such transactions can lead to margin calls over the life of the product, investors must ensure that they have sufficient liquid assets before entering into such transactions.

Option Transactions

Options are derivative instruments the value of which tracks the evolution of the value of the underlying asset. The purchaser of an option receives, after having paid a premium to his counterpart, the seller of the option, the right to purchase (call) or to sell (put) the underlying asset at maturity or during a certain period for a strike price determined in advance. The characteristics of the option can be standardized or defined on a case-by-case basis between the purchaser and the seller.

Characteristics

- *Duration*: The duration of the option starts from the day of the subscription until the day of the maturity of the option right;
- *Link between the option and the underlying asset*: This link underlines the number of units of the underlying asset that the holder of the option has the right to purchase (call) or to sell (put) by exercising his option right;
- *Strike price*: The strike price is equal to the price agreed upon earlier at which the holder of the option may purchase or sell the underlying asset when he exercises his option right;
- *Strike date:* Options which can be exercised on any trading day up until the maturity date are called 'American style' options. Options which can be exercised only on their maturity date are called 'European style' options. The latter can nonetheless be traded on the secondary market before their maturity if the market is liquid;
- *Conditions of exercise:* the option can be with physical settlement, in which case the buyer of a call option can demand physical delivery of the underlying asset against payment of the strike price or the buyer of a put option can deliver to the seller of the option the underlying asset, against payment of the strike price by the seller. The option can also be with cash settlement, in which case the difference between the strike price and the market value of the underlying asset is due, provided nonetheless that the option is 'in-the-money';
- *Options 'in-the-money', 'out-of-the-money', 'at-the money':* A call option is 'in-the-money' if the market value of the underlying is higher than the strike price. Conversely, a call option is 'out-of-the-money' if the current market value of the underlying asset is lower than the strike price. A put option is 'in-the-money' if the market value of the underlying asset is lower than the strike price. Conversely, a put option is 'out-of-the-money' if the current market value of the underlying asset is higher than the strike price. When the market value and the strike price are the same, the option is 'in-the-money';
- *Price of the option:* The price of an option depends on its intrinsic value as well as on a variety of factors (time value), in particular the remaining life of the option and the volatility of the underlying asset. The time

value reflects the chance that the option will be 'in-the-money'. Therefore, this latter value is higher for long duration options with a very volatile underlying asset.

- *Margin:* Over the lifetime of an option, the seller must provide as collateral, either the corresponding amount of the underlying asset or another form of collateral. The margin is determined by the bank. Markets stipulate a minimum margin for listed options. If the margin cover provided by the investor proves to be insufficient, the bank is entitled to request additional collateral, sometimes at a very short notice;
- *Form:* Option certificates (warrants, listed options) – the rights and obligations associated to the relevant option are securitized. They are sometimes listed on the market. Traded options – these are standardized options for which the rights and obligations are not securitized and which are traded on certain specific markets. Over-the-counter (OTC) options – these are options traded outside a stock-exchange or agreed directly off-market between the parties. Their level of standardization depends on market practices. They can also be tailor-made to meet investors' needs. This type of option is not listed and rarely takes the form of a certificate;
- *Leverage*: Every change in the price of the underlying asset entails a proportionally higher change in the price of the option right;
- *Purchase of a call or a put*: The buyer of a call option speculates on a rise of the price of the underlying over the life of the option, which causes an increase in the value of his option right. Conversely, the buyer of a put option benefits from a drop in the price of the underlying;
- *Sale of a call or a put*: The seller of a call option anticipates price drops of the underlying asset whereas the seller of a put profits from a rise in the value of the underlying asset.
- *Information notices:* In addition hereto, the attention of investors is specifically drawn to the information notices relating to option trading, issued by the markets on which such options are traded, and in particular the following documents:
- Characteristics and Risks of Standardized Options available upon request at the bank, and on the Internet website www.cboe.com;
- In signing this document the Client recognises and accepts that the bank may conclusively consider that when transmitting an order relating to options traded on such markets the client has beforehand taken due note of the information notices issued by such markets.

Advantages

Over the lifetime of the option, the beneficiary of the option is granted the right to purchase or sale certain assets. The chances of profits are important due to the leverage effect linked to the use of an underlying asset. For the counterparty, such a transaction mainly permits to increase the return on an existing position.

Risks

(a) *Price risk:* Options may be traded on markets or over-the-counter (OTC) and follow the law of offer and demand. An important point for the determination of the price of an option consists, on the one hand in determining whether there is a sufficient liquidity of the market for the relevant option, and on the other hand in determining the actual or expected evolution of the price of the corresponding underlying asset. A call option loses value when the price of the underlying asset decreases, whereas the opposite is true for put options. The price of an option does not solely depend on the price fluctuations of the underlying asset but a series of other factors may come into play, such as for instance the duration of the option or the frequency and intensity of the fluctuations in the value of the underlying asset (volatility). Consequently, drops in the value of the option may appear although the price of the underlying asset remains unchanged.

(b) *Leverage risk:* Due to the leverage effect, price modifications of the value of the option are generally higher than the changes in the price of the underlying asset. Thus, during the lifetime of the option, chances of gains for the holder of an option as well as risks of losses are higher. The risk attached to the purchase of an option increases with the importance of the leverage effect of the relevant option.

(c) *Purchase of an option:* The purchase of an option represents a highly volatile investment and the likelihood that an option reaches maturity without any value is relatively high. In this case, the investor loses all the funds used for the payment of the initial premium as well as commissions. Pursuant to the purchase of an option, the investor can maintain his position till maturity, he can enter into an opposite transaction or, for 'American-style' options, exercise the option before maturity. The exercise of the option may either entail the payment in cash of a differential amount or the purchase or the delivery of the underlying asset. In case the option's object consists in futures contracts, its exercise causes the taking of a position in futures, which supposes the acceptance of some obligations concerning security margins.

(d) *Sale of an option:* The sale of an option entails, generally speaking, higher risk-taking than its purchase. Indeed, even if the price obtained for an option is fixed, the losses that the seller may incur are potentially unlimited. If market prices of the underlying asset vary in an unfavorable way, the seller of the option will have to adapt his security margins in order to maintain his position. If the sold option is an 'American-style' option, the seller may be required at any moment to settle the transaction in cash or to purchase or deliver the underlying asset. If the underlying of the option consists in futures contracts, the seller will take a position in futures and will have to respect obligations concerning security margins. The seller's risk exposure may be reduced by keeping a position on the underlying asset (financial instruments, index or other) corresponding to the sold option.

(e) *Purchase of the underlying asset in case of short sale:* The seller of an uncovered call option does not have a corresponding quantity of the underlying asset at his disposal upon the conclusion of the contract (short sale). In the case of options with physical settlement, the potential loss for the investor amounts to the difference between the strike price paid for the delivery of the underlying assets in case the option right is exercised and the price he will have to pay to acquire the relevant underlying asset. For options with cash settlement, the risk of loss for the investor amounts to the difference between the strike price and the market value of the underlying. Since the market value of the underlying can move well above the strike price when exercising the option, the risk of loss for the investor cannot be determined in advance and is, theoretically at least, unlimited. This risk is more important for 'American-style' options which may be exercised at any time and thus at a highly unfavorable time for the seller of the option. Another risk for the investor selling the option is also to be unable to obtain the requested underlying when the option is exercised or to have the possibility to obtain it only at very unfavorable conditions (in particular for costs) due to the situation of the markets. In this context, it must be reminded that the potential loss can also be greater than the value of the margin cover provided by the investor.

(f) *Specific risks associated to options traded over-the-counter (OTC):* A position arising from the purchase or the sale of an OTC option can only be closed with the approval of the counterparty.

(g) *Specific risks associated to combined options:* A combination consists in the conclusion of two or more option contracts based on the same underlying, which differ in the option type or the characteristics of the option. The number of possible combinations is important. Therefore, the risks involved by any particular combination cannot be described in the present document. Consequently, the investor must inquire about the specific risks associated to the contemplated combination. It can nonetheless be noted that for any combination, the cancellation, at a certain point, of one or more options may entail substantial changes in the risk position of the investor.

(h) *Specific risks associated to 'exotic' options:* These options are subject to additional conditions or agreements. Their payment structures cannot be obtained by using a combination of transactions. They can take the form of tailor-made OTC options or warrants. The range of exotic options is unlimited so that it is impossible to describe the risks entailed by each 'exotic' option in this book.

Forward Transactions

Futures are contracts traded on a market and standardized as regards the quantity of the underlying asset and as regards the maturity date of the transaction. Over-the-counter (OTC) or forward contracts are contracts that are not traded on a market and which may be standardized or individually negotiated between purchaser and seller.

Characteristics

- *Initial required margin:* Be it a future purchase or sale of an underlying asset, an initial margin is fixed when the contract is concluded. This margin is generally expressed in percentage of the value of the contract;
- *Variation margin:* During the entire life of the contract, a variation margin is periodically determined and required from the investor. It represents the accounting benefit or loss, derived from the modification of the contractual price or the price of the underlying asset. The variation margin may exceed the initial required margin by far. The computation method for the variation margin, be it during the life of the contract or at closing, depends on the stock – exchange rules and on the specific contractual provisions of each contract. The investor must immediately provide the bank with variation margin upon request from the latter;
- *Liquidation:* In general, the investor may, at any time during the life of the contract, sell off or liquidate the contract before maturity, either by selling the contract or by entering into an opposite contract as regards the delivery and reception obligations. In this latter case, the provisions of the opposite contract will be such as the delivery and reception obligations arising from both contracts cancel one another out. The liquidation puts an end to the risk positions incurred: gains and losses accumulated until liquidation are realised;
- *Settlement*: Contracts that have not been sold off until settlement must be performed by the relevant parties. Contracts having as underlying tangible property assets may be performed by effective delivery of the assets as well as by cash settlement (although physical delivery settlement is more common) while contracts having as underlying reference rates (to the exception of currencies) cannot be performed by actual delivery of the underlying. In case of an effective delivery of the underlying, the contractual obligations need to be performed in full, whereas for cash settlement contracts, only the difference between the price agreed upon when concluding the contract and the market price upon performance of the contract is payable. Therefore, investors need

more available funds for contracts providing for the actual delivery of the underlying asset than for contracts providing for cash settlement.

Advantages

Chances of gains are important depending on the market value of the underlying upon maturity, especially because the principal amount originally invested is low. Such products may also permit to secure existing positions.

Risks

(a) *Modification of the value of the contract or the underlying asset:* The investor incurs a risk if the evolution of the actual value of the contract or of the underlying is not in line with the evolution forecasted by the investor when concluding the contract. Despite a rise in the price of the contract or the underlying, the forward seller will have to deliver the underlying asset at the initially agreed upon price, which may be far lower than the current price. For the seller, the risk is equal to the difference between the price agreed upon when concluding the contract and the market value on maturity date. As the market value may theoretically rise in an unlimited manner, the loss potential for the seller is unlimited and may considerably exceed the required margins. In case the value of the contract or the underlying asset decreases, the forward purchaser will still have to accept the underlying asset at the price agreed upon in the contract which can be potentially very much higher than the current market value. Therefore, the buyer's risk consists in the difference between the price agreed upon when concluding the contract and the market value on the maturity date. Thus, the maximum the purchaser may lose is the initially agreed upon price. This loss may however exceed by far the required margins. Transactions are regularly evaluated (mark-to-market) and the investor will need to have permanently at his disposal a sufficient margin cover. In case the margin becomes insufficient during the forward transaction, the investor will have to provide a variation margin at very short notice, failing which the transaction will be liquidated before due term, generally at loss.

(b) *Difficult or impossible sell off:* In order to limit excessive price fluctuations, a stock exchange may fix price limits for certain contracts. In such a case, the investor has to keep in mind that, whenever a price limit is reached, it may be very difficult if not momentarily impossible to sell off the contract. Thus, every investor should, before entering into a forward contract, make an inquiry concerning the existence of such limits. It will not always be possible (depending on the market and the terms and conditions of the transaction) to sell off contracts at any moment in order to avoid or to reduce the risks of a pending transaction. Stop-loss transactions, if they are possible, may only be performed during office hours of the bank. They do not allow to limit losses to the indicated amount, but they will be performed once the threshold is reached in the market and they become at that time an order to perform such a transaction at the then current market price.

(c) *Purchase of the underlying in case of short sale:* To sell an underlying on a forward basis without owning it when concluding the contract (short sale) entails the risk that the seller will have to buy the underlying asset at an extremely unfavorable market price in order to be able, upon maturity, to perform his obligation to deliver effectively the underlying.

(d) *Specific risks associated to over-the-counter transactions (OTC):* For standardized OTC transactions, the market is in general transparent and liquid. Therefore, the selling off of contracts can normally be done. However, no market exists for OTC transactions agreed individually between the purchaser and the seller. That is why the closing-out is only possible with the agreement of the other party.

(e) *Specific risks associated to forward exchange products:* A forward exchange transaction allows the selling or the purchase of a currency at a future date and at a price fixed when the contract is concluded. This type of investment permits to eliminate the exchange risk. Moreover, no premium has to be paid upon conclusion of the contract. The main risk for the investor is the loss of profit in the event the evolution of market rates is more favorable than the evolution of exchange rates anticipated when concluding the contract.

(f) *Specific risks associated to combined transactions:* The number of possible combinations is important. Therefore, the risks involved by any particular combination cannot be described in this book. Consequently, the investor must inquire about the specific risks associated to the contemplated combination. It can nonetheless be noted that, generally, the risks associated to such combined transactions may vary when elements of this combination are sold off.

Structured Products

Structured products are combinations of two or more financial instruments, forming together a new investment product. At least one of them must be a derivative product. Structured products with capital protection are the most frequently traded. Such products can be traded either on the market or over the – counter (OTC). Due to the important number of possible combinations, each structured product has its own risks since the risks associated to each of the elements of this combination can be reduced or even eliminated or enhanced due to such a combination. Consequently, the investor must inquire about the specific risks associated to the relevant structured product. Such information is available, for instance, in the commercial brochures or form sheets describing the product.

Structured Products with Capital Protection

Characteristics

- *Two elements: Such products consist generally of two elements*: A fixed-income investment (*e.g.*, bond or money market investment) and an option or combination of options. This enables the investor to participate in the price movements of one or more underlying assets while at the same time limiting potential losses. The capital protection component may, if applicable, only cover a portion of the capital invested. Moreover, the participation and protection elements can be separated into two separate components in order to ensure the independency of the two components or even to permit to sell them separately;
- *Capital:* Fully or partially secured (upon maturity). The capital protection component determines how much of the nominal value of the structured product will be paid out to the investor, irrespective of any price movements in the option component;
- *Yield:* The option component or direct investment in a risky underlying asset determines how and to what extent the investor can benefit from price movements in the underlying. Therefore, this component determines the potential return over and above the capital protection component;
- *Flexibility:* These products can be tailored to suit the needs of each client and are adaptable to all types of underlying.

Advantages

Such products enable the investor to invest on a market while reducing the risk of losing capital which would exist if he invested directly on the same market. Returns may be higher than those of monetary or bond investments with an equivalent level of protection.

Risks

(a) *Risks at the level of the capital protection component:* The capital protection is linked to the nominal value of the product rather than its issue price or purchase price on a secondary market. Therefore, the investor benefits from a guarantee only up to the nominal value of the product with the consequence that capital protection does not necessarily mean 100 per cent repayment of the capital invested. Consequently, the protection will be reduced if the issue/purchase price is higher than the nominal value and, conversely, increases if the issue/purchase price is lower than the nominal value, in particular if the product has been purchased at a price which was different from *par* or after the original issue. The level of protection depends on the creditworthiness of the issuer. The capital is therefore protected only if the issuer of the protection can meet his obligations. The maximum loss is thus limited to the difference between the purchase price and the amount of the capital protection upon maturity. However, over the life of the product, its price can fall below the level of the capital protection amount, which increases the risk of loss in case of sale prior to expiration. Capital protection is only guaranteed for the investor if the latter holds on the product until maturity but is not ensured if early repayment is requested. Upon maturity, if the capital is not guaranteed up to 100 per cent, the investor will not be repaid the full amount originally invested.

(b) *Risks at the level of the option/direct investment component:* Depending on the evolution of prices in financial markets, this component can expire without value. The risks associated to this component are the same as the risks associated to the relevant option or option combination or direct investment used. Due to the existence of a capital protection, the investor may obtain a lower return than the return he would have obtained if he had invested directly in the underlying.

(c) *Liquidity risk:* The liquidity of the investment is usually ensured only above a certain amount, subject most of the times to a bid/offer spread and/or a penalty in case the product is not held on until maturity.

Structured Products without Capital Protection

Convertible Reverse or Discount Certificate

Characteristics

- *Term product:* The investor receives a guaranteed coupon in a given currency but accepts a risk on his capital on maturity;
- *Underlying assets:* Shares, indexes, baskets, etc;
- *Capital:* Protected if the market value of the underlying is not lower than the strike price on maturity;
- *Repayment:* In cash or by delivery of the underlying, at a strike price determined in advance, if this strike price has fallen or been exceeded. On the maturity date, if the price of the underlying asset is higher than the strike price, the investor receives the guaranteed coupon plus 100 per cent of the capital initially invested (in cash). If the price of the underlying asset is lower than the strike price, the investor receives the guaranteed coupon plus the underlying asset at the strike price;
- *Flexibility:* Such product easier to assess potential earnings.

Risks

(a) *Risks at the level of the capital:* The capital protection is not guaranteed if the investor receives the underlying asset instead of the capital invested upon maturity. The capital risk is closely linked to the evolution of the price of the underlying asset.

(b) *Liquidity risk:* The liquidity of the investment is usually ensured only above a certain amount.

(c) *Exchange rate risk:* For the products denominated in currencies other than that of the underlying asset, the investor is exposed to an additional exchange risk.

Specific Case of Certain Credit Derivative Instruments

Credit Linked Notes ('CLN')

Characteristics: An investment in a CLN can be compared to a direct investment in a floating rate note issued by the same entity.

Risks

(a) *Dual risk:* An investor in a CLN bears the credit risk of both the issuer of the CLN itself and of the underlying credit reference entity/ies. In case of a credit event, the investor receives either a debt instrument (*i.e.*, a bond or a loan) issued or guaranteed by the relevant credit reference entity or a cash settlement amount linked to the market price of such debt instrument, calculated on the basis of the relevant credit event.

(b) *Risk enhanced by the scope of the notion of 'credit event':* The term credit event is defined in broad terms and encompasses more than simply a bond default of the relevant reference entity. Indeed, this concept encompasses, for example, an extension of the repayment date of a loan or a decrease in the rate of interest payable on such loan. Therefore, the holder of a CLN can suffer a loss due to a credit event even though a traditional bond default did not occur. In other words, the probability that a credit event occurs is higher than the probability that a bond default occurs.

(c) *Scope of the risk of loss:* A credit event might result in a CLN suffering a greater loss than the average loss suffered by bonds from that same reference entity since the issuer of the CLN generally has a wider choice of the debt instruments to be delivered on a default and could choose to deliver the lowest priced debt instrument. This risk is mitigated in some structures through pre-defined recovery rates, which determine in advance for instance the loss in case of a credit event. Moreover, a higher loss may occur as a result of a delivery of a bond or loan with a duration longer than the duration of the CLN itself or in case of a valuation using such a bond/loan. However, major rating agencies are aware of these two characteristics and incorporate them into their ratings of CLNs.

Collateralized Debt Obligations (CDO)

Characteristics: Collateralized debt obligations are also structured products based on an underlying basket or portfolio of debt instruments, which can be bonds, loans and/or credit default swaps. A CDO is usually divided into several tranches providing different levels of risk exposure for the basket of underlying debt instruments. Commonly, the most junior tranche is an 'own funds' tranche and the tranches then go up in increasing seniority and correspondingly higher credit ratings.

Advantages: Through these synthetic structures the investor gains exposure to underlying credits which are not always available through direct bond investments.

Risks

(a) *Risks related to the system of tranches:* Losses on the portfolio are borne firstly by the holders of the 'own funds' tranche and subsequently by the holders of the various tranches in order of seniority. The holders of a senior tranche only incur a loss due to a relevant credit event if all the own funds and the capital of the more junior tranches have been lost. Therefore, tranches which are not 'own funds' tranches have some degree of protection against losses whereas the 'own funds' tranche and the more junior tranches represent a leveraged exposure to the fluctuations of the underlying portfolio. Credit events on a small portion of the underlying portfolio can lead to significant or total loss of the capital invested in the 'own funds' tranche and the more junior tranches.

(b) *Risks related to the long-term nature of the product:* The value of any credit derivative can vary significantly before maturity depending on factors including, for instance, the occurrence of credit events and movements of credit spreads in the portfolio. Moreover, like any debt instrument, the initial rating of any credit derivative can be upgraded or downgraded. A credit rating of a particular instrument reflects the (long-term) default risk of that instrument until it matures, and not short-term market risk. Investors in a credit derivative should generally have a long-term investment perspective and the ability to hold the product until maturity.

(c) *Risk related to the low liquidity:* Such instruments are generally illiquid even though a secondary market may exist.

Synthetic Products

Synthetic products – essentially covered options and certificates – are characterized by their identical or similar profit and loss structures when compared with specific traditional financial instruments (shares or bonds). They result from the combination of two or several financial instruments in the same product. Basket certificates, based on a specific number of selected shares, are one typical example. Synthetic products can be traded either on a market or over-the-counter (OTC). Due to the important number of possible combinations, each synthetic product has its own risks. However, generally, the risks associated to synthetic products are not always the same as the risks associated to the financial instruments they contain. Consequently, before an investment in such products, the investor must make thorough inquiries about these specific risks, for instance by consulting the product description.

Covered Options

Characteristics

- *Limited loss:* When purchasing a covered option, the investor purchases an underlying asset (share, bond or currency) and, at the same time, writes a call option on that same asset. In return, the investor is paid a premium. The latter limits his loss in case the price of the underlying falls;
- *Limited potential gain:* The potential return from any increase in the underlying asset's market value is limited to gains up to the option's strike price;
- *Collateral:* For traditional covered options, the investor must lodge the underlying asset as collateral, thus becoming a passive investor;
- *Synthetic covered options:* This type of product is based on the idea of duplicating or reproducing traditional covered options. But this duplication is achieved by means of a single transaction. Both the purchase of the underlying asset and the writing of the call option are carried out synthetically using derivatives. The purchase price of such a product is identical to that of the underlying minus the premium received for the sale of the call option. Hence, the synthetic product is sold more cheaply than its underlying;
- *Settlement*: Either cash settlement or physical delivery of the underlying are possible upon maturity: If the market value of the underlying is higher than the strike price, the investor is paid a specified cash amount as settlement. If, however, it is lower than the strike price, the investor receives physical delivery of the underlying asset.

Advantages

By writing a call option (traditional covered option) or by the return from the sale of a call option included into the product price (synthetic covered option), any loss in the price of the underlying triggers a lower loss than that which could be suffered in case of a direct investment in the underlying asset.

Risks

Unlike structured products with capital protection, synthetic covered options do not contain a hedge against losses in the market value of the underlying. Therefore, if the price of the underlying increases and that upon maturity, it is higher than the strike price of the option, the investor will receive the price originally agreed upon in the form of a cash payment. If the price of the underlying upon maturity is lower than the price contemplated by the investor when purchasing the product, the yield of such product may be lower than the return of an investment on the monetary market with the same maturity. If the price of the underlying, upon maturity, is equal or lower than the strike price of the option, the investor will receive the underlying. The potential loss that may be suffered by the investor is thus linked to a possible drop in the market value of the underlying until maturity.

The risk of loss is therefore unlimited, as if the investor had invested directly in the underlying asset. However, the premium of the option mitigates the consequences of a potential loss of profit in relation to the underlying.

Certificates

Characteristics

- *Diversification:* A certificate entitles an investor to purchase a right which is based on several underlings or has a value derived from several indicators;
- *Main types of certificates:*
  - *index certificates*: these reflect a whole market being based on an official index;
  - *region certificates*: these are derived from a series of indexes or companies from a certain region
  - *basket certificates*: these are derived from a selection of national or international companies active in the same sector (*e.g.*, biotechnology, telecoms, etc.), indexes, bonds or other underlings;
- *Guarantee:* These certificates are securitized;
- *Maturity and trading:* The maturity of these certificates usually ranges between one to three years. However, these certificates can be traded at any time;
- *Limited duration:* They are incorporated in an instrument and thus these certificates have a limited duration;
- *Investor's rights:* No voting right and no right to dividend/interests in relation to the underlying assets;
- *Repayment:* Repayment occurs upon maturity and equals:
  - a set amount per index point for an index certificate;
  - the difference between the market value upon maturity and the strike price for a region or basket certificate.

Advantages

For a minimum of capital investment, the investor can achieve diversification over a broad range of instruments or risk factors and thus mitigate the latter. This type of product offers the same potential of gains or losses than a similar direct investment in the underlying assets but, due to the diversification of the index, it is possible to limit or even eliminate the risks specific to the companies composing this index and thus to limit the risk of loss of the full amount invested. They are usually low-cost products (in particular because they have no rights to dividends/interests or voting rights vested in them).

Risks

(a) *Transfer of risk:* Investments in index, region or basket certificates basically involve the same level of potential loss as direct investments in the corresponding shares themselves. However, they offer greater risk diversification. However, this does not mean the risks are eliminated – they may simply be transposed onto the market or sector on which the certificate is based.

(b) *Absence of rights:* In contrast to direct investments, certificates do not confer any voting rights nor do they entitle the investor to payments of dividends or interests in relation to the underlying assets. Therefore, a drop in the price of the certificate cannot be counter balanced by payments of dividends or interests.

(c) *Issuer risk:* In addition to the risk of insolvency of the companies constituting the underlings of the certificate, the investor is exposed to the issuer risk, that is to say the risk of insolvency of the credit institution issuing the certificate.

(d) *Leverage risk:* Due to the leverage effect, price modifications of the value of the certificate are generally higher than the changes in the price of the underlying assets. Thus, during the lifetime of the certificate, chances of gains as well as the risks of losses are higher. The risk attached to the purchase of a certificate increases with the importance of the leverage effect of the relevant certificate. Such certificates are usually more volatile instruments than normal certificates and can lose their entire value very quickly.

DEBT *VS.* EQUITY INSTRUMENT

We already have seen the basic characteristics and risks associated with the financial instruments in the previous section. Now let's have a look on the debt and equity instruments and valuation in financial marketing.

Financial instruments can be classified by the type of claim that the holder has on the issuer. When the claim is for a fixed cash amount, the financial instrument is said to be a *debt instrument*. In contrast to a debt obligation, an *equity instrument* obligates the issuer of the financial instrument to pay the holder an amount based on earnings, if any, after the holders of debt instruments have been paid. Common stock is an example of an equity claim. A partnership share in a business is another example. Some securities fall into both categories in terms of their attributes. Preferred stock, for example, is an equity instrument that entitles the investor to receive a fixed amount. This payment is contingent, however, and due only after payments to debt instrument holders are made. Another 'combination' instrument is a convertible bond, which allows the investor to convert debt into equity under certain circumstances. Both debt instruments and preferred stock that pay fixed dollar amounts are called *fixed-income instruments*.

CHARACTERISTICS OF DEBT INSTRUMENTS

As will become apparent, there are a good number of debt instruments available to investors. Debt instruments include loans, money market instruments, bonds, mortgage-backed securities, and asset-backed securities. There are features of debt instruments that are common to all debt instruments and they are described below.

Maturity

The term to maturity of a debt obligation is the number of years over which the issuer has promised to meet the conditions of the obligation. At the maturity date, the issuer will pay off any amount of the debt obligation outstanding. The convention is to refer to the 'term to maturity' as simply its 'maturity' or 'term'. There may be provisions that allow either the issuer or holder of the debt instrument to alter the term to maturity. The market for debt instruments is classified in terms of the time remaining to its maturity. A *money market instrument* is a debt instrument which has one year or less remaining to maturity. Debt instruments with a maturity greater than one year are referred to as a *capital market debt instrument*.

Par Value

The *par value* of a bond is the amount that the issuer agrees to repay the holder of the debt instrument by the maturity date. This amount is also referred to as the *principal, face value, redemption value,* or *maturity value*. Bonds can have any par value. Because debt instruments can have a different par value, the practice is to quote the price of a debt instrument as a percentage of its par value. A value of 100 means 100 per cent of par value. So, for example, if a debt instrument has a par value of $1,000 and is selling for $900, it would be said to be selling at 90. If a debt instrument with a par value of $5,000 is selling for $5,500, it is said to be selling for 110.

Coupon Rate

The *coupon rate,* also called the *nominal rate* or the *contract rate,* is the interest rate that the issuer/borrower agrees to pay each year. The dollar amount of the payment, referred to as the *coupon interest payment* or simply *interest payment* is determined by multiplying the coupon rate by the par value of the debt instrument. For example, the interest payment for a debt instrument with a 7 per cent coupon rate and a par value of $1,000 is $70 (7% times $1,000). The frequency of interest payments varies by the type of debt instrument.

Zero-Coupon Bonds

Not all debt obligations make periodic coupon interest payments. Debt instruments that are not contracted to make periodic coupon payments are called *zero-coupon instruments*. The holder of a zero-coupon instrument realises interest income by buying it substantially below its par value. Interest then is paid at the maturity date, with the interest earned by the investor being the difference between the par value and the price paid for the debt instrument. So, for example, if an investor purchases a zero-coupon instrument for 70, the interest realised at the maturity date is 30. This is the difference between the par value (100) and the price paid (70). There are bonds that are issued as zero-coupon instruments. Moreover, in the money market there are several types of debt instruments that are issued as discount instruments. There is another type of debt obligation that does not pay interest until the maturity date. This type has contractual coupon payments, but those payments are accrued and distributed along with the maturity value at the maturity date. These instruments are called *accrued coupon instruments* or *accrual securities* or *compound interest securities*.

Floating-Rate Securities

The coupon rate on a debt instrument need not be fixed over its lifetime. *Floating-rate securities*, sometimes called *floaters* or *variable-rate securities* have coupon payments that reset periodically according to some reference rate. The typical formula for the coupon rate on the dates when the coupon rate is reset is:

Reference rate ± Quoted margin

The quoted margin is the additional amount that the issuer agrees to pay above the reference rate (if the quoted margin is positive) or the amount less than the reference rate (if the quoted margin is negative). The quoted margin is expressed in terms of *basis points* A basis point is equal to 0.001 or 0.01 per cent. Thus, 100 basis points are equal to 1 per cent.

To illustrate a coupon reset formula, suppose that the reference rate is the 1-month AB interbank offered rate (ABIBOR) and the quoted margin is 150 basis points. Then the coupon reset formula is:

1-month ABIBOR + 150 basis points

So, if 1-month ABIBOR on the coupon reset date is 5.5 per cent, the coupon rate is reset for that period at 7 per cent (5% plus 200 basis points).

The reference rate for most floating-rate securities is an interest rate or an interest rate index. There are some issues where this is not the case. Instead, the reference rate is the rate of return on some financial index. There are debt obligations whose coupon reset formula is tied to an inflation index. Typically, the coupon reset formula on floating-rate securities is such that the coupon rate increases when the reference rate increases and decreases when the reference rate decreases. There are issues whose coupon rate moves in the opposite direction from the change in the reference rate. Such issues are called *inverse floaters* or *reverse floaters*.

A floating-rate debt instrument may have a restriction on the maximum coupon rate that will be paid at a reset date. The maximum coupon rate is called a *cap*. Because a cap restricts the coupon rate from increasing, a cap is an unattractive feature for the investor. In contrast, there could be a minimum coupon rate specified for a floating-rate security. The minimum coupon rate is called a *floor*. If the coupon reset formula produces a coupon rate that is below the floor, the floor is paid instead. Thus, a floor is an attractive feature for the investor.

Provisions for Paying off Debt Instruments

The issuer/borrower of a debt instrument agrees to repay the principal by the stated maturity date. The issuer/borrower can agree to repay the entire amount borrowed in one lump sum payment at the maturity date. That is, the issuer/borrower is not required to make any principal repayments prior to the maturity date. Such bonds are said to have a *bullet maturity*. An issuer may be required to retire a specified portion of an issue each year. This is referred to as a *sinking fund requirement*.

There are loans, mortgage-backed securities, and asset-backed securities pools of loans that have a schedule of principal repayments that are made prior to the final maturity of the instrument. Such debt instruments are said to be *amortizing instruments*. There are debt instruments that have a *call provision*. This provision grants the issuer/borrower an option to retire all or part of the issue prior to the stated maturity date. Some issues specify that the issuer must retire a predetermined amount of the issue periodically. Various types of call provisions are discussed below.

Call and Refunding Provisions

A borrower generally wants the right to retire a debt instrument prior to the stated maturity date because it recognises that at some time in the future the general level of interest rates may fall sufficiently below the coupon rate so that redeeming the issue and replacing it with another debt instrument with a lower coupon rate would be economically beneficial. This right is a disadvantage to the investor since proceeds received must be reinvested at a lower interest rate. As a result, a borrower who wants to include this right as part of a debt instrument must compensate the investor when the issue is sold by offering a higher coupon rate. The right of the borrower to retire the issue prior to the stated maturity date is referred to as a 'call option'. If the borrower exercises this right, the issuer is said to 'call' the debt instrument. The price that the borrower must pay to retire the issue is referred to as the *call price*.

When a debt instrument is issued, typically the borrower may not call it for a number of years. That is, the issue is said to have a *deferred call*. The date at which the debt instrument may first be called is referred to as the *first call date*. If a bond issue does not have any protection against early call, then it is said to be a *currently callable issue*. But most new bond issues, even if currently callable, usually have some restrictions against certain types of early redemption. The most common restriction is prohibiting there funding of the bonds for a certain number of years. *Refunding* a bond issue means redeeming bonds with funds obtained through the sale of a new bond issue.

Many investors are confused by the terms non callable and nonrefundable. Call protection is much more absolute than refunding protection. While there may be certain exceptions to absolute or complete call protection in some cases, it still provides greater assurance against premature and unwanted redemption than does refunding protection.

Refunding prohibition merely prevents redemption only from certain sources of funds, namely the proceeds of other debt issues sold at a lower cost of money. The bondholder is only protected if interest rates decline and the borrower can obtain lower-cost money to pay off the debt.

Prepayments

For amortizing instruments – such as loans and securities that are backed by loans – there is a schedule of principal repayments but individual borrowers typically have the option to pay off all or part of their loan prior to the scheduled date. Any principal repayment prior to the scheduled date is called a *prepayment*. The right of borrowers to prepay is called the prepayment option. Basically, the prepayment option is the same as a call option.

Options Granted to Bondholders

There are provisions in debt instruments that give either the investor and/or the issuer an option to take some action against the other party. The most common type of embedded option is a call feature, which was discussed earlier. This option is granted to the issuer. There are two options that can be granted to the owner of the debt instrument: the right to put the issue and the right to convert the issue. A debt instrument with a *put provision* grants the investor the right to sell it back to the borrower at a specified price on designated dates. The specified price is called the *put price*. The advantage of the put provision to the investor is that if after the issuance date of the debt instrument market interest rates rise above the debt instrument's coupon rate, the investor can force the borrower to redeem the bond at the put price and then reinvest the proceeds at the prevailing higher rate. A convertible debt instrument is one that grants the investor the right to convert or exchange the debt instrument for a specified number of shares of common stock. Such a feature allows the investor to take advantage of favorable movements in the price of the borrower's common stock or equity.

VALUATION OF FINANCIAL INSTRUMENTS

Valuation is the process of determining the fair value of a financial instrument. Valuation is also referred to as 'pricing' a financial instrument. Once this process is complete, we can compare a financial instrument's computed fair value as determined by the valuation process to the price at which it is trading for in the market (*i.e.,*, the market price). Based on this comparison, an investor will be able to assess the investment merit of a financial instrument.

There are three possibilities summarized below along with their investment implications.

Market Price *vs.* Fair Value	Investment Implications
Market price equal to fair value	Financial instrument is fairly priced
Market price is less than fair value	Financial instrument is undervalued
Market price is greater than fair value	Financial instrument is overvalued

A financial instrument that is undervalued is said to be 'trading cheap' and is a candidate for purchase. If a financial instrument is overvalued, it is said to be 'trading rich'. In this case, an investor should sell the financial instrument if he or she already owns it. Or, if the financial instrument is not owned, it is possible for the investor to sell it anyway. Selling a financial instrument that is not owned is a common practice in some markets. This market practice is referred to as 'selling short'. The two reasons it is possible for an investor to sell short are.....

1. the investor must be permitted or authorized to do so; and
2. the market for the financial instrument must have a mechanism for short selling.

BORROWING FUNDS TO PURCHASE FINANCIAL INSTRUMENTS

Some investors follow a policy of borrowing a portion or all of the funds to buy financial instruments. By doing so an investor is creating *financial leverage* or simply leverage. First the principles of leverage is described and then explain how an investor can create a leveraged position in financial markets.

Principles of Leverage

The objective in leveraging is to earn a higher return on the funds borrowed than it cost to borrow those funds. The disadvantage is that if the funds borrowed earn less than the cost of the borrowed funds, then the investor would have been better off without borrowing.

Here is a simple example. Suppose an investor can invest $100,000 today in a financial instrument. The investor puts up his own funds to purchase the financial instrument and this amount is referred to as the *investor's equity*. Suppose that the financial instrument at the end of one year provides a cash payment to the investor of $5,000. Also assume that the value of the financial instrument has appreciated from $100,000 to $110,000. Thus, the investor's return is $5,000 in the form of a cash payment plus capital appreciation of $10,000 for a total of $15,000. The return this investor realised is 15 per cent on the $100,000 investment. Instead of an appreciation in price for the financial instrument, suppose its value declined to $97,000 then the investor's return would be $2,000 ($5,000 cash payment less the depreciation in the value of the financial instrument of $3,000) or a 2 per cent return.

Now let's see where leverage comes in. Suppose that our investor can borrow another $100,000 to purchase an additional amount of the financial instrument. Consequently, $200,000 is invested, $100,000 of which is the investor's equity and $100,000 of which is borrowed funds. Let's suppose that the cost of borrowing the $100,000 is 7 per cent. In the case where the financial instrument appreciated, the investor's return on equity is summarized below:

Investment in financial instrument	=	$200,000
Cash payment	=	$10,000
Values of financial instrument at end of year	=	$220,000
Appreciation in value of financial instrument	=	$20,000
Cost of borrowed funds	=	$7,000 (7% x $100,000)
Return = $10,000 + $20,000 – $7,000	=	$23,000
Return on investor's equity	=	23 per cent (= $23,000/ $100,000)

Thus the investor increased the return on equity from 15 per cent (when no funds were borrowed) to 23 per cent (when $100,000 was borrowed). The reason should be obvious. The investor borrowed $100,000 at a cost of 7 per cent and then earned on the $100,000 borrowed 15 per cent. The difference of 8 per cent between the return earned on the money borrowed and the cost of the money borrowed accrued to the benefit of the investor in terms of increasing the return on equity.

Let's try this one more time assuming that the investor borrowed $200,000 at a cost of 7 per cent and the value of the financial instruments increased. The results are summarized below:

Investment in financial instrument	=	$300,000
Cash payment	=	$15,000
Value of financial instrument at end of year	=	$330,000
Appreciation in value of financial instrument	=	$30,000
Cost of borrowed funds	=	$14,000 (7% x $200.000)
Return = $15,000 + $30,000 – $14,000	=	$31,000
Return on investor's equity	=	31 per cent (= $31.000/ $100,000)

By borrowing $200,000, the investor has increased the return on equity compared to the case of no borrowing or borrowing just $100,000.

That is the good news and occurs if the return earned on the borrowed funds exceeds the cost of borrowing. But there is a risk that this will not occur. For example, take the case where the investor borrows $100,000 but the financial instrument's value declines. Then we have the following situation:

Investment in financial instrument	=	$200,000
Cash payment	=	$10,000
Value of financial instrument at end of year	=	$194,000
Depreciation in value of financial instrument	=	$6,000
Cost of borrowed funds	=	$7,000 (7% x $100,000)
Return	=	$10,000 -6,000 - $7,000 = – $3,000
Return on investor's equity	=	-3 per cent (= -$3,000/ $100,000)

The return on investor's equity in this case is -3 per cent. This is less than the investor would have realised if no funds were borrowed (2%). The reason is that the investor earned 2 per cent on the $100,000 borrowed and had to pay 7 per cent to borrow the funds. The difference of 5 per cent between the cost of borrowing and the return on the $100,000 borrowed works against the investor in terms of reducing the return on the investor's equity. It is easy to see why the more borrowed in this scenario, the more it would have decreased the return on investor's equity.

Collateralized Borrowing in the Financial Markets

How does an investor create leverage? One obvious way is to take out a loan from a financial institution. However, there is a standard mechanism in most sectors of the financial market that allows an investor to create leverage. The investor can use the financial instrument purchased with the borrowed funds as collateral for the loan.

In the stock market, the form of collateralized borrowing is referred to as 'buying on margin'. In the bond market, there are various forms of collateralized borrowing. For individual investors, typically the mechanism is buying on margin. For institutional investors, a repurchase agreement is used. It is actually a short-term investment to the entity that wants to lend funds (hence it is called a money market instrument) and a source of funds for an investor who wants a collateralized loan. There is a specialized type of repurchase agreement in the mortgage backed securities market called a dollar roll.

DERIVATIVE MARKETS

So far we have focused on the cash market for financial instruments. With some financial instruments, the contract holder has either the obligation or the choice to buy or sell a financial instrument at some future time. The price of any such contract derives its value from the value of the underlying financial instrument, financial index, or interest rate. Consequently, these contracts are called *derivative instruments*.

The primary role of derivative instruments is to provide investors with an inexpensive way of controlling some of the major risks that will be described in this book. Unfortunately, derivative instruments are too often viewed by the general public – and sometimes regulators and legislative bodies – as vehicles for pure speculation (that is, legalized gambling). Without derivative instruments and the markets in which they trade, the financial systems throughout the world would not be as efficient or integrated as they are today.

Derivatives serve an important function of the global financial marketplace, providing end-users with opportunities to better manage financial risks associated with their business transactions. The rapid growth and increasing complexity of derivatives reflect both the increased demand from end-users for better ways to manage their financial risks and the innovative capacity of the financial services industry to respond to market demands.

Types of Derivative Instruments

The two basic types of derivative instruments are futures/forward contracts and options contracts. A *futures contract* or *forward contract* is an agreement whereby two parties agree to transact with respect to some financial instrument at a predetermined price at a specified future date. One party agrees to buy the financial instrument; the other agrees to sell the financial instrument. Both parties are obligated to perform, and neither party charges a fee.

An *option contract* gives the owner of the contract the right, but not the obligation, to buy (or sell) a financial instrument at a specified price from (or to) another party. The buyer of the contract must pay the seller a fee, which is called the *option price*. When the option grants the owner of the option the right to buy a financial instrument from the other party, the option is called a call option. If, instead, the option grants the owner of the option the right to sell a financial instrument to the other party, the option is called a put option. Derivative instruments are not limited to financial instruments. Moreover, there are other types of derivative instruments that are basically 'packages' of either forward contracts or option contracts.

FINANCIAL INTERMEDIATIONS

Perhaps the most powerful trend in today's financial world is the versatility and diversity of products, institutions, people and ideas present in the industry. It's a time when the global operating financial model is changing, with an increased number of operations conducted with a different approach at a pace that is difficult to follow. The model being created is more complex and diversified than ever before. New products, new markets and new locations all create huge opportunities for businesses. However, it is sensible to presume that the stability of current market conditions 'lies on very thin ice'. Managing such change reducing risk and ensuring consistency across hugely diverse locations and operations requires appropriate regulation and control. The presence of pertinent institutions, a reliable and up-to-date regulatory system and consequently transparency and equality among the participants of financial markets is critical to successfully achieve a sound and stable financial condition. The key for success thus, lies on the ability to cope with all the changes that are having effect appropriately.

A financial intermediary is an entity that connects surplus and deficit agents. The classic example of a financial intermediary is a bank that transforms bank deposits into bank loans. Through the process of financial intermediation, certain assets or liabilities are transformed into different assets or liabilities.

As such, financial intermediaries channel funds from people who have extra money (savers) to those who do not have enough money to carry out a desired activity (borrowers). Banks carry out the following intermediation function.

1. *Denomination Intermediation:* By accepting small amounts of savings from individuals, and by pooling those funds to make large loans, extended principally to corporations and governments that have frequent and large amount funding requirements.
2. *Default Risk Intermediation:* Banks issue safe and liquid securities, in the form of deposits to individual borrowers, and in turn make loans to riskier borrowers with the funds it has attracted, and the bank absorbs any problems with the loans while depositors continue to receive safe, uninterrupted monthly interest payments.
3. *Maturity Intermediation:* Means borrowing comparatively short-term funds from savers, who often cannot commit their funds over long periods, and making long-term loans to borrowers (corps., governments, real estate mortgages) who require long-term committed funds.
4. *Liquidity Intermediation*: Checking and saving accounts are highly liquid in such that they are convertible to cash with little risk of loss and low transaction costs for savers yet, the bank accepts illiquid direct claims from borrowers which may entail considerable risk and high transaction expenses.
5. *Information Intermediation:* Financial institutions use their skills in gathering and processing information from the financial marketplace compared to an individual borrower who may not have the expertise nor the time to determine the credit suitability of a borrower or investment. Savers delegate the task of professional management to ascertain and monitor borrowers to the financial intermediary however; conversely, they give up yield in exchange for the service.
6. *Risk Pooling/diversification Intermediation:* The intermediary invests in a wide variety of loans and assets with a corresponding wide variety of risk and returns characteristics and maturities, and through diversity obtains stability of earnings. Small investors have limited funds and cannot diversify their investments thus it relies on the intermediary to pool the funds, thus lowering risk for all savers. As the size of the bank and its operation increases, the intermediary also lower costs for all savers.

Advantages of Financial Intermediaries

There are two essential advantages from using financial intermediaries in general:

(i) *Cost advantage*: over direct lending/borrowing.
(ii) *Market failure protection*: the conflicting needs of lenders and borrowers are reconciled, preventing market failure.

The cost advantages of using financial intermediaries include:

1. Reconciling conflicting preferences of lenders and borrowers.
2. Risk aversion: intermediaries help spread out and decrease the risks.
3. Economies of scale: using financial intermediaries reduces the costs of lending and borrowing
4. Economies of scope: intermediaries concentrate on the demands of the lenders and borrowers and are able to enhance their products and services (use same inputs to produce different outputs).

FINANCIAL MARKETS

A financial market is a market where financial instruments are exchanged (*i.e.*, traded). Although the existence of a financial market is not a necessary condition for the creation and exchange of a financial instrument, in most economies financial instruments are created and subsequently traded in some type of financial market. The market in which a financial asset trades for immediate delivery is called the *spot market* or *cash market*.

Role of Financial Markets

Financial markets provide three major economic functions. *First*, the interactions of buyers and sellers in a financial market determine the price of the traded asset. Or, equivalently, they determine the required return on a financial instrument. Because the inducement for firms to acquire funds depends on the required return that investors demand, it is this feature of financial markets that signals how the funds in the financial market should be allocated among financial instruments. This is called the *price discovery process*.

Second, financial markets provide a mechanism for an investor to sell a financial instrument. Because of this feature, it is said that a financial market offers 'liquidity', an attractive feature when circumstances either force or motivate an investor to sell. If there were not liquidity, the owner would be forced to hold a financial instrument until the issuer initially contracted to make the final payment (*i.e.*, until the debt instrument matures) and an equity instrument until the firm is either voluntarily or involuntarily liquidated. While all financial markets provide some form of liquidity, the degree of liquidity is one of the factors that characterize different markets.

The *third* economic function of a financial market is that it reduces the cost of transacting. There are two costs associated with transacting: search costs and information costs. *Search costs* represent explicit costs, such as the money spent to advertise one's intention to sell or purchase a financial instrument, and implicit costs, such as the value of time spent in locating counterparty. The presence of some form of organized financial market reduces search costs. *Information costs* are costs associated with assessing the investment merits of a financial instrument, that is, the amount and the likelihood of the cash flow expected to be generated. In a price efficient market, prices reflect the aggregate information collected by all market participants.

The financial markets today encompass not only traditional banking institutions, but also many other financial entities such as insurance companies, pension funds, mutual funds, venture capital funds and stock and commodity exchanges that perform the function of financial intermediation. This development has been accompanied by the advent of market-based instruments of the stock and bond markets, financial products such as asset-backed securities, financial futures and derivative instruments. While reducing the dependence of investors on bank credit to fund their investments, these have also contributed to reallocation of risks and putting of capital to more efficient use. Financial markets also serve the need for greater financial inclusion. The recent experience from the global financial crisis, has however, shown that, despite the variety of instruments and the sophistication of the markets, they may not remain immune to crisis, if the investors/institutions do not pay adequate attention to the fundamentals or if the pricing of risk and the ratings for these instruments are not transparent, and if the regulatory oversight is poor. An efficient and healthy financial market, should therefore avoid the shortcomings as gleaned from the experience of the global financial markets. The deepening and broadening of financial markets also underscores the importance of institutional safeguards for monitoring and analyzing the domestic as well as external developments to ensure that the regulatory system is efficient and effective.

Types of Financial Markets

Different financial markets serve different types of customers or different parts of the country. Financial markets also vary depending on the maturity of the securities being traded and the types of assets used to back the securities. For these reasons it is often useful to classify markets along the following dimensions:

(i) *Physical Asset vs. Financial Asset Markets*: Physical asset markets (also called 'tangible' or 'real' asset markets) are those for products such as wheat, autos, real estate, computers, and machinery. Financial asset markets, on the other hand, deal with stocks, bonds, notes, mortgages, and other claims on real assets, as well as with derivative securities whose values are derived from changes in the prices of other assets. A share of Ford stock is a 'pure financial asset', while an option to buy Ford shares is a derivative security whose value depends on the price of Ford stock.

(ii) *Spot vs. Futures Markets*: Spot markets are markets in which assets are bought or sold for 'on-the-spot' delivery (literally, within a few days). Futures markets are markets in which participants agree today to buy or sell an asset at some future date. For example, a farmer may enter into a futures contract in which he agrees today to sell 5,000 bushels of soyabeans six months from now at a price of $5 a bushel. On the other side, an international food producer looking to buy soyabeans in the future may enter into a futures contract in which it agrees to buy soyabeans six months from now.

(iii) *Money vs. Capital Markets*: Money markets are the markets for short-term, highly liquid debt securities. The New York, London, and Tokyo money markets are among the world's largest. Capital markets are the markets for intermediate or long-term debt and corporate stocks. The New York Stock Exchange, where the stocks of the largest U.S., corporations are traded, is a prime example of a capital market. There is no hard and fast rule on this, but when describing debt markets, 'short term' generally means less than 1 year, 'intermediate term' means 1 to 10 years, and 'long-term' means more than 10 years.

(iv) *Primary vs. Secondary Markets:* Primary markets are the markets in which corporations raise new capital. If GE were to sell a new issue of common stock to raise capital, this would be a primary market transaction. The corporation selling the newly created stock receives the proceeds from the sale in a primary market transaction. Secondary markets are markets in which existing, already outstanding, securities are traded among investors. Thus, if Jenkins decided to buy 1,000 shares of GE stock, the purchase would occur in the secondary market. The New York Stock Exchange is a secondary market because it deals in outstanding, as opposed to newly issued, stocks and bonds. Secondary markets also exist for mortgages, various other types of loans, and other financial assets. The corporation whose securities are being traded is not involved in a secondary market transaction and, thus, does not receive any funds from such a sale.

(v) *Private vs. Public Markets*: Private markets, where transactions are negotiated directly between two parties, are differentiated from public markets, where standardized contracts are traded on organized exchanges. Bank loans and private debt placements with insurance companies are examples of private market transactions. Because these transactions are private, they may be structured in any manner that appeals to the two parties. By contrast, securities that are issued in public markets (for example, common stock and corporate bonds) are ultimately held by a large number of individuals. Public securities must have fairly standardized contractual features, both to appeal to a broad range of investors and also because public investors do not generally have the time and expertise to study unique, no standardized contracts. Their wide ownership also ensures that public securities are relatively liquid. Private market securities are therefore more tailor-made but less liquid, whereas publicly traded securities are more liquid but subject to greater standardization. Other classifications could be made, but this breakdown is sufficient to show that there are many types of financial markets. Also, note that the distinctions among markets are

often blurred and unimportant except as a general point of reference. For example, it makes little difference if a firm borrows for 11, 12, or 13 months, hence, whether we have a 'money' or 'capital' market transaction.

A healthy economy is dependent on efficient funds transfers from people who are net savers to firms and individuals who need capital. Without efficient transfers, the economy simply could not function: Carolina Power and Light could not raise capital, so Raleigh's citizens would have no electricity; the Johnson family would not have adequate housing; Carol Hawk would have no place to invest her savings; and so on. Obviously, the level of employment and productivity, hence our standard of living, would be much lower. Therefore, it is absolutely essential that our financial markets function efficiently – not only quickly, but also at a low cost.

MARKETING CHALLENGES FOR FINANCIAL SERVICES

Financial products and services are a particular type of good that pose special challenges to marketing. These challenges include the following:

- *Intangibility:* Financial services meet a general monetary rather than a specific tangible need. Accordingly, financial service providers must get their message across effectively and ensure an attractive image. A financial service cannot appeal to a depositor's senses, but rather provides them with an intangible benefit.
- *Inseparability:* Financial services are produced and distributed at the same time. The main concern of the marketer is therefore to provide the right service at the right place and time. This requires close proximity to customers. In addition, the packaging of the savings product is very important.
- *Limited Differentiation:* Financial services are very much alike. Reasons for choosing one provider over another are often related to convenience. This is especially true for small depositors whose demand for a savings product is often not excessively dependant on interest rates.
- *Trust:* Financial service provision involves an intimate relationship between the producer and the consumer. Thus, financial relationships are often built over a long period of time and are very sensitive to changes in mutual trust.
- *Geographic Dispersion*: Because proximity is a key factor in financial service provision, large financial institutions must offer a wide branch network, numerous sales points, or doorstep services to ensure the satisfaction of regional and local needs. Except in the case of recent high-tech developments such as internet banking, financial institutions cannot hope to serve a large customer base if they only distribute their products and services centrally.

- *Growth Balanced with Risk:* Selling financial products, particularly loan products, involves risk. Accordingly, organizational growth must be well balanced with the capacity of a financial institution to manage risk.
- *Fiduciary Responsibility:* The primary responsibility of a depository is to guard the interests of the depositors. Systems and procedures, as well as financial services, must be structured accordingly.
- *Labor Intensity:* Financial service provision is highly labor intensive. While automation, especially computerization, can effectively make transaction management more efficient, financial services, particularly savings services, remain dependent on the personal relationship between customers and the front-line staff of the institution.

MARKETING CHALLENGES FOR MICRO-FINANCE INSTITUTIONS

Micro-finance institutions (MFIs) around the world face very different market situations. Increasing competition becomes evident on the supply side when new players enter the market and on the demand side when clients begin choosing between services, demanding increased product sophistication, and requesting tailor-made products. These signs indicate developing or maturing Micro-finance markets.

Depending on the stage of the development of their markets, MFIs face different marketing challenges. Grant (1999) distinguishes three stages of Micro-finance market development that impact client characteristics.

A major challenge for MFIs is to balance their social goals with their financial goal of profitability. The corporate culture of many MFIs is based on humanitarian goals. Orienting these institutions to concentrate on client satisfaction and understanding the needs of their target markets can therefore pose a challenge. This is especially true for MFIs that began as non-governmental organizations (NGOs).

Institutional history and legal status also pose challenges to MFIs and marketing. While commercial banks that enter Micro-finance markets often have substantial marketing experience from their traditional operations, new entrants to formal financial markets may find marketing a new and low-priority task. State-owned organizations and those strongly influenced by the state may find it difficult to implement a customer-oriented approach because political and administrative decisions have dominated past activities. The state owned characteristics of MFI's clientele also significantly impact their marketing approach.

The traditional markets of most MFIs include poorer segments of the population, which are often illiterate, live in remote areas, and may be more attached to traditional and religious values. Micro savings products are likely to be geared toward a higher number of customers than traditional savings products because per-client volumes are lower. These aspects require considerable adaptations of traditional bank marketing.

Table 7.1: Stages and characteristics of clients

Stage	Client Characteristics
New Market	Customers have rarely had any contact with financial institutions and are not used to accessing formal financial products. Customers are unaware of the range of financial products that could be available.
Growth Market	Customers are becoming aware of the availability of financial services. Many customers have heard about services even if they are not yet available in their area. Customers are beginning to compare the products offered by different MFIs.
Maturing Market	Customers are increasingly sophisticated. They are aware of different institutions and different products. Individual customers may select financial services from more than one MFI. Customers may become more demanding about the quality and price of services. Customers are more apt to leave one institution for another with better products.

COMMERCIAL BANKS

BANKING: UNDERSTANDING THE BASICS

A bank is defined by Merriam-Webster's online dictionary (www.merriamwebster.com) as "an establishment for the custody, loan, exchange, or issue of money, for the extension of credit, and for facilitating the transmission of funds". While they are simple to describe, the roles of banks, bankers, and banking are – for some – not as simple to understand. 'Banking' can be defined as 'the business of banking' a vibrant business that continually evolves to meet the latest financial needs and economic conditions. In order to understand how banking evolves, it is important to gain a broad understanding of financial concepts, fundamental banking functions, and the banking business in a technology driven world.

From Barter to Payment Systems

Money is the basis of banking. And the basis of money is the need for a substitute for directly bartering for everything we need. 'Barter' is defined as trading without the use of money – and it can be traced back to the very origin of civilization. Can we imagine how our economy would operate if we didn't use money? We would either have to be completely self-sufficient or have to produce a good or service that we could trade for whatever we could not produce ourself. Most of us would spend our time making almost everything we needed (including growing food, building shelter, and making clothes) or working at a specialty that others needed so we could trade for many of the necessities of life. The specialties would be few. Our technological advances would be restricted by an incredibly inefficient system of exchanging goods and services.

The development of money was a significant advance over barter as a payment system. But today we have extended the concept of payment systems way beyond the original concept of money. One of the first steps into more sophisticated payment systems was the development of checks and checking accounts.

Money is a symbol of value, and cheques are a symbol of money. We give another person a cheque when we want to give him or her money. The other person then takes that cheque and sends it through the cheque clearing system so that the money it represents is transferred from us to him or her. It is fact, prior to the age of computers, banking employees posted transactions on individual account cards. Banks had to close for business early in the afternoon so that several hours could be devoted to recording and reconciling the day's transactions. The early computer systems used in banking seemed like a tremendous advance over manual systems. But today they seem like pocket calculators compared to the computing power that the banking industry and customers depend on and, frankly, take for granted.

Computers have changed the face and complexion of the banking business. Computers have changed how customers use banking services, how banks operate internally, and how banks interact with the rest of the financial system. Technology has revolutionized banking and continues to do so at a fiercely accelerating speed. Computers, the Internet, mobile technology, wireless access, and other improved communication systems give banking great flexibility and efficiency. All of this growth continues to create new opportunities to reinvent banks and, in particular, banking careers.

Banking also fulfills a valuable role in society by:

- Playing a key role in financial intermediation.
- Creating financial products and services that benefit businesses and consumers.
- Driving a thriving financial system regulated by state and federal governments.
- Facilitating the creation of money.
- Being involved in the transfer of funds.
- Reinventing the financial future – the future of banking.

In order to understand the business of banking, it is useful to understand one of its key elements of financial intermediation as we discussed in the previous section.

Satisfying Customers' Needs – A Service Business

While banks play a critical role in financial intermediation and in the creation of money, banking's primary focus is the satisfaction of customers' financial needs. Banking services satisfy financial needs such as:

- Earning a return on idle funds.
- Borrowing money to achieve goals.

- Preventing losses.
- Managing money conveniently and efficiently.

To be successful, banking must meet the financial needs of customers. But most customers need assistance to wade through the bewildering array of banking products and services. Many customers are not aware of all the different services available and may not have a good understanding of whether a particular service would be useful to them. Often customers are overwhelmed at the vast array of products and services. Banking professionals are the link between these products, services, and customers. Bankers act as interpreters between the banking products and services and help customers evaluate their financial needs. Bankers suggest services that meet those needs. An important part of the job of a banker is to promote banking products to customers in a sales consultant capacity, not as a cashier. In other words, bankers help customers select the right services for them rather than simply ringing up the sale.

High Tech *vs.* High Touch

Banking went through revolutionary changes when computers were introduced many years ago. Today, if we are reading this book, it is quite likely that we use a computer to connect to the Internet on a regular basis, so we are already aware of the powerful effect of electronic communication in our society. Some people would argue that technology is reducing the human element in banking ('high tech' *vs*. 'high touch'). While this is true, technology is also enriching the human interaction in banking. Technology reduces boring tasks or processing of simple transactions that aren't 'high touch' anyway. What technology is doing for the high-touch side of banking is making sure that interaction between customers and banking professionals are valuable for both sides.

Customers can use automated systems such as ATMs, online banking, wireless access, and telephone banking programmes to process transactions quickly and get basic information. When their needs extend beyond these mechanical aspects of banking, the banking professional is there to help with the real questions, such as which checking account would be lowest cost for the customer or which loan plan would best meet the customer's needs. Helping customers with these needs is also more rewarding and satisfying for most banking professionals. Over the years, various banking products have been developed as an outgrowth of the bank's role in financial intermediation. Many years ago, few types of banking products and services existed – primarily checking accounts and commercial loans provided to businesses and consumers. Over time, however, the number and variety of products and services have increased dramatically.

Banking Products and Services

Let's look at these products and services a little closer. To understand financial intermediation and the role of the bank, common bank products and services, including banking deposit accounts and various types of loans and lines of credit are defined. Also discussed various other types of accounts, such as cash management and retirement accounts.

The following categories of products and services are explained:

Deposit and transaction accounts such as:
Savings accounts
Money market accounts
Real estate loans
Credit cards
Construction loans
Other services such as:
Cash management services
Payment processing

- Checking accounts
- Certificates of deposit
- Loans and credit accounts such as
- Installment loans
- Commercial loans
- Agricultural loans
- Retirement plans
- Funds transfer services
- Debit cards

- *Deposits:* Traditional banking deposit products can be divided into four categories:
  1. Transaction accounts.
  2. Savings accounts.
  3. Certificate accounts and others.

The features of these accounts vary considerably depending on the type of account, its restrictions, and the specific policies of the bank where they are offered. A common characteristic of these accounts is deposit insurance provided by the Federal Deposit Insurance Corporation (FDIC), which allows customers to conduct day-to-day business and keep their funds in a safe place.

- *Transaction Accounts:* Transaction accounts are defined as deposit accounts on which customers can write an unlimited number of cheques. These types of account include:
  - Interest-earning checking accounts.
  - Non-interest-earning checking accounts.

Customers use transaction accounts for daily expenses because the funds are easily accessed and cheques are a widely accepted method of payment. Customers may need to maintain a minimum balance in a checking account. Due to the transactional nature of these accounts, the maintenance and processing costs of these accounts are higher than other deposit accounts. Therefore, customers may need to pay monthly and other fees to use the accounts. Also, the interest paid on interest-earning checking accounts is usually a low rate.

- *Savings Accounts:* Savings accounts are interest-earning deposit accounts that usually have few restrictions on deposits and withdrawals. Two types of savings accounts offered most frequently are regular accounts and money market deposit accounts (MMDAs). Regular savings accounts usually pay a low rate of interest and require a minimum balance. Customers often use regular savings accounts for emergency funds and to supplement the funds maintained in a checking account. Regular savings accounts are often the first account individuals open when they begin saving money beyond their daily needs. Money market deposit accounts offer higher rates of interest that usually fluctuate according to changes in interest rates offered on investments available from other sources. MMDAs require a higher minimum balance than regular savings accounts and customers can write only a limited number of checks each month. With MMDAs, customers can make deposits at any time and can make unlimited withdrawals by mail or in person; however, MMDAs are not intended to operate as a checking account. As a result, there are restrictions on the number of transfers allowed per month (electronic or check). The benefit of an MMDA is a higher rate of interest with relatively easy access to the funds. Customers may use an MMDA to hold large amounts of cash temporarily between investments. For example, a customer could receive an inheritance and place the funds in an MMDA while making decisions about how else to invest it.

- *Certificate Accounts:* The third category of deposit accounts is certificate accounts. Certificate accounts are accounts that typically require a higher minimum balance and offer higher interest rates for a fixed period of time or term. Interest rates are often fixed for the term and therefore produce a predictable return. A critical feature of certificates is a monetary penalty on early withdrawal. If the customer redeems the certificate before the end of the agreed-upon term (the maturity date), the customer must pay a penalty (at the bank's option) that is often based on the interest rate of the account (*e.g.*, an amount equal to 90 days of interest).

Certificates may be negotiable or nonnegotiable. Negotiable certificates can be sold and resold to other businesses or individuals. Nonnegotiable certificates can be presented for payment only by the original owner. In general, customers use these accounts to hold funds for long-term goals.

- *Other Types of Accounts:* Banking includes other types of deposit accounts, such as holiday club accounts or vacation club accounts, but these are often variations of the accounts just described.

Loans and Other Credit Services

Loans and other credit services are an important source of income for banks. There are two major categories of loans: *(i)* business and *(ii)* consumer. Business loans can be secured or unsecured and are primarily classified into three categories:

1. Short-term.
2. Long-term.
3. Line of credit.

Short-term business loans typically have a term of less than one year and may be used for the purposes such as purchasing inventory or for a seasonal need. Long-term business loans are made for a term longer than one year and may be used for purposes such as expanding a business or purchasing equipment. They are usually repaid from business income in installments. A line of credit is essentially a preapproved credit limit against which the business borrows.

A line of credit can be closed or open end. In a closed-end line of credit, the business borrows and repays the funds within a certain time limit. In an open-end line of credit, the business can borrow any amount up to the approved limit, make repayments, and borrow again up to the limit.

Loans can be secured or unsecured. A secured loan is one in which an asset, such as inventory or property, is pledged against repayment of the loan. For example, a secured line of credit used to purchase inventory can be secured by that same inventory. An unsecured line of credit used to purchase the inventory is not secured by the inventory; rather, the line of credit is granted primarily because of the good credit history of the business. Consumer loans can be divided into two categories: *(i)* installment credit and *(ii)* mortgage loans. Installment credit is essentially a loan or credit account on which the payments (including interest) are made at regular intervals. If the interest rate is fixed for a set term (such as a car loan) the payments are for a fixed amount, and the loan amount and interest are fully repaid by the end of the term.

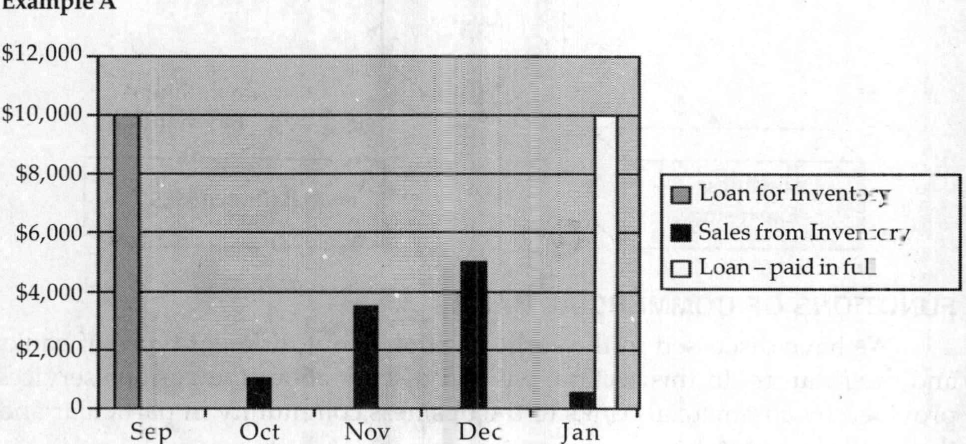

A business obtains a loan to purchase a large inventory shortly before the end-of-year holiday season. The items are sold during the season, and the loan is repaid in a lump sum

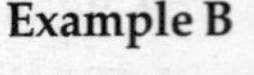
Example B

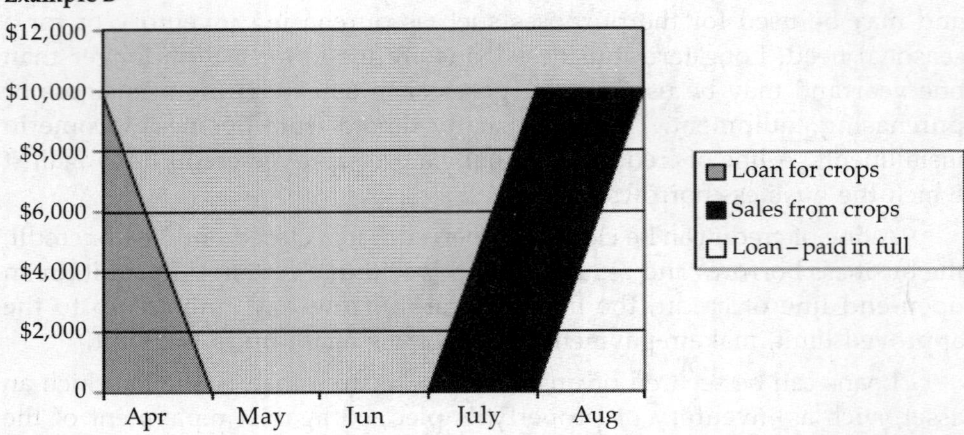

A farm obtains a loan to purchase seed and fertilizer at the beginning of the growing season. The loan is repaid when the harvested crops are sold.

Long-term Business Loans

Example A	Example B
A business has outgrown its current location and the owner needs to build an addition or a new building. The additional income generated by the expansion of the business is a source of installment payments on the loans.	A farm needs to purchase large equipment or new grain storage facilities and finance the purchase through a long-term loan.

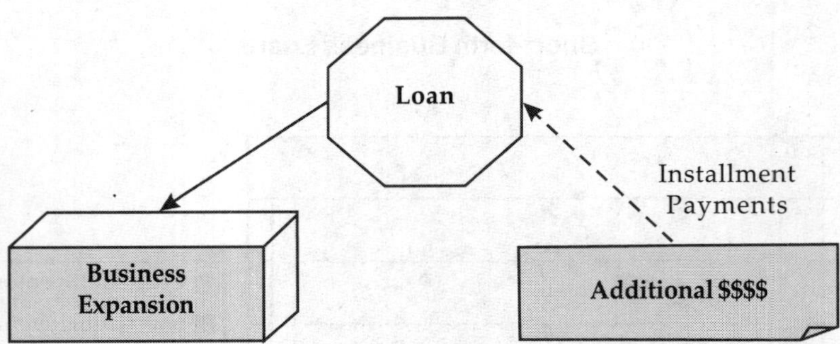

FUNCTIONS OF COMMERCIAL BANKS

We have discussed in the earlier section about different types of banks and their nature. In this section, we will discuss about the various services provided by commercial banks to the business community in particular and the public in general.

The functions of commercial banks are divided into two categories:

(i) primary functions; and

(ii) secondary functions including agency functions.

1. ***Primary Functions:*** The primary functions of a commercial bank include:
   (a) accepting deposits; and
   (b) granting loans and advances;

(a) *Accepting deposits:* The most important activity of a commercial bank is to mobilize deposits from the public. People who have surplus income and savings find it convenient to deposit the amounts with banks. Depending upon the nature of deposits, funds deposited with bank also earn interest. Thus, deposits with the bank grow along with the interest earned. If the rate of interest is higher, public are motivated to deposit more funds with the banks. There is also safety of funds deposited with the bank.

(b) *Grant of loans and advances:* The second important function of a commercial bank is to grant loans and advances. Such loans and advances are given to members of the public and to the business community at a higher rate of interest than allowed by banks on various deposit accounts. The rate of interest charged on loans and advances varies depending upon the purpose, period and the mode of repayment. The difference between the rate of interest allowed on deposits and the rate charged on the Loans is the main source of a bank's income.

(i) *Loans:* A loan is granted for a specific time period. Generally, commercial banks grant short-term loans. But term loans, that is, loan for more than a year, may also be granted. The borrower may withdraw the entire amount in lump sum or in installments. However, interest is charged on the full amount of loan. Loans are generally granted against the security of certain assets. A loan may be repaid either in lump sum or in installments.

(ii) *Advances:* An advance is a credit facility provided by the bank to its customers. It differs from loan in the sense that loans may be granted for longer period, but advances are normally granted for a short period of time. Further the purpose of granting advances is to meet the day to day requirements of business The rate of interest charged on advances varies from bank to bank. Interest is charged only on the amount withdrawn and not on the sanctioned amount.

Modes of Short-term Financial Assistance

Banks grant short-term financial assistance by way of cash credit, overdraft and bill discounting.

(a) *Cash Credit:* Cash credit is an arrangement whereby the bank allows the borrower to draw amounts up to a specified limit. The amount is credited to the account of the customer. The customer can withdraw this amount as and when he requires. Interest is charged on the amount actually withdrawn. Cash Credit is granted as per agreed terms and conditions with the customers.

(b) *Overdraft:* Overdraft is also a credit facility granted by bank. A customer who has a current account with the bank is allowed to withdraw more than the amount of credit balance in his account. It is a temporary arrangement. Overdraft facility with a specified limit is allowed either on the security of assets, or on personal security, or both.

(c) *Discounting of Bills:* Banks provide short-term finance by discounting bills that is, making payment of the amount before the due date of the bills after deducting a certain rate of discount. The party gets the funds without waiting for the date of maturity of the bills. In case any bill is dishonored on the due date, the bank can recover the amount from the customer.

2. ***Secondary Functions:*** Besides the primary functions of accepting deposits and lending money, banks perform a number of other functions which are called secondary functions. These are as follows:

   (a) Issuing letters of credit, traveler's cheques, circular notes etc.

   (b) Undertaking safe custody of valuables, important documents, and securities by providing safe deposit vaults or lockers.

   (c) Providing customers with facilities of foreign exchange.

   (d) Transferring money from one place to another; and from one branch to another branch of the bank.

   (e) Standing guarantee on behalf of its customers, for making payments for purchase of goods, machinery, vehicles etc.

   (f) Collecting and supplying business information.

   (g) Issuing demand drafts and pay orders.

   (h) Providing reports on the credit worthiness of customers.

Different Modes of Acceptance of Deposits

Banks receive money from the public by way of deposits. The following types of deposits are usually received by banks:

(i) Current deposit.

(ii) Saving deposit.

(iii) Fixed deposit.

(iv) Recurring deposit.

(v) Miscellaneous deposits.

(i) *Current deposit:* Also called 'demand deposit', current deposit can be withdrawn by the depositor at any time by cheques. Businessmen generally open current accounts with banks. Current accounts do not carry any interest as the amount deposited in these accounts is repayable on demand without any restriction. Banks usually charge a small amount known as incidental charges on current deposit accounts depending on the number of transaction.

(ii) *Savings deposit/savings bank accounts:* Savings deposit account is meant for individuals who wish to deposit small amounts out of their current income. It helps in safe guarding their future and also earning interest on the savings. A saving account can be opened with or without cheque book facility. There are restrictions on the withdrawals from this account. Savings account holders are also allowed to deposit cheques, drafts, dividend warrants, etc., drawn in their favors for collection by the bank. To open a savings account, it is necessary for the depositor to be introduced by a person having a current or savings account with the same bank.

(iii) *Fixed deposit:* The term 'Fixed deposit' means deposit repayable after the expiry of a specified period. Since it is repayable only after a fixed period of time, which is to be determined at the time of opening of the account, it is also known as time deposit. Fixed deposits are most useful for a commercial bank. Since they are repayable only after a fixed period, the bank may invest these funds more profitably by lending at higher rates of interest and for relatively longer periods. The rate of interest on fixed deposits depends upon the period of deposits. The longer the period, the higher is the rate of interest offered. The rate of interest to be allowed on fixed deposits is governed by rules laid down by the National Reserve Bank.

(iv) *Recurring deposits:* Recurring Deposits are gaining wide popularity these days. Under this type of deposit, the depositor is required to deposit a fixed amount of money every month for a specific period of time Each installment may vary from place to place like bans to banks or more per month and the period of account may also vary from 12 months to 10 years. After the completion of the specified period, the customer gets back all his deposits along with the cumulative interest accrued on the deposits.

Different Methods of Granting Loans by Banks

The basic function of a commercial bank is to make loans and advances out of the money which is received from the public by way of deposits. The loans are particularly granted to businessmen and members of the public against personal security, gold and silver and other movable and immovable assets.

Commercial bank generally lends money in the following form:

(i) Cash credit.

(ii) Loan.

(iii) Bank overdraft.

(iv) Discounting of Bills.

(i) *Cash Credit:* A cash credit is an arrangement whereby the bank agrees to lend money to the borrower up to a certain limit. The bank puts this amount of money to the credit of the borrower. The borrower draws the money as and when he needs. Interest is charged only on the amount actually drawn and not on the amount placed to the credit of borrower's account. Cash credit is generally granted on a bond of credit or certain other securities. This is a very popular method of lending.

(ii) *Loans:* A specified amount sanctioned by a bank to the customer is called a 'loan'. It is granted for a fixed period, say six months, or a year. The specified amount is put on the credit of the borrower's account. He can withdraw this amount in lump sum or can draw cheques against this sum for any amount. Interest is charged on the full amount even if the borrower does not utilise it. The rate of interest is lower on loans in comparison to cash credit. A loan is generally granted against the security of property or personal security. The loan may be repaid in lump sum or in installments. Every bank has its own procedure of granting loans. Hence a bank is at liberty to grant loan depending on its own resources. The loan can be granted as:

(a) *Demand loan:* Demand loan is repayable on demand. In other words it is repayable at short notice. The entire amount of demand loan is disbursed at one time and the borrower has to pay interest on it. The borrower can repay the loan either in lump sum (one time) or as agreed with the bank. Loans are normally granted by the bank against tangible securities.

(b) *Term loans:* Medium and long-term loans are called 'Term loans'. Term loans are granted for more than one year and repayment of such loans is spread over a longer period. The repayment is generally made in suitable installments of fixed amount. These loans are repayable over a period of 5 years and maximum up to 15 years. Term loan is required for the purpose of setting up of new business activity, renovation, modernization, expansion/extension of existing units, purchase of plant and machinery, vehicles, land for setting up a factory, construction of factory building or purchase of other immovable assets. These loans are generally secured against the mortgage of land, plant and machinery, building and other securities. The normal rate of interest charged for such loans is generally quite high.

(iii) *Bank Overdraft:* Overdraft facility is more or less similar to cash credit facility. Overdraft facility is the result of an agreement with the bank by which a current account holder is allowed to withdraw a specified amount over and above the credit balance in his/her account. It is a short-term facility. This facility is made available to current account holders who operate their account through cheques. The customer is permitted to withdraw the amount as and when he/she needs it and to repay it through deposits in his account as and when it is convenient to him/her. Overdraft facility is generally granted by bank on the basis of a written request by the customer. Sometimes, banks also insist on either a promissory note from the borrower or personal security to ensure safety of funds. Interest is charged on actual amount withdrawn by the customer. The interest rate on overdraft is higher than that of the rate on loan.

(iv) *Discounting of Bills:* Apart from granting cash credit, loans and overdraft, banks also grant financial assistance to customers by discounting bills of exchange. Banks purchase the bills at face value minus interest at current rate of interest for the period of the bill. This is known as 'discounting of bills'. Bills of exchange are negotiable instruments and enable the debtors to discharge their obligations towards their creditors. Such bills of exchange arise out of commercial transactions both in internal trade and external trade. By discounting these bills before they are due for a nominal amount the banks help the business community. Of course, the banks recover the full amount of these bills from the persons liable to make payment.

Agency and General Utility Services provided by Commercial Banks

Besides the primary activities, commercial banks also render a number of ancillary services. These services supplement the main activities of the banks. They are essentially non-banking in nature and broadly fall under two categories:

(i) Agency services, and

(ii) General utility services.

(i) *Agency Services:* Agency services are those services which are rendered by commercial banks as agents of their customers. They include:

(a) Collection and payment of cheques and bills on behalf of the customers,

(b) Collection of dividends, interest and rent, etc., on behalf of customers, if so instructed by them,

(c) Purchase and sale of shares and securities on behalf of customers,

(d) Payment of rent, interest, insurance premium, subscriptions etc., on behalf of customers, if so instructed,

(e) Acting as a trustee or executor,

(f) Acting as an agents or correspondents on behalf of customers for other banks and financial institutions at home and abroad.

(ii) *General Utility Services:* General utility services are those services which are rendered by commercial banks not only to the customers but also to the general public. These are available to the public on payment of a fee or charge. They include:

(a) Issuing letters of credit and travelers' cheques,

(b) Underwriting of shares, debentures, etc.,

(c) Safe-keeping of valuables in safe deposit locker,

(*d*) Underwriting loans floated by government and public bodies,
(*e*) Supplying trade information and statistical data useful to customers,
(*f*) Acting as a referee regarding the financial status of customers,
(*g*) Undertaking foreign exchange business.

ACCESSING AND MANAGING AGRICULTURAL FUNDS

There are different ways to categorise the various funds financial intermediaries use for lending or for other banking activities (Table 7.2): We can distinguish funds by sources (creditors and owners), by conditions (*e.g.*, interest rates, maturity) and by procedures of mobilization (internal or external, deposited or borrowed).

Table 7.2: Categorisation of funds use for lending

1. *Sources*	International development agencies, national government, central bank, depositors, shareholders etc.
2. *Conditions*	Commercial or concessionary, voluntary or compulsory deposited, long-term or short-term, fixed interest rate or variable rate
3. *Procedures*	Outside or self-financing, actively borrowed or from deposits

Each loanable fund appears on the *liabilities and equity* side of the balance sheet as a separate entry. In annual reports of financial institutions they are usually amalgamated to blocks of deposits, borrowings, debt instruments and equity. *Deposits* are funds left with a financial institution for safekeeping or to earn interest. The depositor rather than the borrowing institution takes the initiative to place the fund. Similar to deposits, *trust funds* are left with a financial institution with certain purposes and procedures defined by the creditor (usually the government or an international donor agency). *Borrowings* are funds voluntarily raised by financial institutions. Unlike in the case with deposits, it is the financial institution, which takes the initiative to mobilize these funds. *Debt instruments* are written documents (bills, bonds, debentures etc.) used to raise funds. Bonds for instance are usually in form of fixed interest securities and sold against public loans or mortgages. Debentures are unsecured promises to pay. *Equity*, also called net value or net worth, is total assets less total liabilities and comprises paid in capital, retained earnings and reserves. Main output of financial intermediation is the loan portfolio. The asset side of the balance sheet provides information regarding the use of all funds.

Balance sheets, however, do not disclose full information on origin and conditions of funds. Table 7.3 summarizes the main creditors (first column) and the categories under which their funds may appear in the balance sheet of financial institutions (first row). The second row distinguishes them by selected conditions. In this way we obtain a comprehensive image of all possible funds various financial institutions use for agricultural lending.

Table 7.3: Simplified balance sheet of financial institutions

Assets	Liabilities and Equity
Cash Reserves in central bank Loan portfolio Bills, bonds etc. Investments	Deposits • Current accounts • Savings accounts • Time deposits • Compulsory deposits • Trust funds
	Borrowings • Commercial loans • Government loans • Central bank loans • Donor loans
Land, building, equipment etc. Total assets	Debt instruments (debentures, bonds) Equity • Paid-in capital • Reserves • Retained earnings Total liabilities and equity

Table 7.4: Sources and features of agricultural lending

Founds for agricultural lending – Sources and features							
Founds Creditors	Borrowings		Deposits		Trust Founds	Debt Instru-ments	Equity
	Com-merical	Conces-sionary	Volun-tary	Compul-sory			
Donors		A			B		C
Government		D		I	E		F
Central bank		G					
Savers			L	K		O	
Banks	M			H			
Fin. markets						N	P
Self-finance							R

(A) Credit lines of development agencies.
(B) Donor trust funds (*e.g.*, revolving funds).
(C) Technical and financial aid (grants, risk capital).
(D) Government credit lines.
(E) Government trust funds.
(F) Operational subsidies and equity grants.
(G) Central bank credit lines.

(H) Compulsory funds from other banks.
(I) Accounts of state-owned entities.
(K) Compulsory deposits from loan clients.
(L) Deposits from the general public.
(M) Inter-banking loans.
(N) Debentures (unsecured or bonds).
(O) Negotiable Certificates of Deposits.
(P) Share capital.
(R) Retained earnings, reserves and paid in capital.

It has to be underlined that only resources that increase the total balance are considered loanable funds. Cash received by selling assets such as bills, securities or property or loan repayments do not enlarge the balance total and are therefore excluded. In practice, changes of the asset structure are common activities of managing liquidity. In this sense, central bank rediscount is not part of the analysis of the various sources of funds. Rediscount is usually a means of liquefying assets but not of enlarging liabilities.

OUTSIDE AND SELF FINANCING

- *Outside Financing:* Financial institutions can raise their funds *externally* (outside financing) or *internally* (self-financing). However, unlike manufacturing or commercial enterprises, financial institutions are basically financed by outside funds. Main sources of external funds are individual savers, other banks, insurance companies and large-scale enterprises, national governments, international donor agencies, central banks and local or international capital and money markets. Usually savings deposits are the most significant part of total liabilities. In some publications savers are classified as internal sources of funds. This classification might be justified in savings and credit co-operatives where savers are also shareholders/owners of the enterprise. However, even co-operatives differentiate between savings accounts and share accounts. When computing the capital adequacy of mutually owned institutions, savings are not classified as equity.
- *Direct and Indirect Self-financing:* Since the paid-in capital is usually limited, outside financing is the dominant instrument in practice. However, in addition to a *direct* increase of equity through new share issues or new co-operative members, retained earnings constitute a significant part of the self-financing capacity. Retained earnings are built up by the yearly net profit after taxes. Therefore, each income or subsidy financial institutions accumulate leads *indirectly* to a broader base of loanable funds.

Schreiner (1997) classifies six different forms of subsidies potentially obtainable by financial institutions. They all increase net worth – in other words they enlarge the equity basis of the firm. Since, in particular, public financial institutions in many cases receive multiple subsidies, their retained earnings are inflated.

Exhibit 7.1: Financing of Financial Institutions

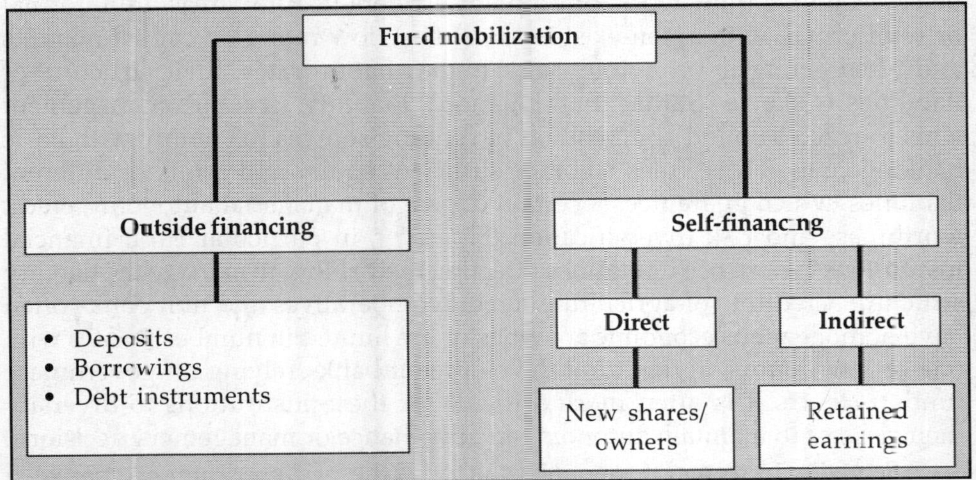

CHALLENGES OF RESOURCE MANAGEMENT

Each financial institution faces several challenges regarding its management of financial inputs and outputs. We can distinguish four specific areas of *asset-liability management*:

1. Availability and composition of funds (liability structure management).
2. Interest margin/spread (interest rate risk management).
3. Foreign exchange risk management.
4. Liquidity risk management.

Default or credit risk management and related activities (like hedging or asset diversification) are basically output oriented management tasks. However, decision making in the field of resource mobilization is strongly linked to the financial institution's output side. The liability structure of banks determines the asset allocation and vice versa. This general statement applies above all to financial institutions operating in a hostile macroeconomic environment as well as to institutions in their first stage of evolution (like most lenders in rural areas). In terms of the four generic fields of asset-liability management, emphasis will be placed on the specific problems of mobilizing and operating.

Firstly, the availability of funds and thereby the composition of funds within a lending institution involved in agriculture depends a lot on the type of lender. Usually the spectrum of possible funds increases with the lender's grade of formality. Chartered financial institutions ruled by banking law are able to mobilize all kinds of funds (deposits, commercial borrowings, debentures and equity), although not automatically at favourable conditions. At the bottom end are informal lenders (individual and self-help groups) who are faced with many restrictions regarding access to deposits, commercial borrowings and debt instruments. Other decisive factors regarding access to certain funds are the performance of a financial institution and the macroeconomic framework. Since many lenders in rural areas are informal or semiformal, with a non-existent or, at best, low rating on capital markets and often acting in economies with high inflation rates, their structure of liabilities is skewed rather than balanced. Liability structure management aims to reach a sound composition of funding sources to comply with basic banking rules. These rules embrace sufficient equity and a mix of different liabilities, which guarantees a certain degree of managerial autonomy, credit worthiness and risk diversification. However, in particular rural financial institutions experience limitations affecting their ability to manage the liability structure. Creditors of agricultural credit co-operatives and unit banks often have homogeneous economic activities or are limited in number (NGOs with one or few donors, agricultural development banks relying on government funds). Hence, it is often more difficult for these institutions to diversify their risks or to maintain autonomy in governance or management decisions.

Secondly, in terms of the *interest margin* (the pricing difference between interest earning assets and interest paying liabilities) institutions lending to agriculture are faced with interest rate risks. In many developing countries margins for agricultural lending are set by governments, which impose ceilings on deposit and loan rates. Agriculture is a politically sensitive sector. These externally defined ceilings are all too liable to inadequate adjustment under changing economic conditions. Moreover, a long-term loan portfolio has to be refinanced several times, if no long-term funds are available that match exactly the term structure of the outstanding loans. However, the interest rates of funds in future refinancing periods are unknown. Therefore, long-term loans expose financial institutions to higher risks than a loan portfolio characterized by short-terms and a high turnover.

Thirdly, the foreign exchange risk is associated with international borrowings. Many NGOs and agricultural development banks raise offshore funds for local lending. This bears a high currency risk and may turn even concessionary loans into a heavy burden.

Fourthly, the liquidity risk management of institutions lending for agricultural purposes needs to be more sophisticated than when lending to commerce or to diversified urban economic activities. Agricultural production and investments require customized loan products with longer terms and adapted conditions. Cash flow patterns of farm households usually differ from urban or peri-urban enterprises. This does not apply to every rural household since many try to diversify their sources of income flows through off-farm activities or salary earning. Moreover, some types of livestock production realise a steady flow of income, making these ventures more flexible than crop production. However, investments in horticulture, plantations, irrigation, and land purchase are long-term and cannot be financed by short-term credit. Crop production has a clear seasonal cash flow pattern and requires special loan repayment terms.

Financial institutions involved in agricultural lending have to address these specific requirements. They have to arrange their liability structure or/and the internal liquidity management in order to solve the problem of unmatched maturities of funds and loans. Both tasks are difficult. Many financial institutions, especially unit banks and informal institutions in rural areas are not able to mobilize sufficient long-term funds. Government or donor funding is in many cases unpredictable. Reliance on offering higher interest on term deposits may also not elicit sufficient response from savers who prefer short-term savings products. Moreover, the capabilities of managing liquidity risks are still under developed in many financial institutions, due to inadequate management information systems or weak banking skills. The table 7.5 summarizes the challenges of fund mobilization and management of institutions which are involved or want to get involved in agricultural lending.

Table 7.5: Challenges of fund mobilization for agricultural lending

Asset-liability management goals	Challenges of fund mobilization for agricultural lending
Sound liability structure (*e.g.*, sufficient equity, appropriate mix of creditors, compliance with banking laws and standards)	• No or limited access of informal and semi-formal lenders to various type of funds (*e.g.*, savings deposits, debentures). • Dominance of one creditor or homogeneous creditors (*e.g.*, in the case of agricultural banks, credit co-operatives). • Deposits in rural financial markets are less interest rate sensitive and costly to raise.
Low exposure to interest rate risks	• State interventions in interest rate policy for deposits and agricultural loans. • High refinance risks of long-term loans. • Limited access to fixed interest liabilities bonds, time deposits).
Low exposure to foreign exchange risks	• High percentage of off-shore funds but no or only low percentage of assets in foreign currency.
Low exposure to liquidity risks	• High demand for long-term credit, but limited access to long-term funds. • Need for sophisticated liquidity management. • Higher risks of massive deposit withdrawals after crop failure, animal diseases, etc. • Refinance risks due to withdrawal or cut of public funds.

CHANGING PARADIGM AND POLICY OBJECTIVES: PRACTICAL REVIEW IN RURAL FINANCE

Since the mid 1980s, there has been a paradigm shift in financial policy (including rural finance) in the world from subsidized credit to financial systems development. The old paradigm of sector-directed, supply-led and subsidized credit has been based on faulty assumptions about the willingness and ability of poor farmers and other entrepreneurs to pay for financial services, which led to faulty policy design and implementation.

The new paradigm departs not from the need, but from the demand (*i.e.,* willingness and ability to pay market prices) for savings, credit and insurance services by farmers and other entrepreneurs. Instead it focuses on building sustainable financial institutions and systems, and introduced the operational policy objective of financial sustainability of MFIs. The new paradigm recognises that high transaction costs and risks that partly result from information asymmetries and moral hazard problems for both financial intermediaries and clients are some of the root causes of the gap between demand and supply. Therefore, the new paradigm places emphasis on searching for technological and institutional innovations (including suitable governance and incentive structures) to reduce the costs and risks of financial intermediation. The new paradigm recognises the possibility of market as well as government failure (*i.e.,* institutional failure in general), and negates the thesis put forward by proponents of market liberalization that a 'financial system which is not repressed would by itself function optimally'. The new paradigm in contrast sees financial market liberalization (*e.g.,* with respect to interest rate formation) as a necessary but not sufficient condition for deepening financial systems. Moreover, as the required technological and institutional innovations needed to deepen the financial system and to serve poorer segments of the population can be readily copied by for-profit financial institutions, the resulting free-rider problem prevents the private sector from sufficiently investing (compared to socially optimal levels) in such innovations. In conclusion, public investment in pro-poor (and pro-rural) financial innovation is required.

Learning from Informal Demand and Supply

At first glance, many might be tempted to say that the poor, earning incomes of less than a dollar per day, are neither credit worthy nor are they able to save; nor can they pay for insurance against any of the risks they face. That these common assumptions are wholly unfounded has been demonstrated time and again by empirical research on informal financial markets and the risk-coping behaviour of households. During the past fifteen years, these myths should have been laid to rest by the recognition of an increasing number of successful institutional innovations that provide savings, credit and insurance services to poor women and men in developing countries who were previously thought of being unbendable and uninsurable. False assumptions about the demand for financial services by poor households and smallholder farmers were one of the major reasons why the old paradigm of directed, subsidized credit was accepted for so long. Most financial policy until the end of the 1980s and even today has been based on these faulty premises, leading to well-meant, but inefficient and costly policies with negligible outreach to smallholder farmers and rural dwellers. Past policy neglected to provide savings and insurance services (which are especially relevant for poorer clientele), and much, if not all of the emphasis was put on 'giving and forgiving' loans in great numbers. The old paradigm ignored the fact that by using informal contracts 'many of the poor borrow, save, and all insure'. The old paradigm ignored this ranking of importance. The ranking actually gets more pronounced with increased levels of poverty, female head of household, higher risk aversion, and greater exposure to food insecurity and other risks Most, if not all so-called credit projects quickly degenerated into transitory income transfer programmes with doubtful coverage of the poor, but with never-ending need for injecting public resources to keep state-driven banks and savings and credit co-operatives from collapsing. Faulty perceptions about the clientele and its demand serve as excuses for inaction or lead to policy recipes promoting ill-adapted services, institutions and market structures

- *Lending among Relatives, Neighbors, and Friends:* Borrowing from socially close lenders within the moral economy is often the first recourse that poor households have in financing expenses, especially those related to essential consumption expenditures. Transactions are collateral-free and in most cases interest is not charged. These are essentially informal mutual aid schemes that have the principle of reciprocity at the core of transactions. Hence, both the lender (deposit-taker, or insurance provider) and the client gain from the transaction, and the process is self-sustaining.

The borrower is able to finance urgently needed expenditures quickly and with few transactions costs: a lengthy appraisal process does not exist, little or no paperwork or travel time is involved, and the terms of the transactions are well understood. The lender gains a right to reciprocity in that she or he can lay claim to in the future. Furthermore, the risk of loan recovery is at a minimum since the lender only lends to persons who are part of her or his social network, within which contracts can be enforced. For each partner, therefore, the long-term gains associated with maintaining borrowing privileges is greater than the short-term gain of reneging on the payback.

- *The Rotating Saving and Credit Associations (ROSCAs):* Found in many countries are also network-based. These associations, which may even operate under a designated, sometimes remunerated manager, pool savings from members each period and rotate the resulting pot among them using various rules. The process is repeated until the last member receives the pot. Because of the rotation rules, these schemes are less suited to address household risk unless the timing of the receipt coincides with unexpected events. Other ROSCAs auction the fund. Still some others allow the fund to be paid out earlier in times of crisis of one of its members, at times requiring a premium payment. Also, unlike demand deposits, once the saving is committed, it cannot be withdrawn immediately and the member is required to wait his/her turn. The main purpose of a ROSCA is to accumulate savings and channel this to borrowers in some pre-specified order, thereby fulfilling an important intermediation function. Informal financial self-help groups exist in many countries, and have inspired to some extent the innovations in solidarity group lending as well as linkage banking.

- *Informal Moneylenders and Pawnbrokers:* Typically, they are approached when the amount demanded (*e.g.*, loan amount and its timing, sometimes need for confidentiality) cannot be fulfilled by socially close lenders, such as friends, neighbors, or ROSCAs. Moneylenders charge explicit interest rates in order to obtain real positive returns on their capital. In fact, interest rates are usually high, and real rates in the range of 5-10 per cent per month are common. Typically, moneylenders lend only to households about whom they possess enough information. However, they may also lend to others about whom they possess less information if punitive actions against those that default are feasible. Lending may be either secured by physical collateral (*e.g.*, land, movable property such as gold and jewelry, or by production assets such as animals and standing crops), or by social collateral, such as third-party guarantees or loss of reputation in one's social network. These collateral substitutes are effective in sustaining the informal lending business because contract enforcement is legitimized by social norms. Member-based institutions, such as village banks, groups, and savings and credit co-operatives have a comparative advantage over socially distant banks in using social capital for the enforcement of their contracts. Also, deposit-taking institutions have a comparative advantage in using informal enforcement mechanisms compared to institutions that lend 'cold' money.
- *Tied Credit:* Informal, but socially and/or spatially distant lenders frequently tie their loans to complementary transactions in land, labor or commodities as they lack adequate information about the creditworthiness of the borrower or suitable physical or social collateral. Thus, traders disburse input and consumption credit to farmers in exchange for the right to market the growing crop; shopkeepers increase sales by providing credit for food, farm inputs, and household necessities; and landowners secure access to laborers to whom they lent in the hungry season. The important feature of these types of transactions is that the lender also deals with the borrower in a non-lending capacity and is able to use this position to screen applicants and enforce contracts at relatively low transaction costs compared to a pure money-lending contract. In the complementary non-financial contract, the lender often exercises near-monopoly power (such as often occurs

between landlord and tenant or employer and laborer) that may feature usurious, *i.e.*, monopolistically priced interest rates. Tied credit has frequently been used by state owned marketing boards that monopolize agricultural input supply and output marketing. It is also used by agribusiness processing firms that control critical bottlenecks in the production or marketing of agricultural and often perishable products. However, the deregulation and liberalization of agricultural markets has reduced the scope of using tied contracts as collateral substitute in rural lending.

These four informal institutions provide valuable financial services, and much may be learned from them. However, they should not be romanticized. Lending among family members and friends as well as ROSCAs may bear a high risk for poor people, for example with respect to default or social exclusion. Information tends to be segmented and to circulate within specific groups or networks excluding others. Communities can be driven by vested interests of the local elite. Moreover, *all of the above institutions have serious limitations with respect to term and size transformation, liquidity, and risk diversification* because they are based on personal relationships and reciprocity and deal in socially, culturally, economically or geographically limited sectors.

THE TRIANGLE OF MICRO-FINANCE: FINANCIAL SUSTAINABILITY, OUTREACH, AND WELFARE IMPACT

Internationally agreed principal objectives of development cooperation are the United Nations' Millennium Development Goals (MDGs). These set targets to reduce poverty and make improvements in the various dimensions of poverty (or welfare) such as education, health, nutrition and women's empowerment. Following the concept of a logical framework, (financial) sector policy objectives need therefore to be consistent with these principal objectives. Micro-finance as well as rural financial policy has to be evaluated against three objectives: *financial sustainability, breadth and depth of outreach, and the welfare impact.*

Financial sector policy can support the Millennium Development Goals (and thus poverty reduction) in two ways:

- *Indirectly,* through supporting a sustainable financial system as a precondition for economic and social development. This indirect pathway includes causal chains that can be summarized under the thesis of *poverty reduction through economic growth.* An example of one of these causal chains is that owners of wealthier enterprises who use the financial services create additional demand for goods and services of the poor thus increasing their income.
- *Directly,* by increasing the access of poor people to financial services.

Within this direct pathway, distinguishes three sub pathways of how access to financial services can influence the poor's income generation and consumption stabilization.

Governments and donors may differ in their perceptions about the relative effectiveness and efficiency of the two pathways. Indeed, which one may receive more emphasis has to necessarily vary with country - specific conditions. It follows that governments and donors also differ in their relative emphasis on the three objectives in micro and rural finance, *i.e.,* financial sustainability, depth of outreach, and welfare impact. This, of course, influences their view on the relative efficiency of different types of financial institutions, and thereby influences how financial policies are designed in practice and how the institutional landscape evolves. Because of market imperfections, the state has a legitimate role for investing in financial systems development.

8

Regulatory and Policy Issues

A policy can be best described as a framework or strategy, giving a broad outline of the direction and overall strategy for the development of a particular sector. It is formulated by central government, from within a particular ministry to regulate the performance of individual sectors. In this chapter we will discuss the policy framework of credit and finance policy that affecting the formulation of agricultural and rural finance; regulation of financial markets; money markets and monetary policy; principles for responsible lending; and micro-finance policy.

POLICY FRAMEWORK

Policies often focus on creating a strategy which will arrest the decline of a specific sector or redress the imbalances which have occurred as a result of market forces. It is usually possible to identify a number of different functional sectors which normally correspond with the division of the government into ministries or departments. However, the formulation or re-definition of an effective policy for rural finance does not refer to a single sector, but rather to three main policy spheres which are closely interconnected and include the prevailing macroeconomic parameters, the agricultural sector and the financial sector. Moreover, during rural finance policy analysis and formulation, international and regional trade should be considered in view of the current increasing globalization of the world economy.

All three policy areas have their own impact on the effective provision of financial services. Generation of an effective agricultural and rural finance policy depends on the definition of a clear overall rural finance policy framework and strategy. Tensions and contradictions do occur between each of these policy areas, which need to be debated and addressed through effective and continuous policy dialogue.

FIELDS AFFECTING THE FORMULATION OF AGRICULTURAL AND RURAL FINANCE POLICY

The existence of a favorable and stable macroeconomic environment is imperative for the development of a country's economy.

Macroeconomic Environment

The macroeconomic policy conditions and legal framework that exist in a developing country can either enhance or impede the development of agriculture and the financial sector. Governments and donor agencies presently acknowledge the necessity of an enabling environment for private sector development, but all too often in the past they have supported direct government interventions and supply-led credit programmes to achieve short-term social equity objectives, which in most cases have performed poorly through inefficient management and political interference.

The sequencing of structural adjustment measures in a liberalized market environment has strong implications for the development of both the agricultural and financial sector. In the standard model of structural adjustment, demand management stabilization measures should precede conventional structural production adjustment measures. More specifically they argue that domestic financial markets must be liberalized before product markets are reformed, otherwise limited access to effective financial services will hamper the performance of scheduled privatization programmes. Inefficiencies in the financial sector, if not addressed and corrected in time, will arrest, in this case, the development of the non-financial sectors.

Appropriate government policy support measures that facilitate the role of the private sector, and in particular, provide favorable investment opportunities for small-scale farmers, should recognise the interdependence of the financial and non-financial sectors. While measures to create a favorable policy environment for agricultural and rural finance are necessary, they may not be sufficient in themselves. Development of rural financial markets requires a supportive legal and regulatory framework, and direct interventions may be needed to accelerate the building of robust rural financial markets.

Formulating appropriate prudential banking laws, financial contract laws and procedures for the effective enforcement of these contracts are important areas for policy interventions in developing countries and countries in transition, in view of the recent changes in the macroeconomic environment as a result of liberalization and globalization. Financial institutions cannot depend solely on agricultural lending, which faces high risks; indeed the trend is to restructure agricultural banks into universal rural banks. The banking legislation should specify the contractual form for agricultural loans and strengthen their enforcement mechanisms.

Agricultural Sector Policy

Governments must sincerely work for the removal of pricing and supply distortions in agricultural products so that activities supported by credit may be sufficiently remunerative for small farmers.

The crucial issue in agricultural sector policy is the profitability of farming. As long as this remains low, then lending for agricultural production will be risky. It is important that the agricultural sector becomes as profitable as other sectors if it is to attract funds for viable investments. While no simple solution exists, the formulation of effective policies for agricultural sector development is imperative. Appropriate macroeconomic policies and the provision of essential rural infrastructure and support services such as roads, markets, agricultural research and extension are crucial to making farming more profitable in developing countries and countries in transition. Favorable agricultural policies create an environment in which private financial institutions are willing to service farmers. Governments should avoid undue taxation of agriculture. Instead, policy-makers should liberalize agricultural trade and product prices, thus making on-farm investments more profitable and attractive, as well as benefitting the national economy. While accessible credit and deposit facilities may help poor rural people to smooth their production and consumption needs, there may be limited opportunities for farmers and micro entrepreneurs to use these facilities productively, unless accompanied by a broader set of non-financial support services and investments in rural infrastructure.

Financial Sector Policy

Rural financial reforms should be a vital part of financial sector reform. The challenge is to promote a variety of viable financial institutions that are client oriented, that mobilize deposits efficiently, and that provide access to loans to a broad spectrum of farmers, agribusiness entrepreneurs and other rural clients. Policies should facilitate the experimentation and adoption of new financial technologies and development of attractive financial products. In all cases, government should be guided by the principle that any intervention should only be directed to improving the workings of financial markets (Stiglitz, 1994).

The new financial market approach does not ignore the important role of government in reducing risks and increasing confidence, by improving information and providing incentives to improve the performance of financial intermediaries. In particular, the government has specific powers regarding taxation, subsidization, regulation and enforcement that can influence the direction of desired developments. Successful financial intermediation, in particular, is dependent upon transparency and accountability. Financial institutions should have updated and accurate information systems in place, that are readily available not only to management and bank supervisors but also to policy-makers, to assist them in policy revision for improved delivery of agricultural and rural financial services

REGULATION OF FINANCIAL MARKETS

Financial markets are organizational frameworks within which financial instruments can be bought or sold. They are critical for the successful allocation of capital among lenders and borrowers and are in consequence indispensable for the well-being of these days society. Regulation of financial market is tightly related to the confidence investors have in financial markets and therefore, it is key to their performance.

(a) *Changes in Financial Markets:* Now-a-days, banks and other financial institutions are involved in many different activities, offering diversified products to all types of customers and engaging in complex and new transactions. Companies are increasingly raising capital through private deals, as opposed to public equity like the sale of stocks or bonds. This tendency makes it harder for regulators to ensure a 'true and fair view'. Also, the lending of funds is more and more being devised from outside the regulated banking industry by bigger institutions like hedge funds which are only indirectly supervised. The complexity of instruments and operations is a concern to financial stability. A new approach towards the regulatory system is crucial to avoid a potential crisis and possible solutions will be discussed shortly.

(b) *Internationalization and Globalization Effect on Regulatory Frameworks:* Cross-border financial transactions reflect a trend that is increasingly overtaking the way businesses and financial institutions exercise their operations. The globalization of markets is not to be overlooked when designing a regulatory system. Local events, which used to affect only their surrounding areas, now have the ability to disrupt the whole international financial system. The collapse of one important financial institution or company could cause severe losses in other countries. There is therefore, an important need for global standards in terms of corporate governance, auditing and accounting. In the recent past, a different approach across countries to all these issues made it difficult to converge into global standards. Now-a-days, and especially after the recent scandals that have proven that regulation is not working as it should, global standards appear to be indispensable to maintain cross-border capital flows. Consistency in the way transactions are treated and recorded is essential to compare the performance of an organization either through time of with the performance of other organization in a different location. Different groups of users look for different information. Hence, financial reports need to include all the information that is relevant for each group. The disclosure of high-quality and standardized information which also needs to be 'comparable', 'reliable', 'consistent' and 'transparent' should be a priority for regulators. To safeguard a growing financial international market, a more flexible approach towards regulation, without decreasing its strength, is required.

(c) *Forms of Regulation:* The argument for more regulation is twofold. Some argue that regulation is unnecessary, "in a market-based economy, competitive forces will ensure that those providing information will meet the needs of users". On one hand, one could say that if people do not want to accept the shortcomings of risk, they should not invest in risky businesses. "After all, if rich sophisticated investors want to lose their money by placing it with some mathematical whiz kids who think markets mimic their models, why should regulators intervene?". However a second argument makes the stronger case for regulation. Furthermore, there are a growing number of people who are exposed to these institutions either directly or indirectly *e.g.*, through pension funds. So, the power in the hands of financial institutions implies that the public has an interest in regulators controlling their actions.

(d) *Innovations and Policies to Consider:* There are many several positions as to what should be done to prevent a possible financial crisis due to the lack or misuse of regulatory tools. Some argue that large institutions are the ones that need to be supervised and there is no need to bring institutions like hedge funds under the regulatory umbrella. Others discuss that this type of organizations should be supervised through specific types of institutions such as self regulatory organizations, which are typically run by primary brokers who are close to the market and so, they can keep regulators informed. Also, because many times their money is also at risk (as they are market practitioners), they have a special interest in the appropriate performance of the markets and their participants. "Self-regulation might be better than public regulation and supervision, because norms can be set by those with experience in the business, and can be monitored by those who know how the norms can be evaded". The deregulation that has been taking place in complex markets has increased the uncertainty of how financial institutions would behave in the case of a crisis.

MONEY MARKETS AND MONETARY POLICY

The money markets play a central role in the execution of central banks' monetary policy in many countries Until recently, the job of national central banks, which indirectly seek to regulate the amount of credit in the economy in order to manage economic growth and inflation, involved mainly purchasing and selling government debt to government securities dealers in open-market operations. These operations involve adding money to or draining money out of the banking system, which encourages or constrains banks' lending and thereby affects spending and demand in the economy.

These days, however, central banks in countries with well-developed financial systems often manage monetary policy through the repo market rather than with direct purchases and sales of securities. Under this system, the central bank enters into a repurchase agreement with a dealer. The money it pays the dealer passes to the dealer's bank, adding reserves to the banking system. When the repo matures the dealer returns the money to the central bank, draining the banking system of reserves unless the central bank enters into new repo transactions to keep the reserves level unchanged. If the central bank wishes to drain reserves from the system, it engages in a matched sale-purchase transaction, selling securities from its portfolio to dealers with agreements to repurchase them at future dates.

- *Central Bank Interest Rates:* In many countries, central banks can also lend directly to the money markets by providing credit to financial institutions at posted rates. Such loans are mainly for the purpose of helping institutions that have experienced sudden withdrawals of funds or otherwise face a lack of liquidity. Central bank loan rates are often less attractive than those available in the private sector, so as to encourage financial institutions to borrow in the money markets before turning to the central bank. Central bank rates change much less frequently than rates in the money markets.

Open-market operations have a direct impact on interest rates in the money markets. A central bank is not able to exert direct influence over medium-term and long-term rates, but its use of money-market rates to accelerate or retard economic growth affects investors' expectations of inflation, which in turn influence longer-term rates.

Watching Short-term Interest Rates

Central banks, governments and investors pay close attention to short-term interest rates.

- *Spreads:* In particular, spreads, the differences in interest rates on different instruments, are highly sensitive indicators of market participants' expectations. One important set of spreads is that between uncollateralized loans and repos. As repos are fully collateralized, there is almost no risk that repayment will be disrupted. Uncollateralized loans among banks, however, are at risk if a bank should fail. The spread between these two types of lending thus reflects perceived credit worthiness.

A SYSTEMIC REGULATOR FOR FINANCIAL MARKETS

Financial regulations in almost all countries are designed to ensure the soundness of individual institutions, principally commercial banks, against the risk of loss on their assets. This focus on individual firms ignores critical interactions between institutions. The focus on individual institutions can also cause regulators to overlook important changes in the overall financial system. For example, although the markets for securitized assets and the shadow banking system of lightly regulated financial institutions grew dramatically in the years before the current crisis, the existing regulatory structures did not evolve with them.

The solution to this narrow institutional focus is simple: One regulatory organization in each country should be responsible for overseeing the health and stability of the overall financial system. The role of the systemic regulator should include gathering, analyzing, and reporting information about significant interactions between and risks among financial institutions; designing and implementing systemically sensitive regulations, including capital requirements; and coordinating with the fiscal authorities and other government agencies in managing systemic crises.

What should the Systematic Regulator Do?

The primary role of the systemic regulator should be to prevent financial crises. *First*, the systemic regulator should gather, analyze, and report systemic information. In a related issue, it is argued that a new information infrastructure is needed for regulators to understand trends and emerging risks in the financial industry. This will require reporting from a broad range of financial institutions, with standardized measures of position values and risk exposures. Such information is valueless unless it can be analyzed, and this is a natural function of the systemic regulator. In addition, to enhance general awareness of systemic issues, the systemic regulator should prepare an annual report to Congress on the risks of the financial system. *Second*, the systemic regulator should design and implement financial regulations with a systemic focus. For example, capital requirements for regulated financial institutions should depend on the systemic risk they pose. Large banks holding illiquid assets and relying heavily on short-term debt should be required to hold proportionately more capital than smaller banks with more liquid assets and more stable financing arrangements. The systemic regulator should design and administer these capital requirements, and should negotiate with regulatory authorities in other countries to ensure that capital requirements are broadly comparable internationally. The crisis prevention role of the systemic regulator is paramount. Ideally, crises should be prevented. In the unlikely event that a crisis does erupt, however, a third role for the systemic regulator is to contribute to the management of the crisis. And it is also argued that banks should be encouraged, and possibly required, to issue hybrid securities that have the properties of debt unless and until a financial crisis occurs. At that time, the securities convert to equity if the financial condition of the issuing bank is sufficiently weak, recapitalizing the bank in an efficient manner without any need for an injection of taxpayer funds. The systemic regulator should be responsible for declaring the occurrence of a financial crisis, which is one part of the double trigger for debt-equity conversion. To be sure, the fiscal authority will be ultimately responsible for the use of public funds, but the systemic regulator will be the eyes and ears of the coordinated public response once a financial crisis is under way, as well as the channel for specific policy responses, such as emergency loans, to mitigate the crisis.

Separation of Systemic Regulation from other Financial Regulation

Financial regulators are often asked to protect consumers and to enforce 'conduct of business' rules against insider trading and other market abuses. The skills and mindset required to fulfill these important regulatory roles are fundamentally different from those required by a systemic regulator. Protecting consumers and prosecuting market abuse involve setting and then enforcing the appropriate rules under a transparent legal framework. Such work is primarily done by lawyers and accountants who specialize in rule-making and enforcement. As observed in the current crisis, a legally oriented, rule-enforcing regulator is ill-equipped to cope with a systemic crisis caused by a financial system that has outgrown the existing set of rules. What is needed is a regulator with the expertise to monitor financial innovations, such as the growth of the shadow banking system; to diagnose likely weaknesses in the financial system; and to pursue policies that can head off likely systemic problems.

Central Banks: Serve As A Systematic Regulators

The central bank is the natural choice to serve as the systemic regulator for four reasons. *First*, the central bank has daily trading relationships with market participants as part of its core function of implementing monetary policy and is well placed to monitor market events and to flag looming problems in the financial system. No other public institution has comparable insight and access to the broad flows in the financial system. *Second*, the central bank's mandate to preserve macroeconomic stability is well matched to the role of ensuring the stability of the financial system. Macroeconomic downturns are often tightly connected to the financial system, and similar analyses, drawing on the disciplines of macroeconomics and financial economics, can provide guidance for both types of oversight. As a result, macroeconomic policy and systemic regulation are tailor-made for each other. *Third*, central banks are among the most independent of government agencies. Successful systemic regulation requires a focus on the long run. The respect and independence that central banks enjoy therefore make them natural candidates to be systemic regulators. *Fourth*, the central bank is the lender of last resort. It has a balance sheet that it can use as a tool to meet systemic financial crises. As the lender of last resort, it will be called on to provide emergency funding in times of crisis. No amount of information sharing can substitute for the firsthand information gathered in direct on-site examinations. If a central bank will be asked to lend money to save an institution, it makes sense for the central bank to have firsthand supervisory information. Simply giving a central bank the authority to regulate systemic risk will not ensure that it devotes the appropriate attention and resources to the task. Each central bank should have an explicit mandate to maintain the stability of the financial system so that it properly balances its role as a systemic regulator with its other mandates.

Different central banks operate with different mandates. Some pursue a sole objective, such as price stability or a currency peg. Others pursue a dual mandate, such as the Federal Reserve's joint goals of price stability and maximum employment. Whatever a central bank's current charge, it should be expanded to encompass stability of the financial system. It is recognised the challenges that are introduced when the financial stability mandate is added to the duties of the central bank. The clear focus on achieving output and price stability will become blurred once the central bank also takes account of financial stability objectives. There are also legitimate concerns about the central bank overreaching itself in the resolution stage of a crisis when it greatly extends its balance sheet to lend to private institutions. Finally, recognised the dangers of increased politicization of the central bank's actions due to its role in the resolution stage of a crisis. However, given the importance of the financial stability goal and the fact that some institution must play the role of the systemic regulator, the central bank should take on the task in spite of the difficulties this will pose. Some safeguards can mitigate the difficulties. For example, some central banks have used long-run inflation targets to keep the price stability goal firmly in view. In the resolution stage of crises, a clear demarcation of roles is important, especially when the use of public funds is contemplated. Only the fiscal authority can authorize the use of public funds. The central bank as the systemic regulator assists the fiscal authorities, but it is the fiscal authorities who must ultimately be responsible in any resolution effort.

RECOMMENDATION FOR ESTABLISHING SYSTEMATIC REGULATORS

The discussion above leads to five recommendations.

1. *The Regulatory Structure for Financial Markets and Institutions should Include a Systemic Regulator that Oversees the Health and Stability of the Overall Financial System:* A systemic regulator will be able to limit systemic shocks of the sort that have recently arisen from the shadow banking system and from spillovers between financial institutions.

2. *The Central Bank should be the Systemic Financial Regulator:* Central banks' independence, daily interactions with the markets, focus on macroeconomic stability, and role as lenders of last resort makes them the natural systemic regulator.

3. *The Systemic Regulator (the central bank) should not be Involved in Consumer Protection and Business-practices Regulation:* Those roles should be given to one or more separate agencies. The systemic regulator will be better able to maintain the proper organizational culture and resist political pressure if it is not burdened with these responsibilities.

4. *The Systemic Regulator (the central bank) must be given Adequate Resources:* Without sufficient resources, the systemic regulator will not be able to identify systemic risks and craft the needed regulations to promote

financial stability. During the current crisis, the staff of central banks like the Federal Reserve has been stretched to the limit. Asking central banks to become systemic regulators will stretch already thin resources even thinner, perhaps even compromising the banks' ability to conduct monetary policy successfully.

5. *The Central Bank should be given an Explicit Mandate for Stability of the Financial System:* This will ensure that the central bank properly balances its role as systemic regulator with its other mandates; this would imply a triple mandate – price stability, maximum employment, and financial stability.

Principles for Responsible Lending

(i) Responsible and affordable credit must be provided for all.

(a) Credit is essential for people to participate fully in society.

(b) Banks should not discriminate and should provide real access.

(c) Credit to Consumers and Small Businesses must be supervised.

(ii) Credit relations have to be transparent and understandable.

(a) Competitive transparency requires a standardized mathematically correct form of 'one price' disclosure (the Annual Percentage Rate of Charge or APRC).

(b) Social transparency requires a standardized pre-contractual payment plan.

(c) Consumers should be provided with adequate time for reflection and with access to independent advice.

(d) Consumers should have access to independent financial, credit and debt advice.

(e) Both parties in the credit markets have to take part in a mutually productive process of financial education.

(iii) Lending has at all times to be cautious, responsible and fair.

(a) Credit and its servicing must be productive for the borrower.

(b) Responsible lending requires the provision of all necessary information and advice to consumers and liability for missing and incorrect information.

(c) No lender should be allowed to exploit the weakness, need or naivety of borrowers.

(d) Early repayment, without penalty, must be possible.

(e) The conditions under which consumers can refinance or reschedule their debt should be regulated.

(iv) Adaptation should be preferred to credit cancellation and destruction.

(a) There is a need for effective protection against unfair credit cancellation.

(b) Default charges should be adequate to cover losses only.

(v) Protective legislation has to be effective.

(a) Credit regulation has to cover all non-commercial users.

(b) Credit regulation has to cover all commercial forms of credit provision.

(c) Credit regulation has to cover the whole process of credit extension as experienced by its users.

(d) Credit regulation has to encourage efficient social and economic effects of credit extension.

(vi) Over indebtedness should be a public concern.

(a) Profit-driven systems cannot cope with over-indebtedness.

(b) Consumers should have a right to discharge.

(c) Bankruptcy procedures should lead to rehabilitation and not to re torsion.

(vii) Borrowers must have adequate means to defend their rights and be free to voice their concerns.

(a) There should be adequate individual as well as collective legal procedures to enforce borrowers' rights.

(b) Critical public awareness is crucial for the development a fair and responsible distribution of credit and this requires disclosure of bank services and consumer credit lending patterns to disadvantaged communities.

References

David Downey W. and Steven P. Erickson (1987), *Agribusiness Management*, McGraw-Hill, Inc. New York.

Downey and Erckson (1987), *Agribusiness Management*, Second Edition, McGraw-Hill, Inc. New York.

Gail L. Cramer and Clarence W. Jenser (1994), *Agricultural Economics and Agribusiness*, John Wiley and Sons., New York.

James G. Beierlein and Michael W Woolverton (1991), *Agribusiness Marketing*: The Management Perspective. Prentice Hall, New Jersey.

Jasmer Singh Saini (1998), *'Entrepreneurship Development – Programmes and Practices'*, Deep and Deep Publications, New Delhi.

Kenneth D. Duft (1979), *Principles of Management in Agribusiness*, Vol. 1 and 2, Reston Publishing Company Inc. Reston, Virginia.

Khanka S.S, (2000), *'Entrepreneurial Development'*, S. Chand and Company Ltd., New Delhi.

Kinsey B.H (1987), *Agribusiness and Rural Enterprise*, Croom Helm Ltd., Beken ham, Kent.

Micheal R. Solomon (2003), *Consumer Behaviour*, 5th Edition, Auburn University, New Delhi.

Omri Rawlins (1980), *Introduction to Agribusiness*, Prentice Hall International, Inc. London.

Philip Kotler and Gray Armstrong (2006) *Principles of Marketing*, 11th Edition, Printice-Hall of India, New Delhi.

Rajan Nair N. and Sanjith R. Nair, *'Marketing'*, Sulthan Chand and Sons, New Delhi.

Robert E. Branson and Doglass G. Norvell (1983), *Introduction to Agricultural Marketing*, 1st Edition, McGraw' Hill, Inc,.

Seetharaman S.P and Shingi P.M (1992), *Agribusiness Co-operatives*, Oxford and IBH Publishing Co. Pvt. Ltd., New Delhi.

Sukghpal Singh (2003), *'Rural Marketing Management'*, Vikas Publishing House, New Delhi.

Vanden Ban A.W. and Hawkins H.S. (1996), *Agricultural Extension*, 2nd Edition, Black Well Science Ltd., London.

Vasant Desai, *'Small-Scale Industries and Entrepreneurship'*, Himalaya Publishing House, Mumbai, 2000.

Walter J. Wills. (1973), *An Introduction to Agribusiness Management*, The Inter State Printers and Publishers. Inc. Danville Illinois.

Index